THE LIFE
OF
MUHAMMAD
(PBUH)

ABDUL HAMEED SIDDIQUI

PUBLISHER:

LIBRARY OF ISLAM
P.O. Box 1923
Des Plaines, IL 60017 (U.S.A.)

DISTRIBUTOR:

KAZI PUBLICATIONS INC.
3023 West Belmont Avenue
Chicago, IL 60618 (U.S.A.)

Library Of Congress Cataloging In Publishing Data

Life Of Muhammad
Siddiqui .Abdul H .

ISBN: 0- 934905- 21- 5

Manufactured in the United States of America.

CONTENTS

FOREWORD

Prophet Muhammad (peace be upon him) occupies a unique position in the history of mankind. In him the institution of prophethood found its ultimate fulfilment. The old order reached its finale ; a new era was inaugurated in the life of man. This is what finality of prophethood means.

Man stands in need of Divine guidance, the real source of those absolute values and eternal principles of moral and social system on which ideal individual and collective life can be built. Man has not been left alone by his Creator to grope in the dark in search for such values and principles. The Guidance has come from the inception of mankind. It has come in two forms : Books of God, and His Prophets. All Books essentially carried the same teachings ; all Prophets conveyed the same messages. Books embody eternal Divine guidance ; prophets personify that in space and time. The Message of the Book and the Example of the Prophet go to make up an integrated whole, indivisible and inseparable. And all the Books and all the Prophets are inalienable links of this golden chain. Muhammad (peace be upon him) and the book revealed to him, the Quran constitute its final links. Through them the guidance has been completed and perfected. Man has now been provided with perfect guidance, and his rational faculties have been so awakened and canalised that he can chart out his course of life in the light of these codes of guidance. No *new* revelation is now needed. The Quran and the life-example of Muhammad (peace be upon him) are the eternal guide of man in his unceasing efforts to strive for fulfilment in moral, spiritual and social fields of existence. This makes the life of Muhammad (peace be upon him) unique, and makes it relevant to every human being, wherever he may be.

Although there is a vast body of literature on the life of the Holy Prophet, yet it was being felt that there is no biography in the English language which presents an integrated view of the life, personality and mission of the man who changed the course of history and inaugurated a new era in the life of mankind. Most of the works available in English have come from people who have looked upon the life of the Holy Prophet from certain coloured glasses or limited angles, or who did not have this integrated picture in view. Islamic Research Academy, in collaboration with the Begum 'Aisha Bawany Wakf, undertook this project. Professor 'Abdul Hamid Siddiqui, who was assigned this project, has presented the results of his study and research in two volumes. The first volume, *Prophethood in Islam*, was published in 1968. It gave an exposition of the need of prophethood, and the prophethood of Muhammad (peace be upon him) and its finality. This was a prelude to the present study of the life of the Holy Prophet. Every effort has been made to present the life and message of Muhammad (peace be upon him), relying primarily on original sources. This is not a tract on religious polemics ; what is aimed at is a clear, precise and positive statement of the life and message of the Prophet of Islam. However, certain misconceptions, which have been constantly dinned into the minds of the English readers, have also been rectified in passing.

Finally, a word may be said to our non-Muslim readers. We believe that God's guidance has come in all times and to all peoples. There has been nothing wrong with that Guidance as such ; it came from the same source. The wrong lies the other way round : those who received the guidance or inherited it did not do justice to that. In the past most of them unfortunately destroyed that guidance, and neglected or polluted that. Now another dimension has been added to this attitude—*intolerance towards guidance that comes from a source other than theirs.* When they approach other religions and their prophets—and particularly Islam and its Prophet, Muhammad (peace be upon him), with a kind of concealed antagonism, and distorted vision, they, in fact, deprive themselves of a great source of light and guidance. They are prepared to read lives and works of many social reformers with an openness of mind ; not so, the life and teachings of a prophet, not belonging to their own limited religious tradition. This attitude is as irrational and unscientific as one of not seeing or accepting any piece of molecular or space research which comes from a different source. Why this double standard? We would invite them to study Islam and the life of the Holy Prophet with an openness of mind with which they undertake their other studies. This might help in developing a better appreciation of the message of all prophets, and may assist mankind in finding solution to many of its spiritual, moral and social problems. This would spell good for the entire human race.

In the end we express our gratitude to the Begum 'Aisha Bawany Wakf for the financial assistance they provided for this project and to Dr. Zafar Ishaq Ansari and Khwaja Abdul Wahid for the trouble they took in reading the manuscript and making valuable suggestions for its improvement.

Leicester, KHURSHID AHMAD
U. K.

بسم الله الرحمن الرحيم

In the name of Allah, the Compassionate, the Merciful

PREFACE

Here is a modest attempt on a lofty subject, a subject which is so vast and deep that one cannot fully comprehend it. I have in my own humble way tried to describe some of the aspects of Muḥammad's august personality (peace be upon him). The outcome of my two and a half years' labour is before God and man and certainly it is not for me to pass any judgement on it.

It must be stated with sincere humility that the author has no pretensions to have written a scientific history of the Holy Prophet. He has approached Muḥammad (peace be upon him) not in the spirit of a pedantic critic, but with a simple-hearted form of devotion and love for the benefactor of mankind.

The chronological order of events has not been strictly followed. It has been done with a view to presenting a unified picture of the Prophet's sacred life. Certain interrelated thoughts and facts have been gathered together and discussed at one place instead of leaving them scattered here and there in the course of narration. In this process some events have been considerably shortened, whereas others have been lengthened more than is customary.

No biography of Muḥammad (peace be upon him) is complete which does not mention his teachings and their practical effects on human life. It is of basic importance for the proper understanding and correct appreciation of his Divine Mission. Passing allusions have, no doubt, been made here and there, but it requires another volume to acquaint the people with the ideals, the Holy Prophet preached and the way he transmuted them into reality.

I owe a debt of deep gratitude to Maulana Syed Abul A‘la Maudoodi, Mr. Ebrahim Bawany, Prof. Khurshid Ahmad, Ch.

Ghulam Muhammad, Mr. Misbah-ul-Islam Farooqi, Mr. Shahzad Muhammad, Malik Ghulam Ali, and Dr. 'Abid Ahmad 'Ali for their constant help and encouragement. Prof. Zafar Ishaque Ansari very kindly revised the manuscript and gave me very valuable suggestions. I am deeply obliged to him. Mr. Ghulam Sarwar typed the final draft of the manuscript and Syed 'Ata Husain and Mr. Ashraf Darr prepared it for the press. I am thankful to all of them.

If there is any merit discernible in the work, it is absolutely due to the grace and mercy of Allah, and for all acts of omission and commission, the writer alone is to be held responsible.

ABDUL HAMEED SIDDIQUI

Lahore:
July 8, 1969

بسم الله الرحمن الرحيم

PREFACE TO THE SECOND EDITION

No words are adequate enough to express my deep sense of gratitude to my Lord for the unbounded favour He has shown me in giving this humble attempt of mine popularity beyond my imagination. It has been received well in all quarters as a result of which the book has been printed again. I am deeply indebted to Malik Ghulam 'Ali and Mr. Waqar Husain Gardezi who have very kindly revised the first edition and have given me valuable suggestions. My brother Muhammad Iqbal Shaiq has prepared the index of the book with great skill and has assisted me in many other ways. I feel obliged to him.

Directors of Islamic Publications Ltd. deserve thanks for the keen interest they have taken in the publication of this book.

ABDUL HAMEED SIDDIQUI

Lahore:
26th May, 1975

Chapter 1

Arabia Before Islam

Physical Features of Arabia

Between the Red Sea and the Persian Gulf lies a cheerless continent, arid and well nigh waterless, save where an occasional flood lends to the scene the freshness and charm of an oasis. Most of it is an uninviting place, unfriendly too, from the physical point of view. For miles around there appears to be no end to barren hills, no end to the glittering, blazing desert ; no respite from the fiery heat except for the few green places which abound in palm and water and provide rest to the wandering tribes of the Arabs. The streams are few and seldom reach the sea. Most of them come to life only when swelled by occasional rains and disappear in the sandy plains.

The peninsula was divided by the ancient geographers into "Arabia Petraea", "Arabia Felix" and "Arabia Deserta". "Arabia Petraea" corresponded to the present *Ḥijāz* and eastern part of *Najd* ; "Arabia Felix" to *Yemen* and *Ḥaḍramaut*, and "Arabia Deserta" comprised the rest of the country. In the north lies the hilly tract, once inhabited by the Edomites and Midianites of the Hebrew Testament. Then comes *Ḥijāz* proper which extends along the Red Sea between Syria in the north and Yemen in the south. In this part are situated the famous cities of Mecca, Medina and Jeddah and is dotted by hills extending from the isthmus of Suez to the Indian Ocean.

"There were but a few points at which, in ancient times. Arabia touched the outer world. The northern region, stretching from Syria to Euphrates, was occupied, in the second century, by some of those tribes which had, according to native tradition, about that time immigrated from the south and of whom we frequently hear in the later annals of the Roman empire. To the west, in the Syrian desert with their capital at Palmyra, was the dynasty of the Ghassanides ; and to the east, on the banks of the Euphrates, the kingdom of *Hira* : the former, as a rule, adhered to the Roman, the latter to the Persian empire."[1]

The ancient records of Arab history eloquently speak of the fact that it was but the farther outskirts of the peninsula which came into contact with the civilized world. "The rest of Arabia was absolutely unknown ; and, excepting through the medium of countrymen engaged in merchandise, or settled on the confines of Syria, the Arabs themselves had but little knowledge of anything beyond their own deserts."[2]

Within the bounds of the country, the city of *Mecca* occupied a prominent position. It was but a small town, nestling in a plain amid arid, volcanic rocks, some fifty miles away from the shores of the Red Sea, from which the ground rises gradually towards the great table land of inner Arabia. As a commercial centre and as a sanctuary of great holiness, the *Ka'bah* attracted innumerable people from all parts of Arabia every year.

The control of the *Ka'bah* had been the chief object of ambition for the Arab tribes on account of the great influence its directors exercised over the whole of Arabia. There had been, therefore, constant struggle to secure the eminent position of the custodianship of the "House of *Allah*".

As far as history reveals, we find that the Ishmaelites remained the guardians of the *Ka'bah* for a long time. Afterwards it passed on to the *Jurhamites* and then to the *Amalekites*. Later on, the *Ishmaelites* and the *Jurhamites* joined hands to expel the common foe, *i.e.*, the *Amalekites*, from Mecca and having succeeded in doing so, the *Jurhamites* finally became the guardians of the *Ka'bah.*

Banū Bakr and *Banū Khuzā'ah* envied this privilege of the guardianship of *Ka'bah* and combined to dislodge the *Jurhamites*. After this *Qusayy* conspired with *Banī Kin'ānah*, defeated *Banū Bakr* and *Banū Khuzā'ah* and established their own authority over *Mecca* and the *Ka'bah*.

Thus the control of the *Ka'bah* and Mecca was restored to the *Qurayshites* after the lapse of about four hundred years.

Next, the custodianship of the *Ka'bah* passed first to

---

1. William Muir, *The Life of Muhammad* (1912), p. lxxx.
2. *Ibid*, p. xciii.

'Abd al-Dār and then to his sons and grandsons. To cite Muir :

> The house of *'Abd al-Dār* originally possessed all the public offices ; but in the struggle with Hāshim they were stripped of several important dignities, their influence had departed, and they were now fallen into a subordinate and insignificant position. The offices retained by them were still, undoubtedly, valuable ; but divided among separate members of the family, the benefit of combination was lost ; and there was no steady and united effort to improve their advantages towards the acquisition of social influence and political power. The virtual chiefship of Mecca, on the other hand, was now with the descendants of *'Abd Menāf*. Among these, again, two parties had arisen—the families, namely, of his sons *Hāshim* and *'Abd Shams*. The grand offices of giving food and water to the pilgrims secured to the house of *Hāshim*, a commanding and permanent influence under the able management of *Muṭṭalib*, and now of *'Abd al-Muttalib* who, like his father *Hāshim*, was regarded as the chief of the Sheikhs of *Mecca*.[3]

Thus at the time of Muḥammad's birth this honour was enjoyed by his family, and his grandfather was the venerable chief of the theocratic commonwealth which was constituted round the *Ka'bah*. According to P. De Lacy Johnstone :

> Medina, according to Arab tradition, was originally settled by the *Amalekites*, but these gave way in very early time to Jewish invaders, driven from their own land (probably) by the national disasters wrought by Nebuchadnezzar and later conquerors. Prominent among them were the *Nazir*, *Quraiza*, and *Qainuqaa* tribes. About 300 A.D., the *Aus* and *Khazraj* tribes, of *Azdite* stock, struck back south from their kindred in Ghassan, and at first lived on good terms with Jews who had hospitably welcomed them. But when they grew in numbers and felt their power, they, about the end of the fifth century, rose against their Jewish partners in the Government, massacred the chiefs, seized the best of their lands, and reduced the tribes to subjection. The treachery and

---

3. William Muir, op. cit., p. ciii.

massacre was avenged by *Abu Karib*, a prince, who slew the leaders, and devastated the cultivated lands, but had then to retire. Thereafter followed twenty years of strife between the rival clans ; a truce for half a century, then renewed war, ending after a terrible battle at *Buath* in 616 A.D. (where the strength of Jews divided between the contending tribes, and desert allies joined in the fray) in triumph of the *Khazraj*, whose chief, *'Abdullah ibn Ubai*, was about to be raised to the kingship of Medina, when the exile from Mecca changed the fortunes of the city.[4]

Before the recent gush of oil and the gold that it has brought, the Arabs were living a life of extreme poverty. Their soil was poor ; and constant tilling enabled them to wring only a precarious subsistence. They earned their livelihood either by rearing camels, horses, cattle, and sheep, pitching their tents within certain limits, where water and pasturage were most abundant, or they were engaged in the transport of merchandise along the trading routes through the desert.

The Arab Character :

They were no doubt poor, yet they took life light-heartedly. They were in fact free from all the inner tensions and stresses which are so peculiar to our times. Men of strong passions were they, fiery of temper, ardent in love and bitter in hate, delighting in war, in the chase, and the banquet, not sparing the wine-cup at the feast, but of unmatched forbearance for cold, thirst and hunger when need arose. They were generous in their tongues, and eloquent in their utterances. They could be easily touched by every form of poetry, in praise of themselves, their kindred and their friends, or bitter shafts of blame and satire against their foes.

Writing, of course, there was little or none ; the literature of the desert was preserved 'living on the lips of men and graven on the tablets of their hearts'; the perfect warrior was also the famous poet, and the name of many a poetess adorns the Arab bead-roll of glory :

The staple of their poetry is, however, largely a des-

---

4. P. De Lacy Johnstone, *Muhammad and His Power* (New York 1901), pp. 35, 36.

cription of the joys of battle, the struggle for mastery, and the perils of the long, dark journeyings through the waste : the noble horse and camel, the keen flashing sword in the battle, the deadly lance and arrow ; the swift, sudden storms that sweep over mountain and plain, driving the goats and wild antelopes in panic fear to their fastness, while the lightning flashes and thunder roars, and the rain-torrents hurry down the stony watercourses—these are the themes of their songs. And prefaced to nearly every one of longer poems is a wail of lament over the ashes of a long-deserted encampment, once the home of a beloved maiden, a tearful note of human sorrow to attune the heart of softened melancholy. One type, one theme, is strangely absent from it all,—the devotional. Praise or prayer is seldom heard, though wild and terrible oaths are not wanting. The old Arab was, above all things, self-centred, self-reliant, confident that the cunning of his own strong right hand could conquer fate. His worship did not greatly pervade his life or his thoughts. The warrior would take the arrows of divination, but if the answer squared not with his desire, he would hurl them back wrathfully and scornfully in the face of his idol.[5]

We reproduce here some of the snatches of songs which would give a very clear idea to the readers about the sensuous delights of the Arab, his pleasures and pains, and his metaphysical beliefs :

He is a young boy of charming countenance ;
He looks promising and is growing with the perfection of
Harith

Age and youth blended together.
They are best of men,
What of their fine great ancestors ;
They are the best drunkards.[6]
When she flashes across the eyes of old hermit,
He who lies on the peaks of hill,

5. P. De Lacy Johnstone, op. cit., p. 18.

6. *Ibn Qutaybah, al-Shi'r wa'al-Shu'arā'*, ed. Ahmad Muhammad Shākir, Cairo (1367 H), Vol. I, p. 109.

He too is enchanted by her beauty,
Lends ears to her and comes out of his hut.
Were you not a human being, you would have been a full moon.[7]

There are innumerable verses of pre-Islamic Arabic poetry which are indicative of the fact that despite love for sensuous pleasures, the Arabs were very brave and had the courage to meet all kinds of situations manfully :

Roast flesh, the glow of fiery wine,
to speed on camel fleet and sure.
As thy soul lists to urge her on
through all the hollow's breadth and length.
White women, statue-like, that trail
rich robes of price with golden hem,
Wealth, easy lot, no dread of ill,
to hear the lutes, complaining string,
These are life's joys. For man is set
the prey of Time, and Time is change.
Life strait or large, great store or nought
all's one to time, all men to death.[8]

Now follow part of the dirge which a brave chief sang for himself when, before his death, he faced the foes that had overwhelmed him :

Upbraid me not, yet twain : enough is the shame for me,
To be as I am, no gain upbraiding to you or me.
Know ye not that in reproach is little that profits men ?
It was not my wont to blame my brother when I was free.
Mulaika, my wife, knows well that time when I stood forth
A lion to lead men or face those that rushed on me.
Yea, many a slaughtered beast I gave to the gamers, oft
I journeyed along where none would venture to share my way ;
And of times I slew, to feast my fellows, the beast I rode,
And of times I rent my robe in twain for two singing girls.

---

7. *Ibn Qutaybah, al-Shi'r wa'al-Shu'arā*, ed. Ahmad Muhammad Shākir, Cairo (1367 H), Vol. I, p. 114.

8. Charles James Lyall, *Translations from Ancient Arabian Poetry*, (Edinburgh 1885), p. 64.

And when 'neath the stress of spears our steeds plunged and broke and backed,
Yet mine were the fingers deft then turned from our line their steel.
And hosts like the locusts swarm have swept upon me alone,
And my hand it was that stemmed and gathered in one their spears.
Now am I as though I ne'er had mounted a noble steed,
Or called to my horsemen charge! gain space for our men to breathe,
Or brought for a wealth of gold the full skin of wine or cried
To true hearts at play—Heap high the blaze at our beacon fire![9]

These verses which have been taken from *Hamasah*, speak eloquently of the ideal of Arab virtue which can be expressed in terms of *Muruwwah* (manliness) and *irḍ* (honour). "It is not mere chance," observes Reynold A. Nicholson, "that *Abū Tammām's* famous anthology is called the *Hamasah*, *i.e.*, 'Fortitude', from the title of its first chapter, which occupies nearly half the book. *'Hamasah'* denotes the virtues most highly prized by the Arabs—bravery in battle, patience in misfortune, persistence in revenge, protection of the weak and defiance of the strong; the will, as Tennyson has said,

"To strive, to seek, to find, and not to yield".

As typical Arab hero we may take *Shanfāra* of *Azd* and his comrade in foray, *Ta'abbata Sharr*. Both were brigands, outlaws, swift runners, and excellent poets:

> Of the former it is said that he was captured when a child from his tribe by the *Banū Salaman*, and brought up among them; he did not learn his origin until he had grown up, when he vowed vengeance against his captors, and returned to his own tribe. His oath was that he would slay a hundred men of *Salaman*; he slew ninety-eight, when an ambush of his enemies succeeded in taking him prisoner. In the struggle one of his hands was hewn off by a sword stroke, and, taking it in the other, he flung it in the face of a man of *Salaman* and killed him, thus making ninety-nine. Then he was overpowered and slain,

9. Charles James Lyall, op. cit., p. 64.

with one still wanting to make up his number. As his skull lay bleaching on the ground, a man of his enemies passed by that way and kicked it with his foot ; a splinter of bone entered his foot, the wound mortified, and he died, thus completing the hundred.[10]

The following passage is translated from Shanfāra's splendid ode named *Lamiyyatu'l Arab* in which he describes his own heroic character and the hardships of a predatory life :

'And somewhere the noble find a refuge afar from scathe,
The outlaw a lonely spot where no kin with hatred burn.
Oh, never a prudent man, night-faring in hope of fear,
Hard-pressed on the face of earth, but still he hath room to turn.
To me now, in your default, are comrades a wolf untired,
A sleek leopard, and a fell hyena with shaggy mane :
True comrades : they ne'er let out the secret in trust with them,
Nor basely forsake their friend because that he brought them bane ![11]

The Arabs were also fully conscious of the blessings of unity and they always exhorted their clans to stand together :

Woe be upon you that you are scattered
Whereas the others are united.
The princes of Persia rally together to attack you
They care not the defence of forts,
They are marching upon you armed to the teeth.
They will inflict disgrace upon you,
Gird up your loins and fall upon them.
The one who can stun others finds safety
Select your chief one who is courageous and brave
Who is not indulgent and can admirably stand the onslaughts of hardships
One who is experienced
Who knows how to serve and be served
Strong and formidable

10. *A Literary History of the Arabs* (Cambridge 1933), p. 79.
11. Reynold A. Nicholson, op. cit., pp. 79-80. English translation of the *Lāmiyya* by G. Hughes (London 1896), quoted by *ibid.*, p. 80.

Mature of age, neither old nor weak.[12]

These verses describe the rudiments of Arabian virtues of courage, hardness, and strength. "Arab courage is like that of the ancient Greeks, dependent upon excitement and vanishing quickly before depression and delay."[13] Hence the Arab hero is defiant and boastful, as he appears, *e.g.*, in the *Mu'allaqa* of *'Amr b. Kulthūm*.[14]

A study of the poetry of the pre-Islamic Arabs will reveal that the Arabs were generally cheerful ; but whenever they thought of old age, their cheerfulness at once gave place to despondency. An old poet, *Hārith B. Ka'b*, while lamenting his youth, sings the dirge :

I consumed my youth bit by bit till it was no more :
I wasted hundreds of months
I have seen with my eyes the passing of the three generations.
They were gone ; gone for ever ;
Alas, I have grown old, one :
Who can neither eat to his heart's content
Nor walk easily ; a victim to the helplessness,
I spend my sleepless night in counting stars.[15]

Nābighah also sings with great pathos :

The man longs to live longer,
But the long life is painful for him ;
He is deprived of the cheerfulness of his countenance,
And the cup of life is filled with grief,
The age betrays him terribly
And he finds little joy in life.[16]

Generosity and hospitality were also greatly cherished in the desert and are still prominent virtues of the Arab. A large heap of ashes and bones outside the tent was a mark of high excellence in a chief, for it means that he had entertained many guests. "The Bedouin ideal of generosity and hospitality is personified in

---

12. *Ibn Qutaybah,* op. cit., pp. 153-54.
13. Mahaffy : *Social Life in Greece,* quoted by Nicholson, op. cit., p. 82.
14. Nicholson, *Ibid.,* p. 82.
15. *Ibn Qutaybah,* p. 52.
16. *Ibid.,* p. 111.

Ḥātim of Tay of whom many anecdotes are told."[17]

Ḥātim was himself a poet. The following lines are addressed to *Mu'āwiyah*, his wife :

'O, daughter of *'Abdullah* and *Malik* and him who wore
The two robes of Yemen stuff—the hero that rode the roan.
When thou hast prepared two meals, entreat to partake thereof.
A guest—I am not the man to eat, like a churl, alone :
Some traveller ; thro' the night, or house-neighbour ; for in sooth.
I fear the reproachful talk of men after I am gone.
The guest's slave am I, 'tis true, as long as he bides with me,
Although in my nature also no trait of the slave is shown.[18]

The Arab's generosity consists in ungrudging assistance to people who seek it :

He is generous and gives unhesitatingly
And bears all the oppressions boldly.[19]

This generosity was shown not only to the human beings, but even to the animals and the beasts :

I traversed many a valley on the camel-back
Valleys where even the bravest would die,
There we heard the voices of the owl
As the bells rang in the darkness of night,
There emerge before us the tops of the hills
Near our hearth there came a wolf ;
I threw bone at him and I showed no niggardliness to my companion ;
The wolf turned back moving its joyful head
And looked to be a brave warrior coming back proudly with his booty.[20]

Another aspect of the Arab's life which deserves mention is the Bedouin's deep-rooted emotional attachment to his clan. Family, or perhaps tribal pride, was one of the strongest passions with him.

"All the virtues," remarks Professor Nicholson, "which enter

---

17. Nicholson, op. cit., p. 85.
18 *Hamasah*, 729, quoted *ibid.*, p. 87,
19 *Ibn Qutaybah*, p. 84.
20. *Ibid.*, p .164.

into the Arabian conception of honour were regarded not as personal qualities inherent or acquired, but as hereditary possessions which a man derived from his ancestors, and held in trust that he might transmit them untarnished to his descendants. It is the desire to uphold and emulate the fame of his forbears rather than the hope of winning immortality for himself, that causes the Arab "to say the say and do the deeds of the noble."

Ancestral renown (*hasab*) is sometimes likened to a strong castle built by sires for their sons, or to a lofty mountain which defies attack. The poets are full of boasting (*mafākhīr*) and revilings (*mathālib*) in which they loudly proclaim the nobility of their own ancestors, and try to blacken those of their enemy without any regard to decorum."[21]

The doctrine of unity of blood as the principle that bound Arabs into a social unity was formed under a system of mother kinship, "the introduction of male-kinship was a kind of social revolution which modified society to its very roots."[22]

"Previously house and children belonged to the mothers: succession was through mothers and the husband came to wife, not the wife to the husband."[23] Whatever might have been the nature of kinship, one thing emerges clearly that kinship among the Arabs means a share in the common blood which is taken to flow in the veins of every member of a tribe. In one word, it was the tribal bond which knit men of the same group together and gave them common duties and responsibilities from which no member of the group could withdraw. This bond was a source of great pride for them.

The tribal constitution was a democracy guided by its chief men, who derived their authority from noble blood, noble character, wealth, wisdom, and experience. As a Bedouin poet has said in a homely language:

A folk that hath no chiefs must soon decay,
And chiefs it hath not when the vulgar sway.
Only with poles the tent is reared at last,

21. Nicholson, op. cit., p. 100.
22. W. Robertson Smith, *Kinship and Marriage in Early Arabia* (2nd Edition London 1903), p. 182.
23. *Ibid.*, p. 172.

And poles it hath not save the pegs hold fast.
But when the pegs and poles are once combined,
Then stands accomplished that which was designed.[24]

The enthusiasm with which the tribes' men have been urged to stand united and elect as their leader one who is wise, sagacious and brave, can be seen from the following verses :

Nothing can be achieved without the leader,
The leadership of the ignorant is no leadership,
The matters are set aright by the consent of the wise men.
Or fall in the hands of mischief-mongers.[25]

An Arab was no doubt wedded to his tribe and was deeply attached to his leaders but was not prepared to give up his individuality and follow them blindly. Every man ruled himself, and was free to rebuke presumption in others. If you are our lord (*i.e.*, if you act discreetly as *Sayyid* should) you will lord over us, but if you are prey to pride, go and be proud (*i.e.*, we will have nothing to do with you).

The tribal solidarity was sometimes extended to a kind of confederacy amongst the various tribes. This alliance of the tribes was "brought through either *hilf* (confederacy, mutual oaths) or *jiwār* (the formal granting of protection). For many purposes the *halif* and the *jār*, the 'confederates' and the 'client' were treated as members of the tribe in order to maintain *it in* existence.

"While the tribe or confederation of tribes was the highest political unit, there was also a realization of the fact that the Arabs were in some sense a unity. This unity was based on common language (though with variation of dialect), a common poetical tradition, some common conventions and ideas, and a common descent. Language was possibly the original basis of the distinction between Arabs and 'foreigners'—'Arab and '*Ajam*'."[26]

The Arabs had a keen sense of their being distinct from other peoples and showing their superiority to them but there is no gainsaying the fact that it was the tribal solidarity which

24. Nicholson, op. cit., p. 83.
25. *Ibn Qutaybah*, p. 145.
26. W. Montgomery Watt, *Muhammad at Mecca* (Oxford 1960), pp. 17-18.

formed the bedrock of their unity and governed the action of the best people. One should not, however, lose sight of the fact that even this solidarity was never absolute. An Arab is an individualist to the marrow of his bone and never accepts the position of an automaton which could work ungrudgingly at the gesture of his master.

"Loyalty and fidelity were also the important virtues [of the Arabs]. Ideally a man ought to be ready to spring to the aid of a fellow tribesman whenever he called for help ; he should act at once without waiting to inquire into the merits of the case."[27]

If the Arab was, as we have seen, faithful to his tribe and its leader and was prepared to risk his all for the sake of its honour, 'he had in the same degree an intense and deadly feeling of hatred towards his enemies. He who did not strike back, when struck, was regarded as a coward.'[28]

Humble him who humbles thee, close tho' be your kindred-ship ;
If thou can'st not humble him, wait till he is in thy grip.
Friend him while thou must ; strike hard when thou hast him on the hip.[29]

The obligation of revenge lay heavy on the conscience of the pagan Arabs :

> Vengeance, with them, was almost a physical necessity, which if it be not obeyed, will deprive its subject of sleep, of appetite, of health. It was a tormenting thirst which nothing would quench except blood, a disease of honour which might be described as madness, although it rarely prevented the sufferer from going to work with coolness and circumspection."[30]

They were in fact obliged to exercise their arms frequently, by reason of independence of their tribes, whose frequent jarrings made wars almost continued ; and they chiefly ended their disputes with the help of the sword.

"The whole law of the old Arabs really resolves itself into

---

27. W. Montgomery Watt, op. cit., p. 21.
28. Nicholson, op. cit., p. 22.
29. *Hamasah*, p. 321 quoted by Nicholson, op. cit., p. 93.
30. Nicholson, op. cit., p. 93.

a law of war—blood-feud, blood-wit and booty are the points on which everything turns.[31] The true Arab feeling is expressed in verses like these :

With the sword will I wash my shame away,
Let God's doom bring on me what it may.[32]

We may sum up the Arab character by saying that the pagan Arab "is a cynical materialist with a keenly logical outlook, a strong sense of his own dignity, and a consuming avarice. His mind has no room for romance, still less for sentiment ; he has very little inclination for religion and takes but slight heed of anything which cannot be measured in practical values. His sense of personal dignity is so strong that he is naturally in revolt against every form of authority. On the other hand he is loyal and obedient to the ancient traditions of his tribe ; the duties of hospitality, alliance in war, of friendship, and such like, are faithfully performed on the lines of recognized precedent, he keeps punctiliously the letter of the law, that is to say, of the unwritten law of his own tribal customs, but own no obligation outside the strict letter."[33]

The Arabs had developed no great art of their own except eloquence and perfect skill in their own tongue. "If the Greek gloried primarily in his statues and architecture, the Arabian found in his ode (*qaṣīdah*) and the Hebrew in his psalm, a finer mode of self-expression. The beauty of man, declares an Arabic adage, 'lies in the eloquence of his tongue.'

'Wisdom,' in a late saying, 'has alighted on three things : the brains of the Franks, the hands of the Chinese and the tongue of the Arabs'. Eloquence, *i.e.* ability to express oneself forcefully and elegantly in both prose and poetry, together with archery and horsemanship were considered in the Jahileyah period the basic attributes of the perfect man (*al-Kāmil*).[34] Their orations were of two sorts, metrical and prosaic, the one being compared to pearls strung, and the other to loose ones.

Poetry was esteemed more than prose. It was indeed a great accomplishment with them, and a proof of ingenious

---

31. W. Robertson Smith, *Kinship and Marriage in Early Arabia*, p. 55.
32. *Hamasah*, quoted by Prof. Nicholson, op. cit., p. 93.
33. De Lacy O'Leary, *Arabia Before Muhammad*, pp. 20-21.
34. Philip K. Hitti, *History of Arabs*, pp. 90-91.

extraction, to be able to express themselves in verse with ease, and elegance on any extraordinary occurrence ; and even in their common discourse they made frequent applications to celebrated passages of their famous poets. In their poems were preserved the distinction of descendants, the rights of tribes, and their achievements, the memory of great actions, and the propriety of their language.

Social life of the Arabs

To keep up an emulation among their poets, the tribes of Arabia held once a year, a general assembly at *'Ukāz* a place between *Nakhlah* and *Tā'if.* This fair, however, revived the scenes of Rome's greatest glory in gaiety and licentiousness. Warriors of all tribes, sworn blood enemies for generations, sat in open-air cafes and taverns. Wine goblets were filled and emptied with alarming rapidity. Amidst this merry-making the poets recited their poetical compositions, contending and vying with each other for the coveted first honour. A poet made a name for himself here or nowhere.

Drinking had in fact become a second nature with the Arabs. Wine and woman go together, and as a result of licentious drinking, fornication was very rampant. The caravans which radiated from Mecca with native merchandise to the Byzantine Empire, Syria, Persia and India, returned therefrom with all luxurious habits and vices and imported slave girls from Syria and Iraq who afforded vast opportunities of sensual pleasures to the rich with their dancing and singing and all corruption which usually goes with them. We reproduce below some of the verses which would give an idea of the immoral life which the Arabs of pre-Islamic period were habituated to lead :

> Either evening or morning will bid farewell,
> To thee, so do thou resolve to what state thou wilt resort.
> Verily the engagement with fondling woman from under the curtain (having) lovely eye (with) langour in it—who are profusely anointed with musk and whom fine apparel, easy life and silk (garments) lend charms, like the marble

35. It was apparently considered a sign of luxury that ointments were applied in excess.

statues in the niches or like the egg (ostrich) in the garden whose flowers are blooming—
Does not become thee now that thou hast grown sobermind-ed and
The sign of hoariness has appeared in thy temple.
Turning white of the black (hair) is amongst the warnings of Evil[36]
And is there, after it, any warning for the living ?[37]

This relish for sensual pleasures had made the Arabs profligate voluptuaries. The members of the tribe, including male and female, young and old often met together in order to enjoy drinking, dancing and gambling. Those who shunned such evil practices were considered mean, stingy and unsocial :

"And when I die, marry not one who is humble, weak or who does not gamble, and avoids people."

This is the will left by a husband to his widow. A poet of that time describes the pleasures of these parties :

Come, friend and fellow, come—for some time is folly sweet
So, come, let us greet our band of drinkers aglow with wine
And wash from our hearts sour speech of wisdom with cups abrim
and cut short the ills of life with laughter and joy ![38]

The old Arab poetry has so many tales to narrate of the drinking orgies of the people of Arabia before the advent of Islam. Their parties were in fact wine-bubbling springs converted into a sort of gambling-den. The Arab found solace in wine and felt proud on drinking it :

Sometime in wine was my solace. Good wine I drank of it,
Suaging the heat of the evening paying in white money
Quaffing in goblets of saffron, pale-streaked with ivory
Hard at my hand their companion, the flask to the left of me.

---

36. viz., death.
37. Abi B. Zaid al-Ibadi (480 A.D.), *Early Arabic Odes* by Dr. S. M. Husain (Dacca) 1938, pp. 172-73.
38. Charles James Lyall, op. cit., p. 72.

Truly this bidding squandered half my inheritance ;
Yet was my honour a wide word. No man had wounded it.[39]

Decency and modesty had been swept away from the society by these drinking revelries, so common and so frequent, and by the absence of any social discipline ; the heathen Arabs had little regard for the sanctity of matrimonial relations. They took pride in flouting them and describing publicly their adulterous adventures. *Imra al-Qays*, for instance, brazenly states :

Many a fair one like thee, though not like thee virgin,
Have I visited by night,
And many a lovely mother have I diverted from the care of her
Yearning in fact adorned with amulets,
When the suckling behind her cried
She turned round to him with half her body,
But half of it, pressed beneath my embrace, was not turned from me.[40]

There was in fact no notion of conjugal fidelity among most of the Arab tribes. "In old Arabia, the husband was so indifferent to his wife's fidelity, that he might send her to cohabit with another man to get himself a goodly seed.[41] There was no stain of illegitimacy attached to the child of a harlot.

'The custom of polyandry, *i.e.*, a custom of marriage under which a woman receives more than one man as her husband was very common in Arabia. The oldest and most direct evidence is that of Strabo which throws a good deal of light on the family life of the pagan Arabs' :[42]

> "Brothers have precedence over children, the kinship also and other offices of authority are filled by members of the stock in order of seniority. All the kindred have their property in common, the eldest being lord ; all have one wife and it is first come first served, the man who enters to her leaving at the door the stick which it is usual for

39. *The Seven Golden Odes of Pagan Arabia,* translated by Anne Blunt (London MDCCCIII), pp. 34-35.

40. *Diwan Imra al-Qays* edited by Muhammad Abul Fazl Ibrahim (Cairo, 1958), p. 12.

41. W. Robertson Smith, op. cit., p. 116.

42. *Ibid.*, p. 128.

> everyone to carry ; but the night she spends with the eldest. Hence all are brothers of all (within the stock) they have also conjugal intercourse with mothers ; and adulterer is punished with death ; and adulterer means a man of another stock."[43]

Under such conditions when a woman is considered to be the property of the whole tribe and she has no right to withhold her favours from any of the kinsfolk, 'the idea of unchastity could not exist ; their children were all full tribesmen, because the mother was a tribeswoman, and there was no distinction between legitimate and illegitimate offspring in our sense of the word.[44] Individual fatherhood is a comparatively modern notion which is fully defined and enunciated by Islam. The pagan Arabs "were in fact reckoned to the stock of their mother's lords before they were one man's children."[45]

Social life in Arabia is paradoxical and presents a gloomy picture of striking contrast. The Arabs, on the one hand, were generous and hospitable even to the point of fault, and took pride in entertaining liberally not only human beings, but also animals and beasts. On the other hand, the impending fear of poverty weighed so heavily upon them that they buried their female children alive, lest they should be impoverished by providing for them. In the same way, they had, on the one hand, little or no regard for chastity and would proudly narrate obscene accounts of their immoral exploits. On the other hand there had sprung up in them an utterly false sense of honour that impelled them to the practice of female infanticide, the underlying idea being that womenfolk, particularly daughters, were objects of disgrace.

The famous commentator Zamakhsharī in his note on Sūra *Al-Takwīr,* verse 8, gives an account of how female infants were buried alive in the graves :

> "When the girl attained the age of six, the husband said to the wife : 'perfume her and embellish her with ornaments.' He would then carry the female babe to the relatives of his wife and set forth to the wilderness. There

---

43. Quoted by W. Robertson Smith, op. cit., p. 133.
44. Quoted by W. Robertson Smith, op. cit., pp. 139-40.
45. W. Robertson Smith, op. cit., p. 147.

> a pit was dug. The child was made to stand by it. The father said, "Fix your eyes on it" and then pushed her from behind so that she fell in the pit where the unfortunate soul wept bitterly in a state of utter helplessness. The ditch was covered with clay and then levelled to the ground."[46]

It was said proverbially, "The despatch of a daughter is a kindness," and "the burial of the daughters is a noble deed."[47] Perhaps the most touching lines in Arabian poetry are those in which a father, oppressed by the thoughts of poverty and disgrace, wishes that his daughter may die before his very eyes and thus spare him the pangs of hunger and indignation :

> But for *Umayama's* sake I ne'er had grieved to want nor braved
> Night's blackest horror to bring home the morsel that she craved,
> Nor my desire is length of days because I know too well
> The orphan girl's hard lot, with kin unkind enforced to dwell,
> I dread that some day poverty will overtake my child,
> And shame befall her when exposed to every passion wild,
> She wishes me to live, but I must wish her dead, woe me :
> Death is the noblest wooer a helpless maid can see,
> I fear an uncle may be harsh, a brother be unkind,
> When I would never speak a word that rankled in her mind.[48]

"As to the extent to which child murder was practised as late as the time of the Prophet, we have some evidence in the fact that Sa'sa'a claimed to have saved a hundred and eight daughter.[49] It is recorded that when Muḥammad (peace be upon him) conquered Mecca and received the homage of the women

46. *Al-Kashshaf*, Ed., Mustafa Ḥussain Aḥmad, Cairo, iv. p. 708.
47. Freytag, *Arabum Proverbia*, Vol. I, p. 229, quoted by Prof. Nicholson, in his *A Literary History of the Arabs*, p, 91.
48. *Hamasah*, p. 150, Prof. Nicholson writes :
Although these verses are not pre-Islamic and belong in fact to a comparatively later period of Islam, they are sufficiently pagan in feeling to be cited in this connection. (p. 92.)
49. W. Robertson Smith, op, cit., p. 282,

in the most advanced centre of Arabian civilization, he still deemed it necessary formally to demand from them a promise not to commit child murder.[50]

It was due to the teachings of Islam that this custom of female infanticide, so prevalent amongst some of the Arab tribes and so many other nations of the world, came to an end. Mark with what force the *Qur'ān* condemns this inhuman practice :

> "Surely lost are they who slay their offspring foolishly and without knowledge and have forbidden that which Allah had provided for them ; a fabrication against Allah. Surely they have strayed and have not become guided ones. (vi : 141)
>
> And slay not your offspring for fear of want—We it is Who provide for you and them. (vi : 152)
>
> And slay not your offspring for fear of want. We provide for them and for yourselves. Verily their slaying is a great crime. (xvii : 33)
>
> And when the girl buried alive shall be asked : for what sin she was slain. (lxxxi : 8)

The weaker sex was in fact an unwelcome figure for the Arabs. The news of the birth of a daughter was received with a terrible shock in the family and the whole clan was rocked with anger. The Holy *Qurā'n* has in its own eloquent style drawn a vivid picture of this sad event.

> "They attribute daughters unto God—far be it from Him ! and for themselves they desire them not. When a female child is announced to one of them, his face darkens wrathfully with shame ; he hides himself from his people, because of the bad news he has had ! shall he retain it on (sufferance and contempt) or bury it in the dust ?
> And what an evil (choice) they decided on." (xvi : 59-61)

Not only were the female infants buried alive, but those who were spared, led a life of unspeakable misery and wretchedness. They were a sort of marketable commodity which could be sold in the open market to the highest bidder. At the time

---

50. Ibn al-Athir (Bulaq ed.), II, p. 105.

they were transferred to the custody of the husband their position was still worsened. Marriage for them was a kind of bondage and the marital rights of the husband were a kind of overlordship, and he was free to treat and dispose of his property as he liked. There is a very instructive passage as to the position of married women, which commences by quoting two lines spoken by a woman of the *Banu 'Āmir ibn Sa'sa'a* married among the *Tay* :

> Never let sister praise brothers of hers ; never let daughter bewail a father's death,
> For they have brought her where she is no longer a free woman
> And they have banished her to the farthest ends of the earth.[51]

The contract of marriage entitled the husband to a certain property right which was absolutely his to enjoy, or to transfer at his will. Indeed this right could even be inherited by his heir. It is recorded that in pagan Arabia, widows were inherited by the heirs of the deceased as goods and chattels. It was generally the eldest son who had the strongest claim to lay upon them. But in the cases, where there were no sons, the widows were passed on to the brother of the deceased or to his nephews.[52] Sometime a sheet of cloth was cast on them in order to secure their property rights.[53] The heirs in such cases either took them as their own wives or married them to the other people by getting a good price for them or kept them in confinement unless they redeemed themselves by paying off handsomely. It is this evil practice which has been condemned in the Holy *Qur'ān* in the following verse :

> O ye who believe ! It is not allowed unto you that ye may heir the woman forcibly.[54] (iv : 19)

---

51. Quoted by Robertson Smith, op. cit., pp. 77.
52. Quoted by Ibn Jarīr Tabari in his famous *Tafsir* on the authority of Muḥammad b. 'Ammār, edited by Muḥammad Shākir and Aḥmad Shākir, Cairo, Vol. VIII, p. 107.
53. *Ibid.*, p. 107.
54. "Forcibly" is a mere statement of fact, not a condition precedent. The practice of taking widows in heritage was actually carried on against their will. There is no suggestion here that the practice would become any more the lawful, if the widows submitted to it willingly. A Commentary of the Holy Qur'ān (English) by Maulana 'Abdul Mājid Daryābādi, Vol. I, p. 152.

Females were allowed no share in the inheritance of their husbands, parents and other relatives. "So far as the widow of the deceased is concerned, this is almost self-evident ; she could not inherit because she was herself not indeed absolutely, but quā wife, part of her husband's estate, whose freedom and hand were at the disposal of the heirs."[55]

There was no check on the number of wives that a man could take. One could marry as many women as he liked and dismiss them according to his own sweet will. No restriction was imposed upon man's lust. The pregnant woman was turned out of her husband's house without any claim and was taken by others under agreement with her former husband.

Economic Life

On examining closely the literature of *Sīrah* and *Ḥadīth* one can form a clear idea of the economic life of pre-Islamic Arabia. It should, however, be borne in mind that while it is convenient to speak of "Arabia", we are mainly concerned only with one region of it—the areas surrounding Mecca and Medina, *Ḥijāz* in the wider sense and the adjoining steppe-land of *Najd*.

The nomads who formed an overwhelming majority of Arab population depended upon stock-breeding, especially the breeding of the camel, for their sustenance. Agriculture was practised in the oases and certain favoured spots high up in the mountains. "The chief crop at the oases was date, while in the mountains, as at *al-Tā'if* cereals were important. *Yat̲h̲rib* (later known as Medina) was a large and flourishing oasis in the time of Muḥammad (peace be upon him). There were several Jewish agricultural colonies such as *K̲h̲aybar*. At Mecca, on the other hand, no agriculture at all was possible. The Yemen or Arabia Felix, was a fertile agricultural country where artificial irrigation had been practised from early times."[56]

Mecca, Muḥammad's home for half a century, as we have observed earlier was not fit for agriculture : "The town that had grown up around the well of *Zamzam* and the sanctuary of *Ka'bah*, was advantageously placed at the extreme ends of the Asia of the whites and the Africa of the blacks, near a breach in

55. W. Robertson Smith, op. cit., p. 95.
56. W. Montgomery Watt, *Muhammad at Mecca*, p. 2.

the chain of the *Sana*, close to a junction of roads leading from Babylonia and Syria to the plateaus of the Yemen, to the shores of the Indian Ocean and the Red Sea."[57]

"To *Mecca*, therefore, the nomad came for the goods brought from the four points of the compass by caravans. Originally the Meccans themselves were probably only middlemen and retailers and not the importers and entrepreneurs who organised caravans. But by the end of the sixth century A.D. they had gained control of most of the trade from *Yemen* to Syria—an important route by which the West got Indian luxury goods as well as South Arabian frankincense.[58] Various charges were levied upon the traders who passed through the route of Mecca ; for example, tithes were paid for entering the city, a special tax for securing permits to stay there, and a departure tax while leaving the town. In short, foreign merchants were entangled in a very intricate fiscal system, whether they settled in Mecca, or only passed through it, especially those who did not obtain the *jiwār* or guarantee of a local clan or notability."[59]

"*Mecca* may rightly be called a merchant republic. The financial operations of considerable complexity were carried on in the city. The nobility of *Mecca in Muhammad's* time besides the religious heads, and *Sheikhs* of clans, comprised of "financiers, skilful in the manipulation of credit, shrewd in their speculations, and interested in any potentialities of lucrative investment from Aden to Gaza or Damascus. In the financial net that they had woven not merely were all the inhabitants of *Mecca* caught, but many notables of the surrounding tribes also. The *Qur'ān* appeared not in the atmosphere of the desert, but in that of high finance."[60]

"The women shared these commercial instincts : *Abu Jahl's* mother ran a perfumery business. The activities of *tādjjra Khadijah* are well-known. Hind the wife of Abu Sufyan, sold her merchandise among the *Kalbis* of Syria."[61]

"*Riba* in all its ugliness formed the backbone of the pre-

---

57. *Encyclopaedia of Islam*, Vol. III, Article 'Mecca' (1936).
58. W. Montgomery Watt, op. cit., p. 3.
59. *Encyclopaedia of Islam*, Vol. III, Article 'Mecca' (1936).
60. W. Montgomery Watt, op. cit , p. 4
61. *Encyclopaedia of Islam*, Vol. III, Article 'Mecca'.

Islamic financial and economic system. The usual method adopted for lending and then of its repayment was highly exploitary. The money-lenders lent money to the people on heavy rates of interest, and when the money borrowed was not paid at the stipulated time, it was doubled and then trebled at the expiry of the third year. This is how it was enhanced with the passage of time."[62] In case when the debtor failed to pay loans along with the amounts of interest the credit sometimes took possession of the borrower's wife and children.

"Speculation too was rampant, on the rates of exchange, the load of a caravan which one tried to buy up, the yield of the harvests and of the flocks and lastly the provisioning of the town. Fictitious associations were formed and sales were made on which loans were borrowed."[63]

The other important town, which was commercially the rival of *Mecca* is known as *Tā'if*, the capital of an important tribe *Thaqīf*. It had an advantage over Mecca, that, along with its business activities, it had fertile lands. "The surrounding valleys supplied its export trade with ample materials, particularly easy to market in a region so unfavoured by nature as the *Ḥijāz*; wine, wheat and wood. Its bracing climate, its fruits, its grapes, the famous *Zabib* suggested this city to belong to Syria rather than to the bare landscapes of western Arabia.

"*Tā'if* was also an industrial town and leather was manufactured in its tanneries, which were so numerous, as we are told, as to render the air around foul. At the entrance and exit to the sea of the sands, *Tā'if* offered the ships of the desert provisions in the varied produce of the soil and loads in the products of its industry.

"There was a kind of *entente cordiale* between Mecca and *Tā'if*, an entente cemented by matrimonial alliances between *Quraysh* and *Ahlāf*. Many Meccans lived in Tā'if and had estates there."[64]

The way in which Medina is favoured by nature forms a striking contrast to Mecca. Its noteworthy feature is richness in water unusual in Arabia. The soil is of salty sand, lime and loamy clay and is every where fertile, particularly in the South.

---

62 *Tafsir* Tabari, Vol. IV, p. 55, in connection with Sūra iii A'ya 130.

63. *Encyclopaedia of Islam*, Vol. III, Article 'Mecca'.

64. *Encyclopaedia of Islam*, Vol. III, Article, 'Tā'if'.

It was, therefore, called the city of farmers. The people of Medina were highly skilled cultivators and efficient in the methods of transplantation. There is a tradition in the *Sahih* of *al-Bukhārī* narrated on the authority of *Abū Huraira* which sheds a good deal of light on the occupations of the people of *Mecca* and *Medina* during the time of the Holy Prophet. He observes :

"My brethren *Muhājirīn* (after their migration to *Medina*) were occupied in buying and selling goods in the market, whereas my brethren Anṣār remained busy in cultivation and gardening."[65]

The Jews of *Medina* were, however, interested in trade and industry besides cultivation.

Religion of the pre-Islamic Arabs

No history of pre-Islamic Arabia would be complete without an account of the religion of the Arabs. Unfortunately the material which we possess does not enable us to form a complete and vivid picture of the religion of the ancient Arabs. Whatever we know about it comes to us through isolated statements of Greek writers and from Greek or Semitic inscriptions, poetical compilations of the old poets, the few anecdotes and traditions embedded in the later Islamic literature. Some information may also be gathered from polemical allusions in the *Qur'ān*. Much credit goes to a few early Muslim scholars who laboriously collected and handed down to posterity, in a systematic form, information on heathen mythology and ritual. Among these scholars a specially prominent place must be assigned to *Hishām al-Kalbī*, usually known as *Ibn al-Kalbī* (819-820 C.E.), the author of *Kitāb al-Aṣnām* (The Book of Idols).

Judged by the scanty evidence available, it suffices to show that Muḥammad's (may the peace of Allah be upon him) contemporaries and the generations immediately preceding them, had little of any religion.

> To spiritual impulses he (the pagan Arab) was lukewarm, even indifferent. His conformity to religious practice followed tribal inertia and was dictated by his conservative respect for tradition. Nowhere do we find an illustration of genuine devotion to a heathen deity. A

65. *Bukkari, Kitāb al-Muzara'.*

story told about *Imru'al-Qays* illustrates this point. Having set out to avenge the murder of his father he stopped at the temple of *dhu-al-Khalasah* to consult the oracle by means of drawing arrows. Upon drawing 'abandon' thrice, he hurled the broken arrows at the idol exclaiming, 'Accursed One ! had it been thy father who was murdered thou wouldst not have forbidden my avenging him.''[66]

The Arabs were undoubtedly indifferent towards religion, but that should not lead any one to conclude that they had no notion of religion whatsoever. They have had an idea of an All-Supreme Power controlling the Universe, His wrath and favour, the Life after death and the angels. But all these ideas had been adulterated with idolatry—that yearning of the baser self in a man for a visible object of devotion, something that the eye can see and the hands touch, which finally develops into the worship of the creature more than that of the Creator. That the Arabs had a concept of an All-Powerful Lord can be illustrated from so many verses. *Nābigha*, for instance, says :

> I took an oath, and left no margin of doubt for who else can support man, besides Allah.[67]

Zahīr b. Abī Salamā in his well-known couplet affirms his faith in the day of judgement :—

> The deeds are recorded in the scroll to be presented on the day of judgement ;
> Vengeance can be taken in this world too ;[68]

The Holy *Qur'ān* eloquently testifies the fact that the unbelievers and polytheists of Arabia did not deny the existence of a Supreme Power, nor did they deny the fact that *Allah* is the Sole Creator of the heavens and the earth ; or that the whole mechanism of nature is operated in accordance with His Command, that He pours down the rain, drives the winds, controls the sun, the moon, the earth and everything else. Says the *Qur'ān* :

"And if you ask them, Who created the heavens and

---

66. Phillip K. Hitti, *History of the Arabs* (London, 1951), p. 96.
67. Ibn Qutaybah, *al-Shi'r-wa'al-Shu'arā'*, p. 110.
68. *Ibid.*, p. 88.

the earth and constrained the sun and the moon (to their appointed task) they would say : Allah. How, then, are they turned away ?" (xxix : 61)

"And if thou were to ask them, Who causeth water to come down from the sky, and wherewith reviveth the earth after its death ? they would verily say : *Allah.*" (xxix : 63)

"And if you ask them Who created them they will surely say : *Allah*. How then are they turned away ?" (xliii : 87)

"And if you should ask them, Who created the heavens and the earth ? they would most certainly say : The Mighty, the Knowing One has created them." (xliii : 9)

These verses make it abundantly clear that the Arabs of pre-Islamic period believed in the existence of one Great Deity, but at the same time they entertained the notion that the All-Powerful Lord had delegated His powers to some of His sacred personalities and objects—both animate and inanimate—who serve as the media through which the worshipper could come in contact with Him and thus earn His pleasure. It was under this misconception that they worshipped the idols of saintly persons, heavenly bodies and stones which were sometimes regarded not as divinities, but as the incarnations of Divine Being.

We have seen earlier that the Arabs had deep-rooted love for the tribe to which they belonged. This belief in the greatness and excellence of their tribe led them to carve a deity of their own and they sang hymns in its praise in order to win its favour. The tribe called *Kalb* worshipped *Wadd*, the *Hudhayl* worshipped ***Ṣuwā'***. The tribe of *Madh'hij* as well as the people of *Quraysh* worshipped *Yaghūth*, the *Khaywan* worshipped ***Ya'ūq***. The last-named idol was placed in their village called *Khaywan* at a distance of two nights' journey towards Mecca. Similarly the tribe of *Himyar* adopted ***Nasr*** as their god and worshipped it in a place called *Balkha*. The *Himyār* had also another temple (***bayt***) in *San'ā*. It was called ***Ri'am***, the people venerated it and offered sacrifices to it.'[69]

69. Hisham Ibn Al-Kalbī, *Kitāb al-Aṣnām*, edited by Aḥmad Zāki Pāsha, (Cairo, 1927), pp. 9-14.

The most ancient of all these idols was *Manāh*. The Arabs named their children after them as *'Abd Manāh* and *Zayd Manāh*. *Manāh* was erected on the seashore in the vicinity of Mushallal in Qudayd, between Medina and Mecca. All the Arabs used to venerate her and offer sacrifices to her. The *Aus* and the *Khazraj* were her most faithful devotees.[70]

Another goddess which was ardently worshipped by the Arabs was known as *al-Lāt*. "She was a cubic rock beside which a certain Jew used to prepare his barley porridge (*Sawīq*). Her custody was in the hands of *Banū Attab Ibn Mālik* of the *Thaqīf* who had raised an edifice over her. She was venerated by the Quraysh and almost all the tribes of Arabia and they named their children after her, *e.g.*, *Zayd al-Lāt* and *Taym al-Lāt*. The Arabs worshipped her till the tribe of *Thaqīf* embraced Islam. It was on this occasion that Muḥammad (may the peace of *Allah* be upon him) sent al-Mughīrah ibn Shu'bah to destroy this idol. It is recorded that when al-Lāt was demolished, *Shaddād ibn 'Arid-al-Jushmai* gave in verse a grim note of warning to the tribe of *Thaqīf* :

> Come not for help to al-Lāt, Allah has doomed her to destruction.
> How can you be helped by one who is not victorious,
> Verily, that which, when set on fire, resisted not the flames.
> Nor saved her stones, inglorious and worthless.
> Hence when the Prophet will arrive in your place,
> Not one of her devotees shall be left at the time of his departure.[71]

Still another goddess who was venerated by the Arabs is known as al-*'Uzzā*. She was introduced to the people by a person known as *Zalim ibn As'ad*. Her idol was erected in a valley in *Nakhlat al-Shāmiya* called *Hurad* alongside *al-Ghumyayr* to the right of the road from *Mecca* to *Iraq* about *Dhat-Iraq* and nine miles from *al-Bustān*. A grand superstructure was raised around it where the people would sit and receive oracular communication. It was a common practice with the Arabs to name their children after this goddess. The *Quraysh* were sent to circum-

70. *Ibid.*, p. 14.
71. Hishām Ibn Al-Kalbī, op. cit., p. 17.

ambulate the *Ka'bah* and sing hymns for these goddesses whom they called 'the daughters of Allah'.[72]

By al-Lāt and al-'Uzzā, and Manāh,
The third idols beside, verily they are the most exalted females.
Whose intercession is to be sought after.

The Holy Qur'ān has vehemently repudiated such foolish ideas and said in unequivocal terms :

Have ye seen Lāt and 'Uzzā and another. The third (goddess) Manāh ?
What ? For you the male sex, and for Him, the female ?
Behold, such would be indeed a division most unfair.

"These are nothing but names which ye have devised, ye and your fathers—for which God had sent down no authority (whatever). They followed nothing but fancy and what their own souls desire. Even though there has already come to them guidance from the Lord."

(LIII : 19-23).

The *Quraysh* also had several idols in and around the *Ka'bah*. The greatest of these was *Hubal*. It was carved out of red granite, in the form of a man with the right hand broken off. It stood inside the *Ka'bah*. Beside him stood ritual arrows used for divination by the soothsayer (*Kāhin*) who drew lots. On one of these arrows the word '*Sarih*' was inscribed and on the other was written the word '*Mulsaq*', which means 'consociated alien'. Whenever the legitimacy of a new-born babe was questioned the Arabs would shuffle the arrows and then throw them. If the arrow showed the word pure, it was finally decided that the child was legitimate. If, unfortunately, the arrow bearing the word 'Mulsaq' was drawn, the child was condemned as illegitimate. There were also some other arrows which could help the Arabs in the divination concerning marriage, death or the success or failure of the intending journey.[73]

The idol of *Hubal* was widely venerated by the Arabs, especially by the people of Mecca. It was the same idol which *Abū Sufyān ibn Harb* addressed when he emerged victorious

---

72. *Ibid.*, pp. 26-28.
73. Hishām Al-Ibn Kalbī, op. cit., p. 28.

after the battle of *Uhud* saying : *Hubal* ! be thou exalted (i.e., may thy religion triumph).

At this the Prophet replied :

'Allah is more Exalted, and more Majestic'.[74]

Among other idols *Usaf* and *Nā'ilah* are well-known. One of them stood close to *Ka'bah*, while the other was placed by the side of the *Zamzam*. Later, both of them were set together near the sacred fountain and the Arabs offered sacrifices to both of them. Ibn al-Kalbī writes :

> The Arabs were passionately devoted to the idols and worshipped them with fervour. Some of them erected a temple around which they centred their worship, whereas the others adopted venerated idols. A person who was devoid of means to build the temple for himself or carve an idol to worship it, would fix a stone in front of the sacred House or any other temple according to his desire and then circumambulate it in the same manner in which he would circumambulate around the Ka'bah.[75]
>
> They were so deeply attached to them that when any one amongst them intended to go on a journey, his last act before saying goodbye to the house, would be to touch the idol in the hope of an auspicious journey, and when he returned home the first act that he would perform was to touch it again with reverence in gratitude for a propitious return.[76]

The Arabs called these stones to which they showed veneration as *ansāb*. Whenever these stones resembled a living form they called them idols (*Aṣnām*) and graven images (*awthān*). The act of circumambulating them was called circumrotation (*dawr*).[77]

The Arabs were, however, fully conscious of excellence and superiority of *Ka'bah* to which they turned their steps for pilgrimage and visitation. The worship of the stones during their travels meant to prepetuate the religious ceremonies which they had performed at *Ka'bah* because of their immense devotion to it.

---

74. *Ibid.*
75. *Ibid.*, p. 33.
76. Hishām Ibn Al-Kalbī, op. cit., p. 33.
77. *Ibid.*

This practice originated in the custom of men carrying a stone from the sacred enclosures of *Mecca* when they set out on a journey, out of reverence for the *Ka'bah* and withersoever they went they set it up and made circuits about it as is made around the *Ka'bah* till at the last they adored every goodly stone they saw, forgot their religion, and substituted the faith of *Ibrāhīm* and *Ismā'īl* with the worship of the images and the idols.

It will not be out of place to mention briefly some of the practices at the *Ka'bah*. Amongst these practices, it is interesting to note that some came down from the time of *Ibrāhīm* and *Ismā'īl*, such as the veneration of the House and its circumambulation, the pilgrimage, the vigil (*al-Wukūf*) on *'Arafah* and *al-Muzdalifah*, sacrificing she-camels and raising the voice in the acclamation of the name of the Lord (*tahlīl*) but the *Meccans* had polluted all sacred performances with idolatrous practices, for example whenever they raised their voice in *tahlil*[78] they would declare their implict faith in the unity of the Lord through the *talbiyah*, but it was not unity pure and simple. It was alloyed with the association of their gods with Him. Thus their *talbiyah* was expressed in these words :

> Here we are, O Lord ! Here we are ! there is no associate for Thee except one who is Thine. Thou hast full supremacy over him and over everything that he possesses.[79]

The Arabs, both men and women, circumambulated the *Ka'bah* in a state of nudity with their hands-clapping, shouting and singing[80] and it was thought to be an act of highest piety. The argument which they advanced to justify such an indecent act was that it was unfair on their part to perform this sacred ceremony in those very clothes in which they had committed sins. They vehemently stressed this point by saying : "We will not circumambulate with the dress in which we perpetrated

---

78. The formula of the *tahlil* is——*La-ilāha ill āllah* (There is no god but Allāh).

79. Ibn Kat͟hīr, *Al-Bidāya wa'al-Nihāya* (Cairo, 1932), Vol. II, p. 188.

80. This seems to be implied in the Qur'ānic reference to the pagan Meccan : "Their prayers at the House are nothing else than whistling through the fingers, and clapping of hands." (viii : 35).

crimes. We will not worship Allah in the attire in which we committed heinous acts. We will not circumambulate in attire in which we disobeyed our Lord."[81]

The history of pre-Islamic *Arabia* brings into light the fact that the *Arabs*, besides the worship of idols, worshipped the heavenly bodies, trees and dead heroes of their tribes. "The Sun" (*Shams*) construed as feminine, was honoured by the several *Arabian* tribes with a sanctuary and an idol. The name *'Abd Shams* is found in many parts of the country. In the North we meet with the name *Amr-i-Shams*, "man of the Sun". For the worship of the rising sun, we have the evidence of *'Abd-al-Sharq* 'servant of the Raising one."[82] The heavenly bodies, especially worshipped were Canopus (*Suhail*), Sirius (*al-Sh'irā*), Aldebaran in Taurus with the Planets Mercury '(*Utārid*), Venus (*al-Zuhra*) Jupiter (*al-Mushtrī*), and Sale states that the temple at *Mecca* was said to have been consecrated to Saturn (*Zuḥal*).[83]

The *Arabs'* devotion to the Sun, Moon and other heavenly bodies is unquestionable ; but it is wrong to infer from this that the religion of the *Arabs* or even of the *Semites* entirely rested upon the worship of the heavenly bodies. This theory is not supported by facts. The *Arabs* had so many deities which cannot be explained as astral powers.[84] There were not a few deities which were supposed to possess animal forms, e.g., *Ya'ūq* represented by a horse and *Nasr* thought to have the figure of a vulture (*Nasr*). *Ya'ūq* is said to have been god of the *Hamdan* or of the *Morad* or of both tribes.[85] "*Nasr*, the vulture-god is said to have been an idol of *Himyarites*."[86]

Some of the *Arabian* deities seem to be personifications of abstract ideas, but they appear to have been conceived in a thoroughly concrete fashion. In particular, it is to be noticed that the *Arabs*, from a very early period, believed in the existence of certain supernatural powers which shaped their destiny.

---

81. Dr. Jawād 'Alī : *Tarikh al-Arab Qabl al-Islam*, (matba'al-Ilm al-Iraqi (1955) Vol. V, p. 225.
82. *Encyclopaedia of Religion and Ethics*, Article 'Ancient Arab', Vol. I, p. 661.
83. J. W. H. Stobbart, *Islam and its Founder*, p. 32.
84. *Encyclopaedia of Religion and Ethics*, Article 'Ancient Arab'.
85. W. Robertson Smith ; *Kinship and Marriage in Early Arabia*, p. 208.
86. *Ibid.*, p. 209.

Thus, for instance, time in the abstract form was popularly imagined to be the cause of all earthly misery. The Holy *Qu'rān* also refers to this wrong belief of the *Meccans* :

> "And they say : what is there but life in this world ? We shall die and we live, and nothing but time can destroy us. But of that they have no knowledge. They merely conjecture." (xlv : 24)

The Arab poets had also been alluding to the action of Time (*dahr, Zamān*) which brings sorrows and adversities. Then there is a fate which determines the course of life and irresistibly drives them to their destined ends. No one can change the pattern wrought by fate and no action, howsoever concentrated, can alter that which is unalterable. There is, however, one other expression *Manīyah* which often appears in poetry and throws a good deal of light on the fatalist views of the *Arabs*. The Meccans believed that the universe had been created by the Lord, but after bringing it into existence He had retired to the position of a silent Spectator and now it was the driving force of time and fate which was moving it to its destined end and bringing into being new events and episodes of life.[87]

In addition to these deities the pagan Arabs looked upon their priests with the same reverence as they had for their gods. In this class figured high the care-takers of temples and other sanctuaries. The priest of temple-guard (the *Arabic* word is *Sadin*), was, like the Nordic Code, a venerable man who was regarded as the owner of the sacred precinct. As a rule this privilege of ownership and direction belonged to a clan whose chief was the actual priest, but any member of the tribe could carry out the priestly functions, which, in addition to the guarding of the sacred grove, building of the idols, and the treasury where the *votine* gifts were stored, consisted of the practice of casting lots to determine the will of God, or to obtain His advice concerning important undertakings. The priest also served as an intermediary between the mortal and his Master.

Besides priesthood, there was a certain guild of seers whose members received their esoteric knowledge from spirit. *Kāhins*, as they were called, were supposed to possess the power of

---

87. Sayyid Mahmūd Shākir al-Ālūsī : *Bulugh al-Irb-fi Ahwal al 'Arab* (Cairo), Vol. II, pp. 220-21.

foretelling the coming events and of performing other superhuman feats. Any one who was eager to know what the future had in store for him would go in their presence with presents of food and animals. Sacrifices were offered at their feet and *Kāhin* would then lend his ear to a mysterious "voice from the heaven" known as the "oracle" and communicate it to the person concerned.[88]

The pagan *Arabs* included the poet also in the category of those mysterious beings who are endowed with supernatural knowledge, "a wizard in league with spirits (Jinn) or satans (S̲h̲ayāṭīn) and dependent on them the magical powers which he displayed...the pagan Shā'ir is the oracle of his tribe, their guide in peace and their champion in war. It was to him they turned for counsel when they sought new pastures ; only at his word would they pitch or strike their 'house of hair'."[89]

Not only the idols, the stars and the saints, were worshipped in Arabia, but the demons and *jinn* also were venerated in every section of their society. "These *jinn* differed from the gods not so much in their nature as in their relation to man. The gods are, on the whole friendly ; the *jinn*, hostile. The latter are, of course, personifications of the fantastic notions of the terrors of the desert and its wild animal life. To the gods belong the regions frequented by man, to the jinn belong the unknown and untrodden parts of the wilderness."[90]

The *Arabs* also adored the graves of their forefathers and sought assistance from the departed souls in the hour of distress. They believed that the soul of the dead person had the power to incarnate itself in different bodies, both human and non-human.[91]

The belief in signs as betokening future events, was, of course, found no less among the *Arabs* than among other peoples. Some birds were regarded as auspicious, other as ominous. The animals that crossed a man's path and the direction in which they moved alike conveyed a meaning. Many of these signs were such as every one could understand ; others were intelligible only to persons especially trained. One peculiar art consisted in

88. Dr. Jawād 'Ali, *Tārikh al-Arab*, Vol. V. p. 177.
89. Nicholson : *A Literary History of the Arabs*, pp. 72-73.
90. Hitti, *History of the Arabs*, p. 98.
91. Jawād 'Alī, *Tār kh al-Arab*, Vol. V, p. 40.

scaring birds and drawing omens from their flight ; this operation was known as *Zajr*.[92]

The pages of history reveal the fact that fire was also worshipped in *Arabia* as a symbol of Divine power. This practice seems to have penetrated in the Arab lands from their neighbouring country Persia, where it had been rooted deeply. The Magian religion was popular particularly with the tribe of Tamim.

The Jews who fled in great numbers into Arabia from the fearful destruction of their country by the Romans made proselytes of several tribes, those of *Kinanah, al-Hārith Ibn Ka'bah,* and *Kindah* in particular, and in time became very powerful, and possessed of several towns and fortresses. "But the Jewish religion was not unknown to the *Arabs* at least *about* a century before. Abu Qarib Asad who was king of *Yemen* introduced *Judaism* among the idolatrous *Himyarities*."[93]

Christianity had likewise made a little progress amongst the *Arabs* before the advent of *Muḥammad* (may the peace of *Allah* be upon him). How this religion was actually introduced into this land is uncertain, but the persecutions and disorders which took place in the Eastern Church soon after the beginning of the third century, obliged great number of Christians to seek shelter in that country of liberty. "The principal tribes that embraced Christianity were *Himyār, Ghassān, Rabī'a, Tagh'ab, Bahra, Tunukh,* part of the *Tay* and *Kudā'a,* the inhabitants of *Najrān,* and the *Arabs* of *Hīra.* As to the two last, it may be observed that those of *Najran* became Christian in the time of *Dhu Nuwas.*"[94]

Christianity as a religion could not, however, succeed in making a permanent hold in *Arabia* and could not supersede idolatry. The Christian anchorites, dwelling in their solitary cells in the country aided in gaining scattered converts amongst the *Arabs.* This failure of the Christian monks in spreading the Gospel among the people of *Arabia* may be attributed to the

---

92. *Encyclopaedia of Religion and Ethics,* Vol. I. p. 667. Arabs, Ancient (New York, 1908).
93. E. M. Wherry, *A Commentary of the Qur'ān,* (London, 1882) Vol. I, p. 45.
94. E. M. Wherry, *A Commentary of the Qur'ān,* (London, 1882).

fact that by the time of its penetration into *Arabia*, it had ceased to be a living force. It was a mere hotchpotch of dogmas and transcendental hopes having no relationship with the practical life. Its promoters, the clergymen, had degenerated themselves into a class of self-seekers :

> "The clergy by drawing the abstrusest niceties into controversy, and dividing and subdividing about them into endless schisms and contentions, they had so destroyed that peace, love and charity from among them which the Gospel was given to promote, and instead thereof continually provoked each other to that malice, rancour, and every evil work, that they had lost the whole substance of their religion, while they thus eagerly contended for their own imaginations concerning it, and in a manner quite drove Christianity out of the world by those very controversies in which they disputed with each other about it. In those dark ages it was that most of those superstitions and corruptions we now just abhor in the Church of Rome were not only broached but established, which gave great ad vantages to the propagation of *Muhammadism*. The worship of the saints and images, in particular, was then arrived at such a scandalous pitch that it even surpassed whatever is now practised amongst the Romanists".[95]

Such were the real religious conditions of the *Arabs* before Muḥammad (may the peace of *Allah* be upon him). "Causes are sometimes conjured up", observes Muir, "to account for results produced by an agent apparently inadequate to effect them. Muhammad arose, and forthwith the *Arabs* were aroused a new and a spiritual faith ; hence the conclusion that *Arabia* was fermenting for the change and prepared to adopt it. To us, calmly reviewing the past, pre-Islamic history belies the assumption. After five centuries of Christian evangelisation, we can point to but a sprinkling here and there of Christian converts, the *Bani Harith* of *Najran* ; the *Bani Hanifa* of *Yemena* ; some of the *Bani Tay* at *Tayma* ; and hardly any more. Judaism, vastly more powerful, had exhibited spasmodic efforts at proselyt-

---

95. E M. Wherry, *A Commentary of the Qur'ān* (London, 1882), Vol. I, pp. 61-62.

ism ; but as an active and converting agent, the Jewish faith was no longer operative. In fact, viewed in a religious aspect, the surface of *Arabia* had been now and then gently rippled by the feeble efforts of Christianity, the sterner influences of Judaism had been occasionally visible in a deeper and more troubled current ; but the tide of indigenous idolatry and *Ishmaelite* superstition setting strongly from every quarter towards the *Ka'bah* gave ample evidence that the faith and worship of *Mecca* held the Arab mind in a rigorous and undisputed thraldom.''[96]

96. William Muir, *Life of Muḥammad,* p. lxxxv.

Chapter 2

The Dawn

The brightest day follows the darkest night. So it is in the world of living men. *Arabia* was plunged in the darkness of evil and superstition. The rest of the world was no better. But after the gloom of ages there appeared in the person of Muḥammad (peace be on him) a bright sun on the firmament of human history.

The Promise

Prophecies about his advent are met with in the previous sacred books. The *Qur'ān* emphatically asserts that the birth of the Prophet *Muḥammad* was foretold by each and all the foregoing prophets through whom covenant[1] was made with their respective peoples that they would accept him when he came.

> When *Allah* made (His) covenant with the prophets, [He said :] Behold that which I have given you of the Scripture and Knowledge. And afterward there will come unto you a messenger confirming that which ye possess. Ye shall believe in him and ye shall help him. He said : Do you agree, and will ye take up My burden [which I lay upon you in this matter]? They answered : "We agree". He said : "Then bear ye witness. I will be a witness with you."[2]

Similarly, the last of the *Israelite* prophets, *Jesus*, promised his people the arrival of a Comforter :

> If ye love me, keep my commandments. And I will pray the Father, and he shall give you another Comforter, that he may abide with you for ever.[3]

---

1. This covenant refers according to Qurtubi to Holy Prophet. See his *Tafsir-al-Jāmi'al-Ahkam al-Qur'ān* (Cairo, 1957), Vol. IV, p. 125.
2. The Qur'ān, iii : 81.
3. John, xiv : 15-16.

Being aware that the Prophet Muḥammad (peace be on him) was destined to come after him and that he would be a prophet-king, Jesus said :

> Nevertheless I tell you the truth ; It is expedient for you that I go away : for if I go not away, the Comforter[4] will not come unto you ; but if I depart, I will send him unto you. And when he is come, he will reprove the world of sin, and of righteousness, and of judgment.[5]

Referring to the completion of Scriptures and the exposition of all truths by Muḥammad (peace be on him), to his prophecies and to his revelation, Jesus observed :

> I have yet many things to say unto you, but ye cannot bear them now. Howbeit when he, the Spirit of truth, is come, he will guide you into all truth : for he shall not speak of himself ; but whatsoever he shall hear, that shall he speak : and he will shew you things to come.[6]

Again :

> I will raise them up a prophet from among their brethren, like unto thee, and will put my words in his mouth ; and he shall speak unto them all that I shall command him. And it shall come to pass, that whosoever will not hearken unto my words which he shall speak in my name, I will require it of him.[7]

The expression "their brethren" in the verses refers to the children of Ismāʻīl who are the brethren of the *Israelites*.

The Fulfilment

All these prophetic words predict in clear terms the dawn of a spiritual light. This light came in the world on 22 April, 571 A.D., on the ninth of Rabīʻ al-Awwal, of the first year of the Elephant.[8]

---

4. There is a preponderance of evidence in support of the view that the original word which has been translated *Periklutos*, meaning praised and illustrious, meant the same as the words Muḥammad and Aḥmad : not *Parakletes* meaning comforter as is amply shown by Rev. Heorne in his *Introduction to the Critical Study of the Scriptures*.

5. John, xvi : 7.

6. *Ibid.*, 12-13.

7. Deuteronomy, xviii : 18-19.

8. It alludes to the famous Abyssinian attack on Mecca in which the invaders had employed a large number of elephants.

Muḥammad's genealogy has been traced beyond all shadow of doubt to the noble house of *Ismā'īl* in about the fortieth descent. He was the son of *'Abd Allāh* the son of *'Abd al-Muṭṭalib*, the son of *'Abd Manāf*, the son of *Qusayy*, the son of *Kilab*. *Qusayy* was the effective ruler of *Mecca*. The Prophet's mother Āminah was the daughter of *Wahb ibn 'Abd Manāf* of the *Zahrah* family. Thus his father and mother stood eminent in respect of nobility of descent and sublimity of character.

It is recorded that in pursuance of his Divine mission *Muḥammad* (peace be on him) on his return to *Mecca*, sent several envoys to the neighbouring rulers calling them to the fold of *Islam*. One of the noted emperors to whom an emissary was despatched was Heraclius of Byzantine. He treated the messenger with great respect. Before leaving Syria, however, he tried to acquaint himself with the character of the man who had sent him that message. With this objective he summoned some of the *Arab* merchants who had arrived at *Gaza* with a caravan from *Arabia*. Curiously enough, *Abū Sufyān*, who was still a deadly opponent of *Muḥammad* and his Divine mission was among those who had come on a commercial visit. He was also summoned to the court. Among the numerous inquiries that Heraclius made about the character and personality of *Muḥammad* and his teachings, one pertained to his descent. In spite of the grudge that he nursed against Muḥammad (peace be on him), *Abū Sufyān* could not deny the fact that he came of a noble family.[9] At this, Heraclius at once remarked: "The apostles belong to pure and genuine nobility."[10] The stories relating to the base and plebian origin[11] of *Muḥammad* (peace be

9. Ibn Kathīr, *Al-Bidāyah wa'al-Nihāyah*, Vol, II, p. 252.

10. Ibn Ḥajar 'Asqalāni, *Fatḥ al-Bāri*, Vol. II, p. 162.

11. In his book *Muḥammad and the Rise of Islam*, Margoliouth says: "Muhammad came of a humble family ; this crops up in many places. The Kuraish in the Koran wonder why a prophet should be sent to them who was not of noble birth" (p. 47). Margoliouth is perhaps referring to the verse of the Holy Qurān : "And they say : if only this Qurān had been revealed to some great man of the two towns." (xliii : 31) In this verse the "greatness" to which Quraysh referred does not mean the nobility of the family, it is the worldly wealth on which they prided, "Is it they who apportion their Lord's mercy ? We have apportioned among them their livelihood in the life of the world, and raised some of them above others in rank that some of them may take labour from others ; and the mercy of the Lord is better than (the wealth) that they amass." (xliii : 32) [Contd.

on him) are thus calumny of evil minds. These are all baseless, too preposterous to deserve the consideration of any serious person.[12]

Sometime after his marriage, *'Abd Allāh*, the father of the Prophet, *Muḥammad* (peace be on him), set out on a commercial journey to Syria and on his way back he fell ill and passed away at *Medina*. He was hardly twenty-five years[13] of age and *Āminah* was still expectant. The Prophet *Muḥammad* was born as a posthumous child. He was, therefore, left to the care of his grandfather, *'Abd al-Muṭṭalib*, one of the most influential men of *Mecca*, and to his gentle and heartbroken mother *Āminah*. The grand old man received the news of the birth of his grandson with mingled feelings of joy and sorrow. He was glad to be blessed with a male child from the loins of his departed son, but was deeply grieved to see that his son was not alive to share this happiness. He hurried to the house of his son, tears rolling down his cheeks. He took the baby in his arms and went to the Ka'bah; and as he stood beside the sacred house, he gave thanks to God.[14]

The grandfather named the new-born child as *Muḥammad*.[15] This and the other name, *Aḥmad*, which has approximately the same meaning, are both derived from the Arabic root *ḥamd* "to praise."

PROPHET'S CHILDHOOD

The Infant

The infant *Muḥammad*, shortly after his birth, was made over to *Thuwaybah*, the slave girl of his uncle *Abū Lahab* who

---

Ibn 'Abbās, one of the oldest exegetists of the Holy Qur'ān, in his famous Commentary has said in clear words : "The word mercy (Raḥmah) signifies prophethood and the Book (Qur'ān) 'and they amass' means : what the Infidels collect in the form of riches and worldly pomp and show." (p. 387)

12. Zurqāni in his famous book *Sharḥ al-Mawāhib al-Laduniyā* has discussed this point : see Vol. I, p. 61.

13. Ibn Kathīr : *Al-Bidāyah wa'al-Nihāyah*, Vol. II, pp. 263, 264 ; Ibn al-Qayyim, *Zād al-Ma'ād*, Vol. I, p. 32.

14. Ibn Sa'd *Al-Tabqat*, Vol. I, p. 103 and Ibn Hishām, Vol. I, p. 160.

15. According to its derivation, the word signifies an eminent personality who, on account of his great and genuine qualities, is praised with feelings of love and adoration. It also means one who is the best embodiment of the most perfect and admirable qualities.

had lately suckled *Ḥamzah*. Though nursed by her only for a few days, the Prophet retained a deep sense of kinship and always, looked upon her and her family with profound respect and gratitude. When the Prophet was married to *Khadījah*, Thuwaybah would often come to him and she always received from him the love and affection of a loving son. *Muḥammad* could not forget and after his migration to *Medina*, he used to send her clothes and many other gifts as a token of his love and respect. At the time of the conquest of *Mecca*, he inquired about her and her son but they had died and she had left no other relative to mourn her.[16]

It was the general custom of the wealthy Arabs to send their children away to bedouin nurses so that they might grow up in the free and healthy surroundings of the desert whereby they would develop a robust frame and acquire the pure speech and manners of the bedouins, who were noted both for chastity of their language and for being free from those vices which usually develop in sedentary societies and accompany material abundance and prosperity.

The Prophet (peace be upon him) was later entrusted to *Ḥalimāh*, a bedouin woman of the tribe *Banū Sa'd*, a branch of *Hawāzin*. The lady did not accept the child without reluctance, since the care of a fatherless child was less likely to be well rewarded than that of the one whose parents were alive. She proved, however, most faithful to her trust. The infant was carefully and lovingly tended, and was growing up as a healthy and vigorous child when, at the age of five, he was finally returned to her mother's charge. Traditions delightfully relate how *Halīmah* and the whole of her household were favoured by successive strokes of good fortune while the child *Muḥammad* lived under her care. It will suffice to give the best known of the accounts as embodied in *Ibn Hishām*. *Jahim b. Abū Jahim*, the client of *al-Harith b Ḥalib* states that *Ḥalīmah*, the nurse of *Allah's* messenger (God bless him), narrated that she, along with her husband and a suckling babe, set out from her village in the company of some women of her clan in quest of children to suckle. She said :

It was an year of drought and famine and we had

16. Suhaylī, *al-Raud, al-Unuf*, Vol. I, p. 108 and Ibn Ḥajar 'Asqalāni, *Fatḥ al-Bārī*, Vol. IX, p. 124.

nothing to eat. I rode on a brown she-ass. We also had with us an old she-camel. By God we could get not even a drop of milk. We could not have a wink of sleep during the night for the child kept crying because of hunger. There was not enough milk in my breast and even the she-camel had nothing to feed him. At length we reached Mecca looking for children to suckle. Not even a single woman amongst us accepted the messenger of God (may God bless him) offered to her. As soon as they were told that he was an orphan, they refused him. We had fixed our eyes on the reward that we would get from the child's father. An orphan ! What are his grandfather and mother likely to do? So we spurned him because of that. Every woman who came with me got a suckling and when we were about to depart I said to my husband : "By God, I do not like to go back along with the other women without any baby. I should go to that orphan and must take him." He said, "There is no harm in doing so and perhaps God may bless us through him." So I went and took him and I did it simply because there was no other alternative left for me but to take him. When I lifted him in my arms and returned to my place I put him on my breast and to my great surprise, I found enough milk in it. He drank to his heart's content and so did his foster brother and then both of them went to sleep although my baby had not been able to sleep the previous night. My husband then went to the she-camel to milk it and, to his astonishment, he found plenty of milk in it. He milked it and we drank to our fill and enjoyed a sound sleep during the night. The next morning my husband said : "By God, *Ḥalīmah,* you must understand that you have been able to get a blessed child." And I replied : "By the grace of *Allah,* I hope so."[17]

The tradition is explicit on the point that *Ḥalīmah's* return journey and her subsequent life, as long as the Prophet stayed with her, was encircled with a halo of good fortune. The donkey that she rode when she came to *Mecca* was lean and almost foundered ; it recovered speed much to the amazement of *Ḥalīmah's* fellow travellers. By the time they reached the

17. Ibn Hishām, Vol. I, p. 163.

encampments in the country of the clan of *Sa'd*, they found the scales of fortune turned in their favour. The barren land sprouted forth luxuriant grass and their beasts came back to them satisfied and full of milk.[18] The child grew up to be strong and healthy and learnt the pure, chaste *Arabic* of the desert. The Prophet himself was conscious of this attainment. Abū Bakr once said : "O Messenger of God, you are very eloquent in your expression." The Prophet replied : "I was born in a family of the *Quraysh* and suckled by a lady of *Banū Sa'd*."[19]

Muḥammad (peace be upon him) remained for full five years in the desert with *Ḥalimah* and her family in the quiet serenity of the country-side. During these years he developed the habit of meditation and reflection which persisted throughout his life. The handsome child, grateful by nature, loved *Ḥalīmah* and her children and helped them in their daily errands. He developed such a deep attachment to *Ḥalīmah* that he cherished a life long affection for her family. *Ḥalīmah* used to visit him in *Mecca* after his marriage with *Khadījah*. It was an year of drought in which so many cattle heads had perished. *Muḥammad's* affectionate nurse went to *Khadījah* and that generous lady sent her back with the gift of a noble riding camel and a flock of forty sheep.[20] On another occasion the Prophet spread out his mantle for her to sit upon as a token of special respect.[21] Many years later his foster-sister was brought to him along with many other captives in his expedition to *Tā'if*. She claimed that she was his foster-sister. *Muḥammad* (peace be upon him) inquired how he could verify this statement, and she replied : "Once you gave me this bite upon my back, while I was carrying you." The Prophet recognised the mark, spread his mantle, and asked her to sit upon it. He gave her the option of remaining in his house with honour and comfort, but she preferred to return to her people with the gifts the Prophet had given her.

Ir was during his stay with *Ḥalīmah* that the Prophet's heart was purified by the angels.[22] In this again, we see an

18. Ibn Hishām, Vol. I, p. 164.
19. Suhayli, op. cit., p. 109.
20. Ibn Sa'd, Vol. I, pp. 113 f.
21. *Ibid.*, p 114.
22. *Ibid.*, p. 165.

Arabic version of the Psalmist's prayer, "Create in me a clean heart, O Lord."

The Child

Muhammad was hardly six ysars old when his mother died and the charge of the child then fell exclusively on his grandfather *'Abd al-Muṭtalib.* He loved him as dearly as his own life. But *Muḥammad's* sorrows were not yet over. Two years later, his aged grandfather who was now eighty-two also died. The young boy followed the bier of his grandfather at the age of eight, with a heavy and tearful eyes. The charge of the Prophet was now passed on to his uncle *Abū Ṭālib,* who was the brother of the Prophet's father *'Abdullah.* Like all other young boys of his age, the Prophet tended the sheep and goats of *Mecca* and grazed them upon the neighbouring hills and valleys. While in *Medina* he used to remember this period of his life and would remark : "It has a certain similarity with the function of the prophets. *Moses* had tended flocks of goats and the same was the case with *David.* Now I have been commissioned with this office, and I also tended the goats and sheep of my family at the place known as *Ajyād.*[23]

This occupation of tending the flocks is congenial to the thoughtful and meditative temperament which is an indispensable quality of a prophet. "While he watched the flocks, his attention would be riveted by the signs of an Unseen Power spread all around him. The twinkling stars and bright constellations gliding through the dark blue sky silently along, would be charged to him with a special message; the loneliness of the desert would arm with a deeper conviction that speech which day everywhere utters unto day ; while the still small voices, never unheard by the attentive listener, would swell into grandeur and more imperious tones when the tempest swept with its forked lightning and far rolling thunder along the vast solitudes of the mountains."[24]

The Holy *Qur'ān* also calls upon man to ponder over both the world external to him (*āfāq*) and the world within his self

---

23. Ibn Ḥajar, op. cit., Vol. IV, p. 364, of Ijārah. See also Bukhāri, K. al-Ijārah.

24. William Muir : *The Life of Muhammad* (London, 1894), pp. 17-18.

(*nafs*). Therein he will find, according to the *Qur'ān*, not only signs of the Lord, but the eternal principle of harmony and balance :

> We have not created the heavens and the earth and whatsoever is between them in sport. We have not created them except to bear the truth, but most people know it not. (xliv : 38-39)

The *Qur'ān* stresses that there are signs of the Ultimate Reality in the sun, the moon, in the lengthening out of shadows, in the alternation of day and night and in the variety of human complexions and tongues ; in successes and reverses among people, in fact, the whole of nature as revealed to the sense-perception of man and the records of man's past. And it is the duty of every sincere man, who is anxious to be in harmony with the demands of Reality, to reflect on these signs and not to pass by them, "as if he is deaf and blind". This note 'as if he is deaf and blind' is of very great significance. Wherever attention is drawn to the manifestation of life calling for reflection and introspection, expressions as "herein are portents", "herein are signs for the folk who reflect"; "for man of knowledge"; "for the folk who heed"; and for the folk who understand echoes and reverberate only to emphasize the importance which the *Qur'ān* attaches to reflection as a means of obtaining insight : "Show us the nature of things as they really are," is a characteristic prayer of the Prophet. The first step on the road to it is reflection. Thus opportunity for meditation is provided to the prophets by bringing them to the heart of nature.

> There is a tongue in every leaf.
> A voice in every rill,
> A voice that speaketh everywhere,
> In flood and fair, through earth and air,
> A voice, that's never still.

Some Misinterpretations about Prophet's experience as a shepherd

It is, however, significant that the Western biographers of the Prophet, while writing his life-story, have greatly stressed the mental experiences of the Prophet as a shepherd. They want to give the impression that what the Prophet called revelation was nothing but the early reminiscences of his pastoral life. "Thus, we may presume," says William Muir, "was cherished a deep and earnest faith in the Deity as an ever-present, all-directing Agent ; a faith which in after days the Prophet was wont to enforce from the memories, no doubt, of these early days by eloquent and heart-stirring appeals to the sublime operations of Nature and the beneficent adaptations of an ever-present Providence."[25]

This view is absolutely erroneous. The direct contact with nature no doubt provided the Holy Prophet with an opportunity to "see into the life of things" and perceive in its mirror, the presence of a Master Mind. But it is wrong to say that the experiences gathered during this period were later transfigured into revelation. The reflections over the phenomenal world and the world within man's self brighten our intellect and chasten our emotions, delight our senses and raise and soothe our spirits, and thus enable us to appreciate fully the words of *Allah* ; but these cannot serve as substitutes for revelation. These may be regarded, at best, as mental and emotional training in order to prepare a person to receive "the visions of Him Who reigns".

The vision of the physical phenomena may lead us to the right conclusions about the universe and its Creator, but that is not enough. We want to be acquainted with the spiritual principle working at the heart of things, and this we can get neither by means of deductive reasoning, nor is the subject such as to lead itself to direct observation. The only means left is revelation. Matter and energy do not exhaust the contents of the universe. There is "something" beyond them. This 'something', which is most important, perhaps even indispensable, for human life, is neither physical phenomenon nor mere transformation of energy, its ceaseless kaleidoscopic change, but the disclosure of spiritual substance and an Infinite Reality under the flux and reflux of phenomena. No man, not even the Prophet, can obtain, by means of his own intellectual perception, the complete view of this Infinite Reality. The *Holy Qur'ān* informs *Muḥammad* of this important limitation :

> "This is of the tidings of the Unseen which We inspire in thee. Thou thyself knowest it not, nor did thy folk

25. William Muir, op. cit , p. 18.

(know it) before this." (xi : 49)

The *Qur'ān* further states that it is the responsibility of the Creator to illuminate the right path by revealing His message to His prophets (may peace be upon all of them).

It should also be borne in mind that the period of tending the flocks of sheep forms the training ground for the guidance of mankind. The shepherd is always on the alert with regard to his flock and takes full care of the animals so that these may not go astray or fall victims to the beasts of prey. So also is the case with a prophet. He is the shepherd of humanity; always thinking of their welfare and always trying to lead them along the straight path to their well-being. It is from this experience as a shepherd that there sprang up love for man and passion to alleviate the sufferings of mankind steeped in ignorance. Such was the anxiety of the Holy Prophet to bring people to the path of *Allah* that it began telling on his health and he was warned by the Lord in the following words :

It may be that thou tormentest thyself,
(O *Muḥammad*) because they believe not. (xxvi : 3)

Prophet's Youth

When Muḥammad was twelve years old, his uncle *Abū Ṭālib* who was a trader, undertook a business trip to Syria. He was reluctant to take *Muḥammad* with him because of the hardships of the journey. *Muḥammad* was, however, unwilling to remain separated from his uncle. He clung to him and after a good deal of pleading prevailed upon his kind uncle to take him to *Syria* along with him. It was during this journey that he is said to have met *Baḥīra*, a Christian monk. This meeting has been time and again emphasized by several Christian scholars who deduce that it was from Baḥīra that he learnt to hate the idols.

The authentic records of the life-story of *Muḥammad* (peace be upon him) prove beyond all shadow of doubt that there is not a grain of truth in this deduction. That Baḥīra met *Muḥammad* is a fact, but the claim that he learnt from the Christian monk the concept of one God and hatred against idolatry is absolutely baseless. We on the contrary learn that the Holy Prophet in his very first talk showed his utmost contempt for idol-worship that had taken a firm hold on the minds of the people around him. We reproduce below a passage from Ibn Hishām in order to give an idea of what actually transpired between Muḥammad and Baḥīra :

> When *Baḥīra* saw him he began to eye him keenly and to observe the features of his body so as to find out in him the signs (of prophethood) which he already knew (from the Holy Scriptures). Then, when the party had finished eating and had broken up, *Baḥīra* went up to him and said, "Young man ! I adjure you by *al-Lāt* and *al-'Uzzā* to answer my questions." *Baḥīra* said so only because he had heard his people swearing by these two. They say that the Messenger of God (God bless him and preserve him) said to him, "Do not ask by *al-Lāt* and *al-'Uzzā* for by God there is absolutely nothing I detest so much as these two." So *Baḥīra* said to him, "Then, in God's name, answer what I ask you," he said. So *Baḥīra* began to ask him about certain particulars of his condition in sleep. Then the Messenger of God (God bless and preserve him) set about answering him ; and what he said agreed with the description of him in *Baḥīra's* (book) . . .

Then he (*Baḥīra*) went to his uncle *Abū Ṭālib*, and said :

> Return to your own country with your nephew, and take care of him against the Jews, for, by God, if they see him and know what I know about him, they will desire evil ; for great fortune is in store for your nephew. So hurry to your country with him.

His uncle *Abū Ṭālib* set out with him quickly and soon reached *Mecca* on the completion of their trade in Syria.[26]

Muḥammad was hardly fifteen[27] when the "sacrilegious" wars (*ḥarb al-fijār*)—which continued with varying fortunes and considerable loss of human life for a number of years—broke out at *'Ukāz* between the *Quraysh* and the *Banū Kinānah* on the one side and the *Qays Aylān* on the other. In one of these battles

---

26. Ibn Hishām, I, p. 182. Some of the modern critics of Ḥadith and of the early biographers of the Holy Prophet have said that this incident is not authenticated by authentic traditions, but it is not correct. 'Asqalāni says that the incident as recorded in Tirmidhī is authentic even according to the criteria in respect of transmission.
27. *Ibid.*, p. 184.

the Prophet (peace be upon him) attended on his uncles but did not raise arm against their opponents. His efforts were confined to picking up the arrows of the enemy as they fell, and handing them over to his uncles.

At the conclusion of these wars, when peace was restored, people felt the need of forming a confederacy at *Mecca* for suppressing violence and injustice and vindicating the rights of the weak, the indigent, and the destitute. *Muḥammad* played an important role in its formation and this league exercised a strong moderating influence on the different tribes of *Arabia*.[28]

The authorities agree in ascribing to the youth of *Muḥammad* (peace be upon him) a modesty of deportment and purity of manners rare among the people of *Mecca*. During all this time he proved himself to possess a noble and spotless character, to be an absolute believer in one God, and thoroughly trustworthy in respect of his companionship, help and guidance. He was affectionate, kind, and sympathetic to his compatriots ; always considerate, truthful, and sincere ; perfectly faithful in respect of all trusts and promises. He kept himself aloof from gambling, drinking, vulgar wrangling, voluptuousness, and all the vices rampant among his compatriots. He was always fair and honest in all his dealings ; generous and obliging to his friends and benefactors. He walked humbly and thoughtfully in the midst of the arrogant, headstrong and marauding tribes of Arabia. He hated all appearance of show, vanity and pride and would readily attend to the addresses of children and spare no pains in alleviating the sufferings of the poor, old, and the weak. He always impressed his people by his wise, tranquil and piety-inspiring countenance and, by his intimate kindliness and graceful manners, won the heart of everyone who came into contact with him, passing by all the temptations of vice with a majestic indifference. The spotless character and honourable bearing of the unobstrusive youth won the approbation of his fellow-citizens and earned the titles, by common consent, of *al-Amīn* and *al-Ṣādiq*, meaning trustworthy and truthful.

---

28. Ibn Sa'd, Vol. I, p. 129.

The Trader

Thus respected and honoured, *Muḥammad* lived a quiet life in the family of *Abū Ṭālib*. He was never covetous. All through his life he showed no enthusiasm for the pursuit of riches. If left to himself, he would probably have preferred the quiet life. But he was always anxious to help his uncle who had the burden of a large family upon him. So whenever the Holy Prophet found any opportunity he cheerfully helped him.

The account given by *Ibn Sa'*d is as follows :

> When his nephew was five-and-twenty years of age, *Abū Ṭālib* addressed him in these words :
>
> "I am, as you know, a man of scanty means, and truly the time are hard with me. Now there is a caravan of your own tribe about to start for Syria and Khadījah, daughter of *Khuwaylid*, is in need of the services of men of our tribe to take care of her merchandise. If you offer yourself for this enterprise, she would readily accept your services." *Muḥammad* (peace be on him) replied, "Be it as you say." Abū Ṭālib went to her and inquired whether she would entrust this enterprise to his nephew. *Khadījah*, who had already heard of the honesty, trustworthiness, and high moral character of *Muḥammad* (peace be on him) lost no time in accepting this offer and said : "I would give him twice of what I would give to the other men of your tribe."[29]

So the matter was settled and *Muḥammad* (peace be on him) undertook the journey. When the caravan was about to set out his uncle commended him to the men of the company. Maysarah, the servant of *Khadījah*, likewise travelled along with Muḥammad (peace be on him). The caravan took the usual route to Syria, the same which the Holy Prophet had traversed with his uncle known as Basra, on the road to *Damascus*, and he sat down to take rest under a shady tree. A Christian monk who lived near by, on seeing him, rushed to the spot and said : "Right from *Jesus*, the son of *Mary*, none ever sat here but a prophet." He then turned towards *Maysarah* and said : "Do these streaks of light always glisten in his eyes." *Maysarah* replied in the a ffir-

29. Ibn Sa'd, Vol. I, p. 129.

mative. Upon this he remarked : "He is the Prophet and the last of the Apostles."[30]

The Holy Prophet was at that time busy in trade transactions. In the meanwhile there was an altercation with a customer. He asked him to swear by Lāt and *'Uzzā* in support of his contention. "I have never done that," was the prompt reply. "When I happen to pass by their images, I purposely avoid them and take a different course." The man was struck at these words and said : "You are honest, and whatever you contend is absolutely true. By God, here is a man whose glory has been sung by our scholars, and foretold by our books."[31]

This is the full account that we find in the authentic records of *Muḥammad's* (peace be on him) biographies. We do not find any trace of all those stories which have been deliberately fabricated by the Western biographers of the Holy Prophet : that it was to his meeting a Nestorian monk that *Muhammad* (peace be upon him) owed his knowledge of Christian doctrines and wherefrom he imbibed his hatred against idolatry.

Like all other prophets of God, *Muḥammad* (peace be upon him) had a natural aversion to all those evil practices that we find in an idolatrous society. He was instinctively a monotheist and would under no circumstances invoke any other deity except *Allāh*, the sole Creator and Sustainer of the universe.

At that time the concept of monotheism had lost much of its meaning. The way in which the dogma of Trinity was forced upon the people with the misleading and offensive zeal of Eutychian and Jacobite partnership, and the gross form in which the worship of Mary (Mariolatry) was preached to the masses, could hardly make any appeal to *Muḥammad* (peace be upon him) who had been, from the very beginning of his life, an ardent believer in one God.

Muḥammad (peace be upon him) conducted business in Syria with such prudence and sense of duty that he returned from the trade expedition with an amount of profit larger than usual. *Khadījah* was so deeply impressed by the intelligence and integrity of *Muḥammad* (peace be upon him) that she decided to marry him. The conversation that ensued between the maid-

---

30. Ibn Sa'd, Vol. I, p. 130.
31. *Ibid.*

servant of *Khadījah*, who had been deputed to convey the message of marriage and the Prophet clearly reveals that before this offer of marriage, *Mnḥammad* (peace be upon him) had absolutely no idea of this alliance.

Prophet's Marriage with Khadijah

The maid-servant said : "What is it that hinders you from marriage ?" "I have nothing," replied the Prophet, "in my hands with which I can meet the expenses of the wedding." "But if haply that difficulty is removed and you are invited to marry a beautiful and wealthy lady of noble birth who would place you in affluence, would you not desire to have her ?" "And who," said *Muḥammad* (peace be upon him), startled at the novel idea, "might that be ?" "It is *Khadījah*," was the reply. "But how can I have access to her ?" "Let that be my care," said the maid-servant. The mind of *Muḥammad* (peace be upon him) was at once made up and he answered, "I am ready."[32]

She returned and told *Khadījah* the whole story. No sooner was she apprised of his willingness to marry her, *Khadījah* sent a message to his uncle and fixed a time when they should meet. On the appointed day *Muḥammad* (peace be upon him) along with his uncle *Abū Ṭālib* and *Ḥamzah* and several other chiefs of his tribe, went to *Khadījah's* house. *Suhaylī*, a well-known biographer of *Muḥammad* (peace be upon him), asserts that *Khuwaylid*, the father of *Khadījah*, had died before the wars of *Fijār* and it was her uncle 'Amr, son of Asad, who gave her hand in marriage to him.

At the time of her marriage to Muḥammad (peace be upon him) *Khadījah* (may God be pleased with her) was forty years old and the Prophet was hardly twenty-five. From this time on for a quarter of a century *Khadījah* remained his angel of hope and consolation. She gave *Muḥammad* (peace be upon him) ease of circumstances, freedom from the cares of daily life, strength and comfort of deep mutual love, the factors which contributed to the furtherance of the mission of the Prophet.

In spite of conspicuous difference in age, *Muḥammad* (peace be upon him) love for *Khadījah* never wavered. When death parted her from the Prophet, after having shared with him for

32. Suhaylī, op. cit., Vol. I, p. 122.

years the trial and reproach which greeted him the first few years of his preaching, he deeply mourned her death. Once *'Ā'ishah* asked him if she had been the only woman worthy of his love, *Muḥammad* (peace be upon him) replied in an honest burst of tender emotion : "She believed in me when none else did, she embraced Islam when people disbelieved me ; and she helped and comforted me when there was none to lend me a helping hand."[33]

Muḥammad's (peace be upon him) grateful and affectionate remembrance of her persisted till the very end of his life. He was kind to all her friends and occasionally sent them gifts. "Never was I more jealous of any of the Prophet's wives," said *'Ā'ishah*, "than I was of *Khadījah*, although I never saw her ; for the Prophet remembered her much. Once I hurt his feelings on this issue and he replied gravely, 'God has blessed me with her love'."

Khadījah bore the Holy Prophet several children. The first-born was named *Qāsim* after whom, according to *Arab* custom, *Muḥammad* (peace be upon him) received the *kunya*, *Abū al-Qāsim*, "the father of *Qāsim*". Then were born *Tayyib* and *Ṭāhir*. All of them died in their infancy. Amongst the daughters *Ruqayyah* was the eldest ; then came *Zaynab*, *Umm Kulthūm*, and last and best known of them all, *Fāṭimah*.

The Trustworthy

It was before the call that an incident took place which throws light on the wisdom and popularity of the Prophet. The *Ka'bah* was threatened with destruction by a flood and the alarmed *Quraysh* resolved to rebuild it. The work was divided among the leading families and went on in harmony till the time came to put the sacred Black Stone in its proper place. Then strife broke out among the chiefs, each contesting for the honour of placing the stone in its position. Daggers were on point of being drawn and great bloodshed seemed imminent. Luckily, the oldest among the chiefs *Abū Umayyah b. Mughīrah* made a proposal which was accepted by all : He said : "Let him who enters the *haram* first of all tomorrow decide the point." Next morning *Muḥammad* (peace be upon him) was the first to enter

33. Loc. cit.

the sanctuary. When the other people appeared on the scene he was already there. "*Al-Amīn*" (the Trustworthy) has come," they cried with one voice. "We are content to abide by his decision." Calm and self-possessed, *Muḥammad* (peace be upon him) received the commission and at once resolved upon an expedient which was to conciliate them all. He spread his mantle on the ground and placed the Stone in its centre. He then asked the representatives of the different families of the *Quraysh* to lift the stone among them, all together, When it had reached the proper place, *Muḥammad* (peace be upon him) laid it in the proper position with his own hands. This is how a very tense situation was eased and a grave danger averted by the wisdom of the Holy Prophet (peace be upon him).[34]

The last messenger of God had been endowed not only with the highest ideals, but also with the wisdom necessary to translate these ideals into practice.

34. Ibn Hishām, Vol. I, p. 193; Suhaylī, op. cit., Vol. I, p. 127; Ibn Sa'd, Vol. I, p. 146.

Chapter 3

The Call

Muhammad' sheart was restless about the moral evils and idolatry that were rampant among his people. The *Arab* society of his time was torn by dissensions, fratricidal wars and inter-feuds. In other parts of the world the state of affairs was no better. Christianity and Judaism, the chief moral forces of the world, were torn by bitter strife and conflict. The mighty empire of Rome, whose seat had been, three centuries before, moved from the banks of the Tiber to the shores of the Bosphorus, was sinking into decrepitude. The rival empire of Persia had also the vigour of its earlier time. Humanity was, in fact, passing through hard times. Sensitive men everywhere were peering into the turmoil of this turbulent human scene in search of some light through which the future of their race might be divined. They had been eagerly looking forward to a new Master-Word to regulate this life. The world needed a new formula to heal its divisions and to liberate humanity from the worship of false gods and establish an order on the earth.

Craving for the Truth

Muḥammad's heart was perturbed by the sad lot of the human race. He would reflect for hours. Given to solitary musing, he was wont to pass long periods in retirement among the hills and ravines in the neighbourhood of *Mecca.* Of these one in particular was his favourite resort—the cave of *Ḥirā* in the Mount *al-Nūr*.

Muḥammad's soul was struggling to comprehend mysteries of creation, of life and death, of good and evil. Here in the cave he often remained plunged in thought deep in communion with the unseen yet all-pervading God of the universe. He was, however, unaware of the great responsibility which was going to fall on his shoulders. At this stage, when God had not yet sent

His revelation to him, he would catch a glimpse of Reality, not in full consciousness, but lapsing into deep reflection, a state of drawing oneself in the soul-stirring whispers of nature already referred to. It was just a mysterious and sweet-tasting wisdom which often came so clearly to the inmost parts of his soul. He could enjoy it, but he could not apply a name to it, nor communicate it to others. It was in the form of dreams, the dreams which contained Divine mysteries and surpassed the compass of human intelligence that he caught a few glimpses of Reality. Such visions are the states of insight into depths of truth unplumbed by the discursive intellect. They are Divine illuminations, full of significance and importance, but all inarticulate. They are in fact preludes to revelation. It is recorded on the authority of *'Ā'ishah* (may *Allah* be pleased with her) that the beginning of revelation for the Messenger of God was preceded by true visions (*al-ru'yā al-sādiqah*), which used to come like the breaking of the dawn.[1]

Thus *Muḥammad* was quite unaware of the fact that he was to be commissioned by God as the last of prophets. We do not find any hint—direct or indirect—that his mind was preparing blueprints of any religious adventure. His was a quiet life following its natural course in peaceful obscurity, not knowing at all the great assignment coming. The impostors who contemplate spiritual legerdemain at any period of their lives betray their designs in spite of themselves. Their outbursts and activities reveal that they are cooking something in the innermost chambers of their minds ; that they have some enterprise before them to embark upon and some plans to execute. This unawareness of *Muḥammad* (peace be upon him) about his exalted position to which he was going to be elevated, then, is the greatest testimony of his sincerity.

He had no school-learning. The art of writing had just then been introduced into Arabia : it seems true that *Muḥammad* could never write. The *Meccan* life, along with its experiences, constituted all his education. It was after having led such a quiet life that he was suddenly called upon to shoulder the burden of a mighty message. The Holy *Qur'ān* testifies to this in the following words :

---

1. Bukhārī, *Kitāb al-Waḥy*.

> Thou had no hope that the Scripture would be inspired to thee ; but it is a mercy from the Lord, so never be helper to the disbelievers. (xxviii : 86)

Rashid Riḍa has explained this verse in the following words :

> The Almighty God has perfected his blessings on humanity by revealing this Holy *Qur'ān* to you. You could never acquire this position by dint of your knowledge or good deeds and you even never aspired for that. The whole record of the *Ḥadīth* is silent on the point that the Holy Prophet was expecting the prophethood and that he would be chosen by *Allah* to take up this exalted mission.[2]

Preparing for the Assignment

The Prophet was no doubt unconscious of his great assignment but this does not mean that he was allowed to grow up like an ordinary person. His life and all its activities were directly shaped by God and he was thus unknowingly being prepared both mentally and morally for the huge task that lay ahead. From the very beginning the Almighty God had endowed him with those qualities of head and heart which befitted a prophet. Ibn Hishām succinctly remarks :

> The Holy Prophet attained his youth under the direct care of God. His life was free from all the impurities of *Jāhilīyah,* since God had decided to endow him with Prophethood. *Muḥammad* (peace be upon him) achieved perfection in kind and polite behaviour, in forbearance, in truthfulness, and integrity. He had stainless character and was thus recognized as *Amīn* the Trustworthy amongst his fellowmen.[3]

It is narrated on the authority of the Caliph *'Alī* that the Holy Prophet (peace be on him) was once asked if he had ever worshipped an idol. He replied, "Never". He was again questioned, "Have you ever tasted wine ?" He emphatically said, "No", and added, "I always looked down upon these acts as shameful acts of *Kufr*, even during that period of my life when the Holy Book had not been revealed to me and I had no idea

---

2. *Al-Waḥy al-Muḥammadi*, p. 107.
3. Ibn Hishām, Vol. I, p. 62.

of faith (*īmān*)."[4] The Prophet also said on another occasion: "Since my birth I have developed a sense of deep hatred and enmity towards the idols and a dislike for (obscene) poetry."[5]

Ibn al-Qayyim, in his famous book *Zād al-Ma'ād*, has discussed this point at great length. He says that although prophethood is not something which can be acquired and is bestowed by the Almighty, it is however, erroneous to suppose that it is distributed at random by Him. The prophets are raised according to Divine plan but the persons endowed with rare qualities are elevated to this exalted position. There are some intrinsic virtues in the prophets which are prerequisites for this office. It is recorded in the Holy *Qur'ān* that the Quraysh constantly observed the signs of God but they were not prepared to embrace Islam. Whenever they came across a sign of God they said: "We will not believe till we are given that which *Allah's* messengers are given." Upon this God replied: "*Allah* knows best with whom to place His prophethood."[6] This verse clearly elucidates the point that every human being is not competent to hold this exalted position; it is given to those alone whom Allah deems fit.

The Light Comes

It was now the fortieth year of *Muḥammad's* life. He was spending the month of *Ramaḍan* in in prayer *Ḥira* and supplications when one night the light of revelation suddenly burst upon him.[7] A glorious angel aroused him from sleep; three times his mighty voice sounded in his ears and three times a powerful constraining grasp was laid upon him. He was perplexed at the outset and could not decide as to what he should do, but when the angel called him for the third time, the Holy Prophet took up the message of his Lord. This important event has been described in the *Ṣaḥīḥ* of *al-Bukhārī* in the following words:

> After (the period of true visions) solitude became dear to him, and he would go to a cave, *Ḥira* to engage himself

---

4. Jalāl-ud-dīn Suyūṭī, *al-Kasā'is al-Kubrā*, (Ḥaidarābād 1319 A. H.), Vol. I, p. 89.
5. 'Allāma 'Alā-ud-Dīn 'Alī al-Muttaqī al-Hindī, *Kanz al-'Ummāl*, (Ḥaidarābād 1313 A. H.), Vol. I, p. 305.
6. The Qur'ān, vi: 125.
7. Ibn Hishām, op, cit., p. 236.

in *tahannuth* (devotion) there for a certain number of nights before returning to his family, and then he would return to them for provision for a similar stay. At length unexpectedly the truth (angel) came to him and said, "Recite." "I cannot recite," he (*Muḥammad*) said. "Then he took me and squeezed me vehemently and then let me go and repeated the order 'Recite'. 'I cannot recite,' said I, and once again he squeezed me and let me till I was exhausted."

Then he said : 'Recite in the name of thy Lord' ; I said, 'I cannot recite.' He squeezed me for the third time and then let me go and said : 'Recite in the name of thy Lord Who created man from a clot of blood, for thy Lord is Beneficent.' The Prophet repeated these verses. He was trembling with fear. At this stage he came to his wife, *Khadījah* who said : "God will never bring you any disgrace. You unite uterine relations ; you bear the burden of the weak ; you help the poor and the needy, you entertain the guests and endure hardships in the path of truthfulness."[8]

A careful scrutiny of the contents of the very first verses revealed to *Muḥammad* indicates that these are not the outpourings of *Muḥammad's* (peace be upon him) own mind but had been revealed by God. Firstly, if *Muḥammad's* heart had been struggling for such a spiritual experience he would not have been stricken with fear at the sight of the angel. A man develops a sort of spiritual affinity with one whom he expects to appear before him. The angel's unsolicited appearance and the Prophet's fear conclusively prove that his mind was free from all types of hallucinations. The angel was not a product of fantasy. It was an objective reality that came to him. Secondly, one finds a striking difference in the language of the revelation and the one spoken by the Holy Prophet. There is in the *Qur'ān* a supernatural harmony and cadence of expression and beauty of conception that will be determined by the accuracy of the measures, the purity and fitness of the composition and the point and charm of the thought and imagery—and unknown style

8. Bukhārī has narrated this tradition in the Chapter 'Bāb al-Waḥy' and 'Kitāb al-Ta'bīr' and 'Kitāb al-Tafsīr'.

not only for the *Arabs* but whole of the then known world. It is impossible to find in the writing of a human being such influence, sweetness for the heart and attraction for the mind and soul, injunction for good things and prohibition of evil things ; exhortation for entry into heaven and restraining from hell and that too from the lips of a man who was unlettered.

Thirdly, if it is asserted that whatever the Prophet thought or did was the result of the deep-seated agony that the Prophet felt at the sad state of affairs prevailing in his country, then the very first verse should have some reference, even if indirect, to some aspect of the evils which were eating into the vitals of the contemporary *Arab* society. These verses should have embodied an appeal to the Arabs to uproot those evil practices. Moreover, these verses should have expressed the agony of his heart. But we find none of these things in the first verses of the *Holy Qur'ān.* They consist of a calm and solemn statement in which the Prophet has been exhorted to "recite".

Moreover, the first revelation marks a radical departure from the trends of religious thought of that age. People had been accustomed to legends of a supernatural character. If *Muḥammad* (peace be on him) had fabricated these verses himself, he would have composed such verses as might have created awe and wonder in the minds of the people in order to satisfy the supernatural yearnings of their hearts.

Here we find an altogether different note. Instead of claiming to possess supernatural qualities which the people had always expected of a religious leader, *Muḥammad* (peace be on him) says something which, unlike the religious attitude of the Prophet's time, *i.e.*, blind following, exhorts them to awaken their minds and to observe critically the outer and inner experiences of man. The message of *Muḥammad* (peace be on him) was in many fundamental ways incongruous with the religious outlook of the *Arabs* and much advanced for that age. The Arab mind was accustomed to look with awe and wonder upon the religious forces and personalities having supernatural qualities in them.

Whatever the Prophet (peace be upon him) preached seemed to be different from the common trends of his time. *Muḥammad's* (peace be upon him) unique position in religious history is due to the fact that he inspired mankind without laying any claim to supernatural powers or attributes which were not strictly human. This is one of the strongest testimonies of the sincerity of his purpose. In an age when faith meant nothing but the benumbing of the rational faculty of man, is it not strange that one should come forward and ask people to develop their qualities of head and heart and weigh everything in the scale of reason ? This was a step which completely revolutionised the religious outlook of humanity. Then there are so many verses of the Holy *Qur'ān* which conclusively prove that the source of the Holy Prophet's revelation was other than his own mind for example the opening words of *Sūrah 'Abasa* :

> "He frowned and turned away because the blind man came to him. And what would make thee know that he might purify himself." (lxxx : 1-3)

And those of Sūrah al-Taḥrīm :

> "O Prophet ! why dost thou forbid (thyself) that which Allah has made lawful for thee ? Seekest thou to please thy wives." (lxvi : 1)

And again those of Sūrah Tauba :

> "Ask forgiveness for them or ask not forgiveness for them. Even if thou didst ask forgiveness for them seventy times, *Allah* will not forgive them." (ix : 80)

clearly indicate that his acts were not approved by God. If it were left to the option of an individual, he himself would be the last person to give permanence to a reproval for his own act. Hence the source from which the Holy Prophet received his revelation.

Lastly, if the revelations of *Maḥammad* (peace be upon him) had been his own fabrication, he would never have waited for three years when the revelation was suspended. Whether it was a period of preparation, is altogether a different question which we do not propose to discuss here. The important point is that if one were to compose verses by one's personal endeavour, there seems no reason to "wait and see" and thus provide an opportunity to one's enemies to scoff at one. If the revelations were a prompting of his own heart, he must always have been ready to come forward with one, whenever such a demand was made by people. That *Muḥammad* (peace be upon him) had an intense longing for receiving the message from his Lord during this period (*faṭrah*) but no response come from the heavens, is an unchallengeable proof of *Muhammad's* apostleship. This clearly establishes that he did not speak of his own accord. The *Holy Qur'ān* amply testifies to this statement: "Nor doth he (*Muḥammad*) speak of (his own) desire. It is naught save an inspiration that is inspired" (liii 3-4). He thus delivered the Divine Message when it was communicated to him at the behest of the Almighty God. It is one thing to create or evolve, even unconsciously, a mental image of oneself which one vainly tries to pass off as a Divine Message; it is another to discern; even though for a short time, on august presence, other than human, and listen consciously to the words that it brings from the Creator. It is to the inward recogniṭion of this self-revealing object that the Prophet makes his appeal. "What he discerns is at least not a form of his own mind's throwing; while his knowledge is due, not to the penetration of the finite spirit, but to the condescension of the infinite."

At the end of the period of remission or suspension of messages from the Lord, *Muhammad* (peace be upon him) was again visiṭed by the angel Gabriel, who delivered to him the Divine Command to preach to his people and assured him of the truth of his message.

The Prophet (peace and blessings of *Allah* be upon him) then unequivocally asserted that he was a prophet who had been entrusted with a mission for humanity at large. That he was the last of the long line of prophets and a Messenger for the whole of the human race has been time and again stressed in different verses of the *Holy Qur'ān*:

> "We have sent thee, O Prophet! as a Messenger unto mankind and Allah is sufficient as a Witness." (iv : 79)
>
> "Say (O Prophet): O Mankind! surely, I am the Messenger of *Allah* to you all." (vii : 158)

The Mission and the Movement

The Prophet initiated his sacred mission right from his home. The noble *Khadījah* was the first fortunate soul who was informed of his prophethood and, without the least hesitation, she attested the truth of that which had come to him from the

Lord. She was the first to enter the fold of *Islam* and bear hardships for the sake of *Islam*, along with her husband. Next comes *'Alī*, the Prophet's cousin, who had been living with him since his early childhood. *Zayd*, son of *Ḥārithah*, the adopted son and intimate friend of *Muḥammad* (peace be on him), was also one of the earliest converts to Islam. *Khadījah*, *'Alī*, and *Zayd* were all the members of the Prophet's household and were, therefore, very intimately associated with him.

When we step out of the four walls of the Prophet's household, we find *Abū Bakr*, a well-known figure of the *Quraysh*, responding to *Muḥammad's* call to faith. It is believed that amongst the friends of the Prophet *Abū Bakr* was the first to embrace *Islam*. He had long been intimately associated with the Prophet and this intimacy afforded him an opportunity to assess the nobility and truthfulness of his friend and finally to verify his claim as the Apostle of God. The Holy Prophet once remarked :

> I never invited anyone to the faith who did not display any hesitation in embracing it except *Abū Bakr*. As for *Abū Bakr*, when I offered Islam, he showed no hesitation, not even the least.[9]

We can hardly ever find a more perfect example of the great disciple of a great master than that of *Abū Bakr*. He was wealthy, generous, mild, upright, and firm. He rendered marvellous service to Islam and the Prophet, the like of which is rarely to be witnessed in the whole course of human history. The day he professed Islam, he dedicated all his time and energy and all his fortunes to the propagation of the Divine faith. From then on only one purpose dominated his mind : to preach the Message that he had received from his master. He did only as his worthy guide would wish him to do. He invited people to Islam and spent his wealth generously towards the emancipation of the unfortunate slaves who were being persecuted for their attachment to the new Faith : All through his life *Abū Bakr* stood by *Muḥammad* (peace of *Allah* be upon him) ; never for a moment was his faith shaken nor did his love for the Prophet ever waver.

---

9. Ibn Sayyid al-Nās, *'Uyūn al-Athar* (Cairo 1356), Vol. I, p. 95.

After the death of the Holy Prophet when he was elected as the Commander of the Faithful, *Abū Bakr* arried on the mission with enviable zeal and vigour, defended with all his energy the purity of the Islamic doctrines from debasement and defilement, suppressed all the evil forces that were out to disintegrate the solidarity of nascent Islamic society and managed to convey the message of *Islam* to those far-flung regions where the Faith had not by then penetrated.

It is significant that the earliest converts to Islam were those who had been most closely associated with him and, therefore, knew him best, and from whose eyes no failings of his character could possibly have escaped, nor would it have been possible for any veil of hypocrisy, had there been such a veil, to hide his true nature. "It is strongly corroborative of *Muhammad's* sincerity," says William Muir, "that the earliest converts to Islam were not only of upright character, but his own bosom friends and people of his household ; who, intimately acquainted with his private life, could not fail otherwise to have detected those discrepancies which even more or less exist between the professions of hypocritical deceiver abroad and his actions at home."[10] Stanley Lane-Poole is very much impressed by this very aspect of *Muḥammad's* success : "It is impossible to overrate the importance of the fact that his closest relations and those who lived under his roof were the first to believe and the staunchest of faith. The Holy Prophet who is with honour in his own home need appeal to no stronger proof of his sincerity, and that *Muḥammad* was a 'hero to his own valet' is an invincible argument for his earnestness."[11]

Muḥammad's (peace be upon him) own sincerity and the integrity of his purpose and the zeal and enthusiasm of those who believed in him, their high moral character, and their readiness to undergo persecution for their beliefs attracted a small group of devoted followers. The notable amongst them were *'Uthmān b. 'Affān, Zubayr b. al-'Awwām, 'Abd al-Raḥmān b. 'Awf, Talḥah b. 'Ubaid Allah, Sa'd b. Abī Waqqās, Arqam b. Abī Arqam, 'Ubaydah b. Ḥārith, Sa'īd b. Zayd, 'Amr b. Nufail* and his wife *Fāṭimah*, daughter of *al-Khaṭṭāb* (the sister of *'Umar*), *Asmā*, the

10. William Muir, op. cit., p. 54.
11. Stanley Lane-Poole, op. cit., p. 8.

daughter of *Abū Bakr, 'Abd Allāh b. Mas'ūd, Ja'far b. Abī Ṭālib* and so many other noble souls.

Having got together around him a group of such selfless companions, *Muḥammad* (peace be upon him) took another step. There was nothing new in respect of the doctrines he had so far preached. He was not the preacher of a new religion, but the restorer and reviver of a faith which had been preached by *Adam, Noath, Moses* and *Jesus*—in fact by all the messengers of God.

He was, therefore, not the founder of a new religion but the standard-bearer of one which had been propagated by the Arabs, though subsequently they had forgotten its real purport. It had been overlaid by idolatry and superstitions that had grown up and had veritably put an end to the pure worship of *Allah* to which the great patriarch *Abraham* dedicated the Holy House of *Mecca*, the *Ka'bah*.

A Call to the Nation

For full three years *Muḥammad* (peace be upon him) had been content to teach within a rather narrow circle consisting of the members of his family and his intimate friends and just a few strangers. The time had, however, come to preach openly the faith of the Lord. The angel *Gabriel* had brought down a further revelation of God's Will to proclaim that which thou art commanded, and withdraw from the idolaters "

> "Indeed, We suffice to defend thee, from the scoffers, who associate other gods with *Allah*. We know that thy bosom is at times oppressed by what they say."
>
> (xv : 95-98)

Along with this it was also stressed :

> "Warn thy kinsmen, thy near ones. And lower thy wings (*i.e.* treat kindly) unto those believers who follow thee. And if they disobey thee, say : verily I am innocent of what they do." (xxvi : 24-26)

In obedience to these commands, *Muḥammad* (peace be upon him) rallied his kinsmen to the little hill of *al-Ṣafā*. Standing on the peak of the hillock, *Muḥammad* (peace be upon him) cast a glance at the men and women who waited questioningly and said : "O people of *Quraysh* ! Were I to tell you that an army was advancing to attack you from the yonder hills, would you believe me?" "Yes", everyone answered, "we have always known you to be truthful."

Muḥammad (peace be upon him) inclined his head. Then raising his voice, he continued: "I have come to you as a warner, and if you do not respond to my warning, punishment will fall upon you."[12] Looking at the crowd of listeners he called each sub-division of the *Quraysh* clan, "O *Banū 'Abd al-Muṭṭalib*! O *Banū 'Abd Manāf*! O *Banū Zahrah*! I have been commanded by God to warn you, my kinsmen, and I cannot protect you in this world, nor can I promise you aught in the next life unless you acknowledge that there is no god but *Allah*." *Abū Lahab*, his uncle, interrupted him and said impertinently: "Did you invite us for this very purpose?"

Muḥammad (peace be upon him) was not at all dismayed. He invited the family of *'Abd al-Muṭṭalib* to a feast, after which he intended to deliver his solemn message. The first such attempt was defeated by *Abū Lahab*. But in the next attempt he secured audience and delivered a short speech explaining quite cogently what was at stake. He said: "I know no man in the land of *Arabia* who can place before his kinsfolk a more excellent offer than that which I now make to you. I offer you the happiness of this world and that of the next."[13]

For three long weary years, the Holy Prophet laboured quietly to wean his kith and kin from the worship of their idols but apparently he could achieve no substantial results. It is significant to note, however, that even in this society which had fallen a prey to polytheism there were some known as Ḥunafā' who went about in search of the religion of *Abraham*. It is indicative of the fact that monotheism, which is deeply rooted in the nature of man, even though it is at times overlaid with idolatry, was not yet completely banished from their souls. And this is quite natural. Man, by his very nature, is monotheistic; it is the influence of a corrupt environment which deflects him from the path of true belief. The Holy Prophet has succinctly summed up this fact in one of his famous sayings: "Every child is born

12. Ibn Sa'd, op. cit., Vol. I, p. 133.
13. Suyūṭī, op. cit., Vol. I, p. 123.

true to nature ; it is his parents who make him Christian, Jew or Magian." There is no gainsaying the fact that in the enveloping darkness of the Arab society, there were a number of spots of light such as *Abū Bakr*, *'Uthmān b. Maz'ūn*, *Abū Dhar al-Ghifārī*, etc., who had already served as guiding stars to the wandering tribes of *Arabia*. They were all pious and were free from the evil practices which were so common in that society. It seems that they were instinctively yearning for a religion which could satisfy their spiritual urge.

The Early Converts

Among the first to have been attracted to the faith of *Muhammad* (peace be upon him) was a group of those who had been ardent believers in the unity of God. Even though they were not conversant with the concept of monotheism which *Islam* enunciated, yet one could easily find in them the spark of righteousness which could easily develop into flames. *Zayd b. 'Amr*, whose son *Sa'īd* became a very devoted follower of the Prophet, was one of those famous men who belonged to this group.

There was also a group of men who stood, in fact, outside the clan system, though nominally attached to some clan. Either the clan did not recognize their affiliations to be a matter of great importance, or the clan considered itself too weak to offer them protection against the high-handedness of the tyrants. These men were in no way inferior to the proud men of *Quraysh* both physically and mentally, but they had unfortunately no strong clan at their back to support them. They lacked power and prestige. Amongst them were *'Ammār*, *Khabbāb*, *Abū Fukaiha Ṣuhayb* (may God be pleased with them). These innocent souls were ridiculed and jeered in season and out of season. Referring to such people the high-brow *Quraysh* aristocrats asked the Prophet with scorn and jest :

> "Are these the only persons who have been blessed by *Allah* amongst us ?" vi : 1

There were a few amongst the *Muslims* who, in the words of the Holy *Qur'ān*, were *mustaḍ'afūn*. Ibn Sa'd characterises them as "those who had no clan to protect them.[14]"

---

14. Ibn Sa'd, op. cit., Vol. I, p. 177.

Having formed some idea of the sort of men who responded to *Muḥammad's* call, let us consider more fully the treatment meted out to them and to the Holy Prophet by their Meccan compatriots and the possible reasons for their doing so.

In the beginning the *Meccan* leaders did not care much for *Muḥammad* (peace be upon him) and his teachings. An orphan as he was, they did not see in him the strength and power of a revolutionary who stood much of a chance of success. To them he was a zealot But this attitude of indifference soon changed into active hostility. They could ill afford to observe as silent spectators to the growth of this movement. They were watching its ownward march with grave concern and rallied all their resources to put a stop to its tidal wave. It was not, however, till three to four years of his ministry had elapsed that a full scale opposition to *Muḥammad* (peace of Allah be upon him) was organized. They first contacted *Abū Ṭālib* and apprised him of the situation which had been created by his nephew. They said : "O *Abū Ṭālib* ! your nephew curses our gods ; finds faults with our way of life, mocks at our religion and degrades our forefathers ; either you stop him, or allow us to get at him, for you are in the same position as we are in opposition to him : and we will rid you of him." *Abū Ṭālib* tried to appease their wrath by giving them a polite reply. The Holy Prophet continued on his way preaching God's religion and calling men hitherto. The *Quraysh* were further infuriated and approached *Abū Ṭālib* for the second time and insisted him to put a stop to his nephew's activities which, if allowed unchecked, would involve him into severe hostility. *Abū Ṭālib* was deeply distressed at the breach with his people and their enmity, but he could not afford to desert the apostle too. He sent for his nephew and told him what the people had said ; "Spare me and yourself and put not burden upon me that I can't bear." Upon this the Holy Prophet replied, "O my uncle ! by God, if they put the sun in my right hand and moon in my left on condition that I abandon this course, until God has made me victorious, or I perish therein, I would not abandon it." The Holy Prophet got up. As he turned away his uncle called him and said : Come back, my nephew, and when he came back, he said, "Go and preach what you please, for by God I will never forsake you."[15]

When the *Quraysh* perceived that *Abū Ṭalib* had refused to yield before their demand and he was resolved to protect him, they themselves organized a campaign of persecution against him and his companions. It was started right from the holy precinct of the *Ka'bah* to which the *Quraysh* were deeply attached. It was their shrine, their centre of devotion, the focus of their idolatrous religious worship. Hence it had to be protected at all cost from the ever-increasing influence of Islam. *Muḥammad*, on the other hand, had a strong desire to cleanse this sacred House of God from idolatry. It is narrated that once the Prophet went into the sanctuary of the *Ka'bah* and summoned the people to the unity of God. There was sudden uproar and attack upon him from every side. *Ḥarith ibn Abī Hālah* rushed to the spot and tried to save the life of the Holy Prophet. A sharp quarrel arose between them, a sword struck the head of noble *Ḥārith* and he fell dead on the ground. He was the first martyr to lay down his life for the sake of Islam.

Persecutions

Muḥammad (peace and blessings of be upon him) *Allah* was ridiculed on every occasion. Sometimes the wicked people assembled in the streets and pointed at him slightingly as he passed and shouted : "There goes the fellow from among the sons of *'Abd al-Muṭṭalib* who speaks about the heavens." Dirt was thrown at him. His path was strewn with thorns and filth. Once, while he was praying in the *Ka'bah*, *'Uqbah*, son of *Abī Mu'ayt*, made his sheet into a rope, cast it round the neck of the Holy Prophet and then twisted it so as to choke the Prophet's throat, and when he prostrated on the ground, he pulled it hard. But the Prophet continued with his prayer with his usual calmness. In the meantime *Abū Bakr* arrived at the spot, pushed back *'Uqbah* and exclaimed : "Do you slay a person because he says : My Lord is *Allah*, and has come to you with clear signs ?"[16]

It is narrated on the authority of *Ṭāriq ibn 'Abd Allah al-*

---

15. Ibn Hishām, op. cit., Vol. I, pp. 265-66.
16. *Saḥīḥ Buhhāri*, Part XV, chapter under the heading, 'Ma Laqiya al-Nabī (Sallalāhu 'alaihi wa Sallam) min al-Mushrikīn.'

Muhāribi that he once saw the Prophet preaching, 'There is no god save Allah.' A man followed him and ruthlessly flung stones at him. The Prophet was profusely bleeding and the wicked fellow cried : "O men, be on your guard, he is a liar."[17] It is also recorded that once *Abū Jahl*, the staunch enemy of the Holy Prophet, threw dust on his sacred head and shouted : "O people, do not be taken in by his words. This man wants you to abandon the worship of *Lāt* and "*Uzzā*". The Prophet, however, paid no heed to him.[18]

'Uthmān ibn 'Affān says : "I once saw the Prophet walking around the sanctuary of *Ka'bah*. In every round a band of mischief-mongers headed by *Abū Jahl* passed some sarcastic remarks and then there was a laughter. The Prophet remained unmoved. On the third round, when they repeated the same act, the Prophet stopped there. The complexion of his face underwent a change and he emphatically remarked, "You will never give up these misdeeds until the calamity comes to you from the heavens." *'Uthmān* continues : "At this everyone shuddered." The Holy Prophet stepped back to his place and we followed him. In the way he said : 'I give you a tidings that God shall certainly grant supremacy to His "faith", fulfil His word and shall help His *dīn*. The people whom you find powerful today shall be killed by your hands.' *'Uthmān* observes : "By God we saw with our own eyes that *Allah* destroyed them through our hands."[19]

Once when the Prophet was prostrating while praying in the *Ka'bah*, *Abū Jahl* asked his companions to bring the dirty foetus of a she-camel and place it on his back. *'Uqbah ibn Abī Mu'yat* was the unfortunate man who hastened to do this ignoble act. A peel of laughter rose amongst the infidels. In the meanwhile Fātimah, the daughter of the Holy Prophet, who was hardly four or five years old, happened to pass that way.[20] She removed the filth from her father's back. The Prophet invoked the wrath of God upon them, especially upon *Abū Jahl*,

---

17. *Kanz al-'Ummāl*, Vol. VI, p. 302.
18. *Musnad* of Aḥmad b. Ḥanbal, (Cairo 1306 A.H.), Vol. IV, p. 63.
19. 'Uyūn al-Athar, Vol. I, p. 104.
20. *Ṣaḥīḥ Bukārī*, 'Kitāb al-Jihād.'

'Utbah b. Rabī'ah, Shaybah ibn Rabī'ah. Walīd ibn 'Utbah, Umayyah ibn Khalaf and *'Uqbah ibn Abī Mu'ayt.* It is recorded in the *Ṣaḥīḥ Bukhārī* that most of them were killed in the battle of *Badr.*[21] The Prophet once remarked with deep anguish : "I lived amongst two worst types of neighbours : one of them was *Abū Lahab* and the other was *'Uqbah ibn Abī Mu'ayt.* Both of them used to throw filth at my door."[22]

Mission to Ta'if

The stone-heartedness of the *Meccans,* however, forced the Prophet (peace be upon him) to turn his attention to Ṭā'if, where he hoped the people might respond to him. He went there with a companion of his, *Zayd,* the freed slave, and approached the family of 'Umayr who were reckoned among the nobility of the town. But, to his disappointment, all of them turned a deaf ear to his message. For ten days he stayed there delivering his message to several people, one after another, but all to no purpose. "Stirred up to hasten the departure of the unwelcome visitor, the people hooted him through the streets, pelted him with stones and at last obliged him to flee from the city pursued by a relentless rabble. Blood flowed down upon his legs ; and *Zayd,* endeavouring to shield him, was wounded in the head. The mob did not desist until they had chased him two or three miles across the sandy plains to the foot of the surrounding hills. There, wearied and exhausted, he took refuge in one of the numerous orchards, and rested against the wall of a vineyard. That day little did even his unwavering faith anticipate that in less than ten years he would stand upon the spot at the head of a conquering army, and that great idol of *Ṭā'if* despite the entreaties of its votaries, would be demolished at his command."[23]

Near by was the vineyard belonging to *'Utbah* and *Shaybah,* sons of *Rabī'ah,* the wealthy citizens of Mecca. They watched with pain the condition of the Holy Prophet and moved by compassion, sent to him one of their Christian servants with a tray of grapes. The Holy Prophet accepted the fruit with pious invocation : "In the name of the Lord." The Christian servant

21. *Ṣaḥiḥ Bukhāri,* 'Kitāb al-Salāt,' and Zurqānī, Vol. I, p. 253.
22. *Musnad* of Aḥmad b. Ḥanbal, Vol. IV, p. 63.
23. William Muir, op. cit., p. 106.

Addas was greatly impressed by these words and said : "These are the words which the people of this land do not generally speak." The Prophet inquired of him whence he came and what religion he professed. *Addas* replied : "I am a Christian by faith and come from *Nineveh.*" The Prophet then said : "You belong to the city of righteous *Jonah* son of *Matta.*" *Addas* asked him anxiously if he knew anything about *Jonah.* The Prophet significantly remarked : "He is my brother. He was a prophet and so am I." Thereupon *Addas* paid homage to *Muḥammad* (peace be upon him) and kissed his hands. His masters admonished him at this act but he replied : "None on the earth is better than he. He has revealed to me a truth which only a prophet can do." The masters again reprimanded him and said : "We forewarn you against the consequences of abandoning the faith of your forefathers. The religion which you profess is far better than the one you feel inclined to."

At a time when the whole world seemed to have turned against him, *Muḥammad* (peace be upon him) turned to his Lord and betook himself to prayer and the following touching words are still preserved as those through which his oppressed soul gave vent to its distress. He was weary and wounded but confident of the help of his Lord :

> O Lord ! To Thee alone I make complaint of my helplessness, the paucity of my resources and my insignificance before mankind. Thou art the most Merciful of the mercifuls. Thou art the Lord of the helpless and the weak, O Lord of Mine ! Into whose hands wouldst Thou abandon me : into the hands of an unsympathetic foe who would sullenly frown at me, or to the enemy who has been given control over my affairs ? But if Thy wrath does not fall upon me, there is nothing for me to worry about . . . I seek protection in the light of Thy Countenance, Which illuminates the heavens and dispels every darkness, and Which controls all affairs in this world as well as in the Hereafter. May it never be that I should incur Thy wrath, or that Thou shouldst be wrathful to me. And there is no power nor resource, but Thine alone.[24]

No one can read this prayer without having deepened within

---

24. Ḥāfiz Ibn Qayyim, op. cit., Vol. II, p. 124.

him a sense of the Majesty of God, the completeness of His over ruling providence, His concern with the minutest detail of human life. This prayer affords an insight into the working of the Prophet's mind and one can easily read in it the loftiness of his thinking, the purity of his spirit, and the nobility of his feelings. There is no prevarication, no hiding or suppression of truth, no luxuriant display of poetic fancy but a spontaneous expression of his deep love for God, his implicit faith in His mercy and help, and his cheerful resignation to the Will of the One Who dwells in majesty over all the creation in invisible, inseparable omnipotence, far above the humanly conceivable—the eternal Cause of all effects.

It is hard to believe that an impostor can give vent to emotions so noble. Only a prophet who has direct communion with his Creator is capable of giving utterances to such things. They seem to have emanated direct from the inner springs of life. He is homeless, miserable, yet so calm and so firm. His words, pure and simple, eminently reflect that *Muḥammad* (may *Allah*'s blessings be upon him) had none of those painful cleavages of the spirit, those phantoms of fear, greed, and inhibition that are commonly found in the outpourings of the impostors. "All earnest souls will ever discern in it the faithful struggle of an earnest soul towards what is good and best. Struggle often baffled, sore baffled, down as into entire wreck ; yet a struggle never ended ; even with tears. repentance, true unconquerable purpose, begun anew."[25]

"There is something lofty and heroic," observes William Muir, "in the journey of *Muḥammad* to *Tayif* ; a solitary man, despised and rejected by his own people, going boldly forth in the name of God like *Jonah* to *Nineveh*, and summoning an idolatrous city to repent and support his mission. It sheds a strong light on the intensity of his belief in the divine origin of his calling."[26]

Muḥammad (peace be upon him) had been tortured in numerous ways, but as he had a strong and influential family, the Banū Hāshim, at his back, he was generally not subjected to any severe bodily violence for fear that such action would pro-

---

25. Thomas Carlyle, *On Heroes and Hero-Worship*, pp. 62-63.
26. *The Life of Muhammad*, p. 109.

voke retaliation. Among his followers, the brunt of the physical torture was borne by slaves such as *Bilāl* and *'Amir b. Fuhayrah.*[27]

Sacrifices of the Early Companions

Bilāl the slave of *Umayyah b. Khalaf,* was severely beaten by his master when the latter came to know of his conversion to *Islam.* Sometimes a rope was put around his neck and street boys were made to drag him through the streets and even across the hillocks of *Mecca.* At times he was subjected to prolonged deprivation of food and drink, at others he was bound up, made to lay down on the burning sand and under the crushing burden of heavy stones. Similar other measures were resorted to in order to force him to recant. All this proved in vain. On one such occasion, *Abū Bakr* was passing by ; moved by pity, he purchased and emanicipated him from slavery.

Another victim of the high-handedness of the *Quraysh* was *'Ammār,* the son of *Yāsir.* Both had no influential tribe to back them since they were not the original inhabitants of Mecca. *'Ammār* too was made to lie on the burning sand and was beaten so severely that on occasions, he became senseless. Sometimes he was tossed upon embers. The Prophet was greatly moved by the atrocities which were being perpetrated upon 'Ammār and his family. He comforted them and raised his hands in prayer.[28] It is narrated on the authority of *'Alī* that the Prophet once remarked that *'Ammār* was the repository of faith.[29] 'Ammār, along with his other companions, had retained to the end of his life the scars of wounds inflicted during this period. The same inhuman treatment was meted out to his aged father, Yāsir, and his ailing mother, Sumayyah. "*Khabbāb* and *'Ammār* used to exhibit, in later days, such marks of suffering and constancy to a wondering generation, in which fortune and glory had well nigh effaced the very thought of persecution as a possible condition of *Islam.*"[30]

Outrages were not confined to the helpless men like Ṣuhayb, *Abū Fukaihah, Yāsir, 'Ammār* but the free men of noble descent

---

27. Ibn Hishām, op. cit, Vol. I, p. 205.
28. Ibn Sa'd, op. cit., Vol. I, p. 178.
29. *Fatḥ al-Bārī,* Vol. III, p. 72.
30. William Muir, op. cit., p. 66.

and even chiefs were also victims of similar outrages on every possible occasion. *'Uthmān b. 'Affān*, the third Caliph, was brutally treated by his uncle. Some Muslims of rank and position were wrapped in the raw skins of camels and thrown away and others were put in armours and cast on burning sand in the scorching sun of *Arabia*.

Migration to Abyssinia

To escape these indignities and intolerable persecutions *Muḥammad* (peace be upon him) permitted those of his followers who lacked effective tribal support, to seek asylum abroad. "Yonder," said the Prophet, pointing to the West, lies the country of Abyssinia, there rules a king in whose realm no one is wronged. It is a land of righteousness. Depart to that and remain at that place until Allah provides conditions favourable for return.[31]

In the seventh month of the fifth year of prophethood, eleven men and five women left for Abyssinia which was governed by a Christian king called Negus (*Najāshī*). Among the emigrants were *'Uthmān b. 'Affān* and his wife, *Ruqayyah* (the daughter of the Holy Prophet), *'Abd al-Raḥmān b. 'Awf, Zubayr b. 'Awwām, Abū Ḥudhafah* and his wife, *Mus'āb b. 'Umayr, Abū Salāmah* and his wife *Umm Salāmah, 'Uthmān b. Maz'ūm, 'Āmir b. Rabī'ah* and his wife, *Suhayl b. Bayda, Abū Sabra,* son of *'Amr* and *Ḥātib b. 'Amr*.[32]

This small party of refugees demonstrated to the world that the faith which they had adopted was much more important to them than hearth and home and ties of blood, that they could not forsake it at any cost, and that it had given them a nobility of spirit far more precious than material possessions. They were received warmly by the *Najāshī* (Negus) and his people and lived there in peace and comfort. Traditions give us a good account of the discussion that took place in the court of the *Najāshī* between these emigrants and the envoys of the *Quraysh*,

---

31. Ibn Hishām, op. cit., Vol. I, pp. 321-22.
32. There is some difference in regard to the number of refugees. In *Fatḥ al-Bārī*, the list includes only ten men and four women, whereas in *'Uyūn al-Athar* there are eleven men and five women. See *Fatḥ al-Bārī*, Vol. VII, p. 143, and *'Uyūn al-Athar*, Vol. I, p. 115.

who demanded their extradition.

The two envoys of the *Quraysh* had brought with them valuable gifts for the king and his courtiers, and had been able to win some of the chiefs over to their side. The king, however, resolved to hear the viewpoint of both the parties, and held an audience for that purpose. The pagan envoys claimed that the *Muslim* refugees should be expelled from Abyssinia and made over to them, on the ground that their leader had abandoned the religion of his forefathers, and was preaching a religion different from theirs and from that of the king.

The king summoned the *Muslims* to the court and asked them to explain the teachings of their religion. At this, *Ja'far b. Abī Ṭālib* stood up and addressed the king in the following words :

> O king ! we were plunged in the depth of ignorance and barbarism ; we adored idols, we lived in unchastity ; we ate dead bodies, and we spoke abominations ; we disregarded every feeling of humanity ; and the duties of hospitality and neighbourhood ; we knew no law but that of the strong, when God raised among us a man, of whose birth, truthfulness, honesty, and purity we were aware ; and he called us to the Unity of God, and taught us not to associate anything with Him. He forbade us the worship of idols ; and enjoined us to speak the truth, to be faithful to our trusts, to be merciful and to regard the rights of neighbours ; he forbade us to speak evil of women, or to eat the substance of orphans ; he ordered us to fly from the vices, and to abstain from evil ; to offer prayers, to render alms, to observe fast. We have believed in him, we have accepted his teachings and his injunctions to worship God, and not to associate anything with Him. For this reason our people have risen against us, have persecuted us in order to make us forego the worship of idols of wood and stone and other abominations. They have tortured us and injured us, until finding no safety among them, we have come to thy country, and hope thou wilt protect us from oppression.[33]

---

33. Ibn Hishām, op. cit., Vol. I, p. 336, as quoted by Syed Ameer 'Alī in his *The Spirit of Islam* (London 1961), pp. 29-30.

The king was very much impressed by these words and asked the *Muslims* to recite some of the Divine revelation. *Ja'far* recited the opening verses of the chapter entitled *'Mary'* (xix) wherein is told the story of the birth of both *John* and *Jesus Christ,* down to the account of *Mary* having been fed with food miraculously. Thereupon the king and the bishops of his realm were moved to tears and the Negus exclaimed : "It seems as if these words and those which were revealed to Jesus are the rays of the light which have radiated from the same source."[34] Turning to the crest-fallen envoys of the *Quraysh* he said, I am afraid, I cannot give you back these refugees. They are free to live and worship in my realm as they please."

On the morrow, the two envoys again went to the king and said that *Muḥammad* (may peace of *Allah* be upon him) and his followers blasphemed Lord Jesus Christ. Again the Muslims were summoned and asked what they thought of Jesus. Ja'far again stood up and replied : "We speak about Jesus as we have been taught by our Prophet, that is, he is the servant of God, His apostle, His spirit and His word breathed into virgin Mary."[35] The king at once remarked, "Even so do we believe. Blessed be ye, and blessed your Master." Then turning to the frowning envoys he said : "You may fret and fume as you like but Jesus is nothing more than what *Ja'far* has said about him." He then assured the *Muslims* of full protection. He returned to the *Quraysh* envoys the gifts they had brought with them and sent them away. The *Muslims* lived in Abyssinia unmolested for a number of years till they returned to *Medina.*[36]

It is, however, significant in this connection that the persons who had emigrated to Abyssinia were all free men and the caravan included none of the helpless slaves who were put to unspeakable tortures by the *Meccans.* It is recorded on the authority of *'Urwah b. Zubayr* that *Ja'far* said to the Negus :

> "It is through you, sire, that I want to put some of the questions to these envoys who have come all the way to incite you against us."

Negus allowed *Ja'far* to do so and the following questions

---

34. Ibn Hishām, op. cit., Vol. I, pp. 336-37.
35. *Ibid.*, p. 337.
36. *Fatḥ al-Bārī*, Vol. VII, p. 182.

were asked of them by *Ja'far* : "Are we slaves who have fled away from their masters ? If it is so, we should be forced to return."

The Negus ordered *'Amr b al-'Āṣ*, one of the *Quraysh* envoys to reply. He said : "They are not slaves. They are all free men."

Ja'far : "Have we committed murder ?"

'Amr : "There is not a drop of blood that they have shed."

Ja'far : "Do we owe anything to the people of *Mecca* ?"

'Amr : "No, not even a single penny."[37]

William Muir, while discussing the emigration of the *Muslims* to Abyssinia significantly remarks :

> On this occasion the emigrants were few, but the part they acted was of deep importance in the history of Islam. It convinced the *Coreish* of the sincerity and resolution of the converts, and proved their readiness to undergo any loss and any hardship rather than abjure the faith of *Muḥammad*. A bright example of self-denial was exhibited to the whole body of believers, who were led to regard peril and exile in the cause of God, as a privilege and distinction. It may also have suggested the idea that the hostile attitude of their fellow-citizens, combined with the merits of their creed, might secure for them within the limits of Arabia itself a sympathy and hospitality as cordial as that afforded by the Abyssinian King ; and thus given birth to the idea of a greater "Hegira", the emigration to *Medina*.[38]

The Aim of the Oppressors

The persecution of the helpless *Muslims* and the manner in which the emigrants to Abyssinia were ruthlessly pursued by the chiefs of *Mecca*, can give us an idea of the deep hatred which consumed the Meccans. The following description of *Abū Jahl* by *Ibn Isḥāq* seems to depict the situation correctly :

> It was the wicked *Abū Jahl* who used to incite the men of *Quraysh* against them (the *Muslims*). When he heard of the conversion of a man of high birth with powerful friends he argued with him, criticised him

---

37. Ḥāfiz Nūr-ud-Dīn 'Alī b. Abī Bakr al-Haithami *Majma' al-Zawā'id wa Manba' al-fawā'id* (Cairo, 1353 A. H.), Vol. VI, p. 30.
38. *Life of Muhammad*, p 68.

vehemently, put him to shame, recklessly slung mud at him and said to him : "You abjured the religion of your father. He was far superior to you. We will degrade your prudence and intellect, undermine your judgement and drag your honour in the mire. If he were a merchant he was threatened with dire consequences and warned that in case he embraced Islam, his goods would be boycotted and his assets would thus be lost. If he were not an influential person, he was beaten and people were incited against him."[39]

Social Boycott

These words of *Abū Jahl* clearly show that the opposition was neither accidental nor confined to a particular section of society. It was deliberate and well organized and on all fronts. Every possible attempt was made to check the onward march of *Islam*. From the tenth month of the seventh year of *Muḥammad's* mission till the tenth year,[40] for a period of three years, *Muḥammad* (peace be upon him) and the whole of *Banū Hāshim* were confined within a pass at some distance from *Mecca*. None of the other clans was to have any business dealings with them and there was to be no inter-marriage. The supply of food was almost stopped and the people in confinement faced great hardships. The condition of children was especially miserable. There was no regular supply of food and the people were, at times, forced to eat leaves of trees.

This ultimately created dissension amongst the various *Meccan* factions who were tied with the besieged people by blood relations. Neither *Mūḥammad* (peace be upon him) nor his companions, in spite of their unspeakable sufferings, had shown any signs of giving in and the feud among the Meccan people was causing embarrassing situations. This brought to an end the siege and the Holy Prophet and his companions were permitted to return to their homes.

A Great Personal Loss

Not long after the end of boycott, and within a short span

---

39. Ibn Hishām, op. cit., Vol. I, p. 320.
40. Ibn Sa'd, op. cit., Vol, I, p. 209.

of time, *Muḥammad* (peace be upon him) lost his uncle and protector *Abū, Ṭālib* and his faithful wife and helpmate *Khadījah.*

Muḥammad (may peace of Allah be upon him) remained with *Abū Ṭālib* to the end. He did his best to persuade his octogenarian uncle to make profession of the new faith. But the old man remained obdurate. He was, however, very much attached to *Muḥammad* (peace be upon him). "For forty years *Abū Ṭāblib* had been his faithful friend—the prop of his childhood, the guardian of his youth and in later life a very tower of defence. The sacrifices to which *Abū Ṭālib* exposed himself and his family for the sake of his nephew, while yet incredulous of his mission, stamp his character as singularly noble and unselfish. They afford at the same time strong proof of the sincerity of *Muḥammad. Abū Ṭālib* would not have acted thus for an interested deceiver ; and he had ample means of scrutiny."[40]

The death of his beloved wife *Khadījah* was also a grievous affliction. For five and twenty years she had been his counsellor and support. She was the first to believe in his prophethood and to offer him ungrudging support in the propagation of faith. She stood firmly by his side during the stormy period of persecutions and hardships. Her devotion and fidelity appear all the more remarkable when we bear in mind the prosperous life she had led prior to having become the wife of *Muḥammad* (peace be upon him). Her love for the Prophet never wavered and her faith in him was never shaken. She breathed her last in the month of *Ramaḍān* ten years after her husband's commission as a Prophet. She was sixty-five at the time of her death and her husband fifty. The Prophet's grief at her death was very profound. To the end of his life he retained the tenderest recollections of her love and devotion.

The death of *Khadijah* left the Holy Prophet lonely. The name of *Sawdah* was suggested to him for marriage which the Prophet accepted. This lady had suffered many hardships for the sake of *Islam* . She was an early convert to the new faith and it was by her persuasion that her husband had embraced *Islam*. On the second *Hijrah* to Abyssinia *Sawdah* had accompanied her husband. Her husband died on their way back to

---

40. William Muir, op. cit., p. 103.

Mecca leaving her in aterrible state of destitution. Small as the Muslim community was, where could an old lady of fifty-five look for a more respectable shelter than the household of the Holy Prophet ? Thus her marriage was an act of great compassion and generosity on the part of *Muḥammad* (peace be upon him).

Chapter 4

Propaganda Campaign Against The Holy Prophet

(May peace and blessings of Allah be upon him)

Apart from the pressure on *Banū Hāshim* and the persecution of the Companions of the Holy Prophet, a good deal of criticism was levelled against the Prophet's claim that he had received revelations from God—in fact against the very idea of revelation itself. This criticism was directed along four different channels.

Firstly, *Muḥammad* was subjected to mental torture by suggesting other explanations of his religious experience than that it was a revelation from God.

Secondly, the opponents could not believe that a human being who did not claim to possess any supernatural power could ever become the messenger of God.

Thirdly, if a human being were to be elevated at all to this exalted position, there were so many other persons who were richer and far more influential than *Muḥammd.* Why was it, the sceptics argued, that God ignored all of them altogether and crowned the helpless *Qurayshite* orphan with prophethood ?

Lastly, *Muḥammad* had nothing extraordinary, nothing dramatic, to parade to substantiate his claim to prophethood.

We will consider these allegations in the following pages and will note the way in which the Holy *Qur'ān* repudiates them.

Critics, Old and New

The commonest allegation against *Muhammad* was that he was a ***majnūn***, that is, possessed by a *jinn.*[1] They also suggested

1. The Qur'ān, lxxxi : 22, etc.

that he was a *kāhin*, or soothsayer,[2] a *sāḥir*, that is, magician or sorcerer,[3] and *shā'ir*, that is a poet.[4]

It is significant to note in this connection that the common allegations which the *Meccans* levelled against *Muḥammad* are repeated even to this very day. Professor Macdonald has attempted, though in vain, to explain *Muhammad's* prophethood in terms of epilepsy and psycho-pathology. He also believes that *Muḥammad* was a genius. But this aspect is not well defined. The key to *Muḥammad* is that "he was a poet" of the old *Arab* type without much of poetic skill, with all his being given to the prophetic side of poetry, and that he had a "strange jumble of Jewish and Christian conceptions"[5] as material for his prophetic use.

The view of Macdonald that *Muḥammad* was a poet is slightly different from that of Muir who ventures the suggestion that the supernatural influence, which appears to have acted upon the soul of the *Arabian* prophet, may have proceeded from the "Evil One" and his emissaries,[6] yet the spirit in which the prophetic consciousness of *Muḥammad* manifests itself is not the same. Macdonald asserts that just as *Ḥassān* the poet had his female *jinni* who overpowered him and pressed verses out of him, so *Muhammad* had his companion (*qarin*) who was the source of his inspiration.[7] *Muḥammad*, he continues, is not really a prophet in any exalted sense : "I know nowhere in the Semitic world any appearance like that of the great prophets of the Hebrew."[8] "Rather, this first of all *Moslem* is in part a combination of 'soothsayer' adviser and admonisher, and a hurler of magical formulae against his enemies,[9] although possessed of ideas which raised him above the common place and suggest that *Muḥammad* a devout soul, if ever there was one and a mystic in spite of his creed—was adrift himself on that sea,

---

2. The Qu'ān, lii : 29 ; lxix : 42.
3. *Ibid.*, xxxviii : 4.
4. *Ibid.*, lii : 30 ; lxix : 41.
5. See Macdonald, *Religious Attitude and Life in Islam* (Khayats, Beyrout 1965), p. 20.
6. *Life of Muhammad*, p. 90.
7. Macdonald, op. cit., p. 19.
8. *Ibid.*, p. 14.
9. *Ibid.*, p. 17.

and was nearing that shore."[10]

The Allegations Refuted

I have given long excerpts from Macdonald's book in order to give an idea that in spite of the great difference of time there has been no change in the nature of the allegations hurled at the Prophet. The modern critics of *Islam*, like the *Meccans* of the olden days, believe that what the Prophet claims to be a revelation or the word of *Allah* is nothing else but the frenzied expression of the ecstatic state of his mind.

The Holy *Qur'ān* has vehemently refuted this charge and has explained that the utterances of the Holy Prophet (peace be upon him) are the revelations of the Lord and their nature and contents provide a bold challenge to those who attribute his prophetic expressions to some base origin, at times to the mental throes of a dreaming reformer, at others to the effusion of a frenzied poet or the incoherent drivellings of an insane man. The Holy *Qur'ān* categorically repudiates, for instance, the allegation that the Prophet is a poet : "We have not taught him poetry nor is it meet for him."[11] At another place the Holy *Qur'ān* explains the reasons why it is absurd to call *Muḥammad* a poet. A poet is commonly a mental rambler who tries to transform into beautiful verse his wayward whims and fleeting emotions. He is primarily concerned with abstract and remote issues and speculations which have no bearing on the practical problems of human life.

"As for poets, it is the erring who follow them. Hast thou not seen how they stray in every valley."[12]

Thus whatever the poet says cannot be consistent and closely knit. Being an expression of the fleeting emotions it is impossible to find coherence and harmony in the views expressed by a poet. Moreover, there is a world of difference between the practical life of a poet and his poetical utterances. His poetry merely expresses his emotional moods and therefore a poet is not required to transform his thoughts into living facts : "And how they (the poets) say that which they do not."[13]

---

10. Macdonald, op. cit., p. 39.
11. The Qur'ān, xxxix : 69.
12. *Ibid.*, xxvi : 325.
13. *Ibid* , xxvi : 226.

A prophet, on the other hand, is a practical reformer. He says what he means and means what he says. Whatever he professes is also transmuted by him into practical reality. In his great personality the ultimate values which he preaches take flesh and blood.

Besides, there is complete harmony between the various components of the Prophet's teaching, each message being in entire unison with the whole of his revelation. There is nothing inconsistent, nothing superfluous.

Lastly, unlike poets, the actual impact of the Prophet's activity is the purification and ennoblement of the human beings. A spiritual Armageddon is fought out by the prophets on the plains of history. Humanity, rent with national antagonism and riven with class-conflicts and threatened by the tyranny of materialism, is freed by the prophets from the servitude of these evil forces and learns to live as the family of God. The prophets restore peace amongst the different sections of the human race and bring harmony within man. The greed, selfishness, love for material gains, lust for power—all these base urges are purified and in their place human beings learn to live as self-less and God-fearing men whose uppermost desire is to serve humanity and weed out corruption and tyranny from human society.

Can a poet achieve all this ? Is he capable of expressing something which is consistent and is not in collision with any other aspects of his own preachings ? The reply of history to this query seems to be conclusive and the attestation of human experience abundantly clear—and both of them in the negative.

The allegation that the Holy Prophet was under the influence of the evil spirits has also been categorically repudiated by the Holy *Qur'ān*. How is it that a man who is controlled by a demonic being or a supernatural power of low grade, quite other than the Power that reigns over the universe, can set for himself the sublime purpose of destroying the spell of superstitions which had been interposed between man and his Creator, of restoring the rational and sacred idea of Divinity amidst the chaos of material and disfigured gods of idolatry and of effecting a moral regeneration of a society which had touched a low ebb of degradation, and of giving to humanity a superb code of conduct which does not guide man merely in the sphere of individual righteousness but also in the spheres of politics and economics, law, and morality. It is impossible for anyone who studies the life and character of *Muḥammad*, who knows what he taught and how he lived, to feel anything but reverence for that noble soul—the greatest of the apostles of *Allah* ? Can a person under the control of an evil spirit develop such deep consciousness of his inner self, and all its different aspects, the consciousness of God Almighty with His numerous attributes, the awareness of the sublimity of his mission, and the stern obstacles that stood in his way, the awareness of the qualities of his friends and the stubbornness of his foes—and yet perfect harmony within himself ? Such rare qualities of head and heart are never to be found in those who are under the influence of evil spirits. History shows not a single example of such-like persons whose message created one of the most balanced and noblest civilisations of the world. The Holy *Qur'ān* says :

> Shall I inform you upon whom the devils descend ? They descend on every sinful, false one. They listen eagerly, but most of them are liars. (xxvi : 221-223)

Similarly, the *Qur'ān* also vehemently repudiates the allegation that *Muḥammad* speaks under the influence of the *jinn*. "Have they not bethought them that their comrade is in no way under the influence of the *jinn*. He is but a plain warner."[14] Here "comrade" stands for the Holy Prophet. The *Qur'ān* exhorts the people to reflect if a man of such great eminence and wisdom, whose whole career was the faithful expression of a fine nature, free of every trace of self-seeking, vanity or affectation, a man of loving personality, of transparent candour and integrity, who successfully guided humanity not only in one aspect of life but in all sectors of life, could achieve such a spectacular success under the influence of the *jinn*. Never in history has a man, influenced by the spirits, been able to attain such glory as *Muḥammad* did in the short span of twenty-three years of his prophethood. Coming from a land and a people who had no glorious past of which they could be proud, he elevated them to the heights of eminence, shattered the great empires, undermined

---

14. The *Qur'ān*, vii : 183.

the position of long-established religions, remoulded the souls of countless men and women and built up a whole new world—the world of *Istam*. How can any sane person conceive that this great revolution, which not only changed the map of the world, but also radiated morality and expanded the frontiers of knowledge, could have been brought about by a man who was under the spell of the *jinn*.

The fact that the opponents who brought forth such allegations were not unanimous in their accusations, is a clear proof of their falsehood. They were thoughtlessly slinging mud at the Prophet (peace be upon him) in the hope that some of it might stick. This is the reason why they could not follow any firm line of criticism. They said all sorts of things. Sometimes they said that he was a poet ; at other times they declared his words to be those of a soothsayer or of a magician. It is indeed quite strange that a person who was unlettered, who had no knowledge of the ancient scriptures, should have been the one through whom the world received a book like the *Qur'ān* which in its sublime composition and its incomparable literary excellence speaks for itself as an irrefutable proof of its Divine origin.

There was also the charge that the Prophet was just an ordinary person who walked in the bazaars, who had his wives and children, that there was nothing unusual or supernatural about him. The Holy *Qur'ān* has discussed this point at some length and conclusively shown that prophets, who are sent to guide humanity to righteousness, are human beings and thus no Divinity should be attributed to them. Indeed the *Qur'ān* itself abounds in statements which stress that *Muḥammad* was essentially a human being :

> Say : I am only a human being like you. My Lord inspires me that your God is only One God. (xviii : 110)
>
> Say (unto them O *Muhammad*) : I am only a human being like you. It is inspired in me that your God is One God, therefore take the straight path unto Him. Seek forgiveness of Him. (xli : 6)

The Holy *Qur'ān* has also mentioned the reason why a prophet should necessarily be raised from among human beings. The Prophet is sent to guide humanity, a function which can be performed only by a human being. He should live as a man, enjoying the pleasures and suffering the ills of human existence, so that those around him could follow in his footsteps. People should be able to see in his personality a living embodiment of virtue and piety. His life should be able to manifest the Attributes of the Creator. His love and concern for humanity should be sublime. He reflects the ideal pattern of human existence. This purpose can be achieved only if a prophet, as human being, exemplifies that pattern in his actual life. It is only as a human being that he could show the right path to the people and could inspire in them the religious devotion and piety.

There is a misconception under which people have been labouring since time immemorial that a person who claims no divine powers for himself cannot be deputed by God to reform and regenerate the human race. The Holy *Qur'ān* has winnowed out this mistaken notion and has pointed out that the angels, who do not share human feelings and sentiments, cannot prove themselves to be good guides for humanity. Human beings can learn from the actions and practical wisdom of those alone who share human feelings and appreciate the different problems of human life. It is human beings alone, therefore, who have been deputed to deliver to humanity the words of God and to explain their practical implications by leading their lives in perfect accord with the behests of the Creator. Whatever the prophets say or do is ideal in every respect, because they live in constant fellowship with the Great Reality. The Holy *Qur'ān* says:

> And naught prevented mankind from believing when the guidance came unto them save that they said: Hath Allah sent a mortal as (His) messenger? Say: If there were in the earth angels walking secure, we had sent down for them from heaven an angel as messenger. (xvii : 94-95)

These verses clearly show that a human being alone is competent to guide humanity because his life offers them a practical guidance. Since this world is primarily inhabited by human beings and it is for their regeneration that the prophets are sent, human beings alone can therefore successfully accomplish this great task.

At another place the Holy *Qur'ān* states that even if this task was assigned to the angels, they would present themselves before humanity in the garb of mortals, because it is only in the form of human beings that their lives can provide lessons for their guidance :

> They say : Why has not an angel been sent down unto him. If We sent down an angel, then the matter would be judged ; no further time would be allowed them (for reflections). Had We appointed an angel (Our messenger), We assuredly would have made him a man.
>
> (vi : 8-9)

Another line of propaganda adopted by the opponents of the Prophet to ridicule his revelations was to assert that the revelations were completely human production, the work either of *Muḥammad* himself or that of his human assistants or these were merely the stories of the past. The Holy *Qur'ān* has repudiated this charge in the following words :

> Those who disbelieve say : This is naught but a lie, which he hath invented, and other folk have helped him in it, so that they have produced a slander and a lie. And they say : Fables of the men of old which he hath had written down so that they are dictated to him morning and evening. Say (unto them, O *Muḥammad*) : He Who knoweth the secret of the heavens and those of the earth hath revealed it. Verily, He is Ever-Forgiving, Merciful.
>
> (xxv : 4-6)

The charge has been quoted repeatedly in other verses of the Holy *Qur'ān* in different ways :

> And We know well what they say : Only a man teacheth him. The speech of him at whom they falsely hint is outlandish, and this is clear Arabic speech.
>
> Verily, those who disbelieve the revelation of *Allah*, *Allah* guideth them not and theirs will be a painful doom.
>
> (The Prophet invents no lie) only they invent falsehood who believe not Allah's revelations, and (only) they are liars. (xvi : (103-104)

Amongst the various attempts to deride the *Qur'ān*, it was one of the most powerful charges. It is significant that it has been summarily dismissed by saying that it is nothing but a bare lie. The charge is so foolish and hollow that it hardly deserves any consideration.

The persons who have been referred to in this connection are *Jabir*, *Yāsir*, *Aish*, or *Ya'īsh*, *Qais*, *Addas*. They were the helpless slaves of powerful Arab masters. It is indeed strange that these persons who had been allegedly teaching *Muḥammad* (peace be upon him) the craft of prophethood and had been preparing him for this avocation by narrating to him anecdotes of the past should have been among the first to believe in the divine source of the *Qur'ān* and should have been willing to suffer persecutions at the hands of their masters for this very belief.

Moreover, none of them was an *Arab* by descent. They were all aliens who had been sold as slaves in the markets of *Arabia*. It is indeed surprising that *non-Arabs* should have been able to produce a book like the Holy *Qur'ān* which in respect of the elegance of its language, the superb structure of its words and sentences, in the peculiar style of its narration, in the extraordinary beginning and ending of its verses, in its flow of thought, in the introduction of parables and description of events, in the forms of its admonitions and warnings and in the manner of its reasoning and arguments, is unparalleled in the whole range of human history. The composition of the *Qur'ān*, in spite of its concern with a variety of subjects, is remarkable. The *Arabs* were accustomed either to prose or to poetry. Their prose was divided into rhymed and unrhymed. The intellectuals practised in verse. As for prose, its use was for the common people. The *Qur'ān* did not resemble either the prose or the poetry of the period, for the endings of its verses were different from the rhymes of poetry and the *saj'* of prose. The Holy *Qur'ān*, in fact, introduced a new style of expression which was not within the reach of the common man.

Thus every sensible man must acknowledge *Muḥammad's* unalloyed sincerity in his claim that what he called revelation was not the secret learning from the Christian slaves, but that it came to him from God alone. "The *Qur'ān*," observes Harry Gaylord Dorman, "is a literal revelation of God, dictated to *Muḥammad* by *Gabriel*, perfect in every letter. It is an ever-present miracle witnessing to itself and to *Muḥammad*, the Prophet of God. Its miraculous quality resides partly in its style, so perfect and lofty that neither men nor jinn could produce a single chapter to compare with its briefest chapter, and partly in its content of teachings, prophesies about the future and amazingly accurate information such as the unlettered *Muhammad* could never have gathered of his own accord."[15]

Another line of attack was that *Muḥammad* (peace be upon him) was not the sort of person to whom revelations should have come. He was not sufficiently competent for that. The *Arabs* in general could not imagine that a man who was a posthumous child and had been deprived even of the love of the mother in early childhood, who had lost the support of the important men of his tribe, who had no riches to display, could be elevated to the position of a prophet. They thought that prophethood should have been bestowed upon one of the wealthy chiefs of the tribes :

> And they say : If only this *Qur'ān* had been revealed to some great man of the two towns (*Mecca* and *Ṭā'if*). (xliii : 31)

In refutation of this criticism, the Holy Qur'ān points out that prophethood is a special favour of God and He knows well on whom it should be bestowed. No human being, therefore, has any right to question the choice of *Allah* and no one is entitled to dictate to Him whom to choose and whom to ignore.

It is they who apportion their Lord's mercy ? (xliii : 32)

The unbelievers said that they would not believe in the prophethood of *Muḥammad* unless they were also enabled to enjoy the prophetic experiences themselves :

> And when a token cometh unto them, they say : We will not believe until we are given that which *Allah's* messengers are given. (vi : 125)

The *Qur'ān* spurns it as a fantastic demand and says that Allah is the best to decide correctly on whom His favour should be showered. Allah knoweth best whom to endow with His Message.[16]

The *Qur'ān* stresses this by pointing out :

> And thus have We inspired in thee (O*Muḥammad*) a

---

15. H. G. Dorman, *Towards Understanding Islam* (New York 1948), p. 3.
16. The *Qur'ān*, vi : 125.

spirit of our Command. Thou knewest not what the Scripture was, nor what the Faith. But We have made it a light whereby We guide whom We will of our bondmen. And thou verily dost guide unto a right path. (xliii : 52)

Then in the chapter entitled *Jumu'ah* (Congregation) this point has been further elucidated :

He it is Who hath sent among the unlettered ones a messenger of their own, to recite unto them His revelations and to purify them and to teach them the Scripture and Wisdom, though heretofore they were indeed in error manifest.

Along with others of them who have not yet joined them. He is the Mighty, the Wise. That is the bounty of Allah, which He giveth unto whom He willeth.

(xlii : 2-4)

The Demand for Miracles

The last group of opponents comprised those persons who expected revelation to have supernatural accompaniments observable by all. When they saw that *Muḥammad* (peace and blessings of *Allah* be upon him) was no more than a person walking in the bazaars like all other human beings, procuring articles for his daily use, protecting himself against the cold blasts of the winter and the scorching heat of the summer, they were attempting to establish that a man who shared the life of other mortals and had nothing unusual about him, could not be a messenger of God. For them a prophet was necessarily superhuman who had hardly anything in common with ordinary human beings. The disbelievers, therefore, expressed their doubts about the prophethood of *Muḥammad* and said

What a strange messenger is he, that he eateth food and walketh in the streets, why is not an angel sent down unto him to be a warner with him ?

Or (why is not) a treasure thrown down unto him, or why hath he not a garden from whence to eat ? And the evil-doers say : You are but following a man bewitched.

(xxv : 7-8)

In the chapter entitled *Banu Isrā'īl* the demand for the

supernatural signs in *Muḥammad* (peace be upon him) are even more pressing :

> They say : We shall not give thee credence till thou causest for us to bubble up from the earth a spring ;
>
> Or until thou hast a garden of palm and vine, and thou causest in the midst of it rivers to gush forth ;
>
> Or until thou causest the heaven to fall upon us as fragments as thou hast said, or thou producest God and angels ascending ;
>
> Or until thou hast a house adorned with gold, or thou ascendest into the heaven ;
>
> Nor shall we give credence to thy ascent until thou bringest down to us a writing which we may read.
>
> (xvii : 90-93)

There is some variation in the precise nature of what is expected or demanded of *Muḥammad* (peace and blessings of *Allah* be upon him), but underlying assumption is that a prophet should possess some supernatural powers by virtue of which he should be able to suspend or disrupt the working of the natural order whenever he desires. In answer to these demands God commanded *Muḥammad* to announce :

> Say : Glory be to my Lord ! I am nothing but a human being (sent) as a messenger. (xvii : 93)

This verse beautifully explains the reason why the demand that the Divine can be manifested in time only through a serious disturbance of the natural order is foolish. *Muḥammad* is only a warner and as such does not command the supernatural powers of the universe. The sudden bubbling up of springs from the earth, the gushing forth of rivers, the falling down of the sky and the abrupt appearance of a magnificent building made of pure gold, are not the essential accompaniments of a true prophet. On the contrary, the qualifications of a true prophet are his extremely pious and virtuous life, his perfect integrity, his shining and spotless character, his selflessness, his love for humanity and his unfailing and sustained devotion to the cause of *Allah* and His noble teachings.

The Holy *Qur'ān* has explained this point at numerous places. In the first instance, it emphasises that the performance of miracles does not lie in the hand of the Prophet :

> And it was not given to any messenger that he should bring a portent save by *Allah's* leave but when *Allah's* commandment cometh (the cause) is judged aright, and the followers of vanity will then be lost. (l : 78)

The Prophet himself confesses his inability to perform miracles at his own sweet will, because it rests with the Almighty God. He says in very clear terms that the Prophet is only a messenger of God who honestly carries out the behests of his Master :

> Say (O *Muḥammad* to the unbelievers) : I say not unto you (that) I possess the treasure of *Allah*, nor that I have knowledge of the unseen, and I say not unto you : verily, I am an angel. I follow only that which is inspired in me. (vi : 50)

> Say : For myself I have no power to benefit, nor power to hurt, save that which *Allah* willeth. Had I knowledge of the unseen I should have gathered abundance of wealth, and adversity would not touch me. I am but a warner, and a bearer of good tidings unto folk who believe. (vii : 188)

"It must be said," observes Ameer *'Alī*, "to the credit of the disciples of the Arabian Teacher that they never called for a miracle from *their* Master. They—scholars, merchants, and soldiers—looked to the moral evidences of his mission. They ranged themselves round the friendless preacher at the sacrifice of all their worldly interests and worldly hopes, and adhered to him through life and death with a devotion to his human personality to which there is scarcely a parallel in the history of the world."[17]

He further elucidates this point by adding :

> In an age when miracles were supposed to be ordinary occurrences at the back of the commonest saint, when the whole atmosphere was surcharged with supernaturalism, not only in *Arabia*, but in the neighbouring countries

---

17. *The Spirit of Islam*, p. 31.

> where civilization had made a far greater progress, the great Pioneer of rationalism unhestitatingly replies to the miracle-seeking heathens—"God has not sent me to work wonders ; He has sent me to preach to you. My Lord be praised ! Am I more than a man sent as an apostle ?" . . . No extraordinary pretensions, no indulgence in hyperbolical language, no endeavour to cast a glamour around his character or personality. "I am only a preacher of God's words, the bringer of God's message to mankind," repeats he always. From first to last no expression escapes him "which could be construed into a request for human worship" [The *Qur'ān*, lxii : 1-10] ; from first to last there is unvarying soberness of expression, which, considering the age and surroundings, is more marvellous ; from first to last the tone is one of simple, deep humility before the Creator.[18]

The Prophet disclaims every power of working wonders and bases the claim for the truth of his divine mission entirely upon his teachings. He never resorts to the miraculous to assert his influence or to reinforce his warnings. It is recorded in Ḥadīth that some of the Prophet's companions took the eclipse of the sun as a disturbance of the natural order on the death of his son *Ibrāhīm.* He plainly told his followers that the sun and the moon observed the commands of *Allah* and they had nothing to do with the death of his son. He emphatically remarked : "Indeed the sun and the moon are two out of the numerous signs of *Allah.* They do not eclipse due to birth or death of anyone. When you find them in this state, pray to *Allah* and celebrate His glory.[19]

Instead of creating a halo of awe and mystery around himself, the Prophet appeals to the inner consciousness and credulity. "Look around yourself (the *Qur'ān* says in effect), this wonderful world, the sun, the moon and the stars, holding their swift silent courses in the blue vault of heaven, the law and the system prevailing in the universe ; the rain-drops falling to revive the parched earth into life ; the ships moving across the ocean,

---

18. The Spirit of Islam, pp. 31-32.
19. Ibn al-Qayyim, Zad-ul-Ma'ad, Vol. I, p. 225.

beladen with what is profitable to mankind ; the beautiful palm covered with its golden fruit—are these the handiwork of your wooden or stone gods ?''[20]

"Fools ! do you want a sign when the whole creation is full of the signs of God ? The structure of your body, how wonderfully complex, how beautifully regulated ; the alternations of night and day, and of life and death ; your sleeping and awakening ; your desire to accumulate from the abundance of God ; the winds driving abroad the pregnant clouds as the forerunners of the Creator's mercy ; the variety of the human race, and yet their close affinity ; fruits, flowers, animals, human beings themselves—are these not signs enough of the presence of a Master Mind ?''[21]

The proofs of *Muḥammad's* truth are not philosophically recondite. They do not require any great or profound speculative power to apprehend them. If they did, it would be extremely unfortunate for the masses of mankind—the common people who must of necessity be hewers of wood and drawers of water. To see and feel the force and cogency of some of these proofs demands to an extent the cessation of a strictly philosophic struggle with problems, and the exercise instead of what one calls "wise passiveness" along with the possession of sundry moral virtues, such as reverence, candour, and openness of mind to evidence when it is presented *ab intra*, as well as *ab extra*. To the Prophet *Muḥammad*, as to the seers of the past, it was not only through intellectual scrutiny that they could find "the secret of the universe" but through honest thinking and making use of a heart that watches and receives. The Holy Qur'ān has beautifully expressed this state of mind in the following words :

> Say (unto them, O *Muḥammad*) : I exhort you unto one thing only : that ye awake, for *Allah's* sake, by twos and singly, and then reflect. (xxiv : 46)

But to all the exhortations of the *Qur'ān*, the *Quraysh* turned a deaf ear. They were blind to the signs of God, deaf to the call of the Prophet towards righteousness and towards shun-

---

20. The *Qur'ān*, xxv : 45-59 ; l : 9, etc. Translation taken from Syed Ameer 'Alī, *Spirit of Islam*, p. 35.

21. Syed Ameer 'Alī, op. cit., p. 33. The *Qur'ān*, vi : 96-99 ; li : 20 ; xv : 50-57 ; xxiv : 20-28, 39, etc.

ning corruption and abominations. In the language of the *Qur'ān* they "have hearts wherewith they understand not, and have eyes wherewith they see not, and have ears wherewith they hear not. They are as cattle—nay, they are worse! These are the neglectfull." (vii : 179)

Then the Holy *Qur'ān* also points out the fact that the demand of the unbelievers for miracles was not based on sincerity. The noble life of the Holy Prophet and the sublimity of his Divine message are sufficient to convince any sincere man that *Muḥammad* is a true prophet of God. It is the vanity of the infidels, their grudge against his teachings and their inherited bias that prompted them to make such fantastic demands. Had they been sincere in their quest for truth they would have found ample proofs to believe in the prophethood of *Muḥammad* :

> And those who have no knowledge say : Why doth not Allah speak unto us, or some sign come unto us? Even thus, as they now speak, spake those (who were) before them. Their hearts are all alike. We have made clear the revelations for people who are sure. Verily We have sent thee (*Muḥammad*) with the truth, a bringer of glad tidings and a warner. (ii : 118-119)

In reply to the pressing demand for miracles the *Qur'ān* says that the extraordinary pious life of *Muḥammad* and the wonderful Book revealed to him are themselves the two great miracles which testify to the truth of his claim. Is it short of a miracle that a helpless man, having no material resources, braves for many years the hatred of his people, without any selfish motive whatsoever, and when people rally round him, instead of making them his own bondsmen, he persuades them to bow down before *Allah*, the sole Master of the universe? Then this very person, who had no schooling whatsoever, presents to the people a Book, which is all wisdom, which contains a code of laws, a manual of prayer and ethics, and is reverenced to this day by a great portion of the human race, as a miracle of elegance of style, of sublimity of message and of truth. These are the great miracles ; and miracles indeed these are. The Holy *Qur'ān* stresses this point :

> And they say : Why are not portents sent down upon him from his Lord? Say, Portents are with *Allah* only, and I am but a plain warner.

> Is it not enough for them that we have sent down unto thee the Scripture which is read unto them ? Verily, herein is mercy, and a reminder for the folk who believe. (xxix : 50-51)

In these verses the Holy *Qur'ān* is claimed to be the greatest miracle of *Muḥammad* which pours forth in an inspired tongue "all the revelations of nature, conscience and prophecy. Ask you a greater miracle than this, O unbelieving people ! than to have your own tongue closed as the language of that incomparable Book, one piece of which puts to shame all your golden poesy and suspended songs to convey the tidings of universal mercy, the warnings to pride and tyranny."[22]

The Holy *Qur'ān* further reveals that the advent of *Muḥammad* is not unexpected.[23] All the prophets and the revealed Books that preceded him proclaimed his glorious coming, sang his praise, exhorted their followers to obey him, prophesied extraordinary and unparalleled reforms and wonders to be worked by him, announced the sublimity and perfection of his teachings and declared themselves to be the simple harbingers of the final dispensation, destined for *Muḥammad* :

> Is it not a token for them that the doctors of the children of *Israel* know it ? (xxvi : 197)
>
> And they say : If only he would bring us a miracle from his Lord ! Hath not there come unto them the proof of what is in the former Scriptures ? (xx : 133)

The *Qur'ān* also reveals the fact that the disbelievers were pressing for miracles, not because they were sincere in their demand, but because they wanted to subject *Muḥammad* and his followers to mental torture by talking all sorts of foolish things. Amidst all kinds of doubts and misgivings, when they found themselves drifting to Reality, their obstinacy and self-interests stood in their way. They were unwilling to abandon their religion, because they knew that it would deprive them of so many sources of exploitation and self-aggrandisement. They realised that with the acceptance of Islam as their code of life they would be required to exercise so many restraints on their untamed lusts and surrender, so many material benefits which

---

22. Syed Ameer Ali, op. cit., p. 34.
23. The *Qur'ān*, vii : 157.

they had been enjoying since long by unjust and immoral methods. They had been avoiding Islam purposely and had been trying to check its tidal wave and in this they actually had ulterior motives. Even if miracles were performed before them, they would attribute some low motive to them in order to belittle their value as a sign of *Allah's* power.

The Holy *Qur'ān* is replete with examples showing that when miracles were shown by the prophets, the stubborn amongst the unbelievers brushed them aside by telling people that they were nothing but feats of magic. For instance, when the prophet Moses performed miracles the unbelievers tauntingly remarked that they were merely magical tricks with the help of which he wanted to dupe them :

> But when our tokens came unto them, plain to see, they said : This is mere magic.
>
> And they denied them, though their souls acknowledged them, for spite and arrogance. Then see the nature of the consequence for the wrong-doers. (xxvii : 13-14)

In the same way when miracles were shown at the hand of the Holy Prophet, the unbelievers rejected them outright and said it was just a magic :

> Then turned he away in pride and said : This is naught else than magic from the old. (lxxiv : 23-24)

In this verse *Allah* has also given the reason why unbelievers did not come to the fold of *Islam*. It was their arrogance and spite which kept them away from adopting the path of righteousness.

Such was the obstinacy of unbelievers that when the moon was split in twain by *Allah* at the gesture of *Muḥammad*, they paid no heed to it and overlooked it altogether by saying that it was just an illusion :

> The hour drew nigh and the moon was rent it twain. And if they behold a portent they turn away and say : Prolonged illusion. They denied (the everything Truth) and followed their own lusts ; and every affair is settled.
>
> (liv : 1-3)

The *Qur'ān* further explains that since the unbelievers were fanatics and their visions were cramped and narrow, they could not, therefore, judge wisely between right and wrong.

The portents and signs of God, however manifest, had no appeal for them, since their reasoning faculties had become almost dead due to arrogance which they had been constantly showing in their attitude towards the Messenger of *Allah* :

> Never came unto them a sign of the signs of *Allah*, but they did not turn away from it. (vi : 4)

The Holy *Qur'ān* again points out their stubbornness in clearer words :

> Had We sent down unto thee (O *Muḥammad*) a Writing upon parchment, so that they could feel it with their hands, those who disbelieve would have said : This is naught else than magic. (vi : 7

Apart from some of the above assertions, aspersions were cast on *Muḥammad's* motives. The unbelievers tried to convince people, though vainly, that the religious mission of *Muhammad*, in respect of which he claimed to be actuated by the Command of *Allah*, had some material interests. He, with the help of these religious tactics, wanted to usurp power and prestige and gain pre-eminence over them. The *Qur'ān* emphatically refute all such motives which were attributed to *Muḥammad* and insisted again and again that he was only a warner that his function is simply to warn people and that he had no axe of his own to grind in this sacred cause :

> Say (O *Muḥammad* unto mankind) : I ask of you no reward for this, and I am no imposter. Lo ! it is naught else than a reminder for all peoples. And ye will come in time to know the truth thereof. (xxviii : 86)
>
> Say (unto them, O *Muḥammad*) : whatever reward I might have asked of you is yours. My reward is with *Allah* only. He is the witness over all things. (xxxiv : 47)

The authentic records of the biography of the Holy Prophet show that it had occurred to the *Meccan* leaders to credit *Muḥammad* with ambition. They, therefore, time and again plied him with temptation. One day some of the important men of *Mecca* gathered in the enclosure of *Ka'bah*, sent for *Muḥammad* and addressed him in the following words :

> "We have seen no other man of Arabia, who has brought so great a calamity to a nation, as you have done. You have outraged our gods and religion and taxed our forefathers and wise men with impiety and error

and created strife amongst us. You have left no stone unturned to estrange the relations with us. If you are doing all this with a view to getting wealth, we will join together to give you greater riches than any *Qurayshi* has ever possessed. If ambition moves you, we will make you our chief. If you desire kingship we readily offer you that. If you are under the power of an evil spirit which seems to haunt and dominate you so that you cannot shake off its yoke, then we shall call in skilful physicians to cure you."

"Have you said all ?" asked *Muḥammad* ; and then hearing that all had been said, he spoke forth :

I require none of the things that you offer me. I demand nothing, neither riches nor high status, nor kingship, in return for what I have brought for you. I have been sent to you as a messenger of God, a herald of glad tidings and a warning. I have performed my duty by delivering His message to you which has nothing but goodness for you. If you accept then I assure you the good of this world and the world to come. If you reject, I shall remain patient and watch for the verdict of *Allah*."[23]

We do not find any trace of wavering or despair in the life of the Holy Prophet. A calm and lofty attitude was constantly maintained by him during all the years. The whole tenor of the revelation at this period was marked by a calm confidence, and therein lay the Prophet's strength.

This conversation between the unbelievers and *Muḥammad* clearly brings out the reasons for the opposition of the *Quraysh*. "The grounds of opposition to *Islam*," remarks Montgomery Watt, "were thus, besides self-interest, fear of its political and economic implications, and sheer conservatism. The situation which confronted *Muḥammad* was a malaise which had social, economic, political, and intellectual symptoms. His message was essentially religious in that it attempted to remedy the underlying religious causes of the malaise, but it affected the other aspects, and consequently the opposition had many facets."[24]

---

23. Ibn Hishām. Vol. I, pp. 295-96.
24. *Muhammad at Mecca*, p. 136.

Chapter 5

The Last Phase of Meccan Life

The last years of *Muḥammad's* stay in *Mecca* were very eventful. The tidal wave of Islam had been constantly growing stronger and the Prophet had won a sizeable following in spite of the hostilities of the *Quraysh*. It was during this period that two eminent personalities, *Muḥammad's* uncle *Ḥamzah* and *'Umar*, the son of *Khaṭṭāb* (who later became the Second Caliph), joined the new faith. The pledge of *'Aqabah* took place and the Prophet was asked to undertake his night journey which is known as *Mi'rāj* (ascension).

The New Strength

It is recorded in Ibn *Hishām* that the Holy Prophet was one day seated on the hillock of *Safā* when *Abū Jahl* happened to pass by and accosted the religion preached by him. *Muḥammad* (peace be upon him), however, kept quiet and did not utter a single word. He left the place and came to join a party of the *Quraysh* who were sitting near the *Ka'bah*. It so happened that, shortly after that, *Ḥamzab*, while returning from his hunting expedition, passed by the same way, his bow hanging by his shoulder. A slave-girl belonging to *'Abd Allāh b. Jud'ān*, who had noted the impertinence of *Abu Jahl*, said to him: "O *Abū 'Ummārah* ! would that you witnessed the scene when your nephew was abused by *Abu'l Ḥakam*. He accosted him with reproaches and uttered such words as were most repugnant to *Muḥammad* (peace be upon him), but he did not answer him back." On hearing these words *Ḥamzah* was deeply offended and hurried to the *Ka'bah* and there, in the courtyard of the holy sanctuary, found *Abū Jahl* sitting with a company of the *Quraysh*. *Ḥamzah* rushed upon him and struck his bow upon his head violently and said: "Ah! you have been abusing *Muḥammad* ; I too follow his religion and profess what he preaches. Hit me back if you can." The men of *Band Makhzum* came to his help, but *Abū Jahl* sent them away saying: "Let *Abū 'Ummārah* alone, by God I did revile his nephew shamelessly."[1] Therefrom *Ḥamzah* proceeded direct to the house of *Irqam* and professed *Islam* at the hand of the Prophet. The conversion of *Ḥamzah* to *Islam* proved to be a source of great strength to the new faith and its followers.

Another significant addition to the strength of Islam was *'Umar,* the son of *al-Khaṭṭāb,* a man of dauntless courage and resolution, feared and respected in *Mecca,* and hitherto a bitter opponent of the new religion. The traditional account reveals that the Holy Prophet once raised his hands in prayer and said: "O *Allah* ! give strength to *Islam* especially through *'Umar b. al-Khaṭṭāb.*"[2] The prayer was granted and he embraced *Islam.* The account of his conversion is very interesting.

Oue day *'Umar* set out from his house, sword in hand, with the intention of killing the Prophet. He was in a fit of anger and was fretting and fuming. *Nu'aym b. 'Abd Allah,* a friend of *'Umar,* met him accidentally half way. What had caused so much excitement and on whom was the fury to burst, he inquired casually. *'Umar* said furiously: "To destroy the man *Muḥammad* (peace be upon him), this *Sabean,* who has shattered the unity of the *Quraysh,* picked holes in their religion, found folly with their wise men and blasphemed their gods." "By God, *'Umar,* your soul has deceived you, do you think that *Banū 'Abd Manāf* would let you walk on earth if you slayed *Muḥammad.* Why don't you take care of your own family first and set them right ?" "Which of the folk of my house ?" asked *'Umar* angrily. "Your brother-in-law and cousin, *Sa'īd b. Zayd,* and your sister *Faṭimah,* for by *Allah* they have embraced *Islam* and have chosen to become the followers of *Muḥammad,* so look thou to them."[3] 'Umar directed his footsteps to his sister's house. As he drew near he heard the voice of *Khubbāb b. Aratt,* who was reading the Qur'ānic chapter "*Ṭāhā*" to both of them.

---

1. *Ibn Hishām,* Vol. I, pp. 291-2. *Suhayli, Al-Rouḍ al-Unuf,* Vol. I, p. 185.
2. *Ibn Mājab* and *Ḥahim, al-Mustadrak. Ḥākim,* says that this tradition comes to the standard of *Būkhārī* and *Muslim. Zurqānī,* Vol. I, p. 972.
3. *Ibn Hishām,* op. cit., Vol. I, p. 344.

Khubbāb, perceiving the noise of his footsteps retired to a closet. *Fāṭimah* took hold of the leaf and hid it under her knee. But *'Umar* had already heard the voice. "What sound was that I heard just now" shouted the son of *al-Khaṭṭāb,* entering angrily. Both his sister and her husband replied : "You heard nothing." "Nay," said he swearing fiercely, "I fear that you have become the followers of *Muḥammad* in his religien." He plunged forward towards *Sa'īd b. Zayd* but *Fāṭimah* rushed to the rescue of her husband. Thereupon *'Umar* fell upon his sister and struck upon her head. The husband and the wife could not contain themselves and cried aloud : "Yes, we are *Muslims,* we believe in *Allah* and His messenger *Muḥammad* (peace be upon him) so do what thou will."[4] When *'Umar* saw the face of his dear sister besmeared with blood, he was softened and said : "Let me see what you were reading, so that I may see what *Muḥammad* has brought." *Fāṭimah* hesitated and said : "I feel afraid to trust you with it." *'Umar* swore by God that he would return it to her when he had read it. *Fāṭimah* was satisfied with the assurance but said : "O brother, you are unclean on account of your idolatry, none but pure may touch it. You must at least clean your hands." So *'Umar* arose and washed his hands and took the page and read the opening verses of the chapter *Tāḥā.*

> "We have not revealed unto thee (O *Muhammad*) this *Qur'ān* that thou shouldst be distressed, but as a reminder unto him who feareth ; a revelation from Him Who created the earth and the high heavens, the Beneficent One Who is established on the Throne. Unto Him belongeth whatsoever is in the heavens and whatsoever is in the earth, and whatsoever is beneath the soil. (xx : 2-6)

'Umar read it with great interest and was much entranced with its rhythm, fascinating charm and appeal so that when he came to the verse : "Verily I, even I am thy Lord. There is no god save Me. So serve Me and establish worship for My remembrance,"[5] he remarked : "How excellent it is, and how graceful !" And when he heard that, *Khubbāb* came out of concealment and said, "O *'Umar,* I hope that *Allah* has answered the prayer of

---

4. *Ibn Hishām,* op. cit., pp. 334.
5. The *Qur'ān,* xx : 14.

the Prophet (peace and blessings of *Allah* be upon him) for only yesterday I had heard him say : 'O *Allah* ! strengthen *Islam* through *'Umar.'*" *'Umar* said : "O *Khubbāb* direct me to *Muḥammad* that I may go and submit myself to him."[6]

Khubbāb led him to a house in *Safa* where *Muḥammad* had been living along with his Companions. *'Umar* reached that place with the sword swinging by his arm. He knocked at the door. The Companions of the Holy Prophet turned to see who the intruder was ? One of them peeped through a chink in the door and reeled back exclaiming : "It is 'Umar with his sword." *Hamzah,* the son of *'Abd al-Muṭṭalib,* dispelling the fears of his friends, said : "Let him in. As a friend he is welcome. As a foe he will have his head cut off with his own sword." The Prophet asked his Companions to open the door. In came the son of *Khaṭṭāb.* The Prophet advanced to receive the dreaded visitor and asked him the reason of his visit. At this 'Umar replied : "O Messenger of *Allah* ; I come to you in order to believe in *Allah* and his Apostle and that which he has brought from his Lord." Filled with delight *Muḥammad* cried aloud : "*Allah-u-Akbar*" (Allah is the greatest).[7]

The conversion of *'Umar,* a simple incident, reflects admirably the powerful influence that the Holy *Qur'an* had on the hearts of those who listened to or recited it. It shows how the Word of *Allah* could conquer their souls. Couched in concise and exalted style, its short pregnant sentences, often rhymed, possessed an expressive force which could turn even the bitterest enemy into an ardent admirer. The transmutation of dust into gold seems trivial compared to the overnight transmutation of an avowed foe into a passionate believer. Moreover, this incident also gives us an idea of the deep love the Prophet had for mankind. His calm and dignified personality had a charm of its own. His heart was burning with the keen desire to summon people to the path of righteousness and he was always ready to show the greatest affection even to his most bitter enemy. His mind was absolutely free from all sorts of prejudices.

The conversion of *Ḥamzah* and *'Umar* was a real triumph for the cause of *Islam.* So great and instant was the effect of

---

6. *Ibn Hishām,* op. cit., pp. 344-45.
7. *Ibid.,* p. 345.

their conversion on the situation that the believers who had hitherto worshipped God within their own four walls in secret now assembled and performed their rites of worship openly in that sanctuary itself. This raised their spirits, and dread and uneasiness began to seize the *Quraysh*.

Mi'raj

The last days of the *Meccan* phase of the Prophet's life is noted for his miraculous journey from *Mecca* to the farther mosque at Jerusalem, and an ascent through the sphere of the heavens and then enjoying the company of adoring prophets and angels and getting into immediate presence of God Almighty, far beyond where none except *Gabriel* could ascend.

This important journey is known as *Mi'rāj* which literally means ascent or ascension. In Islamic parlance the ascension of the Prophet *Muḥammad* (peace be upon him) to the heavens is called *Isrā'* which signifies a night journey. This journey is described in chapters 17 and 53 of the Holy *Qur'ān* :

> Glory be to Him, who carried His servant by night from the sacred Mosque to the distant Mosque—the precincts of which We have blessed—in order that We might show him some of Our signs. (xvii : 1)

This verse describes the initial stage of the journey from *Mecca* to Jerusalem, and explains its purpose to be the manifestation of the extraordinary signs of Providence. The noteworthy feature is that the journey took place within a part of the night in spite of the fact that the distance between *Mecca* and Jerusalem is several hundred miles. Another chapter of the Qur'ān which gives an account of *Mi'raj* is liii and it reveals some details of the Prophet's experience in the heavens where he is described as having witnessed the Divine Glory and Manifestation at the closest possible propinquity.

In both these places the events have been described as extraordinary and the Qur'ānic version belies the conclusion that the whole event was merely a dream-experience.

There are many authentic traditions from the Prophet concerning the night journey contained in *Bukhārī* and *Muslim* and other reliable collections of *Ḥadīth*. Here we quote a few of them. The Prophet described that extraordinary experience in the following words :

"I was one night sleeping at *Mecca* in the house of *Umm Hānī*, daughter of *Abū Ṭālib* and a sister of *'Alī*, when *Gabriel* came to me. He rent the roof of the house and brought to *Ḥaṭīm* near the *Ka'bah*. He opened my chest on the side of the heart, washed it with the water of *Zamzam* in a golden basin, filled it with wisdom and mercy and put it back in its place. Then he brought a horse (*Burrāq*) to me, which resembled lightning in swiftness and lustre, was of clear white colour, medium in size, smaller than a mule and taller than an ass, quick in movement that it put its feet on the farthest limit of the sight. He made me ride it and carried me to Jerusalem. He tethered the *Burrāq* to the ring of that temple to which all the prophets in Jerusalem used to tether their beasts, and led two *Rak'ahs* of prayer with them. After that *Gabriel* took me to the heavens on the same horse. When we reached the first heaven, the guarding angel said: "Blessed be thy arrival" and opened the door of the heaven. The angels congratulated me and opened the gate. I visited Jesus and John (peace be upon them) and saluted them. They returned my salutation and said: "Good brother, blessed be thy arrival!" Then they expressed their faith in my prophethood. Then I reached the third heaven and met Joseph (may peace of *Allah* be upon him) and saluted him. He welcomed me and returned my salutation and expressed his faith in my prophethood. Then I was carried to the fifth heaven. There I met prophet *Ha'rūn* (may peace of *Allah* be upon him). I saluted him and he returned my salutation and expressed his faith in my prophethood. Then I reached the sixth heaven. I met Moses there. I saluted him and he returned my salutation. Thence I reached the seventh heaven and met *Abraham* and saluted him. He returned my salutation. Thence I was carried to the *Sidarat al-Muntaha*. Then I was shown the *Bait al-Ma'mūr* which is a *Ka'bah* encompassed daily by seventy thousaud angels, so that the angels who once encompassed it would not have their turn again till the resurrection. I saw paradise and hell. Then *Gabriel* stopped there and I was presented to the Divine Presence and experienced the thrill of witnessing the Divine Glory and Manifestation. Fifty daily prayers were ordained for my followers. On my return, I spoke to Moses that my followers had been enjoined to pray fifty times in a day. Moses said : "Your followers cannot perform so many prayers ; I have already tried the children of *Isrā'il*. Go back to God and ask for a remission in number," I went back to the Presence of God and stated that my followers could not bear (the burden of) so many prayers. The Almighty God, glory be to Him, made a reduction of ten prayers. When I reported this to Moses, he urged me again to request for a further reduction. I again begged my Lord to reduce the number still further. I went again and again in the presence of *Allah* at the suggestion of Moses for reduction in the number of prayers till these were reduced to five only. Moses again asked me to implore for further reduction, but I said : "I feel ashamed now of repeatedly asking God the Holy and High, for the reduction. I accept five daily prayers. God commanded that these five prayers shall be rewarded as fifty prayers."[8]

It is also recorded in *Ḥadīth* that the Prophet led a congregational prayer of the prophets in *Bait al-Maqdis.*[9]

The account of the *Mi'rāj*, as given in the *Qur'ān* and *Ḥadīth*, is clearly indicative of the fact that it was not a dream, but an astounding experience. The description in chapter xvii begins with the glorification of the Lord for the extraordinary favour that He had conferred on *Muḥammad*. Had it been merely a dream, its special mention was absolutely uncalled for and the limited span of time i.e. a part of the night, would have been meaningless, because one can have a glimpse of both the worlds in a state of slumber even in the fraction of a minute.

Moreover, the *Mi'rāj* has been expressed by the word *Isrā'*, which signifies a journey both of body and soul together in a part of a night as it has been pointed out in the Holy *Qur'ān* :

---

8. The account of *Mi'rāj* has been taken from the following books : (1) *Bukhārī, 'Kitāb al-Salāt' 'Kitāb al-Tawhīd', 'Kitāb al-Anbiyā'*, Chapter *'Mi'rāj'*. Chapter *'Sifāt al-Nabī'*, Chapter *'Bad al-Khalq'*, (2) *Saḥīḥ Muslim*, Chapter *'Mi,rāj'*.

9. *Ibn Qayyium, Zād al-Ma'ād*, Vol. II, pp. 125-26.

> The angels said : O Verily we are messengers of the Lord ; they shall not reach thee. So travel with thy people in a part of the night. (xi : 81)

Likewise in another chapter of the *Qur'ān*, it has been clearly stated :

> And We inspired Moses saying : Take away my slaves by night, for ye will be pursued. (xxvi : 52)

Here the word *asra* denotes travel by night, and it is obvious that it refers to bodily movement.

It is also recorded that as the story of the *Mi'rāj* spread around, the unbelievers scoffed at it. Had it been only a dream, there would have been no occasion for such a reaction about it.

The *Qur'ān*, however, tells us that this event raised a good deal of stir among the people and the sceptical audience plied *Muḥammad* with all sorts of questions :

> And We appointed the vision (of thy ascent) which We showed thee as an ordeal for mankind. (xvii : 60)

This verse clearly indicates that this extraordinary event became an ordeal for the people. The ordinary mind could not imagine that a man could ascend through heavens with his body. A dream, however, could never have created such a widespread discussion as this event did. *'Abd Allāh b. 'Abbās*, who had a deep insight in the Holy *Qur'ān*, says that the word *'ru'yā'* as used in the above mentioned verse, signifies the observation with the help of an eye.[10] He emphatically refutes those who claim that it was a vision in the state of sleep.[11]

It is, however, significant to note in this connection that the word *'ru'yā'* is used in the Arabic language both for the vision in dream and seeing with the physical eyes, corresponding to the context of the use of that word. The well-known poet *Muṭanabbī*, while praising *Badr b. 'Ammār*, says :

مَضَى اللّيلُ و الفضلُ الذى لك لا يُمضِي

ورؤ ياك أحلَى فى العيون من الغمضِ

---

10. *Bukhārī, Saḥīḥ*, Vol II, p. 686 ; *Tirmidhī, Sunan*, Vol. II, p. 141.

11. *Qāḍī 'Iyād, al-Shifā'*, p. 87 : *Ibn Kathīr, al-Bidāyah wa'l-Nihāyah*, Vol. III, p. 113.

The night is over, but your praise is not exhausted. Your seeing with the eyes is more enchanting than your vision in a state of slumber.[12]

The Holy *Qur'ān* testifies to the bodily ascension of *Muḥammad* in *Sūrah Najm* as well :

> Then he drew nigh and came down. Till he was (distant) two bows' length or even nearer. And he revealed unto His slave that which He revealed. The heart lied not (in seeing) what it saw. Will ye then dispute with him concerning what it seeth.
>
> And verily he saw him yet another time by the Lote-tree of the utmost boundary, nigh unto which is the Garden of Abode. When that which shroudeth did enshroud the lote-tree. The eye turned not aside, nor yet was over-bold. Certainly he (the Prophet) saw some of the greatest signs of his Lord. (liii : 6-8)

The famous scholar of *Ḥadīth*, *Nauwwī*, in his well-known commentary of *Muslim's Ṣaḥiḥ* succinctly remarks :

> The fact is that an overwhelming majority of the people including the early servants, jurists, *muḥaddīthūn* and the scholars agree that the Prophet ascended to the heavens with his body. Any person who would carefully reflect over the traditions and the accounts narrated by the Companions would be convinced of this truth.[13]

This opinion of the illustrious commentator of *Ḥadīth* clearly points to the fact that the *Mi'rāj* was a unique experience of the Holy Prophet in which both the body and the soul participated. This view is accepted universally by the *Muslim* scholars and mystic philosophers of the various schools of thoughts. The difference, if there is any, is on the issue whether the Prophet saw the Lord with his naked eye or not. In this connection the disagreement rests on the fact that the Companions gave different interpretations of the verse :

> And verily he saw *Him* yet another time descending.

---

12. *Qāfiya dād Shahrah al-Diwan fi tash.l al-bayān*, edited, by Zulfaqār 'Ali Deobandī (Dehli, 1345 A.H.), p. 304.

13. *Commentary on Muslim*, Chapter "*al-Isrā*", Vol. I, p. 91.

'Abd Allah b. Abbās says that "*Him*" stand for God, whereas *Abd b. Mas'ūd* and *'A'ishah* claim that "him" denotes the angel *Gabriel*.[14]

This unique experience of the Holy Prophet led to different reactions. The unbelievers found it a suitable opportunity to jeer at the *Muslims* and their creed. They pestered the Prophet with questions as to the description of the temple at Jerusalem, where he had never gone before and, to the astonishment of many, the Prophet's replies furnished accurate information about that city, etc.[15]

But for the true *Muslims* there was nothing unusual about it. The Almighty God, Who is powerful enough to have created the heavens and the earth by an act of His Will, is surely powerful enough to take His messenger beyond the heavens and show him those signs of His at first hand which are inaccessible to man otherwise. This deep of the *Muslims* in the Omnipotence of *Allah* and in the variety of the Prophet is expressed in the answer of *Abū Bakr*, when he was asked to make his comment about this extraordinary episode. It is recorded in the *Ḥadīth* that the unbelievers came to *Abū Bakr* and inquired whether he believed in the truth of the story of his friend *Muḥammad*, that he went to Jerusalem and then came back within a part of the night. *Abū Bakr* inquired if the Holy Prophet had actually said that. "Yes" they answered. Upon this he said : "Yes, I do verify it." The unbelievers then said : "Do you testify that *Muḥammad* went to Jerusalem and then returned within the short span of a night?" He replied : "Yes, I am prepared to testify to events even more wonder-provoking than this one, i.e., the heavenly messages come to the Prophet day and night. This event (his ascention) is not more astounding than that."[16]

To *Abū Bakr*, therefore, the acceptance of the *Mi'rāj* was just like the acceptance of the prophethood of *Muḥammad*. It was on this occasion that he earned the title of *al-Ṣiddīq* (the verifier of the truth).

The apt reply given by *Abū Bakr* is very meaningful and

---

14. *Zād al-Ma'ād*, Vol. II, p. 126.
15. *Bukhārī*, Vol. I, p. 548,
16. *Mustadrak of Ḥākim*, Vol. III, p. 63. *Dhahabī* says : "This *Ḥadith* comes up to the standard set by *Bukhāri* and *Muslim*."

beautifully epitomises the Islamic point of view about God and the universe and their mutual relationship and the significance of miracles in the scheme of revealed religions.

The Prophet's Miracle

There can be no doubt that one who believes in the prophetic doctrine about *Allah*, the Creator and the Sustainer of the universe, can find no *a priori* difficulty about verifying the miracles of the prophets. These are not unworthy of God, nor are they arbitrary acts. These are in fact occasional expressions of God's special purpose in the universe in connection with His messengers, expressions which are designed to serve as eye-openers against the bindness of a world perverted by sin. These are not so much disturbances in the natural order of the universe as they are acts of the Lord meant to shake people out of their heedlessness and to wrench back a sinful world into its proper order. They are part of a redemptive process which seeks the restoration of the Divine Order in nature, not its overthrow.[17] For the man who holds the mechanistic view of the universe, nature might be a system, closed and complete in itself, and, therefore, the idea of any intrusion into it of anything "from beyond," or the idea of any interruption of its regular law or order is unthinkable. But for a *Muslim*, there is nothing irrational in miracles because he does not look upon the universe as the creation of blind forces, but of an ever-living Lord Who is always concerned with its affairs and Who moulds them according to His Will. There is, no doubt, a uniformity in nature, but this does not mean that the universe is a finished product which left the hand of its Maker at its completion and is now lying stretched in space as a dead mass of matter with which God has now no active relationship. Such a view is repugnant to the spirit of *Islam*. The uniformity in nature signifies the perfect orderliness of God. But the principle of the order of nature should not be taken in the sense of blind mechanism. It denotes perfectly free will of the Supreme God, the Creator.

The idea of moral freedom is not in itself antagonistic to the idea of a perfect law. If nature is to be animated by freedom, and not by a blind necessity, then there is nothing

17. Bishop Gore, *Belief in God* (Pelican Books 1939), p. 231.

unreasonable in miracles because in the heart of this world of determinate and determined forces and laws there lies this mysterious and unique thing—the free Will of the Creator which the modern scientists have failed to comprehend.

There is no gainsaying the fact that a modern man who is exclusively absorbed in the scientific conception of nature as the scene of inevitable law cannot accept the possibility of miracles. But we should bear in mind that science is not the only legitimate avenue to Reality. There is also a moral avenue to Reality which justifies the existence of miracles. It is not contrary to reason to expect from the Almighty God that, under exceptional circumstances, He should show some special signs which might attract the attention of the people quite effectively.

It is true that the testing of faith lies in enduring and seeing Him Who is invisible in the ordinary course of natural life, but when the hearts of men almost fail to perceive the real worth of the teaching of the Prophets, it is quite logical if they are revived with the force of some extraordinary event. It would be sheer arrogance on the part of human reason to hold this to be necessarily impossible.

We find no basis in the *Qur'ān* for encouraging any childish love for the supernatural. But does it not amount to denying reason and power of God, if we were to assert that the Lord is tied to the rigid laws of nature ? When a miracle is performed what happens is that God innovates upon the moral physical order solely in the interest of the deeper moral order and the purpose of human life.

"Miracles, it must be remembered, are very rare. That is of their essence. These are occurrence in the process of nature of something which nature, that is, the experienced order, cannot account for, and which constrains men to recognize a special or extraordinary action of God calling attention to a special purpose."[18]

This definition of miracles is very exhaustive. It tells us that these are not common occurrences, but are quite rare. Secondly, it tells us that they are astounding events. Lastly, that although these are shown at the hands of some prophet, they are actually performed at the behest of God. *Ghazālī* in

---

18. Bishop Gore, *Belief in God* (Pelican Books 1939), p. 218.

his well-known book *Iḥyā' 'Ulūm al-Dīn* observes :

> The *mu'jizah* (miracle) testifies to the truth of the prophets, because human beings fail to perform it. It is a work of the Lord.[19]

Similarly, *Shaykh 'Abd al-Ḥaqq Muḥaddith Dihlavī* remarks :

> Miracle is not the act of the Prophet, but that of the Lord only which is exhibited at the hand of His Messenger.[20]

Imām Ghazālī has further elucidated this point in another work known as *Tahāfat al-Falāsifah.* He believes that miracles are the works of Allah only, but adds that the time qualified for the occurrence of a mlracle comes only when the prophetic resolution is directed to it, and then as a means of strengthening the system of the sacred Law, its appearance becomes a specific condition for the establishment of the system of God.[21] The Holy *Qur'ān* is the greatest miracle of the Holy Prophet, his character, morals and manners are the resplendent proofs of his truthfulness. "The *mu'jizah* (*i.e.*, a departure from the usual course of nature which the human intellect fails to comprehend as a matter of cause and effect)," says *Ibn Rushd*, is not a purpose in itself but it lends support and strength to man's belief in *Allah* and His Apostle.''[22]

Missionary Efforts

The working of miracles was not thus the main preoccupation of the Prophet. His energies were concentrated on preaching the Word of God and he lost no opportunity in calling people to the path of righteousness. He visited all those tribes who were often drawn to *Mecca* or to fairs in the neighbouring towns. He addressed assemblies at *'Ukāz* and other places and preached to the pilgrim encampments at *Mecca* and *Minā*. On these occasions he made fervent appeals to the people to give up idolatry and accept the sovereignty of *Allah*, the sole Creator and Sustainer of the universe, and assured them that the worship and service

---

19 *Ihya al-Ulum* (Egypt 1939), Vol. I, pp. 96-97.

20. *Madārīj al-Nubuwwah* (Nawal Kishore Press, Cawnpore), Vol I, p. 218.

21. *Al-Ghazālī's Tahāfat al-Falāsifah*, translated by Sabīḥ Aḥmed Kamālī, p. 191.

22. *Kitāb al-Kashf* (Egypt 1319), p. 79.

of the true Lord would not only open for them the gates of heaven in the next life, but would secure for them prosperity and dominion here on the earth as well. *Abū Lahab*, the sworn enemy of Islam and that of the Holy Prophet, would shadow *Muḥammad's* steps crying aloud, "O men, this man exhorts you to cast off the yoke of *Lāt* and *'Uzza* from your necks. Do not listen to him."[23]

The Prophet was not dismayed at all. He persisted in his mission for the fulfilment of which he had been commissioned to strive despite all odds. He moved amongst the tribes, he came across, awakened them to the consciousness of the great destiny that beckoned them and hurled defiance at the forces of doubt and darkness that stood in his way.

It was during this period that he got the opportunity of inviting the tribes of *Medina* (then known as *Yathrib*) to *Islam*. It is narrated that he once met a group of six or seven men whom he recognised as visitors from *Medina*. "Of what tribe are you ?" asked the Holy Prophet. "Of the tribe of *Khazraj*," they replied. "Then, why not sit down for a little and I will speak to you." The offer was readily accepted for the fame of *Muḥāmmad* (peace and blessings of *Allah* be upon him) had spread to *Medina* and the strangers were curious to know more of the man who had created a stir in the whole area. The Prophet presented to them an *expose* of his faith, explained its implications and the responsibilities that fell upon the men who accepted it.

Ḥadith further records that both the Jews and the polytheists of Medina were eagerly waiting for the advent of a new prophet. The Jews, however, excelled others both in wealth and knowledge. So, whenever there was any fight amongst them, the Jews always threatened their opponents by telling them that a prophet was about to rise for the time for a new dispensation had arrived. Him they would follow and then smite their enemies as the children of *'Ād* and *Iram* had been smitten.

So when *Muḥammad* addressed a group of pilgrims from *Medina* they testified him and said :

Know, surely, that this is the prophet with whom the

23. *Ibn Hishām*, Vol. I, p. 423.

Jews are ever threatening us : wherefore let us make haste and be the first to join him.

Invitation from *Medina*

They, therefore, embraced *Islam*, and said to the Prophet : "We have left our community for no tribe is so divided by hatred and rancour as they. God may cement our ties through you. So let us go to them and invite them to this religion of yours ; and if God unites them in it, no man will be mightier than you.[24] It is doubtless the *Ansār* had some awareness of the truth when they accepted the doctrines of Islam, but the majority of them presumably became *Muslims* primarily because they believed that God had sent *Muḥammad* with a message to the *Arabs*.[25]

The handful of *Medinese* converts remained steady to the cause and they preached the new faith with full zeal and devotion with the result that they succeeded in winning adherents for Islam from amongst their fellow-citizens. So the following year, on the occasion of the pilgrimage there came a group of twelve faithful disciples ready to acknowledge *Muḥammad* as their prophet. Ten were of the *Khazraj*, and two of the Aws tribe. They avowed their faith in *Muḥammad* as a Prophet and swore :

> We will not worship any but One God : we will not steal ; neither will we commit adultery, nor kill our children, we will obey the Prophet of God (*Muḥammad*) in all that is good.

When they had taken the oath or pledge, *Muḥammad* (peace and blessings of *Allah* be upon him) said : "He who carries it out has Paradise for his reward and he who neglects anything and is afflicted in this world, it may prove redemption for him in the hereafter and if the sin remains hidden from the eyes of men and no grief comes to him, his affair is with *Allah*. He may forgive him or He may not."

This oath is known as the First Pledge of *'Aqabah*, named after a little terraced mound where it was taken.

When the twelve men returned to *Medina*, the Holy Prophet sent *Muṣ'ab b. 'Umayr b. Hāshim* so that he might teach them

24. *Ibn Hishām*, op. cit, pp. 428-29.
25. *Ibid.*, op. cit., p. 433.

the doctrines of Islam and give them practical guidance as he had learnt in his company. He lived in *Medina* with *'Asad* son of *Zurāra.*[26] "So prepared was the ground, and so zealous the propagation that the new faith spread rapidly from house to house and from tribe to tribe. The Jews looked on in amazment. The people whom for generations they had vainly endeavoured to convince of the errors of heathenism were of their own accord casting their idols to the moles and the bats and professing belief in the One True God."[27]

The next year during the pilgrimage season, the converts of *Medina* met the Holy Prophet once more at the same place where they had met a year ago. This time, however, unlike the previous year, their number was eighty-eight as against twelve previously,[28] they pledged their faith to him in the presence of his uncle *'Abbās b. 'Abd al-Muṭṭalib* who (though himself still not a *Muslim*), abjured them not to draw his nephew away from the protection of his own kindred unless they were fully prepared to defend him even at the risk of their lives. He was the first to speak :

> O ye people of the *Khazraj* ! you all know the position that *Muḥammad* (peace and blessings of Allah be upon him) holds among us. We have protected him from our people as much as we could. He is honoured and respected among his people. He refuses to join anyone except you. If you think you can carry out what you promise while inviting him to your town, and if you can defend him against the enemies, then assume the burden that you have taken. But if you are going to surrender him and betray him after having taken him away with you, you better leave him now because he is respected and well defended in his own place.[29]

The Medinese assured *'Abbās* and his companions of their whole-hearted support to the Holy Prophet and the noble cause

---

26. *Ibn Hishām*, op. cit., p. 434.
27. William Muir, *Life of Muhammad*, p. 115.
28. The names can be read from *Ibn al Jawzī, Talqīh, Ibn Hisham* and *'Uyūn-al-Aṭar.*
29. *Ibn Hishām*, Vol. I, pp. 441-42.

for which he stood and then addressing him said : "O Messenger of *Allah* ! It is now for you to speak and take from us any pledge that you want to take regarding *Allah* and His Messenger."

The Prophet once again preached the faith and said : "I call you in the name of *Allah,* to worship none but one God and to give me a pledge that you will give me whole-hearted cooperation in the cause of *Allah.*"

Barā' b. Ma'rūr stretched out his hand and said : "We pledge, O Prophet of God ! that we accept all these conditions."

Then *Abū'l-Haytham b. Tayyihan* said : O Prophet of God ! between us and the Jews there are agreements which we would then sever. If *Allah* grants you power and victory, should we expect that you would not leave us. The Prophet replied :

> Nay, it would never be : your blood will be my blood. In life and death I will be with you and you with me. I will fight whom you fight and I will make peace with those with whom you make peace.

The audience were ready to take the pledge but *'Abbās b. 'Ubādah* son of *Nadla Ansārī* remarked :

> O ye people of the *Khazraj* ! do you know the significance of the pact that you are entering into with this man ? You are in fact avowing that you will fight against all and sundry. If you fear that your property will be at stake or the lives of your nobles will be endangered, then leave him now, because if you do this after the pledge it will be degrading for you both in this world and the world to come. But if you think that you can carry out what you are called upon to do in spite of the loss of precious lives and property, then undertake this heavy responsibility, and I swear by God, that herein lies the good of this world and that of the next."[30]

The people said with one voice : "We accept this even at the cost of our lives and property. But, O Prophet of *Allah* ! if we remain unshaken in our resolution, what will be in store for us ? "Paradise," was the reply. Then they all stretched out their hands and took the pledge which was as follows :

---

30. *Ibn Hishām,* Vol. I, p. 454.

> We all will obey you, O Prophet of *Allah* ! in all sets of circumstances : in plenty as well as in scarcity, in joy as well as in sorrow, that we would not wrong anyone. We will speak the truth at all times ; and that in God's service we would fear the censure of none.[31]

The Prophet of God appointed twelve deputies to preach *Islam* to the people at *Medina* and to guide the respective men of their own tribes in matters relating to the propagation of *Islam*.

Somehow or the other, the news of these secret desert meetings with the Medinese leaked out and, in order to know the facts with certainty, the *Quraysh* interrogated some of the pagans of *Medina*, who answered in good faith that there was no truth in the report.

As time rolled by the *Quraysh* learned more about the pledge and in a fit of rage they pursued the pilgrims from *Medina* but did not succeed in catching hold of anyone except *Sa'd b. 'Ubādah*. They subjected him to unspeakable tortures, but he was later rescued by *Jubayr b. Mut'in* and *Ḥārith b. Harb* with whom he had trade relations and whom he had given shelter before.

Migration to Medina

After the pledge of *"Aqabah Muḥammad* (peace be upon him) began encouraging his followers to migrate to *Medina* . *Abū Salamah* is said to have gone there even before the pledge. This movement aroused the hostility of the *Quraysh* still further. They were unhappy with emigration because it would remove the *Muslims* to a place entirely beyond their reach, and plant them in a safe place whence they might securely work out their plans. The *Quraysh*, therefore, renewed their persecution, and, wherever they had power, they sought either to force the believers to recant, or to prevent their escape by confining them. It was in pursuance of this unwise policy that *Umm Salamah* (who, after the death of *Abū Salamah* was married to the Holy Prophet) was forcibly detained in *Mecca* and her child was also snatched from her. She succeeded in joining her husband along

31. *Ibn Hishām*, Vol. I, p. 454.

with her child at the end of the following year. After this *'Amir b. Rabī'a* and his wife *Laylā*, the daughter of *Abū Hathma* migrated to *Medina*. Then came *Abū Aḥmad bin Jahsh*, and his brother *'Abd Allāh*. This is how a speedy movement of the *Muslims* to *Medina* went on till the entire quarters of the city became deserted: and *'Utbah*, the son of *Rabī'ah* at the sight of these vacant abodes, once so full of life, sighed heavily and recited the old verse: "Every dwelling place, even if it has been blessed ever so long, will one day become a prey to desolation and bitter wind." "And", he sorrowfully added, "all this is the work of the son of our brother, who has scattered our assemblies, ruined our affairs, and created dissension amongst us".[32]

Within two months nearly all the followers of *Muḥammad*, except, *Abū Bakr*, *'Ali*, the Prophet himself and those helpless noble souls who had been detained in confinement or were unable to escape from slavery, had migrated to their new abode. "They were welcomed with cordial and even eager hospitality by their brethren at *Medina*, who vied with one another for the honour of receiving them into their homes, and supplying their domestic wants." In the words of Muir:

> *Kureish* were paralysed by a movement so carefully planned, and put into such speedy execution. They looked on in amazement, as families silently disappeared, and house after house was abandoned. There was here a determination and self-sacrifice on which *Kureish* had hardly calculated.[33]

This situation alarmed the *Quraysh* and at last they convened a meeting to take some effective measures with a view to stopping this tidal wave. Imprisonment for life, expulsion from the city, each was debated in turn. Assassination was then proposed, but assassination by one man would have exposed him and his family to the vengeance of blood. The difficulty was at last solved by *Abū Jahl* who suggested that a band of young men, one from each tribe, should strike *Muḥammad* simultaneously with their swords so that the blood-wit was spread over

---

32. *Ibn Hishām*, Vol. I, pp. 468-71.
33. William Muir, *Life of Muhammad*, pp. 130-31.

them all and therefore could not be exacted.[34]

This proposal was accepted and a number of young men was selected for the sanguinary deed. *Muḥammad* was informed of all that had been conspired against him and the angel *Gabriel* revealed this verse to the Holy Prophet :

> They are devising a plan against thee and I will devise a plan for thee. Wherefore bear with the infidels and let them alone for a while. (lxxxv : 15-17)

How splendidly did it come true ! Eleven of the conspirators were killed shortly after in the Battle of *Badr*, and the remaining three, namely *Abū Sufyān*, *Jābir* and *Ḥākim* were converted to Islam, and the Prophet escaped safely from their hands. Referring to their deliberations the Holy *Qur'ān* says :

> And call to mind when the unbelievers devised their plans against thee, that they might imprison thee or slay thee or expel thee from the city. Yes, they devised plans, but God also devised plans. (viii : 3)

The situation was no doubt critical but *Mnḥammad* was not at all perturbed. *Abū Bakr* was, however, urging the Prophet to depart from *Mecca*. He was also eagerly waiting for an opportunity to accompany *Muḥammad* on this eventful journey. But the Prophet told him that the time had not yet come : the Lord had not given him the command to migrate.

This delay in the command might have been caused by the overpowering desire of *Muḥammad* (peace be upon him) to see all his followers safely go away from *Mecca* before he himself left for *Medina*. Moreover, by deferring his departure God perhaps purposely wanted to show to the people that *Muḥammād* was the Messenger of God and he had been deputed by Him to call people to the path of righteousness and that the Prophet had, therefore, no cause for fear. The events also made it plain that the safety and security of the Prophet's life depended upon God alone and that the Prophet, therefore, need not bank upon the support of any other individual or agency ; that the Almighty Who had the power to create man and the universe also had the power to save *Muḥammad* from the danger that beset him.

---

34. *Ibn Hishām*, Vol. I, pp. 480-82.

In anticipation of the command of *Altah Abū Bakr* had made preparations for the journey. He had purchased two swift camels and had fed them properly so that they could successfully stand the ordeal of the long desert journey.

The Prophet Leaves

Four months rolled by. One day the Holy Prophet came to the house of *Abū Bakr* and informed him that God had commanded him to leave for *Medina.* The faithful admirer of *Muḥammad* (peace and blessing of *Allah* be upon him) shed tears of joy. The hour for emigration had at last arrived and he was to be the companion of the Prophet's journey. *Abū Bakr* offered him one of the camels which he had already bought for the occasion. The Prophet accepted this offer on condition that he would pay its price.[35]

Abū Bakr's daughter *Asmā'* prepared a bag containing meals for the trip. On the other hand, the Meccans were on the alert. As night advanced, they posted assassins around the Prophet's house. Thus they kept vigil all night long, waiting to kill him the moment he left his house early in the morning, peeping now and then through a hole in the door to make sure that he still lay on his bed. *Muḥammad* had with him people's trusts, which he entrusted to his cousin, ' to return *Alī* them safely to their respective owners and assured him full surety under God's protection and told him that no harm would come to him.[36] '*Alī* (may Allah be pleased with him) lay in *Muḥammad's* bed covered with his green mantle. The Prophet came out of the room and cast a handful of dust at the assassins and reciting verses of the Holy *Qur'ān*, passed unperceived through them.

The assassins remained on the watch until the day dawned when they rushed in and to their utter surprise, found that the person lying in the Prophet's bed was '*Alī* rather than *Muḥammad* (peace be upon him). This created a stir in the whole town.

Muḥammad proceeded direct to the house of *Abū Bakr* who

---

35. *Bukhārī*, Chapter on 'Emigration of the Holy Prophet and his Companions to Medina'.

36. *Ibn Sa'ad*, s v. '*Alī*, and *Ibn Hishām*, Vol. I, p. 485.

immediately accompanied him and both set out southward, clambered up the lofty peak of Mountain *Thawr*,[37] and decided to take refuge in a cave. *Abū Bakr* first entered the cave, closed all the holes with pieces torn off from his clothes, cleaned it and then asked the Prophet to step in.[38]

The Prophet and his companion stayed in this cave for three nights. *'Abd Allāh*, the son of *Abū Bakr*, would go to see them daily after dusk and apprise them of the situation in the city. *Amir b. Fuhayrah*, while in the company of other shepherds of *Mecca* tending his master *Abū Bakr's* flock, stole away unobserved every evening with a few goats to the cave and furnished its inmates with a plentiful supply of milk.[39]

The *Quraysh*, on the other hand, were quite baffled and exasperated. A price was set upon *Muḥammad's* head.[40] The news that the would-be assassins had returned unsuccessful, and that *Muḥmmad* (peace be upon him) had escaped made them gnash their teeth in anger and frustration. Horsemen scoured the country. Once they even reached the mouth of the cave where the Prophet was hiding along with *Abū Bakr*. When he saw the enemy at a very close distance *Abū Bakr* whispered to the Prophet : "What, if they were to look through the crevice and detect us ? We are two and unarmed and at the bottom of the cave."

The Prophet in his God-inspired calm replied :

> O *Abū Bakr* ! What do you think of those two with whom the Third is *Allah*.[41]

---

37. This mountain is situated at the distance of about five miles towards the south of *Mecca*.

38. *Ibn Hajar 'Asqalānī, Fatḥ al-Bārī* (Egypt 1959), Vol. I, p. 185.

39. *Ibn Hishām*, Vol. I, p. 486.

40. *Ibid.*, Vol. I, p. 486.

41. *Bukhāri*, Part II, para XIV, Chapter *'Munaqib al-Muhājrin'*, *Abū Bakr* on the authority of *Anas*. Opinions differ as to when these words were actually uttered by the Holy Prophet. The general opinion is that these words were said on the occasion when the Prophet and his companion were hiding themselves in the cave of *Thawr* and the enemies had actually reached upto its mouth. The Holy *Qur'ān* testifies to this opinion in *Surah Tawbah* (Repentance). "When the two were in the cave alone and the Prophet said unto his companion : Grieve not *Allah* is with us." (ix : 40)

—Contd.

Alluding to this important scene of the cave the Holy *Qur'ān* says:

> If ye will not assist the Prophet, verily God assisted him aforetime when the unbelievers cast him forth, in the company of the second only; when the two were in the cave alone; when the Prophet said unto his companion: "Be not cast down, for verily *Allah* is with us! And *Allah* caused to descend tranquillity upon him and srengthened him with hosts which ye saw not, and made the word of unbelievers to be abased; and the word of the Lord, that is exalted, for God is Mighty and Wise." (ix : 407)

For three days *Muḥammad* (may peace of *Allah* be upon him!) and *Abū Bakr* lived in the cave and the *Quraysh* continued their frantic efforts to get hold of them.

'Abd Allāh b. Arqat, who belonged to the family of *ad-Di'l b. Bakr*, and had as yet not embraced *Islām*, but was trusted by *Abū Bakr*, and had been hired by him as a guide, reached the cave after three nights according to a plan. His report satisfied the noble fugitives that the search had slackened.

In the chapter of *Saḥiḥ Bukhāri* on "*Munāqib al-Muhājirin*" it is recorded that the Prophet consoled and comforted Abu Bakr with these words, at the time when *Surāqah b. Mālik b. Jushum*, was about to apprehend them. Apparently there seems to be a contradiction between the Holy *Qur'ān* and the *Hadith* on this issue and some of the eminent scholars in an attempt to reconcile the two have said that in this verse of *Sura Tawbah* (اذ يقول لصاحبه) the word (اذ) 'when' signifies that these words were uctered at a different occasion than the one about which the previous words were said (ثانى اثنين اذ هما فى الغار) "when the two were in the cave alone." But this is a far-fetched idea. The fact seems to be that the Holy Prophet consoled and comforted his companion on both the occasions with these words "Be not cast down, for verily God is with us." The *Qur'āa* refers to the incident of the cave and *Imām Bukhāri* narrates the occasion when the Prophet and his companion were going to be apprehended by *Surāqah* and *Abū Bakr* was perturbed. *Ibn Qayyim*, in his famous book *Zād al-Ma'ād*, says that when the enemy had actually come to the mouth of the cave and *Abū Bakr* said to the Holy Prophet: "What if they were to look through the crevice and detect us?" the Prophet replied, "What do you think of those two, O *Abū Bakr*, with whom the Third is *Allah*?" and then also consoled him by these words: "Be not cast down, for verily Allah is with us." (Vol. II, p. 138, Chapter "Emigration of the Holy Prophet"). (*Suhayli, al-Raud al-Unuf*, Vol. II, p. 4).

The opportunity to depart was come. They could move unobserved, the sooner the better.

They rode the camels, *Muḥammad* (peace be upon him) with the guide and *Abū Bakr* with his servant *Ibn Fuhayra* behind him, and resumed their journey. Having come down from mount *Thawr* and having left the lower quarter of *Mecca* a little to the right, they struck off by a track considerably to the left of the common road and, hurrying westward, soon gained the vicinity of the seashore near by *'Usfān*.

The little caravan travelled during the night and rested in the noon when the heat grew scorching. One day they could find no shelter. *Abū Bakr* cast a glance and found a little shade beside a rock. He cleaned the ground, spread his mantle for the Prophet to lie upon and himself went off in search of food. Coming across a bedouin boy who was tending his goats, *Abū Bakr* asked him to supply milk, which he did.

The *Quraysh*, as we have mentioned above, had declared that whoever would seize *Muḥammad* (peace be upon him) would receive a hundred camels as reward. This had spurred many persons to try their luck. Among those who were on the look-out for the Prophet and his companion in order to win the reward was *Surāqah*, the son of *Mālik*. He, on receiving information that a party of four had been observed on a certain route, decided to pursue it secretly so that he alone should be the winner of the reward. He mounted a swift horse and went in pursuit of them. On the way the horse stumbled and he fell on the ground. On drawing a lot so as to divine whether he should continue the chase or not, as the Arabs used to do in such circumstances, he found the omens unpropitious. But the lust for material wealth blinded him altogether and he resumed the chase. Once more he met with the same fate but paid no heed to it. Again he jumped into the saddle and galloped on at a break-neck speed till he came quite close to the Prophet. *Abū Bakr's* heart agitated and he said to the Prophet : "O Messenger of *Allah* ! we are lost." But the Prophet remarked in his calm and confident tone : "Be not cast down, for verily *Allah* is with us."[42]

---

42. *Ibn Qayyim, Zād al-Ma'ād*, Vol. II, p. 139.

This marvellous steadfastness of the Prophet in the midst of overwhelming perils was due to Divine revelation that strengthened him and comforted him at every step of his life.

The repeated stumbling of *Surāqah's* horse and his falling from it awakened him to the situation and he realised that it was a constant warning of *Allah* for his evil design which he contemplated against the Holy Prophet. His heart was immediately changed and the sworn enemy was converted into an honest believer. He approached the Prophet with a penitent heart and begged of him forgiveness in all humility. The Prophet forgave him and confirmed it with a token written by *Abū Bakr* on a piece of parchment. *Surāqah* showed this writing to *Muḥammad* (peace be upon him) on the day when he entered *Mecca* in triumph. The Prophet rewarded him and said : "It is the day of favour and fidelity."[43] *Surāqah* hurried back to *Mecca* and tried to foil the attempts of those who were running in pursuit of *Muḥammad* (peace be upon him) and his noble companions.

The party continued its journey till it reached the encampment of *Umm Ma'bad al-Khuza'iyah.* She was a gracious lady who sat at her tent-door with a carpet spread out for any chance traveller that might pass that way. Fatigued and thirsty, the Prophet and companions wanted to refresh themselves with food and a few draughts of milk. The lady told them that the flock was out in the pasture and the goat standing nearby was almost dry. The Prophet with her permission touched its udders, reciting over them the name of *Allah,* and to his great joy, there flowed plenty of milk out of them. The Prophet first offered that to the lady of the house and what was left by her was shared by the members of the party.

After having refreshed themselves the emigrants moved further. In the evening when *Abū Ma'bad,* the husband of *Umm Ma'bad,* came to his house, the lady narrated to him this strange incident. Upon this he remarked : "By God, he is the same man whom the people of *al-Quraysh* are searching for. Can you give me his discription ?" *Umm Ma'bad* said :

> "His was an innocently bright and broad countenance. His manners were fine. Neither was his belly

43. *Ibn Qayyim,* op. cit., Vol. II, p. 141.

bulging out nor was his head deprived of hair. He had black attractive eyes finely arched by continuous eyebrows. His hair, glossy and black, inclined to curl, he wore long. His voice was extremely commanding. His head was large and well formed and set on a slender neck. His expression was pensive and contemplative, serene and sublime. The stranger was fascinated from the distance, but no sooner he became intimate with him this fascination was changed into attachment and respect. His expression was very sweet and distinct. His speech was well set and free from the use of superfluous words, as if it were a rosary of beads. His stature was neither too high nor too small so as to look repulsive.

He was a twig amongst the two, singularly bright and fresh. He was always surrounded by his companions. Whenever he uttered something the listeners would hear him with rapt attention and whenever he issued any command, they vied with each other in carrying it out. He was a master and a commander. His utterances were marked by truth and sincerity, free from all kinds of falsehoods and lies."

On hearing these words *Abū Ma'bad* said, "By God, he is the man who is zealously debated about amongst the *Quraysh* now-a-days. I have determined cheerfully to accept his yoke."[44]

Leaving the encampment of *Umm Ma'bad*, *Muḥammad* (peace be upon him) and his companions lost no time and resumed their journey, going through unfrequented paths and suffering great hardships on account of scarcity of water and severity of heat. It was during this time that they met *Zubayr* at the head of a caravan returning from Syria.[45] Warm greetings were exchanged, *Zubayr* gave them the tidings that *Medina* was eagerly waiting for their arrival. He also presented to them two white garments which they thankfully accepted.

As soon as rumours of *Muḥammad's* arrival began to spread, crowds came flocking out of *Medina*. They would come every morning and wait eagerly for his appearance until forced by the

---

44. *Ibn Qayyim*, op. cit., Vol. II, p. 141.
45. *Skibli Nu,māni, Sirat al-Nabi*, Vol. I, p. 277.

unbearable heat of the midday sun to return. One day they had gone as usual and after a long trying watch had retired to the city when a Jew, catching a glimpse of three travellers winding their way to *Medina,* shouted from the top of a hillock : "O ye people of Arabia ! He has come ! He has come ! He, whom ye have been eagerly waiting for, has come !"

The joyful news soon spread throughout the city and people marched forward to greet their noble guest. The shouts of "*Allaho Akbar*" (God is the Greatest) resounded in *Banu 'Amr. Muḥammad's* elation (may peace of *Allah* be upon him) correspondingly increased, but with rare sense of timing and propriety, he called a halt. It was Monday, the eighth day of *Rabi' al-Awwal,* thirteen years after the inauguration of the prophetic career of *Muḥammad* (peace be upon him) i.e. on 20th September 622.[46]

Muḥammad (peace be upon him) stayed in *Qubā,* with *Kulthūm b. Hadam* a hospitable chief of the tribe of *'Amr b.* 'A*wf,* who had already received many of the emigrants on their first arrival. It was here that the party was joined by 'A*lī*. He brought the news that the rest of the family would soon be arriving. *Zayd* was leading one party which included his own wife *Zaynab,* the Prophet's wife *Sawdah,* and his daughters *Fāṭimah* and *Umm Kulthūm. 'Abd Allāh b. Abū Bakr* was bringing his sisters *'Ā'ishah* and *Asmā',* as well as his mother *Umm Rūmān.*

During his period of stay at *Qubā'* which, according to *Bukhāri,* extended to a fortnight, was laid the foundation of a mosque which has been glorified in the *Qur'ān* in the following words :

> The mosque which was founded upon piety from the first day is more worthy that thou shouldst stand (to pray) therein. (ix : 108)

The Prophet worked side by side with his other companions for the construction of the mosque. He even carried stones on his back and helped in setting them in proper place.

---

46 There is some variation in the dates mentioned by different writers. Phillip K. Hitti, in his book *History of the Arabs,* records it as 24th of September 622. William Muir gives it as 28th of June 622.

On the morning of Friday *Muḥammad* (peace be upon him) rode towards Medina amidst the cordial greetings of his Medinese followers who had lined his path. He halted at a place in the vale of *Banū Sālim* and there performed his first Friday prayer. The address which he delivered is marked by matchless eloquence, exhortation and eulogy of the Faith and succinctly sums up the spirit of *Islam* :

> Praise be to *Allah*, I seek His help, guidance and forgiveness and declare my implicit faith in Him and abhor *Kufr*. I declare that *Allah* is One and *Muḥammad* is His Messenger whom his Lord has blessed with guidance, light and wisdom and has sent him to the people at the time when the Apostles had ceased to come and the people had forgotten the teachings of the previous apostles and were led astray. The Day of Resurrection was at hand. Whoever obeys *Allah* and His Prophet finds righteousness and whoever disobeys goes astray beyond doubt, and is in error manifest. I admonish you to fear *Allah*. The best advice that a *Muslim* can give to his brother is to exhort him to observe piety. Avoid that which *Allah* has commanded you to avoid. There is no better precept than that of piety and fear of God. These are the sources of strength and help in the next life. Your relation with *Allah*, whether in the seen or unseen sphere of your life, should be based on truth and fidelity and this objective can be best achieved when you have no other end to pursue except that of seeking the pleasure of *Allah*. Such a course of life will enable you to get honour and fame in this world and it will prove to be a boon in the Hereafter, when man stands badly in need of good actions and wishes that there had been a great distance between him and misdeeds. *Allah* admonishes you with His Power and Authority and this He does because He is very compassionate and Merciful towards His men. *Allah* is Truthful and fulfils His promise as He says in the *Qur'ān*: My words cannot be changed nor am I indeed unjust to *the* slaves" (1. 29). Therefore fear Him in this world and the world to come in the seen and in the unseen since who fears Him, God grants him redemption for his

sins and favours him with great reward. This person alone is, in fact, highly successful. Fear of *Allah* saves man from His wrath, His punishment and anger. This will brighten the faces of people and elevate them on the Day of Judgment. Fear *Allah,* walk on the path of virtue and piety. Do not show any slackness in obedience to God. *Allah* has revealed the Book for your teaching and has made the right path clear for your guidance so that truth can be distinguished from falsehood. Just as *Allah* has shown you His favour, likewise you should obey Him in right earnest. Look upon His enemy as yours and exert your best for winning His favour. *Allah* has chosen you for Himself and has given you the name of *Muslims,* God has ordained that those who are to be destroyed will be swept away and those who are to survive, after the clear signs have come to them, would live with insight and on the strength of evidence (from the Lord). No power is of any avail to any one except that of the Power of *Allah.* Therefore remember God as much as you can and live for the Hereafter. The man whose relation with God is based on sincerity, *Allah* will help him against evil. None will be able to harm him. *Allah's* command is supreme over the people. But people cannot command God. *Allah* alone is the Master of all men and men have no share in his lordship. Therefore keep your relation with *Allah* on the right footing. Do not brother about others. *Allah* is the Greatest Protector. *Allah* is the Greatest and there is no Power but that of Him."[47]

The address is so eloquent that it needs no comment. A man suffers for thirteen years all kinds of insults at the hands of the *Quraysh* ; stones and filth are thrown at him ; he is beaten by the young and the old, and is excommunicated. Then a plot is hatched to put an end to his life and he is forced to leave his hearth and home. He is put to all kinds of torture—physical and mental, for no fault of his. He only says : Surrender yourself to *Allah.* After having been driven from his native place and having suffered hardships and perils of long journey, when he finds an opportunity to address people, not a single word of

47. *Ibn Kathir, Al-Bidāyā wa'l-Nihāyah,* Vol. III, p. 213.

bitterness is uttered by him. He has nothing to say of his personal sorrows and griefs, of the atrocities perpetrated on him by the people of *Mecca*, of the privations that he has constantly suffered. The noble heart is free from all stains of personal anguish. The audience is repeatedly exhorted to develop God-consciousness and adopt the path of righteousness.

The Prophet Reaches *Medina*

After leading the Friday prayer the Prophet resumed his journey towards *Medina*. The tribes and families of *Medina* came streaming forth, and vied with one other in inviting the noble visitor to their homes. It was indeed a triumphal procession. Around the camel of *Muḥammad* (may peace and blessings of *Allah* be upon him !) and his immediate followers, rode the chief men of the city in their best raiment and in glittering armour. Everyone was anxious to receive him and said: "Alight here, O Messenger of God ! Abide by us." *Muḥammad* (peace be upon him) answered everyone courteously and kindly : "This camel is commanded by God, wherever it stops, that will be my abode."

The camel moved onward with slackened rein and entered the quarter of the city inhabited by *Banū Najjār*, a tribe who was related to the Holy Prophet from the maternal side. There it stopped before the house owned by *Abū Ayyūb*. The fortunate host stepped forward with unbounded joy for the Divine blessing appropriated to him, welcomed the holy guests and solicited them to enter his house. *Abū Ayyūb*, out of the profound respect that he had for the Prophet, offered to vacate the upper storey, but the Prophet preferred the lower one, being more accessible to his visitors. The Prophet stayed in this house for seven months until the building of the mosque and his own apartments was completed.[48]

Achievements in *Mecca*

Islam no doubt achieved tremendous success in *Medina*, but the achievements at *Mecca* too were not insignificant. It was in *Mecca* that the new religion was founded and a phenomenal

---

48. The account of emigration is based upon *Bukhāri*, and *Ibn al-Qayyim Zād al-Ma'ād*, Vol. II, pp. 130-46 and *Ibn So'ad*, Vol. I, pp. 225-38.

transformation was brought about in the life and thought of the *Muslims* in the words of Muir :

> Never since the days when primitive Christianity startled the world from its sleep and waged mortal combat with heathenism, had men seen the like arousing of spiritual life, and faith that suffered sacrifice and took joyfully the spoiling of goods for conscience sake ..
>
> ...What a change had those thirteen years now produced ! A band of several hundred persons had rejected idolatry, adopted the worship of One God, and surrendered themselves implicitly to the guidance of what they believed a Revelation from Him ; praying to the Almighty with frequency and fervour, for looking for pardon through His mercy and striving to follow after good works, almsgiving, purity, and justice. They now lived under a constant sense of the omnipotent power of God, and of His providential care over the minutest of their concerns. In all the gifts of nature, in every relation of life, at each turn of their affairs, individual or public, they saw His hand .....*Mahomed* was the minister of life to them the source under God of their new-born hopes ; and to him they yielded an implicit submission.
>
> ...The Believers bore persecution with a patient and tolerant spirit. And though it was their wisdom to do so, the credit of a magnanimous forbearance may be freely accorded. One hundred men and women, rather than abjure their precious faith, had abandoned home and sought refuge, till the storm should be overpast, in Abyssinian exile. And now again a still larger number, with the Prophet himself, were emigrating from their fondly loved city with its sacred Temple, to them the holiest spot on earth, and fleeting to *Medina*. There, the same marvellous charm had within two or three years been preparing for them a brotherhood ready to defend the Prophet and his followers with their blood."[49]

---

49. William Muir, *The Life of Muhammad*, pp. 155-56.

Chapter 6

The Prophet Gains Power

Let us now turn to the story of the Prophet's achievements in *Medina*. *Muḥammad's* mission is spiritual first and spiritual last, his programmes, which to a superficial observer, appear to be "temporal", were fully inspired by spiritual motives. He was the Messenger of God and it was in this capacity as the last of the Messengers that he had transmuted into reality the word of his Creator. All his energies and efforts were directed to this single end. Whatever he thought or planned, whatever he uttered or did was the outcome of the desire that humanity should recognize its Master, i.e. should recognize the perfect guidance vouchsafed by Him and carry out His Will and Commands with full devotion.

Mosque, The Centre of The New Ummah

The first task to which the Holy Prophet attended on his arrival at *Medina* was the construction of a mosque. A suitable site was selected for it and the land which belonged to two orphans was purchased for ten gold coins and then donated to the mosque.[1] The ground was cleared of weeds and shrubs, palm trees and rubbish, and the construction of the mosque commenced. The Prophet joined in the work which encouraged the *Muslims*. Both the *Muhājirūn* and the *Anṣār* laboured hard to complete it as soon as possible. One of the *Muslims* chanted :

If we sat down while the Prophet worked
This action of ours would be the worst.

As they constructed the mosque, the *Muslims* sang a *rajaz*.

There is no life but the life of the next world,
O God ! have mercy on *Anṣār* and *Muhājirūn*.

1. Ibn Ḥajar al-'Asqalāni, *Fatḥ al-Bāri*, Cairo, 1325 A.H., Vol. ii, p. 188.

The Apostle of God, (peace and blessings of *Allah* be upon him) however, changed its rhythm or order and said :

> There is no life but the life of the next world,
> O God ! have mercy on *Muhājirūn* and *Anṣār*.[2]

This mosque was square in form, each side measuring approximately 50 yards, facing towards the north[3] and having three gates on each of the remaining three sides. The southern door was for public entrance and the western gate was called *Bāb al-Raḥmān* and the eastern gate, reserved for the Prophet's household, was called *Bāb al-Nīsā'*.

To the north of the mosque a place was reserved for those companions of *Muḥammad* (peace be upon him) who had neither family nor home. They were known as *Aṣhāb al-Ṣuffāh* (the people of the *Ṣuffah*). This was a kind of seminary attached to the mosque for those who devoted full time to the study of religion. Adjoining the mosque were erected two apartments for the household of the Prophet. The mosque was a monument of simplicity—the walls were made of mud bricks and the roof supported by trunks of palm trees. Being covered with palm leaves and twigs it could not keep out rain, which sometimes made the unpaved floor muddy. This simple mosque was the venue of glorious scenes. It was here that the Holy Prophet imparted his teachings to the *Muslims*. It was here that embassies from different tribes were received. It was here that edicts were issued to kings and emperors. The residence of the Holy Prophet was, however, even simpler than the mosque. Some of the rooms were built of raw bricks whereas the others were mere cells made with the twigs of the palm trees. Worn out blankets were used with a view to providing privacy and seclusion to the inmates of the house. "During the time of the caliphate of *'Uthmān*," observes *Ḥasan b. 'Alī*, "when we visited the residential quarters of the wives of the Holy Prophet, we found their ceilings so low that we could easily touch them." Similarly another observer *Dāwūd b. Qays*, describing the house of *Muḥammad* (peace be upon him) says, "I have had the good

2. *Ibn Hishām*, Vol ii, (Cairo, 1300 A.H.) pp. 141-42.

3. Later on when the direction of the prayer was changed, the southern gate was closed and a door was made in the northern wall for general entrance.

fortune to see with my own eyes the quarters where the wives of the Holy Prophet lived. These were apartments made out of the branches of palm-trees, and blankets of camel-hair hung at their doors. The courtyard was hardly six to seven paces in length and breadth and rooms did not extend beyond ten paces."[4] After the death of the Prophet's wives all these quarters were annexed to the mosque and the land thus acquired was used for its extension. "Were these rooms kept intact, the world would have seen the austere and simple living of the last of the prophets in whose hand had been placed the keys of the worldly treasures",[5] to which the Prophet showed no inclination.[6]

The Adhan

We have noted earlier the persecution of *Muslims* in *Mecca.* They could not even perform their prayers openly. Up to that period these prayers had to be conducted in secret. Every precaution had to be taken not to let it be known that the

---

4. Bukhārī, *al-Adab-ul-Mufrad*, Karachi, Chapter "Construction of Huge Buildings."

5. Zurqānī, *Sharh al-Mawāhib al-Ladunnīyah*, Vol. i, p. 370.

6. *Muḥammad* was the Apostle of God, and was, therefore, head and shoulder above the level at which ordinary men and women live, immune to the temptations of material life. By his words and deeds the Holy Prophet rejected the attitude of world-renunciation and exhorted man to develop his God-given powers and strengthen his individuality through active contact with his material and cultural environment. At the same time, by his personal example, he also stressed that this strong, concentrated individuality, sharpened and steeled through a life of activity and experience, should not be directed toward self-aggrandisement but should be dedicated to the service of the Lord. The Prophet in fact taught humanity a kind of emotional asceticism which does not lead man to spurn the world for its being a source of evil and corruption, but prepares him to use it for the pursuit of noble and worthy ends. This attitude, which is known in Islamic literature and poetry as *faqr* or *istighnā'* has been, in fact, a matter of immense importance in *Islam* and the life of the Holy Prophet (peace be upon him) gloriously exemplifies it. His noble companions including the righteous caliphs and a large number of saints tried to live upto this ideal. This attitude is not a mere philosophical contemplation but it is a power, which saves a man from arrogance and self-intoxication when he obtains worldly resources and authority, and helps him to safeguard his integrity in a world of temptations. It also enables him to defy with contempt all the vested interests, and the forces which stand in the way of his ideals.

prayer service was taking place. In the peaceful conditions of *Medina,* where *Muslims* enjoyed full religious freedom, the problem which figured prominently was how to summon the *Muslims* to the mosque. The Jews summoned their congregations to the ṭemple by blowing trumpets, the Christians by striking gongs. *Muḥammad* (peace be upon him) did not feel drawn at all towards these customs and he considered them inappropriate for such sacred purposes. He felt that the human voice could better communicate the inspiration and emotion which should be dedicated to the solemnity of the occasion. It is narrated that when this problem was discussed, one day *'Abd Allāh b. Zayd* came to the Holy Prophet and told him : I saw last night a visitant in a dream who had a clapper in his hand and I asked him to sell that to me.

When he questioned what I wanted to do with that, I replied that it was to summon people for prayer, whereupon he said : Should I not show you a better way than this ? I replied in the affirmative. Upon this he said, say :

Allāhu Akbar, Allāhu Akbar
Allāhu Akbar, Allāhu Akbar
Ashhadu an lā ilāha illa Allāh
Ashhadu an lā ilāha illa Allāh
Ashhadu anna Muḥammad ar Rasūl Allāh
Ashhadu anna Muḥammad ar Rasūl Allāh
Ḥayya ala al-Salāh
Ḥayya ala al-Salāh
Ḥayya ala al-Falāḥ
Ḥayya ala al-Falāḥ
Allāhu Akbar, Allāhu Akbar
Lā ilāha illa Allāh

(*Allah* is the Greatest. *Allah* is the Greatest. *Allah* is the Greatest. *Allah* is the Greatest. I bear witness that there is no god but *Allah.* I bear witness that there is no god but *Allah.* I bear witness that *Muḥammad* is the Messenger of *Allah.* I bear witness that *Muḥammad* is the Messenger of Allah. Hearken to prayer. Hearken to prayer. Hearken to salvation. Hearken to salvation. *Allah* is the Greatest. There is no god but *Allah*).

The Holy Prophet said : "Your vision, by the grace of God,

is true. Go to *Bilāl* and communicate it to him so that he should call to prayer accordingly." When *'Umar* heard this in his house, he came there dragging his cloak on the ground and said : "By Him Who has sent you with the truth, I have seen precisely the same vision which has been shown to *'Abd Allāh b. Zayd.*" The Holy Prophet said : 'God be praised for that."[7] For the morning prayer, the following reminder was added :

As-Salātu khayrun min al-nawm,
(Prayer is better than sleep)[8]

Every day, at the five appointed times, this familiar call summoned the people to their devotions. For over thirteen centuries the same call has continually sounded from myriad minarets.

It is not only a summons to prayer, but also sums up very concisely the teachings of *Islam.* There is no god but *Allah,* the Sole Creator, the Master and the Law-Giver. *Muḥammad* (peace be upon him) is His Apostle and it is through him alone that we can find out the Will of God which should be followed. Prayer is the basis of religious life and it is through prayer alone that one can find the path of salvation.

Brotherhood

Prayers being thus regulated, the Prophet next turned his attention to cementing the ties of brotherhood amongst the *Muslims* of *Medina,* who were called *Anṣār* and the *Muhājirūn,* i.e., emigrants from *Mecca.* It was a necessary step since the refugees who had left their hearths and homes and had said goodbye to friends and relatives were feeling lonely. To raise the spirits of his homesick and suffering followers, to cast off their feeling of loneliness,[9] and to attune them to the changed circumstances, a new fraternity was established amongst the *Muslims* of *Mecca* and those of *Medina*[10].

---

7. Abū Dawūd, Edited by Muḥy al-Dīn bin 'Abd al-Ḥamīd, Chapter "*Adhan*".

8. Imām Muḥammad b. 'Alī b. Muḥammad al-Shawkānī, *Nail al-Awtār,* Vol. ii, p. 38—Cairo, 1952.

9. Suhaylī, *al-Rauḍ al-Unuf, Cairo,* 1332 A.H. Vol. ii, p. 18.

10 This was in fact the second brotherhood, the first was established [*Contd.*

This brotherhood was indeed unique in the history of the world. The fellow-feeling and love on which this new relationship was established found a wonderful expression. For example *Sa'd b. Sabī'*, a Helper said to his fellow brother *'Abd al-Raḥmān b. 'Awf*, "I am the richest man amongst the Helpers. I am glad to share my property half and half with you. I have two wives, I am ready to divorce one, and after the expiry of *'iddah*, you may marry her." But *'Abd al-Raḥmān b. 'Awf* was not prepared to accept anything : neither property nor home. So he blessed his brother and said : "Kindly direct me to the market so that I may make my fortune with my own hands."[11] The Helpers were extremely generous to their brethren-in-faith. They once approached the Holy Prophet with the request that their orchards should be distributed equally between the *Muslims* of *Medina* and their brethren from *Mecca*. But the Prophet was reluctant to put this heavy burden upon them. It was, however, decided that the refugees would work in the orchards along with the Helpers and the yield would be divided equally amongst them.[12]

These are not solitary expressions of the spirit of selflessness which the Holy Prophet had infused in his followers. It was a common trait of their character which they had developed under the influence of *Muḥammad* (peace be upon him). So strong and cordial was this relation that it surpassed even the relationship of blood. When either of the two persons who had been paired as brothers, passed away, his property was inherited by his brother-in-faith. This practice continued till the following verse was revealed and the regular rule of inheritance was allowed to take its usual course :

> And those who believed afterwards and emigrated and strove hard along with you : these also are of you :

---

amongst the Muslims of Mecca before migration to Medina. Ibn Ḥajar al-'Asqalānī, *Fatḥ al-Bārī*, Cairo, 1325 A.H., Vol, vii, p. 191. See also Ibn Sayyid al-Nās, *'Uyūn al-Athār*, Vol. i, p. 199, which confirms the statement of Ibn 'Abd al-Barr and mentions the names of those pairs who were locked in brotherhood at Mecca.

11. Bukhārī, *Kitāb al-Manāqib*, under the head *Manāqib, al-Anṣār*, Chapter 'The Establishing of Brotherhood amongst *Muhājirūn* and *Anṣār* by the Holy Prophet.'

12. *Ibid.*

> and the kindred by blood are nearer unto one another in *Allah's* decree. Verily *Allah* is of everything the Knower, (ix : 75)

The atmosphere of brotherhood and fellow-feeling created by the Holy Prophet produced very healthy results. Age-long enmities amongst the different tribes, especially those that had existed between the *Aws* and the *Khazraj* were almost forgotten amongst the converts from those tribes. "Acceptance of the faith required that as *Muslims* they should acknowledge not only the spiritual but temporal authority of *Muḥammad* and, holding subordinate every distinction of race and kindred, regard each other as brethren."[13] The Holy *Qur'ān* refers to this brotherhood as a great boon :

> And hold ye fast, all of you, to the cord of *Allah*, and be not disunited, and remember *Allah's* favour unto you, in that ye were enemies, and He joined your hearts together, and so ye became by His favour brethren, and ye were on the brink of an abyss of the fire, and He rescued you therefrom." (iii : 103)

The pages of history bear testimony to the fact that it was a marvellous and spectacular reform. Before the advent of the Prophet the *Arabs* were an uncompromising people, a nation torn into mutually hostile clans and tribes, who were always ready to unsheath their blood-thirsty sword for petty reasons. It was due to the teachings of Islam and the untiring efforts of *Muḥammad* (peace be upon him) that the spirit of brotherhood began to surge across Arabia. The entire past of tribal animosities was obliterated and a new society was summoned into existence which had a deep-rooted sentiment for the brotherhood of man, a consciousness of mutual rights and duties and love, and a humane and noble outlook on life. The Prophet had in fact eminently succeeded in creating a social pattern "which had none of the features of the ancient cults, no priesthood and no ceremonial, which was based on no forms, but upon a spiritual relationship to an Unseen God. It was not designed to give prestige to a social group but to create a universal brotherhood composed of all men of every race who would accept this God

---

13. William Muir, *Life of Muhammad*, p. 174.

and promise loyalty to His Holy Prophet."[14]

The New Treaty

Another important task which attracted the attention of the Holy Prophet was to establish friendly relations between the *Muslims* and non-*Muslim* tribes of Arabia, particularly those of *Banū Naḍīr, Banū Qurayzah* and *Banū Qaynuqā'*. As this was the first political agreement between *Muslims* and non-*Muslims*, we mention only a few of its provisions which would clearly give an idea of the rights of non-*Muslims* in an Islamic state.

> In the name of *Allah*, the Compassionate, the Merciful. This is a document from *Muḥammad*, the Messenger of *Allah*, concerning emigrants and helpers in which he made a friendly agreement with the Jews and established them in their religion and property and stated the reciprocal obligations as follows :
>
> They form one group[15] to the exclusion of other people. The emigrés of *Quraysh* unite together and shall pay bloodwit among themselves, and shall ransom honourably their prisoners. The *Banū 'Awf* unite together, as they were at first, and every section among them pays a ransom for acquitting its relative prisoners. (This clause is repeated with the same phraseology concerning *Banū Sā'ida, Banū al-Hārith, Banū Jusham, Banū al-Najjār, Banū 'Amr b. 'Awf, Banū al-Nabit,* and *Banū Aws*). Believers shall not leave any one destitute among them by not paying his redemption money or bloodwit in kind.
>
> Whosoever is rebellious or whosoever seeks to spread

---

14. Denison : *Emotion as the Basis of Civilization*, p. 174.

15. The words are امـة واحـدة من دون الناس (They are one community *(ummah)* to the exclusion of all men). But this term *ummah* is used here in the sense of confederation rather than in its strict technical sense, because in this very treaty it has also been laid down that the "Jewish tribe will have its own religion, *mawālis*, and persons. Furthermore, the treaty does not indicate that the Jewish tribe as a whole will form a nation by themselves ; rather each Jewish tribe will form a separate nation with the Muslims. The nature of this part of the treaty, therefore, shows that a sort of confederation was established between the Arab and Jewish tribes, with the state of Medina taking the lead and the prominent position." (Majid Khadduri : *The Law of War and Peace in Islam* (London, 1940), p. 87.

> enmity and sedition, the hand of every God-fearing *Muslim* shall be against him, even if he be his son.
>
> A believer shall not kill another believer, nor shall support an unbeliever against a believer. The protection of *Allah* is one (and is equally) extended to the humblest of the believers.
>
> The believers are supported by each other. Whosoever of the Jews follows us shall have aid and succour ; they shall not be injured, nor any enemy be aided against them.

The peace of the believers is indivisible. No separate peace shall be made when believers are fighting in the way of God. Conditions must be fair and equitable to all.

It shall not be lawful for a believer, who holds by what is in this document and believes in God and the Day of Judgement, to help a criminal nor give him refuge. Those who give him refuge and render him help shall have the curse and anger of Allah on the Day of Resurrection. His indemnity is not accepted. Whenever you differ about a matter it must be referred to God and to *Muḥammad* (peace be upon him).

> The Jews shall contribute to the cost of war so long as they are fighting alongside the believers. The Jews of the *B. 'Awf* are one community with the believers. The Jews will profess their religion, the *Muslims* theirs. No one shall go forth to war except with the permission of *Muḥammad* ; but this shall not hinder any one from seeking lawful revenge. The Jews shall be responsible for their expenditure, the Muslims for theirs, but if attacked, each shall come to the assistance of the other. *Medina* shall be sacred and inviolable for all that join this treaty.[16]

These are some of the clauses of the famous treaty. "It appears as a tripartite agreement between the *Muhājirūn* or emigrés of *Mecca*, the *Anṣār* or adherents of *Medina*, and the Jews. A careful examination of the text shows, however, that it was more than a treaty of alliance. The first part indeed reflects to us more than an attempt at reconciliation between the

---

16. *Ibn Hishām*, Vol. ii, pp. 147-50.

tribes ; it is in fact a convention for fusing all the rival attempts of the *Arab* tribes in *Medina* to constitute one nation in distinction from the rest of the people. It is, in other words, a constitution for the Islamic state in its embryonic stage rather than a loose alliance of tribes. In this *Muḥammad* (peace be upon him) had attempted to dissolve the narrow tribal loyalties within a superstructure, by shifting their focus of attention to a new religion and state."[17]

Secondly, this treaty sheds a good deal of light on the position of the Prophet as the controller of the affairs in *Medina*. The constitution states that wherever there is any dispute, it is to be referred to God and to *Muḥammad* (peace be upon him). "It seems likely that it was contemplated in the original agreement between *Muḥammad* and the Medinites that he would be able to act as an arbitrator between rival factions and thus help to maintain peace in the oasis."[18]

The latter part of the treaty, which refers to an alliance between the Arabian tribes constituting one party and the Jews as the other, clearly lays down the broad principles on which cordial relations could be established between *Muslims* and non-*Muslims*.

This treaty, which owed itself to the efforts of the Holy Prophet for establishing peace, is a landmark in human history. "It guaranteed mankind thirteen hundred and fifty years ago, freedom of thought and freedom of worship. Protection of life and that of the property was recognized and the crime in all its forms was legally banned. These are in fact fresh laurels which *Muḥammad* (peace be upon him) eminently won in the realm of civics and politics of that time, for it guaranteed peace and freedom to the people who had been woefully groaning under the heel of tyranny and oppression let loose by despotism and autocracy and anarchy of that age."[19]

---

17. Majid Khadduri, *The Law of War and Peace in Islam* (London, 1940), p. 87.

18. W. Montgomery Watt, *Muhammad : Prophet and Statesman*, Oxford, 1961, pp. 95-96.

19. Muhammad Husayn Haykal : *Hayat Muhammad*, Cairo, 1947 p. 227.

Prophet's Family

After having united all the discordant elements of society, *Muḥammad* (peace be upon him) turned his attention towards his household affairs. He had been living at that time with his wife *Sawdah*, and his daughters *Fāṭimah* and *Umm Kulṯẖūm*.

'A'iṣẖah, his new bride, was just attaining her puberty and was still in the house of her father. She was a precocious girl[20] and was developing both in mind and body with rapidity peculiar to such rare personalities. At the suggestion of *Abū Bakr* and his wife, *Muḥammad* (peace be upon him) decided to consummate the marriage.

Like everything else in *Muḥammad's* life (peace be upon him), the ceremony was simple. *'Ā'iṣẖah* was washed and dressed in clean clothes, *Umm Rumān*, her mother, then took her to a room where some women of the *Anṣār* had been anxiously waiting for the arrival of the bride. The moment *'Á'iṣẖah* stepped in, they prayed: "May you be blessed, your fortune is enviable."[21]

This marriage is significant in the history of *Islam*. It further cemented the ties between *Muḥammad* (peace be upon him) and his devoted friend who always stood by him in hours of distress and who sacrificed his all for the cause of *Islam*. Secondly, by this marriage, a lady of rare qualities, both of mind and heart, was allowed to enter the *ḥaram* of the Prophet at an impressionable age, and thus got an opportunity to penetrate into the innermost recesses of the life of *Muḥammad* (peace be upon him). She shared his sacred company and was thus able to develop her potentialities and refine her taste. Even a glance at the life of this eminent lady clearly bears out the fact that her marriage with the Prophet was a source of immense good to herself and to the world of *Islam* at large. She came into direct contact with the Prophet when her sensibilities were just developing. It was the august personality of the last of the Prophets (peace be upon him) which nurtured them properly and directed their growth to the right channels. This young age was opportune for marriage, as it has been clearly shown in the researches of the psychoanalysts that much of the emotional life

20. Sayyid Sulaymān Nadvī, *Sirat-i-'A'ishah*, p. 12.

21. Bukhārī : *Kitāb al-Manāqib*, Chapter : "The Marriage of the Holy Prophet with 'Ā'ishah".

of a mature person and most of those seemingly unaccountable leanings, tastes and tendencies comprised in the term idiosyncrasies can be traced back to the experiences of his highly formative age, either later childhood, or early adolescence.

Moreover, even from the psycho-sexual stand-point it was a happy union as it is evident from the records of *Hadith*. "When the difference (in ages)" says Th H. Von De Velde, Director of the Gynaecological Clinic at Harlem, "is great e.g., exceeds fifteen or twenty years, the results may be happier. The marriage of an elderly (senescent)—not, of course an old (senile)—man to a quite young girl, is often very successful and harmonious. The bride is immediately introduced and accustomed to moderate sexual intercourse."[22]

Those Western critics of *Islam* who have criticized this marriage lose sight of the fact that this marriage did not involve sexual considerations alone. There was so many other reasons behind it. Firstly, there was the consideration of *Abū Bakr's* honour and status and an expression of due recognition of his glorious services. Then there was the problem of training a young girl who was gifted with penetrating intellect and zest for knowledge so that she might be able to guide young women in different spheres of their lives.

The wives of *Muḥammad* (peace be upon him) with the exception of *'Ä'ishah*, were all of advanced age, and thus could neither share the feelings of the younger generation nor could they properly appreciate their point of view. The difference of age always stood as a barrier between them and the ladies of younger ages. The only lady with whom young women could frankly enter into conversation and discuss their problems without any reserve could be none else but young *'Ā'ishah*. Thus the marriage of the Prophet with *'Ā'ishah* at an age when she was at the threshold of puberty was a great necessity, as it was through her that instructions could successfully be imparted to the young ladies who had newly entered the fold of Islam. *'Ā'ishah* performed this function most eminently and fully justified the choice of the Messenger of God (peace be upon him).

Moreover, this marriage struck at the root of a wrong notion which had taken a firm hold on the minds of the people, that it

22. *Ideal Marriage, its Psychology and Technique*, London, 1962, p. 243.

was contrary to religious ethics to marry the daughter of a man whom one declared to be one's brother. The Prophet, with the help of his personal example, showed to the people that there was great difference between a brother-in-faith and a brother by blood. The marriage which is forbidden in Islam is not that with the daughter of a man who is tied to oneself in the bond of faith, but with one who is one's niece in blood.[23]

The main concern of the Prophet, however, was the spiritual and moral training of his followers. In a relatively free atmosphere though not totally free from the threat of *Meccan* vengeance and aggression the Prophet began to propound the principles of righteous conduct, including rituals of worship.

The Fast of Ramaḍan

At the end of eighteen months after the *Hijra* fasting was established as an obligatory ritual for the month of *Ramaḍan*. The word *ṣawm* which literally means abstinence, is a worship of a very great significance. It serves as an effective means, in the religious system of *Islam*, for bringing about purification of the souls of *Muslims*. A *Muslim*, according to its implication, is strictly forbidden to take food or drink (and even to smoke) or to indulge in sexual intercourse from the moment when the first streak of light on the eastern horizon announces the coming of dawn, until sunset. And this continues for one full month every year. In the words of *Muḥammad Asad* :

> Twofold, I learned, is the purpose of this month of fasting. One has to abstain from food and drink in order to feel in one's body what the poor and hungry feel : thus, social responsibility is being hammered into human consciousness as a religious postulate. The other purpose of fasting during *Ramaḍan* is self-discipline, an aspect of individual morality strongly accentuated in all Islamic teachings (as, for instance, in the total prohibition of all intoxicants, which Islam regards as too easy an avenue of escape from consciousness and responsibility). In these two elements—brotherhood of man and individual self-discipline—I began to discern the outlines of *Islam's*

---

23. Sayyid Sulaymān Nadvī : *Sirat-i-'Ā'ishah*, p. 19.

ethical outlook.[24]

Moreover, fasting is the means whereby our sense of gratitude towards *Allah* is awakened. We can rightly measure and truly appreciate the countless favours of the Lord when we are deprived of them, even though for a short span of time. Thus we can thank our Creator for His infinite bounties that He has so benevolently showered upon us.[25] The following verse of the *Qur'ān* makes a pointed reference to this aspect :

> Ye should complete the number and that you should exalt the Greatness of *Allah* for His having guided you and that you may give thanks. (ii : 185)

Zakat

It was at this stage that the payment of *zakāt*[26] was made obligatory by *Allah* upon all *Muslims*. *Islam* does not leave the orphans, the infirm and the old to subsist on what is called "charity." By making the payment of *zakāt* obligatory for the rich, *Allah* has given the poor a right to share in the wealth of the community. The *Qur'ān* explicitly lays down :

> And in their wealth, is the right of the needy and of those who are deprived of the means of subsistence.
> (li : 19)

This verse clearly establishes that the portion of the wealth which the *Muslims* contribute annually in the form of *zakāt* is a matter of duty for them and, on the other hand, whatever the poor receive is not an act of undue favour for which they should hang down their heads in humiliation. The wealth of the rich that they receive is a matter of right for which they have no reason to feel small. Then the *Qur'ān* has also laid down the purposes for which *zakāt* is to be used. It should be paid, according to the Holy *Qur'ān, inter alia* to those who cannot make an independent living [e.g., the orphans, helpless widows, the infirm, the decrepit, the travellers in distress, and people who have been deprived of the means of sustenance or of oppor-

---

24. Muḥammad Asad, *The Road to Mecca*, London, 1954, p. 188.

25. M. Muḥammad Idrīs Kandhlavī, *Al-Ta'līq al-Sabīḥ 'Alā Mishkāt al-Maṣābīh*, Damascus, Vol. ii, p. 368.

26. The word *zakāt*, means increase, or purity.

tunities of work through natural calamities over which they have no control], the slaves seeking freedom and the debtors who cannot afford to pay off their debts :

> The compulsory alms are only for the poor and the needy and the agents employed therein, and those whose hearts are to be conciliated, and those in bondage and debtors and for expenditure in the way of *Allah*, and for the wayfarer, an ordinance from *Allah*. And *Allah* is Knowing, Wise. (ix : 60)

The *Qur'ān* thus makes it obligatory on those who earn or produce wealth to pass on to the state a specific portion of their savings as God's share to be distributed among the above categories of the members of society. "So great is the stress laid on the levy called *zakāt*, that the compulsory injunction of prayer is always clubbed together with the insistence on the payment of this levy ; so much so that when in the time of the first Caliph *Abū Bakr*, some of the *Muslim Arab* tribes refused to pay *zakāt* to the State Exchequer, he had to wage a *jihad* against them till they yielded"[27] and resumed the payment of *zakāt*.

The Change of Qiblah

It was during this period that a change in the *qiblah*, was also ordered by *Allah*.[28] It is significant that while at *Mecca* and living among the idolaters of *Mecca*, the Holy Prophet (may peace and blessings of *Allah* be upon him) used to pray with his face turned to the holy temple at Jerusalem, but when he came to *Medina*, where the Jewish element was strong and powerful, he was directed by Divine revelation to turn his face to the *Ka'bah* as his *qiblah*. This was a change of far-reaching importance, and it had different reactions in different circles. It strengthened the loyalty of the *Muslims* to *Islam* and the Holy Prophet. They expressed their implicit faith in *Muḥammad* (peace be upon him) as the recipient of Divine revelation and accepted this change most willingly. The pagans of *Mecca* said : "The way *Muḥammad* has changed his direction for prayer

---

27. Sayyid Abdul Latif : *The Mind That al-Qur'ān Builds*, Hyderabad, 1952, pp. 98-99.

28. *Qiblah*, from the root QBL 'to be before', is the point in the direction of which people are required to turn while performing ritual prayer.

towards our *qiblah*, gives us reason to hope that he will eventually come back to our faith also." The Jews were very indignant and said tauntingly : "*Muḥammad* has, in this change of direction for prayer, opposed all the earlier prophets. If he were a genuine prophet, he would have never done like that." The hypocrites (i.e., those who falsely pretended to be *Muslims*) availed themselves of this opportunity to undermine the increasing influence of *Islam*. They were sarcastic in their remarks and said : "We are not sure in which direction the Prophet wants to turn for prayer. If the previous position was correct he has abandoned that ; and if this new position is right, it means that he had erred before."[29]

The Holy *Qur'ān* refers, in its eloquent style, to these different objections raised from the different quarters, and observe :

> And We appointed not the *qiblah*, which you have had, but that We might distinguish him who follows the Apostle from him who turns back upon his heels, and this was surely hard except for those whom *Allah* has guided aright. (ii : 143)

"The change of direction", says Arnold, "has a deeper significance than might at first sight appear. It was really the beginning of the national life of *Islam* ; it established the *Ka'bah* at *Mecca* as a religious centre for all the *Muslim* people, just as from time immemorial it had been a place of pilgrimage for all the tribes of Arabia."[30]

Jihad—Its Nature and Significance

A few words may now be added as a prelude to the coming events which are connected with the unsheathing of the sword by the *Muslims* in the path of *Allah*. *jihād* is a matter of great importance in the history of *Islam*, but it is sad to note that so many doubts and misgivings are centred around it. The true nature and significance of *Jihād* can be well understood, when it is viewed in the context of the teachings of Islam as a whole as well as the objectives which it seeks to realize. Moreover, we also have to consider the role of war, in other words, that of

29. Ibn Qayyim : *Zād al-Ma'ād*, Vol. ii, pp. 147-48.
30. *The Preaching of Islam*, p. 27.

power, as a means for the establishment of a sound social order.

It should be clearly borne in mind that *Islam* does not subscribe to the materialistic world-view which is in vogue among the Western nations. "It is an intense God-consciousness that expresses itself in a rational acceptance of all God-created nature : a harmonious side-by-side of intellect and sensual urge, spiritual need and social demand."[31] It is thus clear that *Islam*, besides, laying a good deal of stress on the problems of belief, ritual and personal morality and as a consequence of that nursing a moral attitude in the individual—the bed-rock upon which is raised the superstructure of *Islamic* society "also aims at translating the moral attitude into a definite social scheme which would ensure to every member of the community the greatest possible measure of physical and material well-being, and thus, the greatest opportunity for spiritual growth."[32]

This important aspect of *Islam*, i.e., its social aspect, is woefully neglected by Western thinkers, while estimating the role of power in a comprehensive view of life. They lose sight of the fact that Christianity in its early history did not aim at setting up a state,[33] whereas *Islam*, from the very beginning, was a politico-religious institution. In order to translate into reality *Islam* had to contend with those evil forces which knew no reasoning and persuasion.

It should be made clear, however, that war in *Islam* is not a casual phenomenon of violence ; it is one of the phases of man's striving (*jihād*) against all that is evil, whether in thought, or feeling or action. The raising of the sword is only one aspect of the all-round struggle to establish *Islam* in the world, and it represents in *Muslim* Law what is known as an 'honest struggle.'

The word (*jihād*) is derived from the word *jahāda*, which means "he exerted himself." Thus literally *jihād* means exertion, striving ; but in juridico-religious sense, it signifies the exertion of one's power to the utmost of one's capacity in the path of *Allah*. This is why the word *jihād* has been used as an antonym to the word *qu'ūd*[34] in *Islam*.

---

31. Muhammad Asad, *The Road to Mecca*, p. 190.
32. *Ibid.*, p. 290.
33. "My kingdom is not of this world", John, xviii, 36
34. *Qu'ūd* means : sitting, desistence, abstention, refraining, renunciation, abandonment.

> Not equal are the holders-back among the believers save those who are disabled, and the strivers in the way of *Allah* with their riches and their lives. *Allah* hath preferred in rank the strivers with their riches and their lives above the holders-back and unto all, *Allah* hath promised good. And *Allah* hath preferred the strivers above holders-back with a mighty reward. (iv : 95)

The above-quoted verse speaks eloquently of the fact that *jihād* (striving) is just the opposite of idleness.

It is necessary to winnow out one mistaken notion which has taken hold of the minds of so many people. The word *jihād* is often confused with the word *qitāl* (fighting) and these are used in one and the same sense, whereas the *Qur'ān* has made a clear distinction between them. *Jihād fī Sabīl Allāh* (fighting in the way of *Allah*) refers to an all-round struggle, while the other signifies only one aspect of that struggle i.e., *fighting*. The verse iv : 95 mentioned above bears ample testimony to this fact. The Holy *Qur'ān* has clearly pointed out that *jihād* denotes two kinds of striving ; striving with the help of God-given faculties, both mental and physical, and striving with the help of resources which he has at his command.

Ibn Rushd maintains that *jihād* is an all-round struggle and makes it obligatory for a *Muslim* to exercise all his powers, may be in the form of intellectual or physical capacities, or his gift of speech or his moral strength, courage and steadfastness in the face of hardship and his worldly riches.[35]

The Holy *Qur'ān* has elucidated this point, i.e., *jihād* as an all-round struggle in various *sūrahs*. We reproduce below a few of them in order to explain the true nature and significance of *jihād* in *Islam* :

> The believers are only those who believed in *Allah* and His Apostle and thereafter doubted not, and struggled hard with their riches and their persons in the cause of *Allah*. Those ! they are the truthful. (li : 15)

> And strive hard for *Allah*, as is due unto Him. He has chosen you, and has imposed no hardship on you in

35. Ibn Rushd, *Kitāb al-Muqaddimat al-Mumahhidat* (Cairo, 1325 A.H.), Vol. i, p. 259.

matter of the religion, the faith of your father *Ibrahīm*
(xxii : 78)

This verse of the Holy *Qu'rān* sums up the spirit of *jihād* in Islam. It is a striving in the way of *Allah*, and has far wider scope than mere fighting. The Holy Prophet once explaining the true qualities of *mujāhid* (the one who strives in the path of *Allah*) significantly remarked :

> The *mujāhid* is one who tries to struggle against his self, i.e., evil self.[36]

Ibn al-Qayyim in his explanation of this aspect of *jihād* has observed :

> The *jihād* against the enemies of *Allah* with one's life is only a part of the struggle which a true servant of *Allah* carries on against his own evil self for the sake of his Lord. This striving against the evil tendencies which have dominated his mind and heart is more important than fighting against the enemies in the outside world. It is in fact the basis on which the struggle in the path of *Allah* can be successfully launched.[37]

Since *jihād* is an all-round struggle, a struggle directed to so many channels, it necessitates the employment of different methods to acquit oneself creditably of its wide and varied responsibilities. According to *Imām Rāghib* a *Muslim* is required to fight against three foes :

(1) against the visible enemy ;
(2) against the devil ;
(3) against his self (*nafs*).[38]

Ibn Rushd maintains that the believer may fulfil this struggle in four ways ; by his heart, by his tongue, by his hands, and by the sword.[39] The first of these implies that a Muslim should develop his sensitivities to the point of excellence, so much so that nothing evil should find its way either in his heart

---

36. Tirmidhī : Chapter, *Abwāb Faḍā'il al-Jihād.*
37. *Zād al-Ma'ād* (Cairo, 1935), Vol. ii, p. 103.
38. Rāghib al-Isfahānī, *Mufradāt, Gharā'ib al-Qur'ān* (Cairo), 1325 A.H.), Vol. i, p. 259.
39. *Kitāb al-Muqaddimat al-Mumahhidat,* Vol. i, p. 259.

or in his mind. He should have a deep-rooted aversion to everything ignoble and a strong desire to fight it tooth and nail, whether it is found in his own self or in the world outside.

Then comes the function of the power of expression which has a vital role to play in the establishment of a sound and just social order, free from all kinds of exploitation. This power has a double responsibility in the sense that it has to clothe in noble words the noble ideals and sentiments which upsurge the mind and heart of man and then by dint of his eloquence, imprint their superiority in the minds of other people. Moreover, this gift of expression is to be used for protesting against evils in human life. The Holy *Qur'ān* shows the way how the powers of expression is to be used for inviting the people to the path of *Allah* :

> Invite (all) to the way of their Lord with wisdom and goodly exhortation and argue with them with that which is the best.[40] (xvi : 125)

In his characteristic style, the Holy Prophet has explained that *jihād* consists not only of using the sword, but that even when a *Muslim* uses his tongue for protesting against the atrocities of tyrants, he is waging *jihād*. He once said :

> Whoever amongst you sees something abominable, he should endeavour to change it with his hand, in case he has the power to do it : but if he lacks the requisite power, he should then use his tongue, and if he is powerless in this also, he must then hate it from the heart, and

---

40. 'Abdullah Yūsuf 'Ali, in his comments on this verse has observed :

"In this wonderful passage are laid down principles of religious teaching which are good for all times......we must invite all to the way of God, and expound His universal will ; we must do it with wisdom and discretion, meeting people on their own ground and convincing them with illustration from their own knowledge and experience, which may be very narrow or very wide. Our preaching must not be dogmatic, not self-regarding, not offensive, but gentle, considerate, and such as would attract their attention. Our manner and our arguments should not be acrimonious, but modelled on the most courteous and the most gracious example, so that the hearer may say to himself, "This man is not dealing merely with dialectics ; he is not trying to get a rise out of me ; he is sincerely expounding the faith that is in him and his motive is the love of man and the love of God."

this in fact is the weakest (state) of faith.[41]

Then in other tradition which is narrated on the authority of *Abu Sa'id al-Khuḍrī* the Prophet is reported to have significantly remarked :

> The best of *jihād* is the uttering of the word of truth in the face of a tyrant ruler.[42]

This would make it abundantly clear that *jihād* in Islam is not an act of violence. It is, in fact, an all-round struggle in the path of *Allah*.

In this all-round struggle, however, which covers all aspects of life, *Islam* has assigned a special place to *qitāl* (fighting) as well. There do arise such occasions in which the use of arms becomes a dire necessity and even a slight show of weakness under these circumstances leads to disastrous results. *Islam* has stressed the need of rising to such occasions and has exhorted its followers to face the dangers that might thus beset them bravely and manfully. Thus the use of force is not only permitted in *Islam*, but its need has been duly stressed in the Holy *Qur'ān* and the *Sunnah*. But it should be made clear that even *qitāl* in *Islam* is not an act of mad brutality. "It represents in *Muslim* law what is known among western jurists as just war."[43]

In order to understand the true nature of *qitāl* in *Islam*, we must first analyse the different motives which incite people to fight :

> (1) The desire for material benefits is the principal impulse to warlike aggression : "Territory, with the attendant booty of various kinds, has been the usual stake in war, coveted alike by peoples and by dynasties."
>
> (2) "The fear of injury as well as the resentment due to actual injury has unfailingly prompted to defensive war when resistance was possible and often when it might well be deemed hopeless. The interests which nations have usually prepared to defend at all costs are, in addition to their territory, their jurisdiction and their honour."[44]

---

41. Ibn Mājah, *"Kitāb al-Fitan"*,
42. *Ibid.*
43. Majid Khadduri, *op. cit.*, p. 20.
44. *Encyclopaedia of Religion and Ethics*, Article "War", Vol. xii, p. 676.

(3) The desire for power and glory has been, in the main, dominant motive of the great conquerors and their armies. It is a fact that ambitious men have again and again resorted to the use of force as a means for appropriating territory and increasing their own wealth and of the people whom they represent, but there is no denying the fact that nations as well as individuals find satisfaction in the exercise of power as an end in itself. "This desire manifests itself positively in the attempt of a nation or class to acquire dominion over others. The love of power for its own sake has been an important factor in the movements which established the great empires of history, and it has been not less conspicuous in struggle for a supremacy among allied states as illustrated in the ancient rivalry of Athens and Sparta, and in the modern contest of the German principalities which issued in the hegemony of Prussia."[45]

(4) "The passions of hatred and revenge have also furnished a relatively independent motive. A nation can take up an attitude that is on a still lower plane than brutal selfishness ; it can become inspired by a hatred of the diabolic kind which makes it disregard even the counsels of self-interest for the satisfaction of inflicting deadly injury on a loathed enemy. The spirit of hatred has sometimes even been engendered by centuries of conflict or oppression. Sometime it has its spring in deep-seated difference of racial character and culture."[46]

Qitāl in *Islam* has no evil design behind it. *Islam* has the greatest respect not only for the lives of human beings but even for those of animals and plants, and it is only for the achievement of some nobler ends and those too, through noble means, that a *Muslim* has been exhorted to lay hands upon them. There are so many verses in the Holy *Qur'ān* which speak eloquently of the sanctity of life :

And there is not an animal on the earth, not a bird that flieth with its two wings, but are communities like

45. *Encyclopaedia of Religion and Ethics,* Article "War", Vol. vii p. 676.
46. *Ibid.*, p. 677.

> unto you. Nothing have we omitted from the Book. Then they (all) shall be gathered to their Lord in the end.[47] (vi : 38)

The Prophet repeatedly emphasised the fact that not to speak of the life of man, even the life of a small bird is extremely precious and cannot be taken without sufficient reason :

> Whoever kills the swallow, or even a more insignificant bird than that, without any reason, shall be answerable to God for this slaughter.[48]

On another occasion he issued a warning to people about the high-handedness that they showed towards animals :

> If *Allah* in His infinite mercy pardons the mal-treatment which is meted out to your animals, at your hands, it means that you have been relieved of the heavy burden of sins.[49]

Such is the value and consideration which *Islam* shows to birds and other animals. It is due to the result of Islamic teachings that animals have been treated with utmost kindness and love throughout the *Muslim* world. "Nowhere in Christendom", says Bosworth Smith, for instance, "with the one exception perhaps of Norway, are beasts of burden and domestic animals treated with such unvarying kindness and consideration as they are in Turkey."[50]

Human life is given still greater security and no one is permitted to lay hand upon it without sufficient reason :

---

47. "Animals living on the earth" include those living in the water—— fishes, reptiles, crustaceans, insects as well as four-footed beasts. Life on the wing is separately mentioned. "Tā'ir", which is ordinarily translated as "bird" is anything that flies, including mammals like bats. In our pride we may exclude animals from our purview, but they all live a life, social and individual, like ourselves, and all life is subject to the Plan and Will of God."

(Abdullāh Yūsuf 'Alī, *The Holy Qur'ān : Text, Translation & Commentary*, p. 298)

48. M. Muhammad Idris Kandhlavi, *At-Ta'līq-us-Sabīh 'ala' al-Mishkāt al-Masābih*, Chapter : Kitāb as-Sayd wa al-Dhaba'ih op. cit., Vol. iv, p. 334.

49. Ahmad b. Hanbal, *Musnad*, Vol. vi, p. 441.

50. Bosworth Smith, *Muhammad and Muhammadanism* (London, 1870), p. 212.

> Those who invoke not, with God, any other god, nor slay such life as God has made sacred except for just cause. (xxv : 68)
>
> On that account ; we ordained for the children of Israel that if any one slew a person unless it be for murder or for spreading mischief in the land—it would be as if he slew all human beings. And if any one saved a life, it would be as if he saved the life of all human beings. (v : 35)

The above-quoted verses show in unequivocal terms the value of human life. The life of every person is sacred and thus its safety is one of the primary duties of society. A well-known scholar of Islam has made the following observations with regard to the above mentioned verses :

> On close analysis of these verses of the Holy *Qur'ān*, we find that human life has been made sacred by God and its security is, therefore, the foremost duty of mankind ; but this clause is also appended with a certain condition, i.e., "except for just cause". Similarly, along with the words : "If any one slew a person it would be as if he slew all human beings," there occurs this conditional phrase : "unless it be for spreading mischief in the land." It means that the safety of human life is guaranteed no doubt but with certain conditions. Justice demands that tyranny and oppression should not be allowed to work havoc in the world ; that wickedness ought to be restrained and punished in human society in the interests of the peace and prosperity of the human race. Human life is sacred so far as its activities are confined to the reasonable limits, but when these transgress them and become a source of terror and aggression and constant peril to the lives of other persons, then it loses its sanctity and its termination becomes indispensable and therein lies the welfare of humanity. That is why the Holy *Qur'ān* says : "Mischief[51] is more grievous than homicide."[52]

---

51. The word *fitnah* is very meaningful as it covers a large number of crimes over and above the grossest forms of idolatry, as treachery, perfidy, wanton persecution of innocent beings and aggression in fighting.

52. Sayyid Abu al-A'lā Maudūdi, *Al-Jihād fi al-Islam*. II Edition, (Lahore, 1948), pp. 19-20.

The Holy *Qur'ān* clearly brings out the fact that *qitāl* is not an end in itself in *Islam*, but a means to a higher and nobler end—the welfare of humanity. That is why *Islam* has exhorted its followers to raise arms not in a spirit of brutality but in a spirit of love for hu manity—a spirit in which the surgeon applies the knife to the blistering sores of the human body. An individual or a community is no benefactor of humanity if it becomes a silent spectator to the atrocities which are prepetrated on innocent people by those who have no feeling for humanity and no consideration for moral principles. A person does not fulfil his responsibilities towards mankind if he does nothing to support the moral order which forms the bedrock of justice in the human race. A man, or a nation, who tries to exterminate evil in all its forms, is the benefactor of humanity in the true sense of the term, for it is even a greater evil to commit injustice with impunity than to be punished for it. The Holy Prophet has beautifully summed up the responsibility of man towards his fellowmen in the following tradition :

> It is narrated on the authority of *Anas* (may *Allah* be pleased with him) that the Messenger of God once said : 'Help your brother whether he is the wrong-doer or the oppressed one.' Thereupon people said to him, 'O Messenger of *Allah*, we can help the man when he is wronged, but we fail to know how a wrong-doer can be helped.' Upon this the Prophet (may peace and blessings of *Allah* be upon him) replied, 'You can do this by holding his hand from an act of oppression.'[53]

---

53. Bukhāri : *Kitāb al-Mazālim wa al-ga'saba*, Vol. ii, p. 66.

Ibn Ḥajar has quoted the same words, though with some change of expression in another *Ḥadīth* :

> "The man said, 'O Messenger of *Allah* ! I can help him if he is an oppressed one, but if I find him an oppressor, how can I lend him my assistance ?' Upon this the Prophet remarked, 'Hold his hand (from wrong-doing) and that is in fact his help'."

Fatḥ al-Bārī (Cairo, 1959), Vol. vi, p. 23.

The learned commentator while discussing the subtleties of the metaphorical expression of the above-quoted words say :

> "The metaphorical words تاخذ فوق يديه imply that the wrong-doer should be practically restrained from doing an act of wrong if persuasion cannot dissuade him. The word *fauq* (فوق) is indicative of the fact that his hand should be checked with power and force."

Fatḥ al-Bāri, Vol. vi, p. 23.

None having a grain of common sense can favour the granting of licence to the wicked people for committing crimes and then letting them go scot free. It is not love for humanity but act of enmity towards it that the weaker elements of society should be subjected to wrongs and injustices and no check should be imposed upon the wrong-doers. "It is absurd to maintain," says W. P. Paterson, "that the rulers of a nation are under obligation, not merely to sacrifice themselves, but to take the responsibility of sacrificing others who instinctively look to them for protection, and of abandoning old men, women and children, to privation, sufferings, and moral perils. The Christian spirit was surely better interpreted in the mediaeval code of chivalry."[54] Herbert Spencer declares :

> The doctrine of non-resistance is anti-social, as it involves the non-assertion, not only of one's own rights, but of those of others, while it holds out no prospect of leading to the desirable end of international peace.[55]

Grotius argues that recourse to war is permitted and approved by the law of nature, by the consent of the manly and of the wise, and by the law of nations, as well as by the divine law which was promulgated and attested by the scriptures.

> The law of nature has two branches, the course dictated by natural instincts, and the principles approved by reason. This law intimates its permission of war through the universal instinct of self-preservation, accompanied as it is by nature's disclosure of purpose in the provision of means of defence to all creatures and also by the voice of reason which makes it clear that the well-being of society is incompatible with the unchecked reign of violence.[56]

These observations make it abundantly clear that the use of force is essential in certain conditions in order to maintain the sanctity of human life and to preserve the moral order in the world. The very first passage which gave the sanction of *qitāl* to the *Muslims* makes a pointed reference to all these noble ideals :

---

54. *Encyclopaedia of Religion and Ethics* ; Article "War", Vol. xii, p. 680.
55. Herbert Spencer, *Social Statics*, new ed. (Lond. 1902), p. 116.
56. *Encyclopaedia of Religion and Ethics*, Article "War", Vol. xii, p. 681.

> Permitted are those who are fought against, because they have been oppressed,[57] and verily to succour them, *Allah* is Potent. Those who have been unjustly driven forth from their abodes merely because they say : "Our Lord is *Allah*". And were it not for *Allah's* repelling or some by means of others, cloisters and churches, synagogues and mosques, wherein the name of *Allah* is mentioned much, would have been pulled down. Surely *Allah* shall succour whosoever succoureth Him. Verily *Allah* is Strong, Mighty.[58]
>
> They are those who, if we establish them in the land, establish the prayer and give the poor-rate and enjoin right and forbid wrong, and unto *Allah* is the end of all affairs. (xxii : 39-41)

The passage sums up in clear terms the aims and objects of *qitāl* in *Islam*. It is neither the acquisition of land, nor of power, nor yet of privilege. The *Muslims* were permitted to use force because their very existence had been made difficult due to persecution by the pagans of Arabia. They had been subjected to unspeakable tortures at their hands ; beaten and insulted, and then driven away from their homes for no other reason than that they worshipped *Allah*. They had as much right to be in their native town and worship in the *Ka'bah* as the other *Arabs*, but nobody was tolerant towards them. The animosity of the *Quraysh* did not end even after having driven the Prophet and his companions out of their native place. The unjust men of *Mecca* had not only given no ear to the heavenly Message delivered by *Muḥammad* (peace be upon him) but would not even let him live if he kept on preaching it. The pagan *Arabs* had evil design in their minds to pursue the innocent souls who left for *Medina* and to exterminate them even in their new abodes. If one were to reflect calmly over this state of affairs one would be convinced that the verdict of all religions and ethical philosophies, both ancient and modern, has been that

57. The word *Yuqātalūna* (يقاتلون) is in the passive voice which means 'against whom war is made,'—not who take up arms against the unbelievers as Sale translates this word.

58. This is the first passage which was revealed to the Holy Prophet in connection with '*qitāl*'. Ibn Kathir : *Tafsīr al-Qur'ān*, Vol. iii, p. 225.

under such circumstances war is not only justifiable but a basic necessity, and non-resistance is blameworthy and even immoral. There has been a practical unanimity as to the moral justification of self-defence when one nation is assailed by the ambition and cupidity of another.

Then the *Qur'ān* also explains the function of war as a moral necessity. It is with the help of force that the ever-mounting evil in human life is curbed, for if it continues to spread unchecked, it would brutally shake the basis of moral order and justice in human society so much so that even the places of worship would not be safe at the hands of the wicked elements of the human race. It deserves to be noted that the *Muslims* have been asked to lay down their lives not only to save their own skins from the atrocities of the opponents, and to save their own mosques, but to save churches, synagogues, and cloisters as well. This means that *Islam* wants to protect the moral order vouchsafed to humanity through the Messengers of God at different stages of human history. The same idea has been expressed in another verse :

> And were it not for *Allah's* repelling people, some of them by means of others, the earth surely would be corrupted, but *Allah* is Gracious unto the worlds. (li : 251)

The above verse reveals that the rise and fall of nations is not a mere accident, but that it follows a definite pattern in the moral order of the universe. If some nations are swept out of effective existence, it is because they have been corrupted to the marrow of their bones and their dominance in the world is a terrible threat to the peaceful existence of the human race. They are, therefore, through the efforts of the other groups of human beings, thrown into an obscure background with a view to saving humanity from their corrupt and unhealthy influences.

The human society always contains a number of anti-social elements which need a check even though this check were to be exercised with the help of force. When the evil becomes parasitic upon the good, that is to say, it begins to flourish by preying upon what is good, it becomes the primary duty of humanity to restrain it with all the means at its disposal. "The philosopher", observes Joad, "cannot philosophize while his neighbour is abducting his wife, nor can the artist paint while the burglar is running off with his canvasses. In this sense all civilized activity is dependent upon a minimum background of ordered security, and the maintenance of this background is a condition of its continuance."[59] The use of the sword is, therefore, required to put a curb on the anti-social activities of the evil elements of the human race. As with individuals, so with nations. A rabid nation should no more be permitted to hold to ransom the humanitarian activities of peaceful men. The downtrodden people who are subjected to the tyranny and oppression of heartless tyrants are to be helped at all cost, and it is the bounden duty of all God-fearing human beings to rescue these helpless folk from the clutches of the enemies of humanity :

> And what aileth you that ye fight not in the way of *Allah*, and for the oppressed among men and women and children who say : 'Our Lord ! Take us forth from the town whereof the people are wrongdoers, and appoint us from before Thee a patron and appoint us from Thee a helper'. (iv : 75)

It is significant that the war which is waged for upholding the cause of the oppressed is named by the *Qur'ān* as "fight in the way of *Allah*". Then, in the succeeding verse a clear distinction is also drawn between the two types of war ; the one which is fought for the sake of *Allah* and the other which is waged in the cause of evil :

> Those who believe fight in the way of *Allah* and those who disbelieve fight in the way of *Satan*. Fight then against the friends of *Satan* ; verily feeble indeed is the cunning of the devil." (iv : 76)

A distinct and clear line of demarcation marks off the "just" from the "unjust" war. Those who fight for self-glorification, self-aggrandisement, or for the exploitation of the resources of the weaker peoples, are in fact the friends of the devil ; whereas the persons who raise arms in order to curb tyranny and oppression and to eradicate evil are the blessed souls who fight in the way of *Allah*. Thus every war which is waged for personal or national glorification at the cost of others is a war in the way

---

59. C. E. M. Joad, *Guide to Modern Wickedness* (London, 1938) Faber & Faber Limited, p. 187.

of *Satan* and is vehemently condemned by *Islam*. On the contrary, the war which is fought in defence of the oppressed, which aims at the eradication of evils and the suppression of those who spread them is a Holy War which is upheld by *Islam*, for it is essential to strike at the very root of the supremacy of the wicked elements in order to establish peace and justice in the world :

> And fight them until there is no more tumult and oppression and religion should only be for *Allah*. So if they desist, then verily *Allah* is the Beholder of that what they do. (viii : 39)

This verse clearly defines the aims and objects of fighting in *Islam*. *Muslims* have been asked to raise arms not for any personal end but purely for the love of *Allah*, so that the rebels, who, by their evil designs, have made life intolerably difficult for the innocent souls, should be forcibly prevented from carrying on their nefarious activities and there should prevail justice, goodwill and fraternity in human society.

The war of *Islam* has been completely purged of the spirit of self-aggrandisement or that of national dominance. It is narrated on the authority of *Abū Musā al-Ash'ari* that once a man came to the Holy Prophet and said : "A person fights for booty, another fights with a view to winning fame and still another raises his arms in order to display his courage and bravery—who among these should be considered as a fighter for the sake of *Allah* ?" To this question the Prophet replied : "He who raises his arm with the sole objective that the Word of *Allah* should become supreme is the one who fights for the cause of *Allah*".[60]

Thus in *Islam*, it is not every war which is sanctified as *jihād*. It is the noble objectives alone which justify a *Muslim* to raise arms against the tyrants and the exploiters of the human race. Such is the importance of this objective behind fighting that *Bukhārī* has assigned a separate chapter to it in which it has been clearly laid down that it is not feasible to assert with certainty whether a man killed in warfare, is a martyr or not ; since martyrdom of a person depends upon the intention with

60. Bukhāri, *Kitāb al-Jihād wa al-Siyar*, Vol. iii, p. 139 ; See section *Man qātala li takūn kalimat Allāh hiya al-'ulyā*.

which he participates in the battle and it is always hidden from the view of human beings. *Allah* alone is, therefore, the right judge in this matter. The Prophet emphatically said :

> *Allah* knows fully well who strives in His cause and sustains injury for His sake.[61]

It is narrated that once in an encounter with the enemies the Prophet had on his side a hypocrite who was known as *Qazmān*. He fought desperately in the battlefield. The *Muslims* were all praise for his valour and one of them said in the presence of the Prophet : "No one has proved himself to be so useful as this man has done." Upon this the Prophet remarked : "His abode is the Hell."[62] *Badr al-Din-al-'Aynī*, the famous commentator of *Bukhārī*, has recorded that when this man was on the point of succumbing to the injuries which he had received, one of the companions of the Holy Prophet, *Qatādah b. Nu'mān* cheered him up and gave him the tidings of martyrdom. Upon this the dying man disclosed the motive of his fighting and said : "By God, I did not fight for the cause of the faith. I was impelled to take arms for the glorification of my tribe and family."[63]

Ibn Ḥajar al-'Asqalānī, while elucidating the implication of relationship between this particular tradition and the section under which it falls in *Bukhārī*, has made the following significant observations :

> Nothing can be said with certainty, except through revelation, whether a man is a martyr or not and that refers to the address of '*Umar* when he said : "You call those people martyrs who fight in the battles ; I advise you not to make such explicit assertions and say as the Holy Prophet said : "One who lays down his life in the way of *Allah* or one who is killed for no fault of his own is a martyr." This assertion is authentic and corroborates the words of the Holy Prophet which have come down to us through another source (*Abū Dharr*). It is narrated

---

61. Bukhāri, *Kitāb al-Jihād wa al-Siyar*, Vol. iii, p. 139 ; See section *Man qātala li takūn kalamat Allāh hiya al-'ulyā.*"
62. *Ibid.*
63. Badr al-Din al-Ayni, *Umdat al-Qārī* (Cairo), Vol. xiv, p. 181.

that the Messenger of God once asked his companions: "Whom do you count as martyrs." They replied: "One who is attacked with a weapon and as a consequence of that he succumbs to the injuries," whereupon the Holy Prophet remarked: "How many persons receive injuries and die, but they are neither martyrs nor are their sacrifices laudable. On the other hand many a man courts natural death in the bed but in the eyes of the Lord, he is a champion of truth and a martyr." These words of the Holy Prophet clearly bring out the fact that it is not appropriate to call anyone a martyr with certainty, but we should speak in a general way, as we have been instructed by the Messenger of *Allah*: "God alone knows the man who fights or receives injury for His sake," *Imām Bukharī* has recorded the tradition relating to the death of *Qazmān* under the section: "None should be called a martyr with certainty", simply because the person concerned did not fight for the sake of *Allah* alone, but he had in his heart an absurdly extravagant pride in his race of tribe.[64]

Such is the noble spirit which underlies *jihād* in *Islam*. It is not an act of aggression for the sake of material interests or a wanton display of national or tribal power, but it is a sacred duty assigned to every *Muslim* in the interests of humanity so that there should be peace and justice in the world. It is this war, which aims at the achievement of noble ends, that is given the name of 'fighting in the way of *Allah*'! This alone has been eulogised in the Holy Book.

It is interesting to note that a war which seeks to serve such a sacred objective, has not only been permitted by all other religions, but has also been lavishly praised by them. The Christian teachings include percepts which, at the first sight, appear to rule out any kind of engagement in war as inconsistent with its moral ideals, but even a little bit of careful study would convince one of the fact that even the Christian Church does not stand for an unqualified condemnation of war. "The Council of Arles in one of its canons appears to have visited ecclesiastical

64. Ibn Ḥajar al-'Asqalāni, *Fatḥ al-Bāri*, Kitāb al-Jihād, Section *Lā yaqul fulān shahid* (Cairo, 1959) Vol. vi, pp. 429-31.

censure on those who abandoned the army even in time of peace from conscientious scruples. Some even thought that the sword might be drawn in a holy war for the extirpation of idolatry. Ambrose eulogised the warlike courage which prefers death to bondage and disgrace and claimed the O. T. warriors as spiritual ancestors. He even adopted the classical maxim that one who does not defend a friend from injury is as much at fault as he who commits the injury. Augustine was forced to face the question by the havoc of the Teutonic migrations and the peril of the empire and his active mind fully explored the subject."[65] His observations are very significant :

The war is sometimes lawful on the Christian principles and the grounds are :

> (a) that it has been and may be waged by appointment of God ; (b) that the case of wanton and rapacious attack by one nation on another falls under the same category as crimes of murder and burglary, and should presumably be similarly dealt with ; (c) that John the Baptist did not require the soldiers to abandon the service, but only exhorted them to do violence to no man and be content with their wages. The implications of the Sermon on the Mount are most fully discussed in the Epistle to Marcellinus which was called forth by the pagan objection that the precepts of non-resistance were inconsistent with public policy and ruinous to the state. The precept to turn the other cheek to the smiter, cannot be taken literally. What it requires is an inward disposition of patient goodwill towards the aggressor, and it does not prescribe any uniform manifestation of the dispositions in act, as appears from the fact that Jesus at least protected himself against violence (Jn. 18^{23} Cf AC 23^{3}). We ought always to cherish the spirit of clemency, and be willing to render good for evil, but many things have to be done in which we have to pay regard not to our kindly inclinations but to the real interests of the others and their interests may require that they should be treated much as they may dislike it with a certain benignant asperity.[66]

65. *Encyclopaedia of Religion and Ethics*, Vol. xii, pp. 678-79.
66. *Ibid.*

In the same way Thomas Aquinas, explaining the view-point of Christianity with regard to war, says:

> Jesus said that he who takes the sword shall perish by the sword. But "to take" means to use without warrant and the words only prohibit unauthorised or private persons from drawing the sword. (b) War is inconsistent with the command that we resist not evil (Matt. 5 : 38) and avenge not ourselves. "But these injunctions are fulfilled by the cultivation of a placable spirit and cannot require us to do mischief by allowing wickedness to go unpunished. If the peace-makers are blessed, war-makers are accused. But war may be the best or the only means of attaining the end of peace.[67]

Luther held that the Gospel presupposed natural rights and duties, and vigorously defended the Christian soldier. Calvin argued that war is branch of the work of retributive justice which has been entrusted by God to the civil magistrate, and that it has the same moral justification as the police measures which protect the citizens against the criminal populations. In Calvin's own words :

> Whether it be a king who does it, or a scoundrel who does it on a small scale, he is equally to be regarded and punished as a robber. It is no breach of the command : 'Thou shalt not kill,' the slaying of the authors of the unjust war is an execution, the judge is God, and the fighting men who defend the right are merely God's instruments. If it be objected that the New Testament does not expressly permit Christians to fight, it is to be observed that NT does not undertake to legislate about civil policy, and that it presupposes the Old Testament in which the greatest men of God, like Moses and David, were mighty men of valour in the service of God.[68]

The views expressed by the famous writers of Christianity eloquently speak of the fact that "war is not always a sin", contrary to what is commonly imagined by some of the ultra-pacifist intepreters of the Christian faith. Such a view rests on a superficial view of the ethical system of Christianity. The

---

67. *Encyclopaedia of Religion and Ethics*, Vol. xii, pp. 678-79.
68. *Ibid.*

doctrine of retributive justice—that wickedness ought to be punished and curbed—fills at least as large a space as the doctrine of non-resistance in the structure of Christian thought.

Since war need not be merely an impulsive outburst of fury and aggression, but can also be a means for the achievement of some lofty ends, it has been completely humanized by *Islam*. It is not allowed to degenerate into an act of savagery, but is required to be carried on as a noble struggle with humane considerations, under the leadership of a responsible and God-fearing man, and directed to weeding out evil and enthroning goodness, charity and benevolence.

Even a cursory glance over the pages of history would reveal, on the other hand, that war has had in the past even as it has today an extremely horrible record. The countries invaded are ruthlessly devastated, the captured cities are sacked and destroyed, and neither age nor sex counts on immunity. Such has been and continues to be the general practice of warfare. If the practice is commonly less than the theory, this is probably due not so much to clemency as to the consideration that a ruined and depopulated country affords less opportunities of exploitation than the populated one. *Islam* is the greatest religion of the world which makes a strong plea for humane fighting and regulates the conduct of war in such a way that it ceases to be a sheer drive for power, a naked exaltation of the tribal passion for fighting, an act of collective gangsterism, but becomes "a thoroughly reformative process."

> And fight in the way of *Allah* those who fight you, and transgress not the limits ; verily *Allah* loveth not the transgressors.[69] (ii : 190)

---

69. Compare and contrast this verse with the war laws embodied in the Bible. "And they destroyed the cities, and on every good piece of land cast every man his stone and filled it ; and they polluted every spring of water and felled all good trees, till the stones in the walls of the capital city were left demolished and the slinger surrounded it and destroyed it. (2 Kings, 3 : 25) Samuel said to Saul, "The Lord sent me to anoint you to be king over His people Israel. Now therefore hearken to the voice of the words of the Lord. Thus says the Lord of hosts : I remember what Amalak did to Israel on their journey when they were coming up out of Egypt.

Now go and smite the Amalakites, and utterly destroy all that they have, and spare them not ; but slay both men, women, young people and infants, oxen and sheep, camels and asses."

The Holy Prophet has clearly set the limits which may not be transgressed in fighting.

Firstly, the belligerents are divided into two classes : combatants, who actually participate in the battle, and non-combatants, who do not or cannot take part in actual fighting or who are incapacitated to do so, for example, women and children, the aged and the infirm, the blind, the imbecile, the travellers, and the man devoted to monastic services. *Islam* has forbidden their killing altogether.[70]

The following instructions of the Holy Prophet lay down the well-defined limits of warfare :

> Neither kill the old verging on death, nor children and babes nor the females. Do not steal anything from the booty and collect together all those things which fall to your lot in the battle field, and do good. *Allah* loves those who do good.[71]

It is narrated on the authority of *'Abd Allāh b. 'Umar* that once the Holy Prophet saw the dead body of a woman who was killed in a battle. He admonished his men and warned them against killing women and children.[72]

It is also recorded that the Holy Prophet (peace and blessings of *Allah* be upon him) once saw in a battlefield that people had surrounded something. He sent one of his men to find out what the matter was. The man returned and told the Messenger of *Allah* that a woman had been slain and the people had gathered around her. Upon this the Holy Prophet said : "The woman did not participate in the battle, then why was she made a victim of your sword ?" The people replied : "*K͟hālid b. al-Walīd* was in the vanguard of the army." The Holy Prophet sent a man to *K͟hālid* and instructed him not to lay hands on any woman or slave.[73] The Prophet also issued a stern warning to his men against the burning of the enemies.

---

70. Sayyid Abu al-'A'la Maudūdi : *Al-Jihād fī al-Islam*, p. 182.
71. Abū Dāwūd : *Kitāb al-Jihād* (Karachi, 1953), Vol. ii, p. 362.
72 *Ibid.*
73. *Ibid.*

The famous commentator of the *Sunan* of Abū Dāwūd, Abū 'Abd al-Raḥmān Sharf al-Haqq, commonly known as Muḥammad Ashraf, in his expo-

[*Contd.*

There is a tradition which has been narrated on the authority of *Ḥamzah al-Aslamī* that the Messenger of *Allah* once appointed him the leader of a battalion and said : "If you find such and such an infidel, kill him, but do not burn him, because it is the Creator of fire alone Who has the right to use it for punishing the wicked people."[74]

It is recorded by *Samurah b. Jundub* that the Holy Prophet (peace be upon him) exhorted us to give charity and forbade us from mutilation of dead bodies.[75]

It is said that once a news was brought to *Abū Ayyūb al-Anṣārī* that *Muslims* killed four prisoners after having tied them in their camp. The famous companion of the Holy Prophet listened to this with a sense of anguish and said : "I heard the Prophet forbidding us to kill our enemies in this way." He also added : "By God, in Whose hand is my life, I would never slay like this even if it were a hen.' "[76]

This, in brief, is the teaching of the Holy Prophet with regard to dealing with the enemy on the battlefield. So great is the respect for humanity in Islam that it has forbidden wanton destruction of even the enemy's crops and property either at the time of invasion or at the time of conquest. While describing the traits of the mischief-monger, the *Qurān* explicitly tells us that :

> When he turns his back, his aim everywhere is to spread mischief through the earth and destroy crops and cattle. But God loveth not mischief and disorder.
>
> (ii : 205)

The above verse succinctly points out the behaviour of one who is dazzled by the allurements of the material world and its momentary pleasures. *Muslims* have been enjoined to refrain from doing any such mischief and those who violate these injunctions are condemnable in the eyes of *Allah*.

---

sition of the implication of this *hadīth* says : "The use of letter ل on 'تقاتل' which is Khabar (predicate) is clearly indicative of the emphasis on the "negative". *Awn al-Ma'būd 'ala' Sunan Abi Dāwūd* (Ansārī Press Delhi, 1318 A.H.), Vol. iii, p. 7.

74. Abū Dāwūd : *Kitāb al-Jihād*, Vol. ii, p. 362.
75. *Ibid.*, Vol. ii, p. 361.
76. *Ibid.*, Vol. ii, 366.

Islam has purged war of all base passions, so much so that the *Muslims* have been ordained to refrain from creating noise on the battlefield as far as possible, and only chant the glory of the Lord, the Creator of the universe. It is narrated on the authority of *Qays b. 'Abd*, that the companions of the Holy Prophet did not like talking loudly on the battlefield.[77]

This injunction speaks eloquently of the sanctity of the occasion. War in *Islam* is not the wild expression of the baser elements of man, but a sacred struggle undertaken to achieve some definite noble ends.

The four righteous Caliphs followed closely the teachings of *Allah* and His Apostle in letter and spirit and did not deviate from the path shown to them by the Holy Prophet. The celebrated instructions which the first Caliph gave to his army while bidding them farewell on their expedition to the Syrian borders are permeated with the Message of *Allah*. He said :

> Do not commit treachery, nor depart from the right path. Do not mutilate, nor kill a child, nor aged man, nor a woman. Do not destroy a palm tree, nor burn it with fire and do not cut any fruit tree. You must not slay any of the flocks or herds or the camels, save for your subsistence. You are likely to pass by people who have devoted their lives to monastic service ; leave them to what they have devoted their lives. You are likely to find, likewise, people who will present to you meals of many kinds. You may eat : but do not forget to mention the name of *Allah*."[78]

It is said that once at the time of conquest a singing girl was brought to *al-Muhājir b. Abī Ummyyia* who had been publicly singing satirical poems about *Abu Bakr*. *Muhājir* got her hand amputated. When the Caliph heard this news, he was rudely shocked and wrote a letter to *Muhājir* in the following words :

---

77. Mullā 'Ali Qāri adds : "Only with the exception of remembrance of Allāh", vide, *'Awn al-Ma'bud, Kitāb al-Jihād*, Vol. iii, p. 4.

Imām Shaukāni observes : "It signifies that raising aloud of the voice, too much talking and shrieking and crying are not liked in the battlefield."

(*Nayl al-Awṭār*), (Cairo, 1357 A.H.), Vol. iii, p. 243.

78. Al-Ṭabarī, *Tarikh al-Rusul wa al-Mulūk*, edited by M. J. de Geoje E. J. Brill, 1879-1901, Series I, Vol, iv, p. 1580.

> I have learnt that you laid hands on a woman who had showered abuses on me, and therefore got her hand amputated. God has not sought vengeance even in the case of polytheism, which is a great crime. He has not permitted mutilation even with regard to manifest infidelity. Try to be considerate and sympathetic in your attitude towards others in future. Never mutilate, because it is a grave offence. God purified *Islam* and the *Muslims* from rashness and excessive wrath. You are well aware of the fact that those enemies fell into the hands of the Messenger of *Allah* who had been recklessly abusing him, who turned him out of his home, and who fought against him, but he never permitted their mutilation.[79]

Another letter written by '*Umar*' the second Caliph, which is addressed to *Sa'd b. Abī Waqqās*, speaks eloquently of the noble spirit with which the *Muslims* have been exhorted to take up arms :

> Always search your minds and hearts and stress upon your men the need of perfect integrity and sincerity in the cause of *Allah*. There should be no material end before them in laying down their lives, but they should deem it a means whereby they can please their Master and entitle themselves to His favour : such a spirit of selflessness should be inculcated in the minds of those who unfortunately lack it. Be firm in the thicket of the battle as *Allah* helps man according to the perseverance that he shows in the cause of His faith and he would be rewarded in accordance with the spirit of sacrifice which he displays for the sake of the Lord. Be careful that those who have been entrusted to your care receive no harm at your hands and are never deprived of any of their legitimate rights.[80]

Such in fact is the humane and noble attitude which *Islam* exhorts its followers to adopt on the battlefield when passions are generally let loose. It is an attitude the like of which is

---

79. Al-Balādhuri, *Ansāb al-Ashrāf*, (Cairo edition), Vol, ix, page 491. Vide *Haḍrat Abū Bakr ke Sarkarī Khuṭuṭ*, edited by Khurshid Aḥmad Fāriq (Delhi, 1960), p. 81, Arabic text on p. 171.

80. Khurshid Aḥmad Fāriq, *Haḍrat 'Umar ke Sarkārī Khuṭūṭ* , (Delhi, 1959), p. 138, Arabic text on pp. 468-69.

not to be found in the history of any other nation. Has the world any code of military ethics more noble and compassionate than this one ? "The moral tone adopted by the Caliph *Abū Bakr* in his instructions to the Syrian army was", says a Christian historian, "so unlike the principles of the Roman government that it must have commanded profound attention from the subject people. Such a proclamation announced to Jews and Christian sentiments of justice and principles of toleration which neither Roman emperors nor orthodox bishops had ever adopted as the rule of conduct."[81]

Western scholars have indulged in a good deal of mudslinging on the question of the use of the sword in *Islam*. But if one were to reflect calmly on this point one would be convinced that the sword has not been used recklessly by the *Muslims* ; it has been wielded purely with humane feelings in the wider interest of humanity. Utmost regard was always shown to human life, honour and property even on the battlefield. That is why in all the eighty-two encounters between the *Muslims* and non-*Muslims* during the life of the Holy Prophet (peace be on him), only one thousand and eighteen persons lost their lives on both sides. Out of this two hundred and fifty-nine were *Muslims* whereas the remaining seven hundred and fifty-nine belonged to the opposite camp.[82] One wonders at the audacity of these writers when one only compares the religious wars of Charles the Great, in which 4500 pagan Saxons were killed in cold blood, when one recalls the "famous answer by which the Papal Legate, in the Albiqennian war, quieted the scruples of a too conscientious general, 'Kill all, God will know His own',—when one recalls the Spanish Inquisition, the conquest of Mexico and Peru, the massacre of St. Bartholomew, and the sack of Magdeburg Tilly."[83]

This ruthless criticism on the use of sword by *Muslims* is matter of great surprise for us when we find that it emanates from those whose hands are soiled in the blood of countless innocent human beings, by those who exult in the techniques of

---

81. Finlay, *Greece under the Romans*, pp 367-68.

82. Sulaymān Manṣūrpūri, in his scholarly discussion on this topic, has critically analysed the real facts and made some very important discussion in this respect.

(See *Rahmatul lil-'Alamīn*, Vol. ii, pp. 220-267).

83. Bosworth Smith, *Mohammad and Mohammadanism*, pp. 218-19.

homicide, who have depersonalized warfare to such an extent that millions of innocent men and women are put to death and numberless are thrown into concentration camps and flogged with steel rods and ox-hide whips, and all this is done without any qualm of conscience. As human beings, we hang our heads down in shame when think of the horrifying atrocities which have been perpetrated by the modern civilized man. It is estimated that in the World War I, ten million soldiers were killed and an equal number of civilians lost their lives, and twenty million died on account of widespread epidemics and famines throughout the world as an aftermath of this war. Economic costs are estimated at $ 338,000,000,000 of which $ 186,000,000,000 were direct costs.[84]

The losses in the World War II were staggeringly greater as compared with the first one. Twenty-two million persons were killed and thirty-four million were wounded. The estimated cost of war was $ 1,348,000,000,000 of which $ 1,167,000,000,000 consisted of direct military costs.[85]

It is significant that in the Korean War, the first instance in which an international organization for establishing peace utilized military force to suppress aggression, more than one million persons were killed which added to the civilian deaths in Korea and totalled about five millions.[86]

84. *Encyclopaedia Britannica* (London), Vol. xxiii, art, 'War', p. 324.
85. *Ibid.*, p. 335.
86. *Ibid.*

Chapter 7

The Prophet on the Battlefield

The *Quraysh,* mortified at the escape of the Holy Prophet along with his devoted companions, and jealous of his growing power in *Medina,* kept a stringent watch over the *Muslims* who had been left behind in *Mecca* (of whom the majority were women or helpless slaves), and persecuted them in every possible way. In addition to all that, they began to make preparations on a large scale for an all out attack on *Medina* which, they believed, would exterminate the nascent power of *Islam.* But before fighting this decisive battle they were anxious to enlist the support and sympathies of the non-*Muslim* tribes living around *Medina.* This objective was achieved by various means, the chief among which was to display their power and thus impress upon them their unrivalled strength as compared with that of the *Muslims.* They believed that the free and unchecked movements of their caravans to Syria passing along the shores of the Red Sea would provide sufficient proof of their might and thus the tribes who were living on those routes would be terrorised and the *Muslims* would therefore be deprived of their support.

In pursuance of this strategy caravans after caravans of *Meccans* went to Syria. These caravans also had shrewd agents who sowed the seeds of discontent and sedition among the people of *Medina* and tried to enlist their sympathies to the cause of wiping *Islam* out of existence.

The Holy Prophet (peace be on him) was quite aware of these manoeuvres. He, therefore, sent small parties with a view to making the *Meccans* realize the formidable presence of the *Muslims* and the headache that they were capable of causing, if *Meccans* persisted in their hostility. The Prophet confidently believed that this method would cast the wind out of their sails.

Muḥammad (peace be on him) received the news of one such

caravan whcih was passing comparatively close to *Medina* under the leadership of *Abū Sufyān.* The Prophet himself led his party in order to intercept its passage and thus make the bubble of *Meccan* glory burst before the expectant eyes of the *Arabs. Abū Sufyān,* on learning the intention of the *Muslims,* led his caravan off the main route, and inclined it towards the Red Sea. By this manoeuvre, he was able to slip past the Medinite ambush and was out of their reach before they found him out. To be on the safe side, he had also sent a messenger to *Mecca* with the news that *Muḥammad* (peace be on him) was personally out to capture the caravan.

The messenger rode fast and as he rode, he exaggerated in his mind what *Abū Sufyān* had told him. By the time he reached *Mecca* he was in a frenzy. Felling himself from his camel, he stood dramatically before the *Ka'bah,* out off the nose and ears of the camel, turned its saddle upside down, tore off his own shirt from front and behind, and cried :

> O *Quraysh* ! your merchandise ! it is with *Abū Sufyān.* The caravan is being intercepted by *Muḥammad* and his companions. I cannot say what would have happened to them. Help ! Help ![1]

The effect of this hue and cry was instantaneous.[2] Soon an excited throng of one thousand soldiers, with seven hundred camels and horses, was clamouring to be included in the army that was to proceed to avenge the rumoured deaths of all those who had been with the caravan, to say nothing of the plundering of its rich merchandise *Abū Jahl* headed the army.

Counsels in *Medina*

The news of the intended attack of the *Meccans* travelled with mysterious rapidity in the desert. *Muḥammad* (peace be upon him) heard simultaneously that the caravan had escaped and that *Abū Jahl* was on his way with a large army. He apprised his men of the gravity of the situation and asked their advice. *Abū Bakr* was the first who spoke on the occasion and assured the

---

1. Muḥamman Ḥusayn Haykal, *Hayāt Muhammad,* Cairo, 1974. p. 256.
2. Zurqānī. *Sharḥ 'al'a al-Mawāhib al-Ladunniyah,* Cairo, 1325 A.H., Vol. i, p. 410.

Prophet of the unreserved obedience to his command. *'Umar* was the next to stand up and supported the views expressed by his noble friend. Then *al-Miqdād* got up and said : "O Apostle of God ! Proceed where God directs you to, for we are with you. We will not say as the children of Israel said to Moses, 'Go you and your Lord and fight and we will stay here ; rather we shall say, 'Go you and your Lord and fight, and we will fight along with you,' By God ! if you were to take us to *Bark al-Ghimad,*[3] we will still fight resolutely with you against its defenders until you gained it." The Prophet thanked him and blessed him.[4]

Then he said, "Advise me my men !" by which he meant the *Anṣār*. Upon this *Sa'd b. Muā'dh* stood up and spoke thus : "O Prophet of Allah ! We believe in you, and we bear witness to what you have vouchsafed to us and we declare in unequivocal terms that what you have brought is the Truth. We give you our firm pledge of obedience and sacrifice. O Messenger of *Aallh,* you set out of *Medina* with a different objective but God ordained otherwise. Do whatever you deem fit. Cement relations with those whom you like ; and sever them with those whom you dislike. Make peace with those whom you prefer and fight against those whom you look upon as your enemies. We will remain on your side under all circumstances. You have every right to obtain out of our belongings as much as you like and spare for us whatever you desire. We would look upon the portion accepted by you far more valuable than that which you spare for us. We will obey you most willingly in whatever you command us. If you order us to go to *Bark al-Ghimad,* we will show no reluctance and by God, Who has sent you with the Truth, if you were to ask us to plunge into the sea we will do that most readily and not a soul will stay behind. We do not grudge the idea of encounter with the enemy. We are experienced in war and are trustworthy in combat. We hope that God will show you through our hands those deeds (of valour) which will please your eyes. Kindly lead us to the battlefield in the Name of *Allāh.*"[5]

---

3. A place in the Yemen, according to others, the fartherest point in Hijāz

4. Ibn Hishām. Vol, ii, p. 266.

5. Zurqānī, Vol. i, pp. 413-14.

The Holy Prophet was impressed with the fidelity and the spirit of sacrifice which his companions showed at this critical juncture. He, therefore, decided to put up resistance against the *Meccans*. The small band of *Muslims*, hastily recruited and ill-equipped, placing their reliance on *Allāh*, thus marched on the road to *Mecca* to check the onslaught of the *Quraysh*. It was inadvisable to let the flames of war approach their homes in *Medina*. It was at *Badr* that the two armies came face to face.

In respect of numerical strength and equipment the *Muslims* were no match for the *Meccans*. But they had implicit faith in the help and power of *Allāh*. The Holy Prophet took all the precautionary measures which he could have taken at that time, *e.g.* he managed to take hold of the spring of sweet water and the command of water was thus secured. He also made his army encamped in the direction where it would be safe from the glare of the sun in the morning. But these worldly measures were quite insignificant in his eyes. His centre of hope was the Benevolence of his Creator and it was to Him alone that he always looked for succour and redress. He, therefore, retired into a small hut set up for him and implored before *Allāh* with tearful eyes :

> O God ! here come the *Quraysh* exulting in their vanity and pride, contending with Thee and calling Thy apostle a liar. O God ! grant the help which Thou didst promise me.[6]

The Holy Prophet spent the whole night preceding the day of battle in prayer and supplication. The *Muslim* army, wearied with its long march, enjoyed sound and refreshing sleep, a mark of the divine favour and of the state of their undisturbed minds.

In the morning the Prophet called his men to offer the prayers and then urged them to fight in the way of *Allāh*.[7]

As the sun rose over the desert, the Prophet drew up his

---

6. Ibn Hishām, Vol. ii, p. 273.

The Holy *Qur'ān* condemns the boastful march of the Meccan army and orders the Muslims to refrain from any such act of pride :

Be not as those who come forth from their dwellings boastfully and to be seen of men, and debar (men) from the way of *Allāh*, while *Allāh*, is encompassing all they do. (vi : 47)

7. Ṭabarī, Series, I, Vol. iii, p. 1289.

small army, and pointing with an arrow which he held in his hand, arranged the ranks.[8]

The Battle of *Badr*

The common procedure followed in the battles of those days was that champions from both sides "stepped out of their ranks, insulted the enemy, recited the achievements of their leaders and finally defied someone to single combat. The second phase was the single combats. The third was the general mix-up when everybody fought everybody else."[9] This approved procedure was followed in the battle of *Badr* also.

Protected by armour and shields with scimitars in their hands, *'Utbah b. Rabī'a* stepped forth between his brother *Shaybah* and his son *al-Walīd b. 'Utba* from the lines of the *Quraysh* and hurled maledictions at the *Muslims* who faced them.

Three youngmen of the *Anṣār* came out against them : *'Awf* and *Mu'āwiyah,* the sons of *Hārith* and *'Abd Allāh b. Rawāḥah.* But the *Meccans* yelled that they had nothing to do with them. They wanted the heads of their cousins, "the renegades of *Mecca*"—if their owners dared to risk them. Upon this the Holy Prophet asked *'Ubaydah b. Hārith, Ḥamzah,* his uncle, and his cousin *'Alī* (may *Allah* be pleased with them) to go forward for the combat. The three duels were rapid. *Ḥamzah* killed *Shaybah,* while *'Alī* killed *Walīd. 'Ubaydah* was seriously wounded but, before he fell, *Ḥamzah* and *'Alī* were able to come to his rescue. *Ḥamzah* fell upon *'Utbah* and with a sweep of his sword, cut off his head. In a few moments three of the most notable *Meccan* warriors had been put to death.[10] The *Muslim* warriors bore away their wounded companion *'Ubaydah* to the Holy Prophet. His leg had been cut off and the marrow was oozing out from it. In this state of pain he said to the Prophet : "Am I not a martyr, O Messenger of God ?" "Indeed you are," was the Prophet's reply. Then *'Ubaydah* said, "Were *Abū Ṭālib* alive he would know that his words :

> 'We will not surrender him (the Holy Prophet) to the enemies, till we lie dead around him, and are forgotten

8. Ibn Hishām, Vol. ii, p. 278.
9. R. V. C. Bodley, *The Messenger,* Lahore, 1954, p 142.
10. Ibn Hishām, Vol. ii, p. 277.

by our women and children,' truly apply to me." He also recited the following couplets :

> If they have cut off my leg, I don't mind. I am a *Muslim* and hope to get much better life through the grace of *Allāh*, in the world to come. And why should I not expect such a life ? I have reason to do so, for *Allāh* himself in His Infinite Mercy has covered me with the garment of *Islam*.[11]

This duel was followed by a few more duels but the *Meccans* suffered terrible defeats in all combats and lost some of their most precious lives.

Then the third phase of the battle began in the typical *Arab* way. The two armies advanced and drew near to each other. The Apostle ordered his companions not to attack until he gave the signal, and if the enemy should surround them, they were to keep them off with showers of arrows.[12]

The *Quraysh* army fell upon the *Muslims*, but the latter were made to hold firmly to their position and repulse them by Divine assistance. Deeds of valour were exhibited on both the sides, but the army of the faithful was borne forward by the power of the enthusiasm which the half-hearted warriors of *Mecca* miserably lacked. During these encounters, *Abū Jahl*, the arch enemy of *Islam*, suffered death at the hands of two youths from among the *Anṣār*.

The date given for this battle is the 17th of *Ramaḍān* in the second year of *Ḥijrah*.[13]

The part that *Muḥammad* (peace be upon him) himself played in this battle is highly significant and remarkable. He was commanding the army, inspiring confidence among his men and exhorting them to fight manfully for the sake of *Allāh*. The spirit he infused into his men is witnessed by the fiery valour of *'Umayr*, a lad of sixteen, who flung away some dates he was eating crying out : "These are holding me back from Paradise." So saying he plunged into the thick of the battle and died fighting bravely.[14]

---

11. Zurqānī, *Sharḥ 'al'a al-Mawāhib al-Ladunniyah*, Vol. i, p. 418.
12. *Ibid.*
13. Ibn Hisham, Vol. ii, p. 278.
14. Ibn Sa'd, Series I, Vol. ii, p. 16.

The task of *Muḥammad* (peace be upon him) as the leader of the *Muslims* and as a courageous and far-sighted general was no doubt an important one, but far more important than this was his mission as the bearer of God's Message and as such he deemed it to be a suitable opportunity to arouse the minds of the people habituated to the regularity of nature to the clear signs of *Allāh* in the form of miracles.

The Miracles at *Badr*

While analysing the causes of the victory of the *Muslims*, historians make observations which imply that it was only due to certain material factors : the lack of unity amongst the *Meccans*, their over-confidence, and in contrast to these the perfect unity in the ranks of the *Muslims*, their enthusiasm, their love for paradise, etc., which led to their victory. But one should not lose sight of the fact that these advantages enjoyed by the *Muslims* over their opponents were insufficient to counter-balance the striking disparity that existed between the material strength of the two armies. The *Muslim* soldiers were only a little more than three hundred and many of them inexperienced in warfare. The *Anṣār*[15] of *Medina* who formed the spine of the *Muslim* army were mainly peasants and were thus no match for the blood-thirsty fighters of *Mecca*. Moreover, the *Muslim* army was meagrely equipped, having only two horses, seven camels and a few swords.[16] On the other hand, the number of the *Meccans* was three times greater than that of the *Muslims*. They were all well-equipped and were fierce and trained warriors. The Prophet was fully aware of this striking disparity and was conscious of the fact that moral strength alone, unaided by God's assistance, could not make up for this big disparity in material strength. He, therefore, implored his Lord to send such help which might, on the one hand, manifestly turn the tables of war against the *Meccans* and, secondly, provide clear and undeniable proof of His existence and His constant vigilance over the affairs of human beings.

The Holy *Qur'ān* had described the day on which the battle

---

15. The *Anṣār* were more than 240 and the *Muhajirūn* were 66 in number. Sulaymān Manṣūrpuri, *Raḥmatul lil-'Alamīn*, Vol. i, p. 136.

16. *Ibid.*

was fought as the day of distinction[17] (*yaum al-furqān*), because it was decisive in the history of mankind in the sense that the truth in spite of its meagre material resources gained clear victory over the falsehood with all its material strength and glory. A different result would perhaps have changed the entire course of human history. On the one side were arrayed the forces of evil with all their might, and on the other side the servants of *Allāh* had appeared on the stage of history to stem their rising tide. They were weak and helpless. It was an anxious moment and if the tidal wave of evil were to sweep away the rising force of *Islam*, it would have given a serious blow to the moral order of human society. The Prophet was fully conscious of the gravity of the situation and, therefore, spent most of his time beseeching the Almighty to intervene in the affair and ensure a decisive victory for truth and thus prove that He is not a silent spectator in the long drawn struggle between good and evil and when He feels that the standard-bearers of truth, despite their earnest endeavours, are too feeble to stand the onslaughts of evil, He strengthens the forces of Truth and helps them defeat the forces of evil and darkness and thus impresses upon the heart of the people a truth which becomes the first step towards the acknowledgement of one Omnipotent Lord. "While nature," observes John Henry Cardinal Newman, "attests the being of God more distinctly that it does His moral governments, a miraculous event, on the contrary, bears more directly on the fact of his moral government, of which it is an immediate instance, while it implies His existence. Hence, besides banishing the idea of necessity, miracles have a tendency to rouse conscience, to awaken to a sense of responsibility, to remind of duty, and to direct the attention to those marks of divine government already contained in the ordinary course of events."[18]

The fervent appeal of *Muḥammad* (peace be upon him) to the Almighty *Allāh* for support of the nascent forces of *Islam* and in response to that the miraculous aid given to the *Muslims* by His

---

17. If ye indeed have believed in *Allāh* and that which We have sent down on our bondmen on the day of distinction, the day whereupon the two hosts met, And *Allāh* is over everything Potent. (vii : 41)

18. *Essays on Miracles* (Longmans, 1911), p. 12.

supernatural agencies, bears ample testimony to this important fact of human life.

This is how the Prophet poured forth his soul before his Creator :

> O Lord ! I beseech Thee, forget not Thy promise and assurance. O Lord ! If this small force of *Islam* is vanquished then there would be none to worship Thee.[19]

The Prophet repeated these words in such humility and pathos that *Abū Bakr,* who was standing nearby, was moved to tears. He put the mantle on the Prophet's sacred shoulders which had slipped down in a state of deep absorption and consoled him thus :

> O Messenger of God ! enough are these entreaties. *Allāh* shall surely grant you victory and fulfil the promise held out unto you.[20]

Immediate was the response from *Allāh,* Who sent down angels from the heavens for the help and assistance of the Prophet and his companions. The Holy *Qurān* observes :

> And recall what time ye implored your Lord and He answered you : verily, I am about to succour you with a thousand angels, rank in rank. And *Allāh* made not this save as a glad tidings and that your hearts might thereby set at rest : and succour cometh not but from *Allāh.* Verily *Allāh* is Mighty, Wise.[21]

The records of *Ḥadīth* speak eloquently of the fact that the angels did appear on this day and they fought on the side of the *Muslims.* At the instance of Gabriel the Holy Prophet took a handful of gravel, cast it at the enemy and said : "Confusion, seize their faces !" As *Muḥammad* flung the dust, a violent sandstorm blew up suddenly. Burning wind came directly from behind *Muḥammad* and blew like furnace blast into the eyes of his enemies ! The *Quraysh* had already begun to waver. Their

---

19. Ibn Ḥajar al-'Asqalānī : *Fath al-Bārī,* (Cairo ?) Vol. viii, p. 291.

20. *Ibid.*

21. *Ibid.,* viii : 10. The verse implies that it is God alone Who was responsible for the victory and He has the power to do it even without any ostensible cause, but in this case He had done it with the help of angels in order to encourage the Muslims.

movements were impeded by the heavy sands on which they stood ; and when the ranks gave way, their numbers added but confusion. The *Muslims* followed eagerly their retreating steps, slaying or taking captive all that fell within their reach. Retreat soon turned into ignominous rout ; and the flying host, casting away their armour, abandoned beasts of burden, camp and equipage. Forty-nine were killed, and a like number taken prisoners. *Muḥammad* lost only fourteen, of whom eight were *Anṣār* and six refugees. Many of the principal men of *Mecca*, and some of *Muḥammad's* bitterest opponents, were amongst the slain. Chief of these was *Abū Jahl*."[22]

The Holy *Qur'ān* has described this miracle in the following words :

> Wherefore ye slew them not, but *Allāh* slew them, and thou threwest not, when thou threwest but *Allāh* threw, in order that He might prove the believers with a goodly proving from Him. Verily *Allāh* is Hearing and Knowing. (viii : 17)

In the chapter *Āl 'Imrān* the Holy *Qur'ān* reminds the Holy Prophet and through his august personality the whole of the *Muslims* community of the special favours of God in the battle of *Badr*. It is through His help alone that the *Muslim* army which was poor in respect of manpower, mounts and arms, was made to gain victory over the *Meccans* :

> And assuredly *Allāh* had succoured you at *Badr*, while ye were humble. (iii : 123)

The *Qur'ān* also makes a pointed reference to the false hopes which the *Meccans* had madly pinned on this battle. They were confident that their superior numbers, their better equipment and greater experience would prove helpful for them and they would be able to inflict a blow on the rising force of *Islam*. But God had ordained otherwise. He had decided to grant victory to the forces of good. With a play upon the word *fatḥ* (victory, decision, judgement) the *Meccans* were told :

> If ye besought a judgement, then surely a judgement hath come unto you. (viii : 19)

---

22. William Muir, *The Life of Muhammad* (London, 1894), p. 219.

Then the *Qur'ān* describes this battle as decisive, as it served to shake the very foundations of evil in this world and establish the supremacy of good :

> And recall what time *Allāh* was promising you one of the two parties that it should be yours and ye would fain have that the one without arms were yours. And *Allāh* willed that He should cause the Truth to triumph by His words and cut off the root of the disbelievers in order that He might justify the truth and falsify the falsehood, however the guilty might oppose. (viii : 7-8)

Humane Treatment of the Captives

It would be in the fitness of things to say a few words about the magnanimous treatment that was accorded to the prisoners of war by *Muḥammad* (peace be upon him) and his companions. This noble attitude which they showed can be fully appreciated if we review it in the context of the circumstances which led to the war. The Prophet and his companions had endured for full fifteen years unspeakable insults and injuries at the hands of the *Quraysh* of *Mecca* so much so that they were obliged to bid good-bye to their native place and seek shelter into a far-off place. The *Meccans* who were thirsty for their blood did not allow them to lead a life of peace even in their new abodes. They fell upon them with all their forces in order to exterminate them root and branch. Fate, however, decided otherwise and they were defeated by a small army of the *Muslims*. Amidst such feelings of bitterness the Prophet (may peace and blessings of *Allāh* be upon him) remained calm and self-possessed. No atrocity was perpetrated upon the prisoners. Out of the seventy-two captives only two were executed, viz., *al-Naḍr b. al-Ḥārith* and *'Uqbah b. Abī Mu'ayt* who were notorious for their unrelenting hostility towards the *Muslims*. The rest of the captives were treated with utmost kindness and consideration. "Blessings on the men of *Medina*," said one of these in later days, "they gave us wheaten bread to eat when there was little of it, contenting themselves with dates." It is not surprising, therefore, that some of the captives, yielding to these influences, embraced Islam and were therefore immediately set free. The rest were kept for ransom. But this was long before *Quraysh* could humble themselves to visit *Medina* for the purpose. The spell of kindly treatment was thus prolonged and left a favourable impression on the minds of those even who did not at once go over to *Islam*."[23]

The ransom of each prisoner varied with his financial position, ranging from one thousand *dirhams* to four thousand.[24] The poor who could not afford to pay were set free without any compensation. Those who could read and write were given the charge of small children. Each one of them had to teach ten of their wards and when they became proficient in reading and writing, their instructor was granted liberty.[25] This condition of securing freedom throws a good deal of light on the value which Islam attaches to learning.

The Consequences of *Badr*

The triumph at *Badr* was a matter of great importance for the *Muslims*. It consolidated the power of *Muḥammad* (peace be upon him) over the wavering minds. Everybody in the land was reflecting calmly over the questions: "How can the Prophet with such meagre strength of men and arms overpower such large hosts, if he does not have the support of God ? How is it that the worst and the most deadly enemies of *Islam* were each and all packed out and slain exactly in the same way as foretold by the Prophet ? Is this not the handiwork of the Divine Power, the Power which is the Creator and the Sovereign of the universe ?" Questions such as these agitated the minds of the *Arabs* and set them thinking. It was as a result of the mental struggle to find suitable answers to such agitating questions that some of them discovered the Truth preached by *Muḥammad* (peace be upon him) and thus accepted Islam as their faith and code of life. The feelings of *Muslims* and non-*Muslims* concerning this historic event can be well imagined from the following :

> *'Alī b. Abī Ṭālib* said : "Have you seen how *Allah* elevated His Apostle with the favour of the Strong, Powerful and Gracious One ? How He brought humiliation on the unbelievers who were put to shame in captivity and death, while the victory of God's Apostle was glorious ? [The Prophet] having been sent by God with righteousness,

23. William Muir, p. 226.
24. Ibn Sa'd, Series I, Vol. ii, p. 11.
25. *Ibid.*, p. 14.

> he brought the *Furqān* (criterion between the right and wrong) sent down from God. Its signs are manifest to men of sense, some believed them and declared their implicit faith in them, some denied them and their hearts were led astray, and the Lord of the Throne brought repeated calamities upon them.[26]

Hind bint 'Utbah b. Rabī'ah, bewailing the death of her father on the day of *Badr* said :

> Fate is against us and has done us wrong,
> But we can do naught to resist it.
> After the death of *Lu'ayy b. Ghālib,*
> Can a man bewail his death or the death of his friend ?
> Many a day did he robe them
> By lavishing gifts morning and evening.
> Give *Abū Sufyān* a message from me :
> If I meet him today I will reprove him,
> It was a war that would kindle another war,
> For every man has a friend to avenge.[27]

Time, however, rolled on. The *Muslims* were happy and thanked *Allah* for His boundless favours upon them. Their defeat was a matter of great shame and grief for *Meccans.* In almost every house there were tears and wailings either for the captives or the dead. The *Meccans* were burning with humiliation and were thirsting for revenge. "Weep not for your slain," was the counsel of *Abū Sufyān,* "mourn not their loss, neither let the bard bewail their fate. If you lament with elegies, it will ease your wrath and soften your enmity towards *Muḥammad* and his followers. And, should that reach their ears, and they laugh at us, will not their scorn be worse than all ? Haply the turn may come, and ye may yet obtain revenge. As for me, I will touch no oil, neither approach my wife, until I have gone forth again to fight with *Muḥammad.*"[28] It was this savage pride which leapt in the breast of every *Meccan.*

It was during this period that the Prophet lost one of his favourite daughters, *Ruqayyah,* the wife of *'Uthmān,* who had

---

26. Ibn Hishām, Vol. iii, p. 11.
27. *Ibid.*, p. 40.
28. William Muir, pp. 229-230.

only recently returned from the Abyssinian exile. *Muḥammad* (peace be upon him) was kind enough to give his other daughter *Umm Kulthūm* in marriage to *'Uthmān*, *Fāṭimah*, the youngest daughter of the Prophet, was married to *'Alī*, his devoted cousin who stood by him under all sets of circumstances.

Umar's daughter, *Ḥafṣāh* had lost her husband at *Badr*. *'Umar* thought it to be a good idea if *'Uthman* consoled himself with *Ḥafṣah*. But he did not seem inclined to the proposal. *'Umar* then approached *Abū Bakr* with the same proposal, but he also declined the honour. This was enough to perturb *'Umar* who informed the Holy Prophet of the cold behaviour of his two notable friends. *Muḥammad* (peace be upon him) calmed him saying : "*Ḥafṣah* was perhaps reserved for some one better. In fact *'Umar*," he concluded, "I'll marry her myself." He did this accordingly.

The Battle of *Uhud*

The defeat at *Badr* was an ignominy which the *Qurayshite* pride could not leave unavenged. Revenge was, therefore, the catch-word all over *Mecca*. Moreover, the *Meccans* had also realized that their prosperity depended to a great extent on their prestige and in order to maintain it they must in no uncertain measure receive what they had lost at *Badr*. From the *Meccans*, therefore, the Prophet could expect nothing but an intensification of the struggle, for in the hearts of the *Meccans* religious hostility had now mingled with personal rancour and thus all burnt for revenge. They were determined to crush the commonwealth of *Islam* once for all. Emissaries were sent to all the tribes to make common cause against the rising faith which was threatening to sweep away the idolatry and the corrupt practices which were common not only in the land of Arabia but in the whole of the then-known world. As a consequence of this they managed to enlist the support of two well-known tribes *Kinānah* and *Tihāmah*. It was also decided by the *Meccans* that the profits of the escaped caravan headed by *Abū Sufyān* should be devoted to providing equipment to the army.[29] The Holy *Qur'ān* has alluded to this decision of theirs in the following words :

Verily those who disbelieve are spending their riches

---

29. Ibn Sa'ds, Series I, Vol. ii, p. 25. (Leiden 1325 A.H.)

in order to hinder people from the path of *Allāh*. So they will go on spending them. Thereafter it shall become an anguish unto them, then they shall be overcome. (viii : 36)

This time the *Meccans* also decided to take their women along with them for they might arouse them to fight manfully. *Hind*, the wife of *Abū Sufyān*, fiercer even than men, was the first to lead this group.

Thus a contingent of three thousand pitched warriors, of whom seven hundred were mailed soldiers, and two hundred well-mounted cavalry with three thousand camels and fifteen women marched towards *Medina*.[30]

The invaders encamped after ten days' march in the rich plains of *Uḥud*, five miles from *Medina*, from which they were separated by some rocky ridges and ravaged the country around, destroying crops and fruit-trees with the object of drawing the *Muslims* into the open and then overwhelming them.

When the Prophet learnt the news of the advance of the *Meccan* army, he convened a meeting in the mosque in order to discuss this issue with his devoted followers. The Prophet was of the opinion that women and children should be brought from the villages within the city walls and the enemy left to exhaust himself without risking a battle. But this decision was later changed on account of the enthusiasm of the believers and it was thought advisable to face the enemy in an open battlefield. It is narrated that at the time when the issue was discussed whether the enemy was to be resisted at *Medina* or given a fight in *Uḥud*, *Num'ān b. Mālik*, a notable *Anṣārī* addressed the Prophet in these words : "O Apostle of God ! Be kind enough not to deprive us of paradise. I forswear by my Lord Who has sent you with the Truth, I will definitely go into paradise." Thereupon the Prophet said : "Upon what basis do you make this claim ?" He replied : "It is because I bear witness to the fact that there is only one God, *Allāh* ; that you are His Messenger, that I do not turn my back from the battlefield."[31] After weighing carefully the pros and cons of the issue, it was decided that the

---

30. *Ibn Sa'd*, Series I, Vol. ii, p. 25 (Leiden 1325 A.H.)
31. *Ṭabarī*, Series I, Vol. iii, p. 1389.

enemy should be resisted outside the city at *Uḥud.*

Ascending the pulpit at the Friday congregational prayer, the Prophet urged the people in his sermon to fight courageously. "If ye remain steadfast," he said, "you will be helped by the Power of the Almighty." Then he commanded his men to make ready for the battle. Most of the people rejoiced greatly.

By the time the afternoon prayer was ended, people had assembled in the court of the mosque, armed for the battle. *Muḥammad* (peace be on him) retired with *Abū Bakr* and *'Umar* to make preparation. In a little while he stepped out of his chamber, clad in mail and helmet, his sword hanging from a leathern girdle and the shield slung over his shoulder. The citizens, seeing him thus accoutred, repented of their rash remarks and said that he should do as he deemed fit and they would follow him willingly. Upon this the Prophet remarked : "It does not become a prophet that once he had put on armour, he should take it off, until God has decided between him and the enemy."[32]

The *Muslim* army which consisted of only one thousand soldiers, among whom were only two horsemen and a hundred men in armour, spent the night at a short distance from the city, the march being resumed at dawn the next morning.

'Abd Allah b. Ubayy, the leader of the hypocrites and a confederate of the Jews deserted the *Muslim* army at this critical juncture, thus reducing the *Muslim* army to 700, which was to face an army four times its number. Though the *Meccan* army was in full sight, the usual morning prayer was offered. At this moment the Prophet again showed his skill as a general. He drew up his little army with their rear protected by the steep rocks of *Uḥud* and guarded a gap by which he might be outflanked with a picked body of archers, to whom he gave positive orders to hold on to their position whatever the course of the main engagement.

This was the usual care with which the Holy Prophet planned the position of his men so as to leave no point of vantage through which the enemy could launch a surprise attack. He then awaited the attack.

Meanwhile the *Meccan* army advanced. *Abū Sufyān* com-

---

32. *Ibn Kathīr, al-Bidāyah wa al-Nihāyah* (Cairo, 1351 A.H.), Vol. iv, p. 13, and *Ibn Sa'd,* Series I, Vol. ii, p. 26.

manded the centre while the right wing was headed by *Khālid* and the left by *'Ikramah.*

When each side drew near to the other, *Hind* rose with the women who were with her and took up tambourines, beat them and sang martial songs inciting their men to fight bravely. They said :

If you advance we hug you
Spread soft rugs beneath you ;
If you retreat, we leave you,
Desert you and no more love you.[33]

The Combat

Abū 'Āmir was the first to open the battle by coming to the front with his followers from the side of *Quraysh.* But a shower of stones soon turned him back. *Ṭalḥah,*[34] the standard-bearer of the *Quraysh,* rushed forward and challenged the *Muslims* for a single combat. *'Alī* responded to the challenge and brought him down with the stroke of his sword. *Ṭalḥah's* brother, *'Uthmān,* who was incharge of the women, then ran forward and seized the banner which lay by the lifeless body of his brother. He chanted :

The standard-bearer hath the right
To dye its shaft in blood,
Till it be beaten in his hand.[35]

So long as the single combat went on the *Quraysh* received shocks one after another by the fall of their warriors. The rapid destruction of their standard-bearers particularly spread dismay and consternation in their ranks. Then a general engagement ensued. Soon it was apparent that, pressed by the dauntless courage of the *Muslims* the *Meccan* army had begun to waver.

Abū Dujānah displayed wonderful skill as a swordsman that day. Even in the thickest of the battle he, like all other *Muslims,* was fully conscious of his responsibilities and of his duties that he owed to *Allāh* and His Messenger. It is narrated

---

33. *Ibn Hishām,* Vol. iii, p. 52.
34. This *Ṭalḥah* is to be distinguished from *Ṭalḥah* the son of *'Ubayd Allāh* who was a devout *Muslim.*
35. *Ibn Sa'd,* Series I, Vol. ii, p. 28.

that on this occasion when a fierce battle was being fought, he raised his sword to kill a person who was inciting the enemy to fight with the *Muslims*. Upon this the person shrieked and lo! it was a woman. *Abū Dujānah* spared her saying: "I respect the Prophet's sword too much to use it on a woman."[36]

Ḥamzah, 'Alī, Zubayr and other heroes displayed wonderful feats of gallantry against the overwhelming odds which stood unparalleled and created consternation and confusion in the unbelieving hosts. The idolaters now staggered and retreated. A roar of victory rose from the side of the *Muslims*. But it rose too soon. The archers, who had been commanded by the Holy Prophet to guard the opening of the key position, deserted their posts and joined the main body of the soldiers. The cleft was undefended. The shrewd *Khālid b. al-Walīd*, the cavalry commander of the *Quraysh* saw the opportunity and rushed to the opening and attacked the *Muslims* in the rear. This changed the condition totally. *Muṣ'ab* was slain. *Waḥshī*, a hired slave of *Zubayr b. Muṭ'im*, who had been watching the movements of *Ḥamzah* from behind a stone, took him unaware and struck him with a javelin with such a force that he lay lifeless on the ground. Many other Muslims of note fell on the battlefield.

The Prophet also sustained serious injuries on his head and cheek but he was protected by *Allāh* through the unrivalled devotion of his companions, one of whom shielded the Prophet from the arrows of the enemy by his bare hands. It was in this state of confusion that some one shouted that the Holy Prophet had been killed. This news spread consternation among his followers. But this vicious report was soon falsified. The joy of the *Muslims* was unbounded at finding that the Prophet was still alive. The rumour did have, for a while, a harmful effect on a few of the followers of *Muḥammad* (peace be upon him). But he himself was unmoved and faced the odds with matchless courage. It is narrated on the authority of *Maiqdād* that the Holy Prophet showed no sign of anxiety or weakness in this trying hour. "I swear by *Allāh*," said he, "Who sent the Prophet with the Truth, that his feet neither staggered nor wavered at this critical juncture." He stood firmly at his place.

36. *Ibn Hishām*, Vol. iii, p. 53.

His companions came to him in groups to see him and then left him for a few moments in order to encounter the enemy. The Prophet himself did not move an inch from his place.[37]

It is noteworthy that even in this hour of anguish when blood was flowing profusely from various gashes of his body and his son-in-law, *'Alī* was washing them, the Prophet's heart was absolutely free from all those feelings of bitterness and rancour which one finds in common people. *'Abd Allāh b. Mas'ūd* describes vividly the Prophet's conduct at this hour of distress when the enemies were out to put an end to his life and as a consequence of that he was severely hit. He says :

> I can still clearly recall to my mind the occasion when the Prophet was narrating the accounts of the earlier prophets who had received injuries at the hands of their peoples. The Holy Prophet was wiping the blood from his face and saying : 'My Lord ! guide my people to the right path, for they know not'.[38]

Nawawī, the commentator of *Ṣaḥīḥ Muslim*, in his elucidation of the above mentioned *ḥadīth* has observed :

> It is indicative of the unbounded gentleness and clemency, dignified resignation, the noble spirit of forgiveness and sympathy that the prophets showed to their peoples.[39]

It is significant to note that the Holy Prophet in this prayer had not used for his blood-thirsty enemies the word "ignorant", but he has called them "those who know not". This speaks of the unparalleled nobility of the Holy Prophet and his deep love for humanity. It also shows that the Prophet's heart was absolutely free from all stains of hatred, for he thought that his enemies were perpetrating atrocities upon him and his followers simply because they did not know the truth. This implies that as soon as the truth would dawn upon them, their hostility would give way to devotion.

It is pertinent to note the turbulent state of the mind of the

---

37. *Sharḥ Zurqānī* (Cairo, 1325 A.H.), Vol. ii, p. 34.
38. *Muslim* : *Kitāb al-Jihād wa al-Siyar.*
39. *Ibid.*

Quraysh at this moment. They had become savage through and through. Intoxicated by joy at the prospect of victory they had lost all sense of decency and respect for human feelings. Terrible acts of brutality were perpetrated not only upon living beings but even on the helpless slain. Their bodies were mutilated. Not to speak of men, women who have more tender feelings than men, were behaving like heartless beasts. *Hind* tore out *Ḥamzah's* liver and chewed it, but could not take it down her throat and therefore threw it out. The dead bodies of so many other martyrs met with the same fate. Beads were made out of the ears, noses and other parts of the dead bodies of *Muslims* and were dragged all the way to *Mecca* as priceless souvenirs.[40]

It is narrated that when the Holy Prophet went out seeking *Ḥamzah*, he found him at the bottom of the valley with his belly ripped up and his liver missing, and his nose and ears cut off.[41]

After gloating over such cruelties for a time, *Abū Sufyān* approached the foot of *Uḥud* and shouted the names of *Muḥammad* (peace be upon him), *Abu Bakr* and *'Umar* (may *Allāh* be pleased with them). Receiving no reply, he exclaimed : "All are slain. Had they been alive, they must have responded." *'Umar* could not restrain himself : "Thou liest, O enemy of God !" was his reply, *Allāh* has secured their lives in order to bring woe upon thee". Then *Abū Sufyān* shouted : "Glory to *Ḥubal* !" Upon this the Prophet Commanded *'Umar* to proclaim in retort · "*Allāh* is the Most Exalted and the Most Mighty." *Abū Sufyān* again shouted : "We have *Uzzā'* on our side and you have none." The Holy Prophet again directed his companions to reply, "The Lord is our Helper and there is none to help you."[42]

With the retreat of *Muslims* to the cover of the mountain, *Medina* was left entirely exposed ; but the *Quraysh* were not bold enough either to attack *Medina* or drive the *Muslims* away from the heights of *Uḥud*. In hot haste, they bent their steps towards *Mecca* and covered a long distance the same day. The harm that they had done to the *Muslims* was sufficient prize for them, which they thought, would retrieve their lost glory.

On his return to *Medina* the Prophet directed a small body

---

40. *Zurqāni*, Vol. ii, pp. 43-44.
41. *Ibn Hishām*, Vol. iii, p. 101.
42. *Fatḥ al-Bārī* (Cairo, 1959), Kitāb al-Maghāzī.

of his followers to pursue the retreating enemy and to impress upon them that though the *Muslims* had suffered on the battlefield, they were not broken in their spirits and were too strong to be attacked again with impunity. The *Muslims* carried out the behests of their master most cheerfully, despite their suffering and exhaustion. *Abū Sufyān* hearing of the pursuit, hastened back to *Mecca.* A curious sight indeed of a victorious army in retreat and the crest-fallen and crippled group of *Muslims* in pursuit ! The Holy *Qur'ān* has referred to this in the following words :

> Soon shall we cast terror into the hearts of the unbelievers for they ascribe unto *Allāh* partners for which He had sent no authority : their abode will be the Fire ; and vile is the abode of the wrong-doers. (iii : 151)

The observations of the Holy *Qur'ān* on the battle of *Uḥud*

The battle of *Uḥud* has been discussed at length in the Holy *Qur'ān* and all its important aspects have been significantly brought out. In his famous book *Zād al-Ma'ād, Ibn Qayyim* has made a pointed reference to them. We reproduce below his brilliant and thoughful elucidation of these different aspects.[43]

(*i*) *Allāh shall help the Muslims so long as they obey the Holy Prophet.*

The reverse in *Uḥud* resulted from the neglect on the part of the archers of the explicit command of the Holy Prophet and leaving the spot which they were ordered to safeguard to the end. The Holy *Qur'ān* has alluded to this incident in the following words :

> *Allāh* verily made good His promise with you when ye routed them by His leave........ until ye flinched and fell to disputing about the order and disobeyed it after He brought you in sight (of the booty) which ye covet. Some of you desired the world and some of you desired the Hereafter, wherefore He turned you away from them, that He might try you. And He has certainly pardoned

43. It is indeed a very scholarly discussion for which one full chapter has been devoted :

I have only given its summary, For details see this Chapter in *Zad al-Ma'ād,* Vol. ii, pp. 248-265.

> you and *Allāh* is Gracious to the believers. (iii : 152)

The above verse states in clear terms that the success of the *Muslims* depends upon their obedience to the Holy Prophet. As long as they carry out his behests, God will help them in facing all kinds of odds. But when they will set aside his commands in their pursuit of worldly riches, they are bound to come to grief.

(*ii*) *Prophets are not gods.*

Secondly, the harm to the Holy Prophet and his companions is indicative of the fact that prophets are human beings. They no doubt win eventually, and the truth which they preach prevails, but they also share, like all other human beings, the pleasures and pains of human existence.

(*iii*) *The Sufferings sifted the Muslims and the hypocrites.*

Moreover, the victory of the *Muslims* in the battle of *Badr* and their sufferings on the field of *Uḥud* provided them opportunities to learn from the life example of *Muḥammad* (peace be upon him) how to remain calm and self-possessed both at the time of joy and in the hour of distress. Neither victory should intoxicate them nor should injury droop their spirits.

With the glorious success of the *Muslims* at *Badr* there had entered many hypocrites in the fold of *Islām* who were not sincerely attached to the Holy Prophet but professed faith in his leadership since he was the symbol of the rising power in Arabia and their alliance with him was likely to secure them some material benefits. It was not the truth of his mission which impressed them but the worldly power which his leadership promised to bring in its train. Sifting between sincere believers and insincere pretenders to faith in *Islām* was necessary since the presence of a large number of hypocrites within its body politic was a constant threat to its very foundations. The sufferings of the *Muslims* at *Uḥud* drew a clear line of demarcation between the true followers of *Muḥammad* (peace be upon him) and the hyprocrites who paid only lip homage to him but were in fact not with him, being shorn of faith. In the words of the *Qur'ān* :

> *Allāh* is not one to leave the believers in the state wherein ye are until He hath discriminated the impure from the pure. And *Allāh* is not one to acquaint you with

the unseen, but *Allah* chooseth him whomsoever He willeth of His apostles. Believe wherefore in *Allāh* and His apostles, and if ye believe and fear, yours shall be a vast reward." (iii : 178)

If a wound has afflicted you, a wound like it has also afflicted the (unbelieving) people. These are (only) the vicissitudes which we cause to follow one after another for mankind to the end that *Allāh* may know those who believe and may choose witnesses from among you ; and *Allāh* loveth not wrong-doers. (iii : 140)

It has been clearly laid down in these verses that in this fight for truth if the *Muslims* had been hurt, their adversaries had previously suffered hurt likewise, the more so as they had no faith to sustain them. The verses made it plain that there was no occasion to grumble over the harm that had come upon them, as they did not see the whole of God's plan. For, success and failure in this world alternate. And above all, it became obvious that it was adversity which proved a man's mettle.

(*iv*) *Martyrdom is the greatest achievement.*

Death is not always a sign of misfortune. The death which is courted for a just and right cause according to the command of *Allāh* is not a matter for grief or sorrow but an enviable privilege and honour, since it leads a believer into the paradise. It should, therefore, not be considered a loss at all.

The *Meccans* had not won a victory but had been given a little rope to proceed heedlessly towards their own destruction, as we find in this battle : "The orgies of cruelty indulged in by them, after what they supposed to be their victory at *Uḥud* filled up their cup of iniquity ; it lost them the support and adherence of the best in their own ranks ; and hastened the destruction of paganism from Arabia."[44]

(*v*) *Precaution against possible reverses in future.*

The battle of *Uḥud* had an object lesson for the *Muslims* to realize fully that *Muḥammad* (peace be upon him) was the true Messenger of God and that he would, therefore, bid good-bye to

44. Yūsuf 'Ali, *The Holy Qur'ān : Text, Translation and Commentary*, p. 158, footnote.

this mortal world sooner or later. The *Qur'ān* stresses upon the *Muslims* to keep this fact always in their mind, for it was noticed on the field of battle that panic had seized a number of *Muslims* the moment the rumour of the Prophet's death spread so much that a few *Muslims* even said in a state of utter despair : "Of what avail is it now to fight when the Prophet is no more amongst us ?" The *Qur'ān* warns against such pessimism and raises the question of faith or disbelief from the plane of devotion to a person to that of devotion to *Allāh* :

> *Muḥammad* is naught but an apostle. Apostles have surely passed away before him. Will ye then, if he dies or is slain, turn back on your heels? and whosoever turneth back on his heels, hurteth not *Allāh* at all, and anon shall *Allāh* recompense the grateful." (iii : 144)

In these verses the *Qur'ān* makes it clear that *Muḥammad* (peace be upon him) like all earlier prophets is an apostle of *Allāh* and as such he must some day taste the cup of death. There is no escape from that. He was not himself immortal but the cause that he held and the mission that he preached was immortal and divine. This verse served an important purpose on the occasion of the death of the Holy Prophet. Seven years later when the soul of the Prophet left for his heavenly abode and his body was lying motionless in the bed, it "produced such a consternation among his devoted followers that they expected the heaven to burst open and the earth to cleave asunder and wondered how long it could be for the end of the world to come. The loving *'Umar* was entirely beside himself. It was a scene of stormy emotions that the tender-hearted but ever tranquil *Abū Bakr* arrived from the suburb of *Medina* where he lived. He said to the assembled crowd with that sureness of conviction that had won him the title of *Ṣiddīq* :

> O men ! he who worshipped *Muḥammad*, let him know that *Muḥammad* has already passed away ; but he who worshipped *Allāh*, let him know that verily *Allāh* is living and shall never die. And then he recited : 'And *Muḥammad* is no more than an apostle . . .

This allayed all doubts and fears, and a great tranquillity ensued. People who had constantly read the verse that *Ab*

Bakr so appositely quoted, stated that when he recited it on this memorable occasion, it seemed as if it had just been revealed.[45]

The misfortune at *Uḥud* was thus as important for the *Muslims* as the victory at *Badr* from the moral, social and political points of view. It showed them the necessity of strict adherence to the commands of the Holy Prophet. It also awakened the believers to grave responsibilities that fell upon them as the standard bearers of the Divine mission and the hardships which they had to face in establishing its supremacy in the world. It also explained the true status of the Prophet as the Messenger of *Allāh* : the unbounded kindness and the Mercy of the Lord. In short what came to pass at *Uḥud* was to serve as a beacon of hope and courage for the succeeding generations, lest they should in time of distress, fall a prey to despair and turn their backs upon the "Religion of *Allāh.*"

Effect of *Uḥud* on the *Arab* and Jewish Tribes

The battle of *Uḥud* had a number of effects on the enemies of *Islām*. They were, on the one hand, very much perturbed by the growing strength of the *Muslims* but the happenings in *Uḥud* had, on the other hand, supplied fresh vigour to their drooping spirits and they had begun to think of the extermination of the Divine Faith.

The Jews found a suitable opportunity to stab the *Muslims* in the back who had already been hit hard in the battle of *Uḥud.* They perceived that their concentrated efforts could easily precipitate the ruin of *Islām*. The first treacherous act that they did was to open secret communications with the *Quraysh* casting aside their agreements with the *Muslims*. Moreover, they strained every nerve to produce general dissatisfaction and bitterness against the Holy Prophet, his teachings and his faithful companions. A campaign of slander was organized against *Islām* and its followers. The sacred words of the Holy *Qur'ān* were deliberately mispronounced in order to pervert their meanings. Satirical poems were enthusiastically sung at public places in

45. Maulānā Muḥammad 'Alī : Quoted by Maulānā 'Abdul Mājid Daryābādī in his English *Translation and Commentary of the Holy Qur'ān* (Taj Co. Ltd., Lahore), Vol. I, p. 94.

which the religion of *Allāh* was abjectly ridiculed. *Muslim* ladies were insulted and offended by obscene and amatory madrigals. Inflammatory poems were recited with a view to keeping the animosity of the hostile tribes alive.

Life was thus made hard for the followers of *Muḥammad* (peace be upon him). The Holy Prophet was keeping a watch over their seditious activities. He first approached the tribe of *Qaynuqā'* and asked its members to honour the pact which they had concluded with him. But they did not pay heed to his advice. They had become over-confident of their power since they had been assured help from other tribes. Their reply was defiant through and they betook themselves to fortified strongholds. The Prophet laid siege to them and kept it for fifteen days after which they became entirely helpless for want of any external help and thus surrendered themselves. The Prophet then ordered them to leave *Medina* and settle somewhere else. Thus banished, they went to *Khaybar* and settled there.

Similar was the treatment meted out to *Banū Naḍīr*, another important Jewish tribe. They were likewise forced to leave their homes as they had not only refused to renew the pact of peace, but had made an attempt on the life of the Holy Prophet (peace and blessings of *Allāh* be upon him).

New Torrents of Hostility

It is important to note that even in this critical situation when the forces of "ignorance" had been invading the *Muslims* from all directions and their very existence was greatly imperilled, the Prophet was doing all that was possible to propagate the religion of *Allāh*. All his energies were directed to this single end. He organised parties of *Muslim* missionaries to spread the light of *Islām* to the various tribes. The enemies of *Islām* lost no time in taking undue advantage of this noble objective. Treacherous people would sometimes invite these zealous preachers of *Islām* under the pretext of learning the teachings of the Prophet (peace and blessings of *Allāh* be upon him) and having them at their mercy, would kill them without compunction. One such treacherous event took place at *Bi'r Ma'ūna* in the month of *Ṣafar* in the year 4 A.H., when a team of seventy missionaries was brutally attacked by the tribes of *Banū 'Āmir* and *Banū Sulaym* and all were put to death with the exception of one man, *'Amr b. Umayyah* who brought the heart-rending news of the slaughter of the companions to the Prophet in *Medina.* The Holy Prophet and his followers were deeply shocked at the brutal treachery of these tribes.

A similar tragedy is recorded to have been enacted at another place, *Rajī'*. Some of the tribes sent a deputation to the Prophet (peace and blessings of *Allāh* be upon him) expressing their desire to learn the principles of *Islām*. The Prophet readily agreed to their request and sent six *Muslims* to teach them the fundamentals of the Divine Faith. But when they reached the *Rajī'*, they were suddenly attacked by an armed band of *Lihyān* youths. Three of the missionaries died fighting bravely and the other three were taken prisoners and sold at *Mecca*. One of them loosened his hands and managed to escape when he was crushed by a rock hurled down upon him. The only two survivors, *Zayd* and *Khubab* were purchased by *Ṣafwān b. Umayyah* and the tribe of *Hārith* respectively in order to kill them and thus avenge the death of the chiefs of their tribes who fell in the battle of *Badr*. The scene of the death of these two ardent lovers of *Islām* is memorable. They cheerfully laid down their lives in the way of *Allāh* and boldly refused their liberty at the price of recantation. *Zayd* was taken to *Tan'īm* in bondage, where in the presence of a large concourse from *Mecca,* he was to be put to death. When they had bound him to the stake *Abū Sufyān b. Ḥarb* said : "I adjure you by God, *Zayd* don't you wish that *Muḥammad* was now in your place and you were sitting in security at home ?" Upon this *Zayd* replied : "By God ! I would not like that even a thorn should prick *Muḥammad* in the place where he is now and that I should be with my family." He was then killed. May *Allāh* be pleased with him and his friends. *Abū Sufyān* often said : "I have never seen a man who was so loved by his companions as *Muḥammad* (peace be upon him)."

Khubab also faced death with the same firmness and boldness as was shown by his friend. He, like his companion, was taken into the open field where a number of people, men, women and children, had gathered to watch this gory spectacle. He asked the executioners to spare him for some time so that he might offer prayers. His request was granted and he prostrated before his Lord in great humility and declared his implicit faith in

Him. He, however, observed his prayer in haste and then addressed the men around him : "Were it not that you would think that I only delayed out of fear of death I would have prolonged my prayer." The tyrants raised him on the wood and bound him. Even in this state of plight he remained unshaken and was fully confident of the truth which he was required to uphold and preach and the tremendous reward which he would get in the Hereafter for the sacrifice of his life. He uttered these words with great enthusiasm : "O God ! we have faithfully delivered the message of your Apostle (peace and blessings of *Allāh* be upon him). So convey to him what has been done to us." The following verses recited by him speak eloquently of the atrocities borne by him and his faith in *Allāh* at this hour of suffering :

> The confederates gathered their tribes around me.
> And summoned all of them who could come
> Every one amongst them was burning with rage
> As I was helpless in their hands.
> They had gathered their women and children
> I am bound firmly to a lofty trunk.
> To God alone I complain of my helplessness and sufferings.
> And of the death the confederates propose for me.
> Lord of the Throne ! give me endurance against their design.
> They cut my flesh bit by bit.
> All hope for life is gone—gone for ever.
> If Lord so desires, He will bless my torn limbs and broken joints.
> They have offered me a choice for infidelity but death is preferable to it.
> Tears roll out of my eyes, but not out of fear,
> I fear not death, who am I to fear ; die I must.
> But I am afraid of the engulfing flames of Hell,
> By God ! I fear not if I die a *Muslim.*
> On what side do I fall for the sake of *Allāh,*
> I will not yield myself to the enemy,
> Nor will I fret and fume since I am returning to my Lord.[46]

---

46. The narration is based on *Ibn Hishām,* Vol. iii, pp 181-86.

This is a typical illustration of the deep attachment which the companions of the Prophet had for him and for the faith that he preached.

To cut a long tale of woe and misery short, the whole of Arabia was seething with spite against *Islam*. Jews, hypocrites, idolaters, in fact, all the forces of ignorance had joined hands with the determination to annihilate the religion of *Islām*. There was not one front at which the Prophet was required to fight but numerous fronts which needed his attention. He stood eminently the test of time and by his divine wisdom faced successfully all odds.

The Battle of the Trench

Banū Naḍīr, as we have seen, had been banished from *Medina* and had gone to live at *Khaybar*. They were a rich community and had as their leader *Huyayy b. Akhtab* an inveterate foe of the Holy Prophet (peace and blessings of *Allāh* be upon him). He sent emissaries all over Arabia and invited the various tribes to join them in the concerted attack upon the Prophet and his followers so that they might get rid of them altogether. The *Quraysh* responded enthusiastically to their invitation and said: "O Jews! You are the first people of the Scripture and know the nature of our dispute with *Muḥammad*. Is our religion the best or that of his?" They replied that their religion was far better than that preached by *Muḥammad* and thus they had a better claim to be in the right.[47] The *Quraysh* were highly delighted at these words and joined hands with the Jews in order to fight the common foe. Funds were raised and the Jews and the *Meccans* donated liberally to the war preparations. There was hardly any tribe of the disbelieving *Arabs* which was not approached to join the federation. It was in fact a decisive battle between the rising force of *Islam* and that of the rest of Arabia.

47. The Holy *Qur'ān* has referred to their stand in the following words:

"Hast thou not observed those unto whom is vouchsafed a portion of the Book, testifying to idols and devils and saying of those who have disbelieved: These are better guided as regards the way than the believers." (iv : 51)

The Jews had fallen to such a level of corruption that they had in their blind enmity towards the Prophet lost all sense of justice. They frankly avowed that they preferred idolatry and paganism to *Islām*.

When the Holy Prophet (peace and blessings of *Allāh* be upon him) heard of their evil designs, he resolved, at the suggestion of *Salmān*, the Persian, to entrench *Medina*, a stratagem as yet unknown to the *Arabs*. The outer line of the houses was built together so compactly that for considerable length they presented a high stone wall in itself a solid defence against the enemy. The task of digging the ditch was undertaken at once and the Prophet himself participated in it like an ordinary labourer side by side with his companions, an unparalleled example of the keen sense of responsibility, sympathy, equality and humility, the distinguishing features of the Prophet's character. He was the last of the Apostles and thus the most favoured Messenger of *Allāh*, the centre of the loyalties and devotion of the *Muslims*, the most pious and most highly respected by all his companions. In spite of all these honours he claimed no special privileges for himself and was prepared to cheerfully discharge the humblest of the duties that lay upon him. He could get all the facilities and privileges which a man could possibly conceive of but he remained absolutely indifferent to these material interests and preferred to live as a poor, hard working, ill-provided man. "There was decidedly something better in him," says Carlyle, "than hunger of any sort, or these wild *Arab* men, fighting and jostling three and twenty years at his hand, in close contact with him always, would not have reverenced him so! They were wild men, bursting ever and anon into quarrels, into all kinds of fierce sincerity, without right worth and manhood, no man could have commanded them. They called him Prophet, you say, Why? he stood there face to face with them; bare, not enshrined in any mystery; visibly clouting his own cloak, cobbling his own shoes; fighting, counselling, ordering in the midst of them, they must have seen what kind of man he was; let him be called what you like! No emperor with his tiaras was obeyed as this man in cloak of his own clouting."[48]

The records of *Ḥadīth* reveal that the *Muslims* dug this ditch under very trying conditions. They had to work with empty stomachs exposed to the blasts of cold wind. The Holy Prophet also shared with his men the pangs of hunger. Whenever any-

48. Thomas Carlyle, *Hero and Hero Worship* (London, 1898), pp. 95-96.

body offered him something to eat, he would never avail himself of that but would share that with his companions. It is narrated on the authority of *Jābir b. 'Abd Allah* that when the Prophet was busy in digging a ditch I found him in the grip of extreme hunger. "I came to my wife," says *Jābir*, "and asked her to slaughter the little ewe that we had and to roast it for the Prophet. When the night came and the Prophet was about to leave the trench, for we used to work at it all day and go home in the evening—I told him that we had prepared bread and mutton for him and I should like him to come with me along with a few of his men to my place." But the Holy Prophet would not eat alone while his followers were undergoing the pangs of hunger. He, therefore, invited all of them to partake of the feast. He also conveyed a message to the wife of *Jābir* not to take off the earthen pot from the fire till he arrived. "My wife," says *Jābir*, "was exasperated at this situation since we had arranged a feast only for a few persons and the Holy Prophet had arrived in the company of his followers. He blessed the food and invoked the name of *Allāh* over it and it so happened that the food proved to be more than sufficient for a number of people exceeding one thousand."[49]

This incident which speaks of the miracle performed at the hands of the Holy Prophet, also throws a good deal of light on the love and sympathy which inspired the Prophet's dealing with his companions. He was prepared to make the greatest sacrifice for their sake and give priority to their requirements over those of his own. It was owing to this keen sense of fellow-feeling and extremely sympathetic attitude towards his friends and his unbounded love for humanity that the Prophet (peace and blessings of *Allāh* be upon him) succeeded in drawing from the various tribes and races and lands people who were devoted to him beyond measure and were prepared to lay down their lives at the slightest gesture from him.

It is worthy of note that the *Quranic* verses through which the enthusiasm of the companions of *Muḥammad* (peace be upon him) had been awakened, integrated with a keen sense of de-

---

49. Ibn Ḥajar al-'Asqalānī, *Fatḥ al-Bārī*, Vol. viii, Kitāb al-Maghāzī, Chapter : "Ghazwa al-Khandaq".

votion to *Allāh* and most of the verses were the same as the ones recited by them at the time, they were building the mosque :

O Lord ! There is no happiness but that of the next Life.
O Lord ! Have mercy on the *Anṣār* and the Refugees.[50]

The faithful followers of *Muḥammad* (peace be upon him), while digging trenches also declared their deep faith in *Allāh*, the prophethood of *Muḥammad* and their unstinted support to the cause of *Islām* :

We start our work in the name of *Allāh*.
How unfortunate it would be for us
If we worship any one else except Him.
How nice and good is our Sustainer.
How fine and excellent is our Religion.[51]
We are those who pledged themselves to *Muḥammad*.
That we will strive, as long as we live.[52]
We are those who pledged themselves to *Islām* so long as we live.[53]

The Holy Prophet himself frequently repeated the following verses :

O Lord ! Without Thee, we could not be guided rightly ! We should neither have given alms, nor yet have prayed. Send down upon us tranquillity and in battle give us endurance. For they have risen against us, and have sought to entangle us in mischief, We refused to be ensnared by that, yea, we refused.[54]

These verses have been quoted in order to give an idea to the readers how *Islām* had maintained the organic unity of the human life. It had destroyed all those artificial barriers which divide the different sectors of life into watertight compartments. Life is an organic whole which cannot stand the ordeal of fragmentation. When a man submits himself to *Allāh*, his whole life is spiritualised and even those of his activities such as the digging of a trench for the purpose of defence, which, to a superficial observer, appears to be almost a worldly action, be-

---

50. Ibn Ḥajar al-'Asqālanī, *Fatḥ al-Bārī*, Vol. iii, p. 397.
51. *Ibid.*, p. 399.
52. *Ibid.*, p. 398.
53. *Ibid.*
54. *Bukhārī*, Kitāb al-Maghāzī.

comes an act of religious devotion. *Islām* does not recognize the religious urge in man as a mere passing phase in his intellectual, moral and physical development, but makes it the ultimate source of all his thoughts, actions and concepts of morality.

Human life is not a series of isolated events, but it is an expression of man's outlook that runs like a golden thread in the warp and woof of the variegated pattern of his many-sided life. There is no scope in *Islām* to argue in the manner of Machiavelli that there is one rule for business and another for religion, since this attitude opens a door to an orgy of unscrupulousness which undermines the very basis of human dignity.

Prophecies About Future Victories

It is narrated by a reliable authority that, while digging the trench, there appeared a very hard rock which could not be broken by the *Muslims*. Seeing the helplessness of his companions the Prophet took up a pick-axe in his hand and got down in the trench. He struck hard at the stone which gave way emitting a spark. The Prophet raised, with a loud voice the cry of *Allahu Akbar* (God is the Greatest) and remarked : "I have been given the keys of Syria. With my own eyes I see the red palaces of that land". He struck another blow, the stone was split and another spark was emitted. He again raised the slogan of *Allahu Akbar* and observed : "I have been given the keys of Persia. By God I see the white palaces of *Madā'in.*" The third attempt broke the stone into pieces and the Prophet announced that he would be given the keys of *Yemen.* "By God ! I have been shown at this place the gates of *San'à.*"[55]

The pages of history bear out the fact that the prophecies of the Holy Prophet came out to be true in all details and these kingdoms which at the time of the prophecy were so formidable that the *Muslims* could, by no stretch of imagination, conceive of their conquests, fell like a house of cards before the rising tide of the *Muslim* power.

---

55. Ibn Ḥajar al-'Asqalānī, *Fatḥ al-Bāri*, Vol. viii, p. 400.

The Actual Fight

The *Muslims* had hardly finished the preparations when the formidable army of the confederates consisting of 24,000 trained warriors, one of the largest forces ever assembled in the history of Arabia, knocked at the gates of *Medina* with the determination to crush *Islām*. The whole of Arabia was thirsting for *Muslim* blood. It was at this critical juncture that a huge number of hypocrites seceded from the Holy Prophet on one pretext or the other. *Banū Qurayzah* who had been his ally, also deserted to the hostile camp since *Huyayy b. Akhtab* the head of the *Banū Naḍīr* had promised them all kinds of concessions and rewards.

Muḥammad (peace be on him) deputed *Sa'd b. Mu'ādh* and *Sa'd b. 'Ubādah* to negotiate with them and persuade them to honour their agreements with the Prophet. All the attempts of these devoted sons of *Islām* proved to be futile. It was an hour of distress for the *Muslims*. The Holy *Qur'ān* has referred to this state of affairs in the following words :

> When they came upon you from above you and from below you and when eyes turned aside and hearts reached the gullets and of *Allāh* ye were imagining various things. There were the believers proven and shaken with a mighty shaking. And when the hypocrites and those in whose hearts is disease were saying : '*Allāh* and His apostle have promised us naught but delusion.' And when a party of them said : 'O inhabitants of *Yathrib*, there is no place for you, so return.' And a party of them asked leave of the Prophet saying : 'Verily our houses lie open'; whereas they lay not open ; they only wished to flee. (xxxiii : 10-13)

But amidst dread and terror, the Holy Prophet could read the fulfilment of what had been promised to him by *Allāh*. He was, therefore, calm and presented an example of supreme fortitude for his companions. Serenity sat undisturbed upon his brow. He made his decisions and gave his orders with astonishing tranquillity.

The allied forces with full supplies of arms and provisions, had besieged *Medina*, while *Muslims*, hungry and weary, guarded the trench day and night. The allies made several attempts to draw the *Muslims* out from their trenches. *Muḥammad* (peace be upon him), however, refused all temptations to fight the enemy, except on his own terms. Every attack upon the moat was repulsed with a heavy loss to the confederacy. Now and again there was a rain of arrows, the charge of horsemen, movement of great companies of men—but, for all their stratagems, the *Meccans* and their allies found *Medina* impregnable.

As each day rolled by, the morale of the confederacy degenerated. Dissension and discontentment appeared in the ranks of the enemy. The siege became increasiagly tiresome. They were also running short of provisions.

About the same time nature also seemed to have entered into a conspiracy against the enemies of *Islām*. A wild wind flapped their tents ominously. Their fires were extinguished, the sand beat hard on their faces and they were panic-stricken by the portents against them. The storm was growing furious. They had already well-nigh fallen out amongst themselves and were about to retreat. The terrific wind proved to be the last straw which broke their backs and the crestfallen and despondent army returned to *Mecca* with its mission unfulfilled. The false gods hung their heads in despair ! The wind thus accomplished for the *Muslims* what they could not do by the strength of their own arms. The Holy *Qur'ān* thus alludes to the incident :

> O ye who believe ! Remember *Allāh's* favour unto you when there came against you hosts, and We sent against them a great wind and hosts ye could not see. And *Allāh* is ever Seer of what ye do. (xxxiii : 9)

Chapter 8

On the Path of Victory

We have seen the march of events in the Prophet's career so far as he tried to defend the Commonwealth of *Islām* against the terrible onslaughts of the enemies.

The Prophet's Home

Before proceeding further let us see what was going on within the home of the Prophet.

The Holy Prophet was kind enough to marry *Zaynab,* the daughter of *Khuzaymah b. al-Hārith.* She was first married to *Jahm b. 'Amr b. al-Hārith,* her cousin, and then to *'Ubaydah b. al-Hārith* who fell a martyr in the battle of *Uḥud.* Noted for her generous disposition, she gained the title of the mother of the poor (*umm al-masākīn*). She survived but a month or two after the marriage and was the only other among the Prophet's wives, besides *Khadijah,* who died in his life-time and was laid to rest in the grave by the Prophet's own sacred hands.

Umm Salamāh was the next to enter the house of the Holy Prophet as his wife. She was the daughter of *Abū Umayyah,* a well-known leader of the *Quraysh.* As a girl she embraced *Islām* and had been married to *'Abd Allah,* one of the earlier converts and a devoted companion of the Holy Prophet. Both husband and wife suffered severe persecution at the hands of the *Meccans* and fled to Abyssinia, whence they returned to *Mecca* and were subjected once again to the same kind of persecution. A few years later when the Prophet and his companions sought refuge in *Medina,* *'Abd Allah* known as *Abū Salamāh* joined the Prophet, but his beloved wife *Umm Salamāh* was forcibly detained by her cruel father. It was a terrible shock for the lady to have been separated from her devoted husband. She, however, prevailed upon her father to grant her permission to migrate. She sped towards

Medina along with her child and joined her husband there.

But her misfortunes were not yet ended. Her husband, *'Abd Allah,* who had sustained several wounds in the battle of *Uḥud,* did not live long to comfort her and share with her the joys of life. He died within a few months, leaving a pregnant wife behind him. It was a terrible blow to the noble lady who had been suffering shock after shock since her conversion to *Islām.* She was prepared to meet the fury of the time rather than that of her father who was a deadly enemy of the Divine Faith. She was helpless with none to fall back upon. The Holy Prophet, who had already been very sympathetic towards her on account of her steadfastness in the path of *Allah* and the persecutions that she had suffered boldly in the cause of *Islām,* was moved to pity at this latest stroke of misfortune which deprived her of the love and care of a noble husband. Noticing her miserable plight, the Prophet decided to marry her. She told the Holy Prophet that her age was sufficiently advanced and her family was large, but the Messenger of *Allah* assured her that these things were immaterial. He would be very glad to take care of her children. This assurance held out to her by the Prophet was fully honoured by him.

Zaynab bint Jahsh

The other marriage of the Holy Prophet was with *Zaynab* the daughter of *Jaḥsh.* This union which was meant to give a fatal blow to the custom of adoptive kinship, has been adversely criticised by the Western critics of *Islām.* The fanciful stories which are narrated in connection with this marriage are the fabrications of their own minds and there is not even an iota of truth in any one of them.

The story of the marriage is quite simple. *Zaynab* (God be pleased with her) was the daughter of the Prophet's aunt. *Muḥammad* (peace be on him) had been deputed by *Allah* to level down all distinctions of caste, creed and colour and to establish universal brotherhood and equality among human beings. He wanted to set an example in his own house and as a consequence of that he proposed to his aunt that her daughter *Zaynab* (who was Prophet's cousin-sister) should be married to *Zayd b. Hā'rithah,* his liberated slave. The whole family and even *Zaynab* wanted that the Prophet himself should accept her as his wife, but yielded under his pressure who was anxious to abolish false distinctions of high birth. The alliance was brought about with great difficulty but it did not prove congenial. Both *Zayd* and his wife were good people in their own way and both loved the Prophet, but there was mutual incompatibility and this proved to be a stumbling block in creating a happy atmosphere of married life.

Both were, therefore, anxious for separation. But the Prophet did not approve of this and they managed to drift along with each other willy-nilly for some time more. They had come almost to the breaking point and had been convinced of the fact that with this glaring difference in their temperaments they could not get on as husband and wife. They, therefore, took to the last resort—divorce, and secured separation from each other.

This separation was indeed a loss to both of them, but it was more shocking for *Zaynab*, who, being the lady of high birth, was divorced by a freedman. The Holy Prophet owed great responsibility to *Zaynab* and her family. It was he who had arranged the marriage when the whole of her family was opposed to it. Now this divorce had humiliated them still further. *Muḥammad* (peace be on him) was generous enough to marry her himself and thus retrieved for her family a lost prestige and also removed the false conception that the divorce of a woman at the hand of a freed slave ever degraded her position.

These were some of the considerations no doubt but the real objective behind this marriage was to bury for ever the un-Islamic custom of adoptive kinship which had taken a deep root in the minds of the people. As the Holy Prophet was the last link in the golden chain of prophethood, he was required to purge human society of all those customs and superstitions which ran counter to the canons of *Islām*.

Thus with this marriage of *Muhammad* (peace be on him) with *Zaynab*, the divorced wife of his adopted son, the custom of regarding the adopted sons as the real sons, was buried for ever. The Holy *Qurān* speaks of this incident in these words :

> Then, when *Zayd* had attained his purpose concerning her, We wedded her to thee, so that there should be no blame for believers in respect of wives of their adopted sons, when they have attained their purpose concerning them. And the ordinance of *Allāh* was to be fulfiled. (xxxiii : 37).

Then the Holy *Qur'ān* also lays down in unequivocal terms the basic fact about the prophethood of *Muḥammad* (peace be on him) that *Muḥammad* is not the father of any male amongst the Believers, he is the last of the prophets and as such he has to uproot all those conventions which are un-Islamic and has to deliver to the human race a Divine Code of Life perfect in all respects, in order to obviate the need of any other prophet as long as the world lasts :

> *Muḥammad* (peace be on him) is not the father of any of your men, but he is the Apostle of God and the last[1] of

---

1. This word is read as (*khatam*) which means 'seal'. Even if this word is taken in the meaning of seal, we find no justification for the claims of those who take it to be a plea for the continuation of prophethood. When a document is sealed, it is complete and there can be no further addition to it. In the Holy Prophet *Muḥammad* (peace be on him), therefore, there has been a culmination and finality of prophethood. No prophet would be raised after him. If the verse is studied in the context in which it was revealed it would become evident that other meaning except the finality of the prophethood in *Muḥammad* becomes a sort of paradox. The Holy *Qur'ān* is giving an account of the marriage of *Zayd* with *Zaynab*, then the dissolution of this union and the Prophet's hesitation to marry the divorced wife of his adopted son : his fears about the stir that it would create in a society where this custom was greatly honoured. Upon this the Prophet is told by God :

> No blame is there upon the Prophet in that which *Allah* hath decreed for him. That hath been *Allah's* dispensation with those who have passed away afore and the ordinance of *Allah* hath been a destiny destined. Those who preached the message of *Allah* and feared Him and feared none save *Allah* and *Allah* sufficeth as a Reckoner.
>
> (xxxiii : 39)

In these verses the Prophet has been reminded of the fact that gross misrepresentation and calumny have been the inevitable lot of all those who were deputed by *Allah* to convey His message to mankind and thus there is no cause for anxiety. He should, however, carry out the behests of his Master without caring a bit for the criticism of the people. He is not the father of any man in relation of blood : he is a spiritual guide for them and his relationship with them is thus entirely different from the blood relationship of fatherhood. And as he is the last of the prophets it is through him alone that even the last remnant of ignorance, i.e., adoptive affinity is to be finished. If from the Word *khatam* (seal) someone ineptly implies a sanction for the advent of other prophets after *Muḥammad* then the next phrase : "that he is the seal of the prophets" becomes superfluous : an expression which does not fit in with the context. When the new prophets are to be raised, this can be done away with at a later stage. The idea expressed in this verse becomes meaningful only when we take it in the sense of finality.

the Prophets ; And God has complete Knowledge of all things. (xxxiii : 40)

Fabrications of the Orientalists

So far as the fanciful stories and calumnies of the Orientalists are concerned, we can only say that these are so absurd that any one having even a grain of sense in him would unhesitatingly reject them as mere fabrications. William Muir and so many others like him state that the Prophet, having seen *Zaynab* by chance through a half-open door, was fascinated by her beauty, and that *Zayd* having come to know of the leanings of his master, divorced her and then she was married to *Muḥammad*[2]. There is absolutely no truth in these stories which have been fabricated in this connection[3]. *Zaynab* was the daughter of the Prophet's real aunt. There was no seclusion of women before her marriage with him and as such he had not only seen the lady when she was still unmarried but knew her well enough on account of her close kinship and her early conversion to *Islām*. The whole family had initially offered her hand in marriage to the Holy Prophet, but he declined to accept this offer and insisted that she should be married to his freed slave in order to give a fatal blow to the distinctions of high birth : "The Prophet's marriage with *Zaynab*." says Bosworth Smith, "raised an outcry among the *Arabs* of ignorance, not because they suspected an intrigue on the Prophet's part to secure a divorce ; but because they looked upon the adopted as though he were real son, and considered, therefore, that the marriage fell within the prohibited degrees. This restriction, which *Muḥammad*, for whatever causes, considered to be an arbitrary one, he abolished by his marriage, not for his own benefit but for that of the *Arabs* at large. In the view, indeed, usually taken of the whole transaction, there is a strange compound of fact and fiction ; and much that was comparatively innocent has been made to wear the appearance of deep guilt."[4] He also says "Anyhow it is certain that *Zaid*, if he had suspected,

---

2. William Muir, *The Life of Muhammad*, p. 281.
3. Ibn Kathīr in his *Tafsīr* has rejected all such stories. See his commentary in connection with the verse :
(33 : 37) اتق الله و تخفی فی نفسک ما الله مبد یه . . . . .
4. *Mohammed and Mohammedanism* (London, 1876), p. 135.

as Christians have done, anything in the nature of an intrigue on the Prophet's part to alienate his wife's affection from him, could not have served him as he did even to the day of death with all the loyalty and devotion of a zealous disciple."[5]

The Treaty of *Hudaybiah*

We again take up the story of the Prophet's strenuous efforts towards the spread of the Divine Faith. *Muḥammad* (peace be on him) was the Messenger of *Allah* and as such all his energies were directed to one end ; that the people should shed ignorance and enter the fold of *Islām*. This was the be-all and end-all of his struggle, the very alpha and omega of his aspirations. He adopted all possible measures to promote this cause. He tried to preach and win adherents to his cause, to defend it against the attacks of the enemy and, if need be, enter into treaties and agreements. The use of the sword was not the only means adopted by him, but so many other peaceful measures were also adopted in order to awaken the minds of the people to the Truth with which he had been sent by *Allah*. The treaty of *Ḥudaybiah* is an important phase of the Prophet's all-round struggle for the propagation of *Islām*.

It was about the sixth year of the *Hijrah* when the Prophet saw in a dream that he had entered the sacred precincts of the *Ka'bah* in security with his followers and was performing the ceremonies of pilgrimage. Their heads were being shaved and the hair cut off. As soon as the Prophet informed some of his companions the contents of his dream, their hearts leaped with joy since they found in it the realization of their deep longing to take part in pilgrimage and its hallowed rites after an exile of full six years.

This month was one of peace—*Dhū al-Qa'dah*—in which *'umra*[6] could fitly be performed. So *Muḥammad* (peace be on him), after inviting the neighbouriug tribes to join him, set forth

---

5. *Mohammed and Mohammedanism* (London, 1876), p. 126.

6. *'Umrah* (عمرة) is the minor pilgrimage, with only a few rites. Literally 'a visit' or 'a visiting', it is technically a religious visit to the sacred place at Mecca with the performance of the ceremony of circumambulation around the *Ka'bah* and the running between *al-Safā* and *al-Marwāh*. *Hajj* differs from it inasmuch as it is held at a particular time of the year and is not complete without the halting at *'Arafāt* on the day of *'Arafah*.

at the head of fifteen hundred of his followers[7] including both the emigrants and the helpers. Elated with joy at the idea of paying visit to the *Ka'bah*, the *Muslims* confidently marched forward and seventy camels were taken along for sacrifice.

As they approached the sacred territory, all donned the *iḥrām*, the pilgrim's garb and shouted, "*Labbayk Allāhumma Labbayk !* (Here are we, O Lord !). They carried no weapons save sheathed swords, and had no intention of fighting. But the *Meccans* were resolved to stop them. A large army was gathered and the road to *Mecca* was completely blocked. On hearing this news *Muḥammad* turned aside to *Ḥudaybiyah* on the border of the *Meccan* territory and encamped there. When the Prophet (peace be on him) had taken rest *Budayl b. Warqā al-Khuzā'ī* came to him with some men of the *Khuzā'ah* tribe and asked him what he had come for. The Prophet replied that it was not for war that he had come forth : "I have no other design," he said, "but to perform the pilgrimage of the Holy Sanctuary". The next man sent for negotiations was *Mikrāz b. Ḥafs b. al-Akhyaf.* He was followed by another emissary known, as *al-Hulays b. 'Alqamah.* He was very much impressed by the spirit of devotion that the *Muslims* had for the Holy *Ka'bah.* He came back to his men and said ; "*Ye men of Quraysh,* it is not for this that we made an alliance and agreement with you. Should a man who comes to do honour to God's house be excluded from it ? By Him Who holds our lives in His hand, either you let *Muḥammad* do what he has come to do, or I shall take away my troops to the last man."[8] *Hulays* was succeeded by *'Urwah* to negotiate with *Muslims.* In the course of discussion he said to the Prophet : "*Muḥammad !* have you gathered around yourself a mixed people and then brought them against your own kith and kin in order to destroy them ? *Quraysh* have come out with their milch-camels, clad in leopard skins, swearing that you shall never enter *Mecca* by force. By God I think I see you deserted by these people tomorrow."[9] At this *Abū Bakr* stood up and expressed his resentment at this imputation. Meanwhile *'Urwah,* during his stay in the *Muslim* camp, had been closely watching the unfathomable love and profound

7. Ibn Qayyim, *Zād al-Ma'ād,* (Egypt, 1373 A.H.). Vol. ii, p. 301.
8. *Ibn Hishām,* Vol. iii, p. 336.
9. *Ibid.,* p. 327.

respect that the followers of *Muḥammad* showed him. He returned to the *Quraysh* and conveyed them his impression that those people could not forsake the Prophet under any circumstances. He expressed his feelings in the following words :

> I have been to Chosroes in his kingdom, and Caesar in his kingdom and the Negus in his kingdom, but never have I seen a king among a people like *Muḥammad* among his companions. If he makes his ablutions they would not let the water thereof fall on the ground : if a hair of his falls down they vie with each other in order to secure that. They will not abandon him for anything in any case. Do what you please.[10]

The High-handedness of the *Quraysh*

Time rolled on. Negotiations went on but with no result. *Muḥammad* (peace be upon him) sent a messenger to meet the *Quraysh* and to impress upon them his desire as well as that of his companions to perform pilgrimage but he was maltreated. The legs of the camel on which messenger rode were cut off. His own life was hardly spared. An armed *Quraysh* detachment also came out to take the *Muslims* by surprise, but was itself taken captive. The *Muslims*, however, had no desire to fight and hence set them free. The Prophet desired *'Umar* to see the nobles of the *Quraysh* on his behalf. *'Umar* excused himself on account of the personal enmity of the *Quraysh* ; he had, moreover, no influential relatives in the city who could shield him from danger ; and he pointed to *'Uthmān b. 'Affān*, who belonged to one of the most powerful families in *Mecca*, as the suitable envoy. *'Uthmān* went to *Abū Sufyān* and other chiefs and told them that they had come only to visit and pay their homage to the Holy House, to do worship there and that they had no intention to fight.

'Uthmān also assured them that after the performance of ceremonies they would soon depart peacefully. But the *Quraysh* were adamant and were not prepared to grant them the permission to visit the *Ka'bah*. They, however, offered *'Uthmān* the permission to perform the pilgrimage, if he so desired in his individual capacity, but *'Uthmān* (may *Allah* be pleased with him) declined the offer saying : "How is it possible that I avail

---

10. *Ibn Hishām*, op cit., p. 328.

myself of this opportunity, when the Holy Prophet (peace and blessings of *Allah* be upon him) is denied of this ?[11]

The *Muslims* anxiously waited for the arrival of *Uthmān* with mingled feelings of joy and fear. But his arrival was considerably delayed and a foul play was suspected on the part of the *Quraysh*. The *Muslims* were greatly perturbed and they took a solemn pledge at the hand of the Holy Prophet that they would sacrifice their lives to avenge the death of their companion and would stand firmly by their benefactor, *Muḥammad*, (peace be upon him) under all conditions. This pledge goes by the name of *Bay'at al-Riḍwān*. It was a resolution of sacrifice in the cause of Truth and an ardent expression of the strong feelings of devotion and love for the Holy Prophet. The *Qur'ān* has referred to this pledge in the following words :

> Certainly *Allah* was well pleased with the believers when they swore allegiance to you under the tree and He knew what was in their hearts, so He sent down tranquillity on them and rewarded them with a victory in the near future [12] (xlviii : 18)

When the *Quraysh* saw the firm determination of the *Muslims* to shed the last drop of blood for the defence of their faith they come to their senses and realized that they could not be cowed down by these tactics. After some further interchange of messages they agreed to conclude a treaty of peace with the *Muslims*. Some dispute arose with regard to the preamble. For example, when the agreement was to be committed to writing, *'Ali* who acted as a scribe, began with the words : *Bi-ism-Allah ar-Raḥmān ar-Raḥīm*, i.e., "In the name of *Allah*, the Beneficent, the Merciful" but the *Meccan* plenipotentiary, *Suhayl b. 'Amr* declared that he knew nothing about *al-Raḥmān* and insisted upon the customary formula *Bi-īsmka Allāhumma*, i.e. "In Thy name, O God !" The *Muslims* grumbled with uneasiness but the Holy Prophet agreed. He then went on to dictate, "This is what *Muḥammad*, the Messenger of *Allah* has agreed to with *Suhayl b. 'Amr*." Upon this *Suhayl* again protested : "Had I acknowledged you as a prophet, I would not have fought against you. Write your own name and the name of your father." The

11. *Ibn Hishām*, op. cit., p. 329.
12. This refers to the victory of Khaybor.

Muslims grumbled as before and refused to consent to the change. The Holy Prophet, however, in the larger interests of *Islām*, attached no importance to such an insignificant detail and dictated the words : "*Muḥammad*, the son of *'Abdullāh*" instead.

The Terms of the Treaty

The following were the terms on which the two parties agreed :

(1) That year the *Muslims* would not perform pilgrimage.

(2) Next year they would be permitted to do so, provided they did not stay in *Mecca* for more than three days.

(3) The *Muslims* should bear no arms except sheathed swords during their next visit.

(4) Whosoever wished to join *Muḥammad* or enter into treaty with him, should have the liberty to do so ; and likewise whosoever wished to join the *Quraysh*, or enter into treaty with them, should be allowed to do so.

(5) If any one went over to *Muḥammad* without the permission of his guardian, he should be sent back to the *Quraysh*, but should any of the followers of *Muḥammad* return to *Quraysh*, he shall not be sent back.

(6) War should be suspended for ten years so that the people might live in peace.[13]

The terms were distasteful to many *Muslims* but most of them kept quiet, thinking that they did not possess the vision wide enough to comprehend fully the mysteries of this truce, which *Allah* had revealed to His messenger. It was during this time, when the *Muslims* were feeling crest-fallen that *Abū Jandal*, the son of *Suhayl* appeared on the scene. He was brutally chained and was staggering with privation and fatigue. The Prophet and his companions were moved to pity and tried to secure his release but *Suhayl* was adamant and said : "To signify that you are faithful to your contract an opportunity has just arrived." "But the treaty was not yet signed," said the Prophet,

13. *Ibn Sa'd*, series I, Vol. ii (Leiden-Brill), pp. 70-71.

"when your son entered the camp." Upon this he burst forth and said, "But the terms of the treaty were agreed upon."

One required to have a heart of stone not to be moved by this tragic spectacle. It was an unbearable sight for the *Muslims* to return *Abū Jandal* to the tyrants. *'Umar* could not help giving vent to the deep-seated agony of his heart. He said to the Prophet, "Arn't you the true Messenger of *Allah* ?" The Prophet replied calmly, "Why not ?" *'Umar* again spoke and asked : "Arn't we on the path of righteousness and our enemies in the wrong ?" Without showing any resentment *Muḥammad* (peace be upon him) replied that it was so. On getting this reply he further argued : "Then we should not suffer any humiliation in the matter of faith." The Prophet was unruffled and with perfect confidence said : "I am the true Messenger of *Allah*, I never disobey Him, He shall help me." "Did you not tell us," rejoined *'Umar*, "that we shall perform pilgrimage ?" "But I never told you", replied the Apostle of *Allah*, "that we shall do so this very year."[14] *'Umar* was silenced but his mind was disturbed.[15] He went to *Abū Bakr* and expressed his feelings before him. *Abū Bakr*, who knew no doubts and was always ready to accept the words of his master as gospel truth, confirmed what *Muḥammad* had told him.

The Prophet Honours his Words

In brief, the *Muslims* were very anxious about the fate of *Abū Jandal*, but it was also a crucial test of the *Muslims'* word of honour. In silent resignation was therefore *Abū Jandal* borne away with his chains. It was indeed an anxious moment. On the one hand, *Abū Jandal* was lamenting at the top of his voice, "Am I to be returned to the polytheists that they may entice me from my religion, O *Muslims* !" but, on the other hand, the faithful engagement was also considered to be necessary, above all other considerations. A word of the Prophet was something holy, something which admitted no ambiguity, a contract could not be broken. The Prophet's heart welled up with sympathy,

14. *Ṣaḥīḥ Bukhārī, Kitāb at-Shurūt*, Section : Shurūt fil-Jihād, (Cairo) Vol. ii, pp. 121-22.

15. This argumentation often rankled in the heart of *'Umar* and he was repentant on this hasty step and performed many religious acts over and above what were enjoined upon him as a *Muslim* for his atonement.

but he wanted to honour his word at all cost. He consoled *Abū Jandal* and said, "Be patient, resign yourself to the will of *Allah. Allah* is going to provide for you and your helpless companions relief and means of escape. We have concluded a treaty of peace with them and we have taken the pledge in the name of *Allah.* We are, therefore, under no circumstances prepared to break it."[16]

When peace was concluded the Prophet slaughtered his animals which he had brought with him and shaved his head, and turned his steps back to *Medina.* Some of the *Muslims* were quite dejected. Midway between *Mecca* and *Medina* God revealed to *Muḥammad* (peace be upon him) the chapter of the Holy *Qur'ān* entitled *Al-Fatḥ* (Victory). The Holy Prophet was extremely happy, for God had told him distinctly in this chapter that the treaty of *Ḥudaybiyāh* was not a humiliation for the *Muslims* but a clear victory and promised him a succession of victories in future and confirmed everything that he had done and consoled the drooping hearts of the faithful :

> "Verily We ! a victory have given unto thee, a manifest victory. That *Allah* may forgive thee that which hath proceeded of thy fault[17] and that which may come later and may accomplish the more favour on thee, and may keep thee guided on the straight path, And that *Allah* may succour thee with a mighty succour."
>
> (xlviii : 1-3)

"And there was never a victory", says *Ibn Hishām*, "greater than this, for, as *al-Zuhri* rightly observes, when it was the state of war, the people were afraid of meeting with one another, but when the truce came and the fears of war were dispelled and there prevailed a sense of peace among the people, they came nearer and entered into discussion with one another. And no man spoke of *Islām* to another but that the latter espoused it, so that there came within the fold of *Islām* in two years (i.e. between the treaty of *al-Ḥudaybiyāh* and the breaking of the

---

16. *Ibn Hishām*, Vol. iii, p. 333.

17. *Dhanb* differs from *ithm* in being either intentional or committed through inadvertence, whereas ذنب is peculiarly intentional, when spoken of in reference to the prophets it means an act of inadvertence, not blameable in itself, but somewhat below their high rank.

truce by the *Quraysh*) as many individuals as had not entered before."[18]

The most distressing clause which was considered objectionable in the *Muslim* camp was regarding the returning of a believer to his guardian if he came to seek refuge in *Medina*. But even this proved to be a great blessing. The *Muslims* sent back to *Mecca*, were not likely to renounce the blessings of *Islām* ; on the other hand *Muslims* going to *Mecca* proved to be the centres of influence for *Islām*. It was impossible to think that they would become apostates or renegades.

Moreover, some of the *Muslims* who were sent back to *Mecca* managed to escape from the grip of their cruel guards and settled on the coast of Arabia. Gradually other *Muslims* who were leading a miserable life under the atrocities of the *Quraysh* joined them till a fair-sized colony was formed and soon sought revenge upon the passing *Quraysh* caravans. The pagans of *Mecca* finding themselves unable to control these exiled colonists, begged the Holy Prophet (peace be upon him) to do away with the clause which governed the extradition : and thus *Allah* found a way as was promised by Him.

The Treaty Proves Advantageous to the *Muslims*

In fact, every clause of this treaty was a masterpiece of practical statesmanship. It was a triumph beyond doubt. No one, except "perhaps *Suhayl*, had thought back as had *Muḥammad* when the *Quraysh* stood before him. No one except these two, recollected the beatings, the stonings, the escape by night, the hiding in the cave. No one thought of the hazardous exile with the seventy followers. The contrast between now and then was unbelievable, miraculous. That the *Quraysh* were willing to deal with *Muḥammad* at all, to recognize him as someone worthy of their attention, to admit him as the ruler of the *Arab* Community was beyond the bounds of all expectation. He was not a man to quibble over small details. If *Suhayl's* limited mentality could not reconcile itself to calling someone who had been a travelling salesman by a grandiloquent title ; it did not really matter. What was important was to have free access to *Mecca*. *Muḥammad* (peace be upon him) knew that the

18. *Ibn Hishām*. Vol. iii, pp. 336-37.

day he and his men could set foot in the Holy City would not be long before they would be there permanently."[19] "The ten years' truce would, therefore, afford opportunity and time for the new religion to expand, and force its claim upon the convictions of the *Quraysh*. The stipulation that no one under the protection of a guardian should leave the *Quraysh* without his guardian's consent, though unpopular at *Medina*, was in accordance with the principles of Arabian society ; and the Prophet had sufficient confidence in the loyalty of his own people and the superior attractions of *Islām*, to fear no ill effect from the counter clause that none should be delivered up who might desert his standard. Above all, it was a great and manifest success that free permission was conceded to the believers to visit *Mecca* in the following year, and to stay in the city for three days undisturbed."[20]

This treaty had a wonderful effect on the local tribes and what the Holy Prophet had foreseen in this connection proved to be perfectly true. Within a few days of signing the document, which had caused a stir among some of his men, chiefs from all around were coming to swear allegiance to him.

The treaty is a specimen of the finest draft in which the clauses of peace were clearly laid down. There is no ambiguity, nothing hazy about it. Every word is pointed, unequivocal and highly meaningful, nothing superfluous, and no playing of words. "The treaty of *Ḥudaybiyāh*," says *Majid Khadduri*, "was looked upon as a model for drawing up the draft of the arbitration treaty."[21]

Islam—the Universal Religion

Who could be more conscious than *Muḥammad* (peace be upon him) of the universal nature of the teachings of *Islām* and the responsibilities that fell on the Prophet for spreading its message in the whole world. The God of *Islām* is *Rabb al-'Ālamīn*, the Lord of the universe : He is the *Rabb al-nās, Malik al-nās, Ilāh al-nās*—the Lord, the King and God of men : not only of Jews, Christians or *Muslims*, alone but the Lord of all the creation ; the Creator and Sustainer of all mankind, and not a

19. R. V. C. Bodley, *The Messenger* (Lahore 1954), p. 219.
20. William Muir, *The Life of Mohammad*, p. 348.
21. Majid Khadduri, *War and Peace in the Law of Islam*, p. 235.

tribal deity who is pre-occupied with the destinies of one particular tribe or nation, adjusting all peoples to the requirements of a chosen few. Just as God is the Lord of the whole universe, similarly His last Prophet (peace be upon him) is the Mercy for all the worlds :

> We have not sent thee save as a mercy to all the created beings. (xxi : 107)

So is the case with the religion that he preached. Its message is universal and transcends all barriers of caste and colour and those created by geography :

> Blessed is He who hath sent down *al-Furqān* upon His servant, that he may be a warner unto all created beings. (xxv : 1)

The Prophet Plans to Spread the Message of *Islam* beyond *Arabia*

The Holy Prophet was fully aware of the responsibilities that he owed to humanity as the last Messenger of God. Thus in the atmosphere of general security which the treaty of *Ḥudaybiyāh* had provided him, he found it a heaven-sent opportunity to turn his attention to other nations beyond Arabia in order to deliver to them the Message of *Allah*. Once he called his companions and addressed them in the following words :

> "O ye men ! God has sent me a blessing to all mankind. Carry the message of *Islām* to all the corners of the world. Differ not as differed the disciples of Jesus, the son of Mary."
>
> "And how did they differ ?" asked his companions.
>
> He replied, "Jesus called them to what I am calling you, but he who was sent on a short journey obeyed and accepted his mission and he who was despatched afar showed reluctant attitude before his Lord and the Almighty awarded them the punishment that thenceforth every one amongst them could speak only the language of the people to whom he was sent."[22]

---

22. Abū Ja'far Muḥammad ibn Jarīr Ṭabarī, *Tārikh al-Rusul wa'l Mulūk* ed. M. J. de Geoje (Leiden 1881-82), Series I, Vol. iii, p. 1560.

Embassies to Foreign Rulers

Envoys were chosen by the Holy Prophet to carry the light of *Islām* to all those corners where darkness prevailed. In order to authenticate the credentials of his envoys, a silver seal was made in which were graven the words : "*Muḥammad* the Messenger of *Allah.*"[23]

The Envoy to Heraclius

The first mission was sent to Heraclius. When the *Muslim* envoy, *Dihyah Kalbī*, reached Palestine, he was informed that the Emperor was celebrating his victory over the Persians by paying a visit to Jerusalem—the cradle of his faith ; and thus it was here that the Prophet's letter was delivered to him. The *Muslim* envoy was received amidst numerous ceremonies. He delivered the following introductory speech before presenting him the letter :

> "O Caesar of Rome ! the one who has sent me as an envoy to you is better than yourself and the Exalted Lord Who has sent him to us as Prophet is the Greatest of All. So listen to me with full attention and give an earnest reply. If you do not pay full heed you may not be able to catch its meaning and if your answer does not come out of sincere heart, it will not be just. O King ! you are well aware of the fact that Jesus, the son of Mary, offered prayers."
>
> The King replied in the affirmative. "Then I invite you," said *Dihyah Kalbī*, "to that Great Lord to Whom Jesus offered his prayers, prostrated himself and Who shaped him in the womb of Mary and Who created the heavens and the earth. Then I invite you to that unlettered Prophet whose advent has been foretold by Moses and Jesus and you have a complete knowledge of all these facts. If you accept the message preached by him you shall get immense reward in this world and the world to come. But in case you reject it, you shall be denied of them. Believe me, there is one Great Master Who punishes the disbelievers and changes their fortunes.''[24]

---

23. *Zurqānī*, Vol. iii, p. 334.
24. Suhaylī, *al-Rauḍul Unuf* (Cairo, 1332 A.H.), Vol. ii, p. 355.

Abu Sufyan's Testimony

Incidentally, *Abū Sufyān*, who by that time had not embraced *Islām*, was summoned to the court and Heraclius asked him many questions about *Muḥammad* (peace be upon him) and the religion which he preached. The testimony which this avowed enemy of the Prophet gave regarding the personal excellence of the Prophet's character and the good that *Islām* was doing to the human race, left Heraclius wonder-struck.

Contents of the Prophet's Letter

Then the Prophet's letter was read aloud, which rendered into English, is as follows :

> In the name of *Allah*, the Compassionate, the Merciful. This letter is being sent by *Muḥammad* to Heraclius, the Emperor of Rome.
>
> Blessed are those who follow true guidance. I invite you to embrace *Islām*. If you do so, you shall be safe and secure. If you come within its fold, God will give you double reward and in case you turn your back upon it, then the burden of the sins of people shall fall on your shoulders.
>
> O people of the Book ! come to the word that is common between us and between you that we shall worship none save *Allah* and that we shall not associate aught with Him and that none of us shall take others as lords besides *Allah*. Then if they turn away, say : Bear witness that verily we are *Muslims*.[25]

The observations of the Emperor and finally the definite and clear-cut exposition of the *Islamic* message could not but create a tense atmosphere amongst the clergy present at the court. The King did not embrace *Islam*—for it was differently ordained but the *Muslim* envoy was returned to *Medina* with the felicitations of the Emperor.

Letter to Chosroes

Not long after, another despatch, bearing the same seal and couched almost in similar terms, was sent to Chosroes, the

---

25. Ibn Qayyim, *Zād al-Ma'ād*, Cairo, edited by Muḥammad Ḥamīd Alfāqī, Vol. iii, pp. 126-27.

Emperor of Persia. The proud monarch was enraged by the style of the letter as the name of the Holy Prophet had been put above his own name. He could not tolerate such an audacity. He tore the letter into shreds and forthwith dictated a command to his viceroy in *Yemen* to send a couple of troopers to arrest the Holy Prophet and bring him to his presence. The Governor, *Bāzān* by name, immediately sent two men to *Medina* for the purpose. In the past it was commonplace for their soldiers to arrest any of the *Arabs*. When the reaction of the King was reported to the Holy Prophet by *'Abd Allah b. Hudhayfah*, the *Muslim* envoy, he calmly replied : "*Allah* will rend and scatter his kingdom into pieces in the same way as he has torn my letter." As soon as the men of *Bāzān* reached *Medina* the Prophet was informed by a divine revelation that *Parvez*, the Emperor of Persia, had been murdered by his son. The Holy Prophet disclosed to them this news and they were stunned. They hurried back to their kingdom and found to their great surprise that the words of *Muḥammad* (peace be upon him) were quite true. *Parvez* had been assassinated and his son had succeeded him. The glory of Persia had departed. *Bāzān* embraced Islām and gladly signified his adhesion to the Holy Prophet.[26]

A Deputation to Abyssinia

The court of Abyssinia stood in a different relation to *Muḥammad* (peace be upon him) from that of the other kingdoms to which he addressed his apostolic letters. There his followers had received hospitable treatment at the hands of the King and had found a refuge against the atrocities of the *Arabs*. The Holy Prophet had a soft corner in his heart for this Christian king and had an admiration for his benevolent behaviour towards the *Muslims*. The following are the contents of the letter :

> "In the name of *Allah*, the Compassionate, the Merciful. This letter is being sent by *Muḥammad*, the Apostle of God, to Negus, the King of Abyssinia. Salutations. Glory be to *Allah*, there is no God but He, the Sovereign, the Holy, the Author of safety, the Giver of peace, the Protector, the Mighty. I bear witness that Jesus, the son

26. Abu Ja'far Muḥammad ibn Jarir Tabarī, *Tā'rikh al-Rusul wa'l-Mulūk* (Leiden), Series I, Vol. iii, p. 1571-75.

of Mary, is the Spirit of God and His Word which cast into Mary, the virgin, the good, the pure, so that she conceived Jesus. God created him from His Spirit and His breathing as He created *Adam* by His hand and breathing. I call you to God, the Unique, without any associate and to His obedience and to follow me and to believe in that which has come to me, for I am the Messenger of *Allah.* I invite you and your men to the Great Lord. Please listen to what I say and accept my advice. Peace be upon him who follows true guidance."[27]

The King receives the Envoy with Veneration

The King received the envoy and the letter with special veneration and sent a very respectful reply in which he confessed his faith in *Islām* and expressed his regret over his liability to join the Prophet's standard in person. We produce below his letter :

> "In the name of *Allah,* the Compassionate, the Merciful. From the Negus to *Muḥammad,* the Apostle of *Allah.* Peace be upon you, O Messenger of *Allah* ! and mercy and blessing from *Allah* beside Whom there is no God. I have received your letter in which you have mentioned about Jesus and by the Lord of heaven and earth Jesus is no more than what you say. We fully acknowledge that with which you were sent to us and we have entertained your nephew and his companions. I bear witness that you are the Messenger of Allah, true and confirming (those who have gone before you), I pledge to you through your nephew and surrender myself through him to the Lord of the worlds."[28]

Envoy sent to *Hauza*

The messenger sent to *Hauza,* the chief of *Banu Ḥanīfah,* a Christian tribe in Yemen, was entertained hospitably. In reply to the Prophet's epistle *Hauza* showed his approval of *Islām* provided he was given a share in the government, a fantastic demand which could not be met. His demand betrayed gross

---

27. Ḥāfiz Ibn Qayyim, *Zād al-Ma'ād,* Vol. iii, p. 127.
28. *Ibn Qayyim,* op. cit., p. 128.

ignorance of the position and status of *Muḥammad* (peace be upon him) and the religion which he preached. The spread of faith is not an expansionist movement launched by a political genius for self-aggrandisement. Nor is it a weapon of power-politics. It is in fact a divine mission which *Muḥammad* (peace be upon him) had to carry on as the Apostle of *Allah*. The question of sharing of power was, therefore, absurd as it was not the game of power politics in which the influential men were to be won over through various baits. It was a matter of one's commitment with one's Creator ! It was an unconditional surrender of oneself before one's Lord ! If *Islām* were to be accepted as the code of life, it had to be done strictly on its own merits, and not hedged about by certain conditions.

The Fall of *Khaybar*

Though crest-fallen, the Jewish tribes remained actively engaged in devising ways and means to harm the *Muslims*. They possessed, at the distance of three or four days' journey to the north-east of *Medina*, a strongly fortified territory, studded with castles, the principal of which, called *al-Kamus* was situated on an almost inaccessible hill. This group of fortresses was called *Khaybar*, a word signifying a fortified place. The population of *Khaybar* included several branches of the *Banū-Nadhir*, and the *Quraiza*, who had taken refuge there. The Jews of *Khaybar* had shown an active and implacable hatred towards *Muḥammad* (peace be upon him) and his followers, and since the arrival of their brethren among them, this feeling had acquired greater force.[29]

The Prophet Marches towards *Khaybar*

The Jews of *Khaybar* united by an ancient alliance with the bedouin horde of *Banū Ghaṭafān*, and other cognate tribes, worked incessantly for the formation of another coalition against the *Muslims*. To forestall their hostilities the Prophet marched with a force of 1,400 men in *Muḥarram* 7 A.H. against *Kbaybar*. He marched by way of *Isr* and a mosque was built for him there. Then he went forward with the army till he halted in a valley called *al-Raji* ; halting between the men of *Khaybar* and *Ghaṭafān*

---

29. *Syed Ameer Ali*, op. cit., p. 86.

so as to prevent the latter from reinforcing the Jews because they had an alliance with them.

When the forts of the *Khaybar* became visible to him the Prophet prayed in these words :

> "O God, Lord of the heavens and what they overshadow ! And Lord of the lands and what they make to grow ! And Lord of the devils and unto what arrows they throw ! And Lord of the winds and what they winnow ! We seek goodness from Thee for this habitation and goodness for the people who live in it and goodness for all that which is found in it. We take refuge in Thee from the evil of this habitation and the evil of the people who reside in it and from all sorts of evil found in it."

Then he ordered his men to march forward in the name of the Lord.[30]

The Actual Operation Begins

The Holy Prophet began the campaign by reducing the minor strongholds one after the other. When this was done, he marched against *al-Kamus*, the main fortress of *Khaybar*. It was a formidable looking structure with frowning walls built of the solid rock. All accesses to the fortress were strongly fortified, and within the ramparts was a well-equipped and well-provisioned garrison. The Jews showed great courage and proved too formidable even to the repeated rushes of the veteran soldiers of *Islām*. Then the standard was given to *'Ali*, the Prophet's cousin and his son-in-law who led his men up the battlements again and again to charge, but they were repulsed by the volleys of arrows which rained from behind the parapets. It was indeed a tough fight. The *Muslims*, however, were not dismayed. They dragged on the siege for twenty days and after constant struggle managed to take hold of the forts. Rich booty fell into the hands of the *Muslims*. Besides vast stores of dates, oil, honey and barley, flocks of sheep and herds of camels, the spoils in treasure and jewels was very large.[31]

Khaybar was well-known for the rich soil and fine orchards and their owners were anxious to keep on cultivating them as

30. *Ibn Hishām*, Vol. iii, p. 343.
31. *William Muir*, op. cit., pp 367-68.

usual. They, therefore, approached the Holy Prophet with the request that they should be allowed to cultivate their lands and they would give half of the produce to the *Muslims*. *Muḥammad* (peace be upon him) was kind enough to accede to their request.

Marriage with *Ṣafiyyah*

The Prophet took further steps to make friendship with them. Among the captives of war, there was *Safiyyah*, daughter of *Huyayy b. Akhṭab*, one of the leading Jews. The Prophet liberated her and took her in marriage.

It is significant to note that despite huge fortunes which fell to the lot of *Muslims* in the battle of *Khaybar*, the Holy Prophet's austere living did not show any change. He was an embodiment of simplicity and contentment having no inclination, whatsoever, towards material possessions. His attitude towards riches can be well imagined from the fact that he was to be married to the daughter of the chief of *Banū Nadhir*, buṭ the ceremony was so simple that the guests of the Holy Prophet were asked to bring their own meals and these constituted the wedding feast. Can history show another instance of a conqueror celebrating his wedding amidst riches of triumph in such a simple manner ?

Muslims Visit *Mecca*

According to the terms of the truce of *Hudaybiyāh* towards the close of the seventh year of *Hijrah*, the Prophet set off for *Mecca* in order to perform the pilgrimage, from which he had been turned back the previous year. He proceeded with 2000 *Muslims* and 70 camels for sacrifice.

The pilgrimage was performed strictly in accordance with the terms of the treaty. No armed man entered the city. These were left with a party of two hundred men at a place some eight miles from *Mecca*. The city was deserted, the *Quraysh* had left the place and retired to their tents on the adjoining hills.

The cavalcade halted outside the House of *Allah* saying *Labbaik Allahumma Labbaik* (here I am ! at thy service O *Allah* !) The Muslims entered the Sacred House in great humility. The Holy Prophet rode first to the corner of the *Ka'bah* and kissed the Black Stone. He then began the seven circuits of the shrine.

This done, *Muḥammad* (peace be upon him) led the way up the hills of *Safā*, where he rode from one end to the other seven times. This part of the pilgrimage commemorates Hagar's frantic rushing to and fro between these two points when she was looking for water for the baby, *Isma'il.*

The sacrificial animals were then slaughtered. After that, all the pilgrims had their heads shaved.

The main body of the pilgrims had now performed the initial rites of the lesser pilgrimage, but there remained those who were entrusted the charge of the weapons. *Muḥammad* (peace be upon him) had these relieved, and they went through the same devotional acts as others.

The next day, the Prophet came early to the mosque and remained there till noon prayers when *Bilal* climbed the roof of the *Ka'bah* and called the faithful to prayers. Two thousand *Muslims* prayed with the Holy Prophet. It was surely a strange sight which at this time presented itself in the valley of *Mecca.* The *Muslims,* after the exile of many years, had visited the House of Lord. No one showed any yearning to enter his abandoned home : *Muslims* had bid them good-bye not for worldly ambitions but for the cause of *Allah.* Their wealth, their hearth and homes were, therefore, quite insignificant in their eyes. They had a longing to visit the Sacred House only. The love of God and His Apostle was the most valuable asset for them against which everything is trash.

The *Meccans* who had been perching on the surrounding hills had been listening to the words proclaiming the unity of *Allah,* the apostlehood of *Muḥammad* (peace and blessings of *Allah* be upon him) the value of prayer and had been keenly watching the movements of the faithful. The sublime proclamation was irresistibly penetrating into their hearts. They wondered at these announcements : God is the Greatest, there is no deity but *Allah.* "What sort of men these *Muslims* are ?" they exclaimed. "They are calm and dignified, no clapping of hands, no whistling, no intermingling of sexes. Why is it that scores of their deities which were still kept in the *Ka'bah* were not protesting against this new form of worship ? None hurled thunderbolts or caused the earth to quake. Could not they revenge themselves on *Muḥammad* (peace and blessings of *Allah* be upon him) who had announced publicly that it is all falsehood ? *Allah* alone is to be worshipped. Are they utterly powerless ?" These and other questions were haunting their minds and agitated them to find satisfactory answers to such searching of their souls. These were in fact shaking their beliefs from their very foundations and had been preparing them to accept one great Truth preached by all the Apostles of *Allah* in their own respective times and was finally delivered to humanity by *Muḥammad* (peace and blessings of *Allah* be upon him).

Some of the *Meccans* expressed the feelings of disgust against idolatry. It was alarming for the notables of the *Quraysh*. Jealously they watched the time and on the morning of the fourth day of the pilgrimage they asked *Muḥammad* (peace and blessings of *Allah* be upon him) to leave the city along with his companions. *Muḥammad al-Amīn* (peace be upon him) could not conceive of violating the terms. He, therefore, ordered his men to depart for *Medina*.

This visit of the *Muslims* proved to be a great blessing for the citizens of *Medina*. The self-restraint, the high moral standard, the scrupulous regard for their pledged word displayed by the believers, combined, of course, with their love for God and deep attachment to and profound respect for the Holy Prophet, created an indelible impression among the *Meccans*, and as a consequence of that, many of those who were most violent among the *Quraysh* in their opposition to *Muḥammad* (peace and blessings of *Allah* be upon him) and to his faith, the men of position and influence who had warred against him, could no longer remain his opponents and they, therefore, embraced *Islām*. Among these persons the most notable were *Khālid b. Walīd* and *'Amr ibn al-Āṣ*.

The Holy Prophet Marries *Maymuna b. Harith*

It was during this visit of the Prophet to *Mecca* for pilgrimage that *'Abbas*, the uncle of *Muhammad* (peace be upon him), offered the hand of his sister-in-law, *Maymūna*, the daughter of *Hārith* to him. She was the aunt of *Khālid*, the famous general of the *Muslim* army. The Holy Prophet was kind enough to accept this offer since it was an effective step towards cementing the ties of relationship between the Holy Prophet and those of the influential men of *Mecca*.

Prophet's Marriages

The marriages of the Holy Prophet have furnished his critics with the chief implement of attack and some of them have gone far beyond the limits of justice and decency. The following, however, are the relevant facts regarding the Prophet's marriages :

Polygamy—an Established Institution of Human Society

Polygamy was an established institution of human society dating from the most ancient times. It was practised in Biblical and Talmudic times. The Mosaic law, far from interdicting it, encouraged it. The renowned patriarchs practised it, and so did the judges, the kings and the more spiritually-minded amongst the Jews. According to the *Encyclopaedia Biblica*, "a common Jew could take as many as four wives and a king up to eighteen."[32]

In ancient India, in the age of great sages, plurality of wives was not only allowed in theory but was also commonly practised. This can be abundantly proved by direct references to the Rig Veda and other religious texts of the Hindus. In the case of the king, four wives are expressly mentioned. The heroes and Brahmans of the epic era are frequently represented as having several wives.[33]

The history of religion clearly reveals the fact that the idea that there is something necessarily impure and degrading in polygamy, or that it must be regarded as a somewhat grudging concession to human weakness finds no place in the teachings of the great religions. Almost all the revered spiritual leaders who are known as prophets, with the exception of only two, *i.e.*, Jesus (who never married) and John, practised polygamy and some of them are known to have had as many as hundred wives.[34]

Notwithstanding the strict inculcation of the general principle of self-denial in Christian teachings, there is nothing to suggest that monogamy is in any way higher or holier than the state of polygamy. If it is to be judged strictly from the example set by Jesus, then one should not marry at all. But we find that some of the Christian reformers and leaders of thought not only favoured marriage, but in certain cases advocated polygamy with

32. Cheyne and Blake, *Encyclopaedia Biblica*, Birck (London), p. 2946.

33. Hasting's *Encyclopaedia of Religion and Ethics*, Article 'Marriage', Vol. viii, p. 452.

34. David (May the peace of Allah be upon him).

religious fervour. "Monogamy, as the unique and exclusive form of marriage," says the writer in the *Encyclopaedia Britannica*, "in the sense that bigamy is regarded as a grave criminal offence and a sin as well as a sacrilege, is very rare indeed. Such an exclusive ideal and such a rigid legal view of marriage is perhaps not to be found outside the modern, relatively recent development of western culture. It is not implied in Christian doctrine even. Apart from such isolated phenomena as the recent Church of Later Day Saints (Mormons) and the heretical sect of Anabaptists (16th century), polygamy, was legally practised and accepted by the Church in the Middle Ages, and it occurs sporadically as a legal institution accepted by Church and state as recently as the middle of the 17th century.[35]

It thus becomes clear that polygamy is an institution recognised by law and religion in all parts of the world and it had none of the disreputable associations around it as we find today in some of the western countries.

Muḥammad (peace and blessings of *Allah* be upon him) purified this institution which had degenerated into unbridled gratification of sexual desire, by limiting the number of wives to four and enjoining upon those who undertake this heavy responsibility to observe equality amongst them :

> "And if ye apprehend that ye may not deal justly with the orphan girls, than marry such as please you, of other women, by twos, and threes and fours ; but if ye apprehend that ye shall not act justly then marry one only." (iv : 3)

Now the question arises : Is it in the human interest that the Holy Prophet allowed polygamy to exist though with certain conditions. The answer is that as a Benefactor of mankind the Holy Prophet has done a great service to mankind in this sphere of life as well as in others. The recent researches by anthropologists have established this beyond any shadow of doubt. "Man", says G. R. Scott, "is essentially polygamous and the development of civilization extends this innate polygamy."[36] "We should remind ourselves at the outset," says Will Durant,

---

35. *Encyclopaedia Britannica,* London (1900), Vol. 14, Article 'Marriage', p. 950.

36. *History of Prostitution,* p. 21.

"that man is by nature polygamous and that only the strongest moral sanctions, a helpful degree of poverty, and hard work and uninterrupted wifely supervision can induce him to monogamy."[37]

Man is Essentially Polygamous

Professor N. W. Ingells in his essay on *Biology of Sex and the Unmarried*, writes:

> Has man always been essentially monogamous or has he come up from a state designated as promiscuous? The available evidence points to the latter. As an animal, in his sexual make-up, and in his beginnings as far as we can reconstruct them, he is anything but monogamous, and one would have great difficulty in explaining biologically such a sudden change of heart, the transition to a single wife."[38]

Polygamy is not only biologically sound and perfectly in consonance with the demand of nature, but as an institution it has great social value. Dr. MacFarlane in his eye-opener book *The Case for Polygamy* observes :

> Whether the question is considered socially or religiously, it can be demonstrated that polygamy is not contrary to the highest standards of civilization. The suggestion offers a practical remedy for the western problem of destitute and unwanted female : the alternative is contained and increased prostitution, concubinage and distressing spinsterhood.[39]

He further remarks :

> The fact that polygamy has been practised is itself a proof that the sexes do not exist in the uniform proportion : and I am yet to learn that any widespread scarcity of women has been experienced in the past as the result of such practice. Even if there were an equal number of men and women in the world, the enforcement of monogamous marriages would involve as its logical corollary the com-

---

37. Will Durant, *The Story of Civilization*, part V, New York 1953, p. 575.
38. *The Biology of Sex and the Unmarried* by N. W. Ingells in "The Sex Life of the Unmarried Adult", edited by Dr. Ira G. Wile (1046), p. 88.
39. Quoted by Khurshīd Aḥmad in *Marriage Commission Report X-Rayed*, p. 265.

pelling of every one to marry. On this point alone, without the aid of any other argument, monogamy as a universal system, stands condemned.[40]

It is not only the preponderance of females over males that necessitates polygamy but there is a variety of other circumstances which require polygamy to be adopted not only for moral but for the physical welfare of society, for instance, marrying a widow of the family with a view to supporting her and her children. Legitimate sexual needs of man may also impel him to resort to polygamy. If the society is to be saved from adultery, promiscuity and immorality, then law and custom must take a realistic view of man's nature and his genuine needs. One may say anything about polygamy, but there is no denying the fact that prostitution—the great evil of modern civilization with its concomitant of illegitimate children—is practically unknown to the countries where the institution of polygamy was adopted.

"There is pretended monogamy in the West," says Dr. Annie Besant, "but there is really a polygamy without responsibility, the mistress is cast off when the man is weary of her, and sinks gradually to be the woman of the street, for the first lover has no responsibility for her future and she is a hundred times worse off than the sheltered wife and mother in polygamous home. When we see thousands of miserable women who crowd the streets of western towns during the night, we must surely feel that it does not lie within western mouth to reproach *Islām* for polygamy. It is better for woman, happier for woman, more respectable for woman, to live in polygamy, united to one man only, with the legitimate child in her arms, and surrounded with respect, than to be seduced, cast out in the streets—perhaps with an illegitimate child outside the pale of law—unsheltered and uncared for, to become the victim of any passerby, night after night, rendered incapable of motherhood, despised of all."[41]

What has been quoted above speaks eloquently of the fact that polygamy is neither biologically unnatural, nor rationally objectionable, nor morally degrading. It has innumerable advan-

---

40. Quoted by Khurshīd Aḥmad in ***Marriage Commission Report X-Rayed***, p. 265.
41. *Ibid.*, pp. 273-74.

tages : physical, social, religious and moral. *Allah*, therefore, in His perfect wisdom showed the last of His Apostles the way how this institution could be purged of the evils which had crept into it and then assimilated by the *Muslim* society and used it as means for eradicating social ills from it .

Marriages of the Holy Prophet

Now we come to the problem of the Holy Prophet's marriages.

He was hardly twenty-five years of age when he married *Khadijah*, who was fifteen years older than himself. It was with her and her alone that he passed all the years of his youth and manhood till she died three years before *Hijra*, when he was already a man of fifty. After the sad demise of *Khadijah*, he again went in for a widow, this time a helpless one in great distress. She was one of the earliest converts to *Islām* who had suffered many hardships for the cause of Truth.

Then the Holy Prophet married *'Ā'ishah*, the daughter of his devoted friend *Abū Bakr*. She was the only virgin wife of *Muḥammad* (peace be upon him).

Events took a very serious turn in *Medina*. The enmity of the *Quraysh* resulted into armed battles in which so many of the noble *Muslims* fell as martyrs. It was, therefore, the bounden duty of the Holy Prophet and his companions to alleviate the sufferings of the widows and the orphans who had been deprived of their husbands and fathers. *Muḥammad* (peace be upon him) undertook the major burden on himself and married *Ḥafṣa*, daughter of *'Umar*, whose husband had died in the battle of *Badr*. It was on this ground of clemency and compassion that the Holy Prophet married *Zaynab*, the daughter of *Khuzaimah*, who had been deprived of her husband in *Uḥud*. Her parents were non-*Muslims* living in *Mecca* and after the martyrdom of her husband there was none to take care of her. The next lady to enter the hospitable household of the Holy Prophet was *Umm Salamāh* whose husband had received fatal injuries in the battle of *Uḥud* and died leaving behind a pregnant widow and a daughter. The Prophet was moved by her pitiable condition and honoured her by taking her as his wife. The events relating to the marriage of *Zaynab bint Jaḥsh* have been discussed in great detail in the foregoing pages and it has been established that this marriage was governed by some important social considerations, *i.e.*, to obliterate the customs of adoptive affinity and also to remove the false notion then prevalent in society that the divorce of a noble lady by a freed slave undermined her prestige.

Besides these widows of his faithful followers, whom it fell to his lot to take under his protection and share their sufferings and sorrows, the Holy Prophet also took three widows of his enemies in marriage. The entry of these three ladies, *Juwayriyah*, *Maymūna* and *Safiyyah* (may *Allah* be pleased with them) in the house of the Holy Prophet became the means whereby relations with various tribes were cemented and this is how hostilities came to an end.

It is quite evident that the marriages of the Holy Prophet were governed mainly by the feeling of compassion for the widows of his faithful followers, who had no means to fall back upon after they were bereft of the love and care of their husbands. This fact has been acknowledged even by the critics of the Holy Prophet. "It should be remembered, however," says Bosworth Smith, "that most of *Muḥammad's* marriages may be explained, at least, as much by his pity for the forlorn condition of the persons concerned, as by other motives."[42]

Other marriages were contracted from the motives of policy, in order to conciliate the heads of rival factions.

Then there was also one more consideration, in no way less important than those discussed earlier, which led to these marriages. *Muḥammad* (peace be upon him) was the bearer of God's message not only for men, but also for women. The womenfolk needed the prophetic guidance, training and instruction in the same way as the males. The Holy Prophet was fully alive to this need of *Muslim* society. He had, therefore, in the best interest of the *ummah*, endeavoured to create a new leadership amongst women, which, like its counterpart amongst men, could by precept and example, help the formation of new type of womanhood representing the teachings of *Islām*. How could this objective be achieved without first preparing the most perfect specimens of *Muslim* womanhood. The Holy Prophet allowed some women, belonging to different social groups, having different tastes and tendencies and different intellectual standards to enter his household as his wives and then by his close personal contact nurture

42. *Mohammad and Mohammadanism*, London, 1876, p. 136.

and train their God-given faculties so perfectly in accordance with the teachings of *Islām* that they could serve as pillars of light not only for the womenfolk of the *Islamic* common-wealth, but for the whole of womankind. One or two women could not undertake this heavy responsibility. A whole group was required to meet this need.

Moreover there is a good deal of difference in the nature of training essential for male and female. Man's life is predominated by social activities, whereas the natural sphere of woman's work is primarily her home. It is the wife alone who shares with the husband even the most secret affairs of life. The Holy Prophet could not prepare the specimen of *Islamic* womanhood unless he allowed some ladies to enter the innermost chambers of his domestic life. In view of the teachings of *Islām* with regard to seclusion of sexes, only the noble wives of the Holy Prophet could be accommodated on this plane and mankind owes a deep debt of gratitude to these noble ladies that they communicated to us most faithfully the sacred account of the Prophet's private life, which like his public career, had so many facets and has been made a model pattern for the believers, both men and women. The injunction of the *Qur'ān* : 'Verily in the Apostle of *Allah*, you have the best example' (xxxiii : 21) covers not only one aspect of his sacred life but his whole life. It was with a view to achieving this objective, *i.e.*, the authentic transmission of the Prophet's home life to the people that a few noble ladies were made to enter his house as his wives.

The *Qur'ānic* verse : 'It is not allowed to take wives after this, nor to change them for others, (xxxiii : 52) implies that the Holy Prophet, like all his other acts, contracted those marriages perfectly in accordance with the will of the Lord. There was a divine purpose behind them and when it was achieved a restriction was placed upon him.

That the Prophet married these ladies as a religious necessity can be well judged from the fact that he spent his youth in the company of one wife, *Khadījah* only. At the age of forty he was commissioned as a Prophet, and during the first twelve years of his prophethood, when he had only to instil in the minds of the people the fundamentals of faith, *i.e.*, Oneness of God, apostlehood of *Muḥammad*, life after death, he did not feel the necessity of marrying any other lady. After the death of *Khadījah* he married *Sawda*, a widow of advanced age. But with the migration to *Medina* when *Islamic* society was established and the *Muslims* were required to conform their social and personal behaviour to the teachings of *Islām*, revelations for practical guidance in all walks of life came from *Allah*. These had to be explained by the life example of the Holy Prophet. There was not one problem but numerous problems concerning all phases of life which needed solution at every step. The way how the Holy Prophet solved them must be made known to the people as it is also an integral part of the faith for 'he does not speak of his own desire' (liii: 37). It is God who speaks through him in whatever he utters by way of spiritual guidance or practical legislation. Now, whatever the Holy Prophet said or did in public could be easily conveyed to the other people for their guidance. But what about his private life which was equally important and divinely inspired and had to serve as an example for the Believers ? It is through the noble wives of the Holy Prophet that the *Muslims* learnt the teachings of *Islām* in their personal concerns. It was not an ordinary work but an important task of vast magnitude which was admirably accomplished by these pious ladies[43] (*Allah* be pleased with them). How can these facts be justifiably ignored in the matter of *Muḥammad's* marriages ?

It is strange indeed that the western critics of *Islām* and of the Holy Prophet in their sordid endeavours to malgin *Muḥammad* (peace be upon him) close their eyes to all those illuminating facts which prove that his was a life of perfect sublimity and single-minded devotion to *Allah*, absolutely free from the taints of base desires. It is narrated on the authority of *Jābir b. 'Abd Allāh* that *Abū Jahl* and some of the chiefs of the *Quraysh* approached the Holy Prophet and said :

> If you are anxious for leadership, we are prepared to declare you our leader, if you need riches, we would collect for you an enormous amount of wealth that will suffice not only for you but even for your descendants ; if you are impelled by sexual urge, you may choose ten

---

43. For detailed study see the note of Jalāl al-Dīn Suyūṭī on *Sunan al-Nisā'i* (Cairo, 1382 A.H.) Vol. vii, pp. 58-60 and Maulāna Ashraf 'Alī Thānwi's book *Kathra al-Azwāj li- Ṣāḥib al-Mi'rāj*. published by Tajjali Press, Delhi, 1850 A.H.

beautiful damsels out of the whole tribe of *Quraysh*. The Holy Prophet kept silent and did not utter a word. When their talks concluded, the Holy Prophet recited the following verse of the *Qur'ān* :

Ḥā Mīm ! A revelation from the Beneficent, the Merciful ; A Book of which the verses are made plain, and *Arabic Qur'ān* for people who know and a bearer of glad tidings and a warner. Yet most of them turn aside so that they hearken not. (xli : 4)

The Holy Prophet recited these verses of the *Qur'ān* and concluded them on the following verse :

Then if they still turn away, say thou ; I warn you of calamity of the *'Ād* and *Thamūd*. (xli : 13)[44]

Even this single event is enough to prove *Muḥammad's* immense love for *Allah*, his devotion to his sacred mission and the insignificance in his eyes of the worldly pleasures. Allurement could not distract him, even for a moment, from the noble cause for which he stood and suffered all kinds of hardships and privations. No opportunity could be more attractive than this offered by the chiefs of *Quraysh* for the satisfaction of sensuous pleasures, if he were so inclined.

The Conquest of *Mecca*

According to the terms of the treaty of *Ḥudaybiyāh*, the *Arab* tribes were given the option to join either of the parties with which they desired to enter into treaty alliance. As a consequence *Banū Bakr* joind the *Quraysh*, and *Khuzā'ah* joined the Prophet. *Banū Bakr*, without caring a bit for the conditions of the treaty, attacked *Banū Khuzā'ah*. The *Quraysh* helped them with men and arms. Pressed by their enemies the tribesmen of *Khuzā'ah* sought the sanctuary of *Ka'bah*, but here, too, their lives were not respected, and, contrary to all accepted traditions, *Nawfal*, the chief of *Banū Bakr*, chasing them in the sanctified area—where no blood should be shed—massacred his adversaries.[45]

---

44. *Maḥmūd Ālūsi* in his commentary of the Holy *Qur'ān "Rūḥ al-Ma'āni"* (Vol. 24, p. 99), (Mureriah Press, Cairo) has recorded this *Ḥadith* from *Sunnan* Baihaqi.

45. *Ibn Hishām*, Vol. iv, p. 32.

When the aggrieved party sought justice from their *Muslim* allies, the Holy Prophet, as their leader, demanded an immediate redress for not only violating the treaty but also slaying his men in the sanctified area. Three demands were made, the acceptance of any one of them was stressed :

(*a*) to pay blood money for the victims of *Khuzā'ah*,
(*b*) to terminate their alliance with *Banū Bakr* ; or
(*c*) to consider the truce to have been nullified.[46]

In the fit of their pride they arrogantly said : "We will neither pay blood money nor terminate our alliance with *Banū Bakr*, but are prepared to declare the truce as null and void."[47]

Later on *Abū Sufyān* tried to gloss over the imprudence of his people and came to *Medina* for a renewal of the truce. He went to the house of his daughter *Umm Habībah* (wife of the Holy Prophet). But as he went to sit on the Prophet's carpet she folded it up. "My daughter," said he, "I hardly knew if you think that the carpet is too good for me or that I am too good for the carpet." She replied, "It is the Prophet's carpet and you are an unclean polytheist."[48]

This reply of the wife of the Holy Prophet (peace and blessings of *Allah* be upon him) speaks eloquently of the unfathomable love and the profound respect which his partner of life had for him. Can an impostor command such affection from one who has a free access to the most guarded sectors of his life ? It is the sincerity, the deep, great, genuine sincerity of *Muḥammad* (peace be upon him) which enabled him to win the admiration of those who stood face to face with him, bare, not enshrined in any mystery of public glamour, those who could see through all his actions and not only peep into but share the innermost feelings of his heart. How could he wear any mask or conceal his designs and ambitions from them ?

Being disgusted at the curt reply of his daughter, *Abū Sufyān* stepped out of her room and went to the Holy Prophet, but he was well aware of his tricks and did not hold him any assurance. He then approached *Abū Bakr*, but he declined to interfere. He contacted *'Umar* also to intercede but he made a

46. Zurqāni, *Sharḥ al-Mawāhib-il-Laddunniya*, Cairo, 1325.
47. *Ibid.*, p. 292.
48. Ibn Qayyim, Vol. ii, p. 292, *Zād al-Ma'ād*, Cairo, 1953, Vol. ii, p. 386.

point-blank refusal. At last he saw *'Alī b. Abī Ṭālib* in this connection, but he also regretted his inability to do anything for him.

Abū Sufyān turned his steps back to *Mecca* in a state of bitter disappointment and submitted the report of his meeting with his daughter, the behaviour of *Abū Bakr*, *'Umar* and *'Alī* (may *Allah* be pleased with all of them) and the meaningful silence of the Holy Prophet. The *Meccans* were dismayed, but did not expect imminent danger.

Preparations for the Attack on *Mecca*

The Prophet ordered preparations to be made for a foray. The expedition was first kept secret but later on he revealed that it was to the city of *Mecca* that he wanted to lead his troops. The neighbouring tribes, who were in alliance with the *Muslims*, were also invited to join the Prophet's army.

For twenty-one long years the *Quraysh* had been perpetrating atrocities on the *Muslims*. They tortured them, inflicted injuries upon them, dragged them in the mire and on the burning sand of blazing *Mecca*, in fact, made their very existence impossible. Hard pressed by these shameless acts, the *Muslims* left their native place in order to seek shelter at *Medina*. But the revengeful *Meccans* allowed them no rest even in that city. They attacked them even in their new abode. The people were, therefore, fully aware what these preparations really meant. There was dread and fear everywhere. It was under such circumstances that *Ḥāṭib*, one of the most trusted followers of the Prophet secretly despatched a female messenger with a letter to *Mecca* containing intimation of the intended attack. The Prophet received news from the Heaven of *Ḥāṭib's* action and sent *'Alī* and *Zubayr b. 'Awwām* with instructions to go after her. They overtook the female messenger, and after a long search discovered the letter carefully hidden in her locks. The Holy Prophet summoned *Ḥāṭib* and asked him what had induced him to this act. He replied, "O Messenger of *Allah*! I have no affinity of blood with the *Quraysh*; there is only a kind of friendly relationship between them and myself. My family is at *Mecca* and there is no one to look after it or to offer protection to it. My position stands in striking contrast to that of the refugees whose families are secure due to their blood ties with the *Quraysh*. I felt that since I am not related to them, I should, for the safety of my children, earn their gratitude by doing good to them. I swear by God that I have not done this act as an apostate, forsaking *Islām*. I was prompted only by the consideration explained above."[49]

'Umar wanted to cut his head off as a hypocrite, but the Prophet accepted his excuse and granted him pardon and addressed *'Umar* in these words :

> "*Ḥāṭib* is one of those who fought in the battle of *Badr*. How do you know, my companion ! that he is a hypocrite, perhaps God looked favourably on those who participated in that battle."

Turning then, to *Ḥāṭib*, he said : "Do as you please, for I have forgiven you."[50]

After making full preparation the Holy Prophet proceeded to *Mecca* at the head of ten thousand soldiers on the 10th of Ramaḍān, 8 H. He encamped at a place known as *Marr al-Zahrān*. The *Quraysh* were quite unaware of the development. But the Holy Prophet did not like to take them by surprise. He, therefore, ordered his men to kindle fire on all sides for cooking purposes. The idea behind this was that the *Quraysh* should be afforded full opportunity to assess the situation correctly in which they were pitchforked and should not endanger their lives by leaping blindly in the battlefield. The Holy Prophet wanted to avoid bloodshed as far as possible and was anxious that the wiser counsel should prevail upon the haughty *Meccans* and they should weigh the pros and cons of the matter before coming forward for an encounter. *'Abbās*, the Prophet's uncle, like his brother *Abū Ṭālib*, had always been friendly to his nephew, *Muḥammad* (peace be on him). He had been giving him timely warning of the *Meccans'* attack on *Medina*. He met the Holy Prophet on the way and discussed the situation with him. *'Abbās* had tender feelings for his kith and kin in *Mecca* and was desirous that they should realise the gravity of the situation and yield before the irresistible tide of the *Muslim* army. Their

---

49. *Ṣaḥīḥ Bukhārī : Kitab al-Maghāzī*, Chapter *'Ghazwa al-Fatḥ'*. Ḥāfiz Ibn Ḥajar 'Asqalānī, *Fatḥ al-Bārī*, Cairo, 1959, Vol. ix, p. 62.
50. *Ibid.*, p; 62.

doom had been sealed, he thought, and it was no use fighting an already lost battle.

Abu Sufyan Visits the *Muslims'* Camp

In the meanwhile, when the *Muslims* had encamped at *Marr al-Zahrān*, *Abu Sufyān* and *Ḥakīm*, one of the nephews of *Khadījāh*, the chief of one of the few local tribes which had remained with the *Quraysh*, went out to reconnoitre.

Before they got anywhere near the camp, the *Muslims* saw a large white figure looming in the darkness. They were wondering what defensive measures to adopt when the creature stopped beside them. To their surprise it was *'Abbās*, the Prophet's uncle. He apprised *Abū Sufyān* of the situation and advised him to accept *Islām* and persuade his people to surrender before *Muḥammad* (peace be upon him) as the battle had already been won by him. The ideal for which the Holy Prophet stood had been gaining adherents and friends from all camps. The *Meccans* were a divided house. Numerous amongst them were disgusted with idolatry and had become silent admirers of the teachings of *Islām*. The idea of One God, the prophethood of *Muḥammad* (peace be upon him), the high standard of morality of the faithful, combined, of course, with the exemplary pious life of their noble leader (peace be upon him), greatly impressed their hearts. They had eyes to see and minds to think of the glaring contrast presented by their lives and the lives of the *Muslims*. Their leaders, by their vicious tricks and false propaganda, could make fools of them for some time, but it was difficult, nay impossible, to bamboozle them for ever. They had their own consciences, their own minds, their own judgement which they could ill-afford to ignore altogether. How could they close their ears to the inner voice of their hearts and shut their eyes to the remarkable moral superiority of the faithful ? Truth is after all truth and is strong enough to make its way even into the hearts of the deadliest foes.

Abbās was fully aware of the change of heart of the majority of the *Meccans* and he succeeded in convincing *Abū Sufyān* of this state of affairs. The Peace of *Ḥudaybiyāh* had provided them a respite to see and think in a calmer atmosphere, and, with unruffled feelings and in a rational frame of mind, the teachings of *Islām* and the great spiritual and moral revolution which it had brought about amongst those who had accepted it. Their hearts had attested the truth of the Divine mission which *Muḥammad* (peace be upon him) had brought. Only a profession in words was to be made.

It was, therefore, in the best interests of *Mecca* that *Islām* should be allowed to take hold of the city without the least resistance and should be accepted as an incontestable truth. Through the intercession of *'Abbās* and the conviction of *Abū Sufyān*, the way had been paved for this "peaceful conquest."

General Amnesty

None could be more anxious to avoid bloodshed than *Muḥammad* (peace be upon him). He, therefore, proclaimed amnesty to the people who had persecuted and tortured him and his followers and had even made several attempts on his life. But he is the "Mercy unto the worlds," and even his deadliest enemies were to be forgiven. "There shall be no reproof against you this day," he declared. He asked *Abū Sufyān* to proclaim : "He who takes refuge in the house of *Abū Sufyān* is safe : whosoever closes the door of his house, the inmates thereof shall be in safety, and he who enters the mosque is safe."[51]

It was in this spirit of clemency that the Holy Prophet entered the city of *Mecca*. "He, who was once a fugitive," says Syed Ameer Ali, "and persecuted, now came to prove his mission by deeds of mercy. The city which had treated him so cruelly, driven him and his faithful friends for refuge amongst strangers, lay at his feet. His old persecutors, relentless who had inflicted cruel outrage upon inoffensive men and women and even upon the lifeless dead, were now completely at his mercy. But in the hour of triumph every evil suffered was forgotten, every injury inflicted was forgiven and a general amnesty was extended to the population of *Mecca*. The army followed his example, and entered gently and peaceably ; no house was robbed, no woman was insulted."[52] "Facts are hard things ; and it is a fact that the day of *Muḥammad's* greatest triumph over his enemies was also the day of his grandest victory over himself."[53]

"One of the more general forms in which the tragedy of

---

51. Ibn Qayyim, *Zād al-Ma'ād*, Cairo, Vol. ii, pp. 389-391.
52. *The Spirit of Islam*, p 89.
53. Stanley Lane-Poole, *The Prophet and Islam*, Lahore, p. 31.

surfeit, outrage, and disaster presents itself is in the intoxication of victory."[54] But here the victory did not mean either the exhibition of ruthless power or the display of military strength. To *Muḥammad* (peace be upon him) and his followers this conquest meant only one thing : the supremacy of the Great Lord rather than ambition for pomp, grandeur and power. Had the Prophet any of such worldly ambitions there was now nothing left in *Mecca* that could thwart them. "If he had worn a mask at all," says Bosworth Smith, "he would now at all events had thrown it off ; if lower aims had gradually sapped the higher, or his moderation had been directed, as Gibbon supposes, by his selfish interests, we should now have seen the effect ; now would have been the moment to gratify his ambition, to satiate his lust, to glut his revenge. Is there anything of the kind ? Read the account of the entry of *Muḥammad* into *Mecca* side by side with that of Marius of Sullah into Rome. Compare all the attendant circumstances, the outrages that preceded, and the use made by each of his recovered power, and we shall then be in a position better to appreciate the magnanimity and moderation of the Prophet of Arabia. There were no proscription lists, no plunder, no wanton revenge."[55]

The Prophet Enters *Mecca*

After having entered the city, the Holy Prophet offered prayer of thanks to the Almighty God Who, out of His immense grace, had granted him a splendid victory. A tent was pitched for him at a spot where he was obliged to spend his days in a secluded quarter of the *Shi'b*, having been excommunicated by his kith and kin. "Wilt thou not alight at thine own house ?" inquired his followers. "Not so," he said, "for have they left me yet any house within the city ?" The great banner was planted at the door of his tent, and he retired to repose therein. He must have recalled to his mind the march of events. It should have been a quaint sight with moments of strange emotions. How he spent his early childhood ! How he was commissioned by his Lord to deliver His message to mankind ! How mercilessly he was treated by his dear and near, rejected,

---

54. Arnold J. Toynbee, *War and Civilization*, London 1951, p. 104.
55. *Mohammed and Mohammedanism*, London 1876, p. 142.

exiled, but now had the rebellious city at his feet ! What boundless Mercy of *Allah* ! his Creator and Master ! He must have been absorbed in these thoughts.

The *Ka'bah* is Purified

But he did not repose long. He got up and proceeded towards *Ka'bah*, the Sacred House, which is an emblem of the Oneness and Supremacy of *Allah*. It was unfortunately infested with idols. He knocked them down and recited the verse of the *Qur'ān* : "Say, the Truth is come and falsehood gone, verily falsehood is ever-vanishing." (xvii : 81)

One by one the stone-gods were dismantled, images and effigies deleted. He then prostrated himself in worship ; and sitting down, sent *Bilāl* to summon *'Uthmān b. Talḥah* with the key of the *Ka'bah*. Ascending the steps of the threshold and unlocking the door he ordered that idols should be destroyed and images obliterated. He entered the sacred hall and there again performed devout prostrations. He then returned to the door-way and, standing upon its elevated step, gazed in thankfulness on the thronging multitude below. It was the 20th of *Ramaḍān*, the eighth year of *Hijrah*, when, on the gate of Holy *Ka'bah*, and with its key held in his hand, he delivered the following address :

> "There is no god but *Allah* alone. He has no associate. He made good His promise that He held to his bondsman and helped him and defeated all the confederates along. Bear in mind that every claim of privilege, whether that of blood, or proper ty, is under my heel, except that of the custody of the *Ka'bah* and supplying of water to the pilgrims. Bear in mind anyone who is slain, even though unintentionally, may be with club or whip, for him the bloodwit is very severe : hundred camels, forty of them to be pregnant. O people of *Quraysh* ! surely God has abolished from you all pride of the time of ignorance and all pride in your ancestry, (because) all men are descended from *Adam*, and *Adam* was fashioned out of clay."

Then he recited to them the verse :

> "O Mankind ! verily We have created you of a male and a female and We have made you nations and tribes

that ye might know one another. Verily the noblest of you with *Allah* is the most God-fearing of you ; Verily *Allah* is All-Knowing, All-Aware." (xlix : 13)

He further added :

> O ye people of *Quraysh* ! what do you think of the treatment that I am about to accord to you ?

They replied :

> O noble brother and son of a noble brother ! we expect nothing but goodness from you.

Upon this he said :

> I speak to you in the same words as Joseph spoke unto his brothers ;
>
> 'This day, there is no reproof against you,'
> Go your way, for you are freed ones.[56]

This address epitomizes beautifully the essence of *Islām*. It is a proclamation of the Oneness of *Allah* : There is none worthy of worship except He, the Creator and Sustainer of the universe. He is the sole Sovereign and Master of the universe. There is none to share His Power and Sovereignty. The late Rev. C. F. Andrews, in one of his writings, observes :

> "One of the greatest blessings which *Islām* has brought to East and West alike has been the emphasis which at a critical period in human history it placed upon the Divine unity. For, during those Dark Ages both in East and West, from 600 to 1000 A.D., this doctrine was in danger of being overlaid and obscured in Hinduism and in Christianity itself, owing to the immense accretions of subsidiary worship of countless demi-gods and heroes. *Islām* has been, both to Europe and India, in their dark hour of aberration from the sovereign truth of God's unity, an invaluable corrective and deterrent. Indeed, without the final emphasis on this truth, which *Islām* gave from its central position,—facing India and facing Europe—It is doubtful whether this idea of God as One could have obtained that established place in human thought which

---

56. Ibn Qayyim, *Zād al-Ma'ād*, Vol. ii, p. 394.

is uncontested in the intellectual world of today.''[57]

Brotherhood of Mankind

The Holy Prophet also imprinted upon the minds of the people the pragmatic value of this fundamental principle of *Islām, i.e.*, Divine unity. This concept strikes at the very root of all types of man-made distinctions, *e.g.*, those of race, colour and language and completely sweeps off all kinds of hierarchical privileges of life, social and political. It was a pronouncement of very great significance. Herein was sounded the death knell of the doctrine of polygenism ascribing multiple ancestry to mankind and the idea of castes or classes forming a barrier to common humanity. There is no distinction between man and man. All are equal, because they are descendants of the same parents. Superiority of one over another in this vast brotherhood does not depend on nationality, wealth or rank, but on one's conscious adherence to the Commands of *Allah*. The Holy Prophet was sent to the world to break off all kinds of chains which the clever amongst the human race had forged in order to keep it in perpetual bondage. The idols of caste, creed and colour were also destroyed along with the idols of stone and clay. Humanity could not have regained its lost dignity if these were not broken. The Holy Prophet, in his declaration, struck at the very root of all kinds of false distinctions and established the brotherhood of mankind.

Tribe, race and nation are convenient labels by which their differing characteristics are known, but they should have none of the imperialistic designs which we find in the aggressive nationalism of the past and the present—a nationalism which is based upon feelings of vanity and arrogance and hatred against others.

The Love of the *Ansar* for the Prophet

After having delivered this address, the Holy Prophet rode to a small hill, *Safā*, not far from *Ka'bah*. Turning his face towards the Holy House, amidst a vast admiring and devotional multitude, he raised his hands in fervent prayer to *Allah*. The citizens of *Medina* who had gathered round him entertained

---

57. Rev. C. F. Andrews in the Journal, *The Genuine Islam*, Singapore, 1836, Vol. x. p. 108.

fear as the Lord had given him victory over his native city, he might choose to stay here. Immediately revelation came upon him and apprised him of the thoughts of the *Anṣār*. He dispelled their fears and assured them in the following words :

> "O *Anṣār* ! Have you entertained such thoughts ?" They replied in the affirmative. Upon this the Holy Prophet remarked : "Bear this in mind, I would never stay here. I am the servant and the Apostle of *Allah* and have migrated to *Medina* at His Command. I will live with you and die with you."
>
> On hearing this the faces of the *Anṣār* gleamed with joy and they said, "O Messenger of *Allah* ! whatever we have said, is due to our attachment with *Allah* and His Apostle since we cannot afford your separation."[58]

The Holy Prophet then received the people who had come to embrace *Islām*. The men pledged the oath of *Islām* by saying : "We shall not adore anyone but *Allah*, and we would carry out His Commands and those of His Apostle to the best of our capabilities."

Abu Bakr brings his aged Father to the Prophet

The father of *Abū Bakr* also approached the Holy Prophet leaning on his son's arm. *Muḥammad* (peace be upon him) accosted him kindly : "Why didn't you leave your aged father in his house, *Abū Bakr*, and I would have gone and seen him there ?" "It was more fitting that he should visit thee, O Prophet ! than that thou shouldst visit him."[59] The Prophet seated the aged man beside him with respect and, affectionately pressing his hand upon his bosom, invited him to make profession of *Islām*, which he readily did.[60]

Women take the Pledge

Women also took the pledge dipping their hands in a cup of water along with the Holy Prophet and said : "We shall not worship anyone but one Lord Who has no partner. We shall not commit larceny, adultery, infanticide, nor utter falsehood, nor

---

58. *Sharḥ Zurqānī*, Vol. ii, p. 233.
59. *Ibid.*, Vol. ii, p 233.
60. *Ibn Hishām*, Vol. iv, p. 48.

speak ill of other women."[61]

Very few people were punished for past wrongs to *Muḥammad* (peace be upon him). Only four who had murdered or had committed the most heinous crimes were executed.

Magnanimity Unparalleled in the Annals of Mankind

Every attempt was made to grant pardon to the people. *Ikrimah, Abū Jahl's* son, who had attacked *Khalid's* detachment at the time of the entry into *Mecca* was forgiven. To *Waḥshī*, the murderer of *Ḥamzah*, the Prophet's uncle, and to *Hind*, who had chewed his liver, was also extended his generous clemency. The same generous treatment was accorded to *Habbar* who had attacked the Prophet's daughter with a spear while on her way from *Mecca* to *Medina*, so grievously that she ultimately died of the fatal injuries.[62]

Only Four Persons were executed

Only four persons out of the whole population of *Mecca* were executed. One of them was *'Abdullah b. Khaṭāl of Banu Taym b. Ghālib*. He had become a *Muslim* and had been deputed by the Holy Prophet to collect *zakāt* in the company of one of the *Anṣār*. They had also a slave with them. *'Abdullah*, in a fit of rage, killed the helpless slave on account of a mere trifling dispute and joined the pagan *Arabs* as an apostate. He also took with him the camels that he had collected as *zakāt*. He was never repentant at this heinous crime but employed two singing girls and incited them to sing satirical songs about the Holy Prophet.[63] The other man who was put to death was *Miqyas b. Hubaba*. He was a *Muslim*. An *Anṣāri* accidentally killed his brother *Hishām*. The Holy Prophet had arranged the

---

61. This pledge was taken on the conditions laid down in the chapter *al-Mumtaḥanah* (lx : 12) :

"O Prophet ! when believing women come to you giving you a pledge that they will not associate aught with *Allah*, and will not steal, and will not commit fornication, and will not kill their children, and will not bring a calumny which they have forged of themselves and will not disobey you in what is good, accept their pledge, ask forgiveness for them from *Allah*. Surely *Allah* is Forgiving, Merciful."

62. *Sharḥ Zurqānī*, Vol. ii, p. 315.

63. *Ibn Hishām*, Vol. iv, pp. 52, 53.

payment of blood money to him, which he had accepted. But his revengeful nature was never appeased, so he killed the *Anṣāri* and went to *Mecca* as an apostate. The Holy Prophet ordered his execution. Similarly, *Huwayrith* and one singing girl were put to death.

Can history furnish such an example of peaceful conquest of a city which had been for years the hot bed of worst type of tyranny and oppression ? Historical records have no instance to quote of such magnanimous forgiveness as shown by the Prophet of *Islām*.

The Problem of Restoration of the Abandoned Property

Demand was made from certain quarters of *Muslim* refugees that their houses and lands which had been, without any legitimate right, usurped by the *Meccans* should be restored to them. Amongst those who had put forward such a reasonable demand was *Abū Aḥmad b. Jaḥsh*. Upon this the Holy Prophet remarked : "As for your land and property of which you have been deprived in the cause of *Allah*. I do not approve of its possession by you." On hearing these words, the immigrants kept silent and did not cherish the possession of the property which they had abandoned for the sake of *Allah*. The Holy Prophet did not make even the slightest reference—direct or indirect—to his own house in which he was born and where he was married to *Khadijah*.[64] None amongst the emigrants liked to stay in his native place. All of them preferred to go back to *Medina*, their new abodes which had given them refuge after they were driven out of their homes for the sake of *Islām*.

Muḥammad (peace be upon him) now saw his mission completed. He despatched his men in every direction to destroy all remnants of idolatry and call the tribes of the desert to *Islām*. They were instructed to carry out this mission with peace and goodwill. These injunctions were loyally obeyed. Only men of *Khālid b. Walid*, killed a few of the *Banū Khuzaymah* bedouins, mistaking them for hostile soldiers. When this news of bloodshed was conveyed to the Holy Prophet, he was deeply grieved, and raising his hands towards the heavens, uttered these words : "O

---

64. Ibn Taymiyah, *Kitāb al-Sārim al-Maslūl 'alā Shātim al-Rasūl* (Hyderābād), pp. 153-155.

Lord ! I am innocent of what *Khālid* has done." He immediately sent *'Ali* to make every possible reparation to the tribes who had been wronged. After a careful inquiry, *'Ali* paid the blood-wit to all those who had suffered loss. The remaining portion was also distributed amongst the members of the tribe in order to alleviate their sufferings. *'Ali* returned and reported to the Prophet what he had done and earned his admiration. Then the Holy Prophet again rose and, turning his face to *Qibla*, raised his arms in prayer and said, "O Lord ! I am innocent before Thee, of what *Khālid* has done."[65]

This is how *Mecca* was conquered, not by means of the sword, but by peace and goodwill. The highly magnanimous treatment of *Muḥammad* (peace be upon him) had not only disarmed all opposition, but had also awakened the *Meccans* to the Call of Truth which the Prophet had preached. Their minds were agitated and their conscience was stirred and they began to reflect calmly over the blessings which the Divine Faith had in store for them. Blind hostility gave way to sober reflection as a result of which the people entered into the fold of *Islām* not by ones or twos, but in crowds. The Holy *Qur'ān* has described this important event in the following words :

> When there came the succour of *Allah* and victory,
> And thou beholdest mankind entering the religion of *Allah* in crowds,
> Then hallow the praise of thy Lord, and ask forgiveness of Him.
> Verily He is ever Relenting. (cx : 1-3)

It is not a victory of man's self-glory, but of humility ; not that of power, but of sincere and constant service to mankind and its Creator ; not a victory of man's selfishness but of man's selflessness and his perfect realization of *Allah's* Grace and Mercy at every step of his life.

65. *Ibn Hishām*, Vol. iv, p. 73.

Chapter 9

Fulfilment of the Mission

Although a large number of *Meccans* and neighbouring tribes had embraced *Islām*, some people still clung to idolatry. They had accepted *Muḥammad* (peace be upon him) as the ruler of *Arabia*, but did not believe in him as the Messenger of God. The Prophet, on the other hand, was concerned to make the people submit to the Almighty God. That was the only objective to which all his energies were directed. He was considering to go out to preach to the people when unexpected news halted him. The Holy Prophet was informed that the tribes of *Hawāzin* and *Thaqif* had formed a powerful opposition and were mobilizing against the Prophet and his followers.

Muḥammad (peace be upon him) was not an impractical idealist. He believed in practical idealism. No sooner did he receive this news than he decided to put a stout resistance to the invading army before it made any headway.

Swiftly he set out at the head of twelve thousand troops—ten thousands that accompanied him from *Medina* and two thousands recruited locally.

The Battle of *Hunayn*

With four thousand warriors, the tribes of *Hawāzin* and *Thaqif*, along with their satellites, marched against *Mecca* and encamped themselves in the valley of *Hunāyn*. Under the advice of their chief, *Mālik b. 'Awf al-Nasari*, they brought all their females, children, camels and cattle with them to the field, with the idea that their presence would prove a check upon them and they would fight to death in their defence.

For the *Muslims* it was one of the biggest armies that had hitherto assembled under the Holy Prophet (peace and blessings

1. Ibn Qayyim, *Zād al-Ma'ād*, Vol. ii, p. 438.

of *Allah* be upon him). So, some of them felt greatly elated with their numbers and with their preparations for war. Someone, out of excitement, broke forth in admiration : "We shall not be worsted this day by smallness of numbers."

The *Hawāzin* were skilled in archery and they had occupied every point of vantage. They had posted the best of their archers on various hills.

After morning prayers, the *Muslim* troops entered the valley. The vanguard composed of *Banū Sulaym* and led by the famous general *Khālid*, marched onward through the steep and narrow pass, when suddenly the enemy sprang from his ambuscade and charged furiously upon them. "Staggered by the unexpected onslaught, column after column fell back and choked the narrow pass. Aggravated by the obscurity of the hour, and the straitness of the rugged road, panic seized the army. They all turned and fled."[2] It appeared that a general rout had taken place. The knoll on which the Holy Prophet stood was now isolated, the archers concentrated their attack upon it ; the enemy was making straight for that spot. But the Holy Prophet, perfectly confident of the promise of Divine help, remained calm and self-possessed at this hour of trial.[3] He showed no excitement, no fear. The same unfailing source of solace—unswerving faith in the power of *Allah* and implicit conviction of the rightness of his cause and its final triumph sustained him now as ever.

The newly recruited from among the *Quraysh* of *Mecca* had almost lost courage and some of them had given vent to the feelings which can be least expected of friends. *Abū Sufyān b. Ḥarb* remarked : "Their flight will not stop before they get to sea." *Jabla b. al-Hanbal* cried, "Surely the sorcery is vain today." *Shaiba b. 'Uthmān b. Abi Talḥa* said, "I will take my revenge on *Muḥammad*"[4] (for his father had been killed at *Uḥud*).

Amidst such adverse circumstances, with the exception of a few of the Prophet's devoted friends and admirers, there was a general confusion. *Muḥammad* (peace be upon him) called out with a loud and dignified voice : "I am the Messenger of *Allah*, I am no impostor, I am the descendant of *'Abd al-Muṭṭalib*."

---

2. William Muir, *Life of Muhammad*, p. 402.
3. Ibn Ḥajar, *Fatḥ al-Bāri*, Vol. ix, pp. 88-93.
4. *Ibn Hishām*, Vol. iv, p. 86.

'Abbās also called out with his commanding voice : "O Hosts of Helpers. O Companions of the acacia tree !" "*Labbaik* !, i.e. Here we are at thy command" was the response from all sides.[5] Gradually the fleeing soldiers tarried, and forming and reforming, closed their ranks, throwing themselves upon the enemy with the frenzy of religious devotion, they stemmed the tide and fought with the spirit to kill or be killed.

The *Muslims* had learnt enough lesson for their overweening confidence or reliance on human strength, their resources and their numbers. They were all repentant. Then came the help of the Lord Who sent invisible hosts to fight along with the *Muslims*. It was a result of this Divine help that what had begun as a disorderly panic turned into a desperate battle. The tribesmen from the hills did their best to put up a valiant resistance, but failed miserably. Their rout was thus complete. The Holy *Qur'ān* has referred to this event in the following verses :

> Assuredly *Allah* hath succoured you on many fields and on the day of *Ḥunayn*, when your number elated you ; and then it availed you naught ; and the earth, wide as it is, straitened unto you ; then ye turned away in retreat.
>
> Thereafter *Allah* sent down His calm upon His Apostle and upon the believers, and He sent down hosts ye saw not and chastised those who disbelieved, and that is the reward of the unbelievers ! (ix : 25, 26)

It was a splendid victory for the *Muslims*. Six thousand prisoners were taken, while a section of the enemy took refuge in the walled fortress of *Ṭā'if*. The booty which fell into the hands of the *Muslims* was colossal judging from the standards of those days ; for the defeated foe left behind twenty-four thousand camels, forty thousand sheep and four thousand ounces of silver.

The prisoners, along with the booty, were sent to a place named *al-Jir'rāna* and men were sent in pursuit of the fleeing army. The *Muslims* pursued them so far as *Nakhlah*, from thence to *Awṭās* and finally to *Ṭā'if*. The fort of *Ṭā'if* was besieged for the whole month. "But the battlements were strong, the

---

5. *Ibn Hishām*, Vol. iv, p. 87.

city well-provisioned, and a plentiful supply of water within the walls. The besiegers were received with showers of arrows so thick and well sustained that they darkened the sky like the flight of locusts. Twelve men were killed and many were wounded."[6]

The siege dragged on. At last the Holy Prophet conferred with his friends and it was thought that the enemy had been so much humbled that it could do the *Muslims* little injury. The Holy Prophet (peace be upon him), therefore, ordered that the siege should be lifted. While retiring the Apostle of *Allah* was asked to invoke Divine wrath on the foe. But he was a Mercy for the worlds. How could he do that? Instead of cursing them, he prayed for them: "O Lord! grant guidance to the tribe of *Thaqīf*, and direct them on to me."[7]

The prayer was granted and before long these people embraced *Islām* voluntarily.

The Booty

On his return from *Ṭā'if*, the Holy Prophet reached the spot where the booty had been collected. He waitad for more than a week for the arrival of any deputation of the enemies in order to secure release of their prisoners. But none turned up. At last the booty was divided as ordained in the *Qur'ān*—one-fifth to *Allah* and His Messenger, and the rest for the soldiers. After this distribution of the booty, the deputations from various tribes presented themselves to him. They recounted the calamities that had befallen them and urged their claim upon his favour. "There, in those huts among the prisoners are your foster mothers and sisters,—they that have nursed thee and fondled thee in their bosoms. We have known thee a suckling, a weaned child, a youth generous and noble, and now thou hast risen to this dignity, be gracious unto us, even as the Lord hath been gracious unto thee."[8] How could *Muḥammad's* merciful heart remain unmoved by this fervent appeal. It welled with pity. But he was not whimsical to be swayed completely by emotions. He had to approach people so that none should be disgusted with his decision. If he so desired he could easily

6. William Muir, *Life of Muhammad*, p. 404.
7. *Tabaqāt Ibn Sa'd*, Series I, Vol. ii, Brill, Leiden, p. 115.
8. William Muir, *Life of Muhammad*, p. 406.

force his companions to surrender the part of the booty that had fallen to their lot. But command and compulsion would have defeated the very purpose of his noble gesture, for it was an act of mercy which had its root in the depth of the human heart. So, instead of issuing commands, the Holy Prophet (peace and blessings of *Allah* be upon him) touched the chords of their hearts. He told them that it was easy for him to release all the prisoners that belonged to him, and to the refugees and helpers but since there were many new converts and idolaters with him, he, therefore, considered it advisable to persuade them to forego the booty fallen to their lot rather than to compel them to do so.

The Prophet told the deputation : "The prisoners who have fallen to my portion and to that of my family, I give them up unto you ; and I will presently speak unto the people concerning the rest. Come again at the midday prayer when the congregation is assembled and ask of me to make intercession with them for you." "At the appointed time they appeared and made their petition. The citizens of *Medina*, and those of *Mecca* also, cheerfully followed the example of *Muḥammad* (peace be upon him) but some of the allied tribes, as the *Fezāra*, with *'Uyaina* at their head, declined to do so. *Muḥammad* (peace be upon him) urged the claims of his new converts and promised that such of the allies as were unwilling to part with their share of the prisoners should be recompensed hereafter from the first booty the Lord might give in their hands at the rate of six camels for every captive. To this they agreed and the prisoners were all released."[9]

"The incident", says Syed Ameer Ali, "which followed after the distribution of the forfeited flocks and herds of the *Hawāzin*, shows not only the hold the Prophet had over the hearts of the *Medinites*, and the devotion he inspired them with, but it also proves that at no period of his career had he any material reward to offer to his disciples."[10] It also furnished a fine example of his superb balance of mind, his clarity of vision, his reasonableness, quality of mercy, his profound respect for the rights of human beings and his remarkable skill in bringing

9. William Muir, *Life of Muhammad*, pp. 406, 407, see also *Ibn Hishām*, Vol. iv, p. 132.

10. Syed Ameer Ali, *The Spirit of Islam*, p. 92.

round his people to his point of view.

This kindness and generosity on the part of the Holy Prophet won the hearts of many people amongst the tribes, who tendered their allegiance and became devoted *Muslims*.

In the division of the spoils a larger proportion fell to the share of the newly converted *Meccans* than to the people of *Medina*. Some of the *Anṣār*, looked upon this as an act of partiality and their discontent reached the ears of the Prophet. He ordered them to be assembled. He then addressed them in these words :

> "O tribe of *Anṣār*, what is the talk that has reached me from you ? What is this anguish that you feel in your hearts ? Did I not find you going astray and *Allah* guided you through me ? You were disunited and fell upon one another. Did *Allah* not unite you through me ? You were needy did *Allah* not enrich you through me ?"

> In response to each of the questions they cried : "*Allah* and His Apostle are bountiful."

> He said, "What prevents you from replying to the Apostle of *Allah*, O tribe of *Anṣār* ?" They said, "What should be the reply, O Apostle of *Allah*, while to the Lord and to His Apostle belong all benevolence and grace."

> The Prophet (peace be upon him) again said : "But by *Allah*, ye might have answered and answered truly, for I would have testified to its truth myself : you came to us belied and rejected, and we accepted you : you came as helpless and we helped you ; a fugitive, and we took you in ; poor and we comforted you. Ye *Anṣār*, do you feel anxiety for the things of this world, wherewith I have sought to incline these people unto the faith in which you are already established. Are you not satisfied, O group of *Anṣār* that the people go with ewes and camels while you go along with the Messenger of *Allah* to your dwellings. By Him in Whose Hand my life is, had there been no migration, I would have been one of the *Anṣār*. If the people would go through a valley and passage, and the *Anṣār* go through another valley and passage, I would go through the valley and passage of the *Anṣār*.

> The *Anṣār* are the inner garment[11] and the people are outer ones. You will surely face, after me, a wave of terrible selfishness. Then have patience until you meet *Allah* and His Apostle. Verily, I shall be on the '*Ḥaudh.*'[12] *Allah* ! have mercy on the *Anṣār*, their sons and their sons' sons."
>
> The audience wept until tears rolled down their beards as they said : "Yes, we are well satisfied, O Prophet of *Allah* ! with our lot and share."[13]

Then the Apostle left the gathering and the people also dispersed.

Muḥammad (peace of *Allah* be upon him) was, of course, perfectly right. These newly converted tribes had little idea of what *Islām* meant. It was, therefore, imperative that they should be given some material wealth in order to captivate their hearts. It was thus done as a temporary measure with the hope that after some time when the beauties of *Islamic* teachings would have unfolded before them, faith would eventually become the most important concern of their lives, and riches and wealth would pale into insignificance in their eyes.

It may be pointed out here that with the *Anṣār* who had been under the direct influence of the august personality of the Prophet, the concern for worldly riches was a momentary lapse. An overwhelming majority of them had been changed into God-worshipping saints of the highest rank. All cares of life and money were really abandoned by them. The firmness of their faith was attested by the Holy Prophet (peace be upon him). What really rankled their minds was that the worldly favours which the Holy Prophet had shown to the new converts might be due to his change of heart towards them. The speech of the Holy Prophet removed all these doubts and convinced them of

---

11. شعار is an inner garment which touches the skin of man, while the outer garment is put over that. It signifies nearness. *Fatḥ al-Bārī* (Cairo, 1959), Vol. ix, p. 113.

12. Means '*Ḥaudh-i-Kauthar*' in Paradise.

13. The different portions of this speech have been collected from the following books :

(*a*) *Ibn Hishām*, Vol. iv, pp. 172-73.
(*b*) *Ibn al-Athīr*, Egypt, 1349 A.H., Vol. ii, p. 185.
(*c*) *Fatḥ al-Bārī*, Vol. ix, pp. 111-117.

the fact that the worldly riches were immaterial for him, and he wished that his followers should rise far above the material temptations of life in their duties towards *Islām*.

The Prophet's Trust in *Anṣar*

The very fact that riches were not showered upon them by *Muḥammad* (peace be upon him) is the conclusive proof of the Prophet's trust in their faith.[14] The noble sentiments, which found expression in tears in response to the address of the Holy Prophet with regard to the distribution of booty, proved, beyond any shadow of doubt, that *Muḥammad's* trust in their selflessness, integrity and love for him was not unjustified. The Holy *Qur'ān* bears testimony to their devotion to *Allah* and His Apostle in the following words :

> "And (as for) the foremost, the first of the *Muhājirs* and the *Anṣār*, and those who followed them in goodness, *Allah* is well-pleased with them and they are well-pleased with Him, and He has prepared for them gardens beneath which rivers flow, to abide in them for ever ; that is the mighty achievement." (ix : 100)

Personal Sorrows

In the ninth year of *Hijrah*, the Holy Prophet lost his daughter *Zaynab* who had never recovered from the effects of ill-treatment which she had suffered on her escape from *Mecca*. *Umm Kulthūm*, whom *'Uthmān b. 'Affān* had married after *Ruqayyah's* death had also died. *Fāṭimah* alone of the Prophet's daughters had survived.

His heart was, however, solaced for a brief space by a male child, *Ibrāhīm*. He was born of Mary, the Copt. The infant advanced in age under the loving care of the Holy Prophet. In the fifteenth month of his life, however, he fell seriously ill and expired in the arms of his illustrious father. His death afflicted his parents deeply and tears rolled down the Prophet's eyes. The by-standers tried to comfort him. They reminded him that he had counselled others to be moderate in grief. "Nay", said *Muḥammad* (peace be upon him), calming himself as he hung

---

14. For details see Ḥāfiẓ Ibn Qayyim, *Zād al-Ma'ād*, Vol. ii, pp. 452-454.

over the expiring child. "I forbade impatient wailing and fulsome laudation of the dead. This that ye see in me is but the working of love and pity in the heart ; he that showeth no pity, unto him no pity shall be shown. We grieve for the child : the eye runneth down with tears, and the heart swelleth inwardly ; yet we say not aught that would offend our Lord. *Ibrāhīm* ! O *Ibrāhīm* ! If it were not that the promise is faithful, and hope of Resurrection sure ; if it were not that this is the way to be trodden by all, and that the last of us shall rejoin the first, I would grieve for thee with a grief sorer even than this." But the spirit had already passed away, and the last fond words of *Muḥammad* (peace be upon him) fell on ears that could no longer hear. So he laid down the little body saying : "The remainder of the days of his nursing shall be fulfilled in Paradise."[15] Then he comforted the child's mother, her sister and other members of the family and bade them, now that the child was gone, to be silent and resigned.

Incidentally there occurred the solar eclipse on the day when *Ibrāhīm* died. People attributed it to the condolence of the heavens over his death. No other occasion could be more fruitful for exploiting the religious susceptibilities of the people than this. It was a rare opportunity for an impostor to impress upon the innocent beings his command over the supernatural forces of heaven. *Muḥammad* (may the peace of *Allah* be upon him), the true Prophet, would therefore, never play with the religious susceptibilities of the human race. He rejected this idea outright. "The sun and the moon," he told his followers, "are the signs of the Lord, they do not suffer an eclipse at the death of any mortal. But when ye see an eclipse take yourselves to prayer until it passes away."[16]

The March on *Tabūk*

Mention might now be made to the *Muslim* expedition to *Tabūk* in Syria, where the Christian vassals of imperial Rome, notably the Arab chieftain of *Ghassān*, *Lakham* and *Jazam*, had

15. William Muir, *The Life of Muhammad*, p. 415, also, Ḥāfiẓ Ibn Ḥajar 'Asqalānī, *Fatḥ al-Bārī*, Cairo 1959, Vol. iii, Chapter "Kitāb al-Janā'iz," Section "*Qaul al-Nabi, inna bika la Mahzunun,*" pp. 415-417.

16. Ḥafiz Ibn Ḥajar 'Asqalānī, *Fatḥ al-Bārī*, Vol. iii, Chapter : "Abwab al-Kusuf " Section "al-Ṣalāt fi Kusūf al-Shams", pp. 180-182.

persuaded their lord to help them in attacking the *Muslims* at *Medina*. The Prophet ordered his followers to make the necessary preparations in order to meet the impending menace. There were, however, many obstacles in the way. The journey was long and the weather burning hot. Crops were ripe and ready for harvesting. Moreover, such a long journey could not be undertaken on foot and there were many who could not afford a ride.

In view of such grim obstacles, the Holy Prophet (peace be upon him) revealed his intention to the *Muslims*. This was done because timely warning was deemed necessary in order that the hardships of the journey might be fully anticipated by his followers.

Those who were weak in faith were reluctant to quit the ease and shelter of their homes and they pleaded inability on frivolous excuses. One of these pretexts, for instance, was like this : 'O Prophet of *Allah* ! grant me permission to stay back at home. By *Allah* my people know it fully well that I have a great weakness for the fair sex. I am afraid that if I see the women of *Banū Asfar*, I shall not be able to control myself." The Holy Prophet granted him exemption. It was about him that the verse was revealed :

> "Among them is (many) a man who says : Grant me exemption and draw me not into temptation. Lo ! into temptation they are already fallen and verily Hell is the encompasser of the infidels." (ix : 49)

Some of the hypocrites said to one another : "Don't go forth in the heat." Upon this *Allah* reminded them of the heat of Hell which was far more painful than the heat of the sun :

> "Say thou (O Prophet) : hotter still is the Hell-Fire. Wouldst that they understood". (ix : 81)

There were very few who showed such an unbecoming behaviour. The overwhelming majority comprised of loyal and sincere *Muslims* responded to the call of the Holy Prophet with usual readiness and zeal in the path of *Allah*. Hardships could not deter them. They had an implicit faith in the truth which the Holy Prophet had brought to them. Their life-long experience had strengthened their beliefs and had rooted deep convictions in their hearts that no power on earth could falsify the words of the Holy Prophet which were Divinely inspired. They were very enthusiastic about participating in the expedition. When the appeal was made for funds, tithes and voluntary contributions poured in from every quarter while the leading companions vied with one another in making generous contributions. *'Uthmān* contributed three hundred camels and ten thousand dinārs.[17] *'Umar* presented half of his total belongings. *Abū Bakr* submitted all that he had. Upon this the Holy Prophet asked, "O *Abū Bakr* ! Have you left anything for your family ?" "*Allah* and his Apostle," was the reply that emanated from the trusted friend. *'Abd al-Raḥman b. 'Awf* brought two hundred ounces of silver. Women gave away their ornaments and poor labourers offered willingly the major portion of their hard-earned earnings.[18]

Such was the enthusiasm of the faithful ! But even these generous contributions did not suffice to meet the expenses of the expedition. It was a terrible shock to those *Muslims* who longed to participate in the holy war, but could make no provision for it. They retired in tears. Their sincerity, longing and helplessness, have been depicted in the Holy *Qur'ān* in the following words :

> Nor (is any blame) on those who, when they came to you to be provided with mounts and you said, "I can find no mounts for you."
>
> They turned back while their eyes streaming with tears on account of grief that they could not find aught to expend. (ix : 92)

Despite all odds, despite the abstention of several tribes and the withdrawal of the hypocrites, a sizable army of people turned out, larger than ever before. Interminably, the ranks swelled before the oasis. A formidable force of 30,000 of which no less than ten thousand formed the cavalry, was formed to accompany the Holy Prophet. At *Badr*, there had been only three hundred ill-armed devotees ; at *Uḥud* seven hundred, at *Khaybar*, only two years earlier, sixteen hundred and now it was thirty thou-

17. Ibn Ḥajar, *Fatḥ al-Bāri*, Vol. viii, p. 54.

18. M. Idris Kandhalwi : *Seerat al-Mustafa*, Vol. iii, p. 128, also, M. 'Abul Barakāt 'Abdur Rauf Danapuri, *Asaḥḥ-al-Siyar*, p. 362.

sand. The Holy Prophet marched towards *Tabūk* leaving the charge of the city in the hands of *Muḥammad b. Maslama. 'Alī* was deputed to look after the household affairs during his absence from *Medina.*

With his usual perverseness *'Abd Allah b. Ubayy* appeared on the parade. As usual, he and his contingent started their march along with the army, but he had his followers deserted as soon as the troops crossed the outskirts of *Medina.*

Besides the hypocrites, there were several *Muslims* also who were slow to make up their minds so that they stayed behind, even though they suffered from no doubt with regard to *Islam* or the Prophet. They were *Ka'b b. Mālik, Murāra b. al-Rabī',* and *Hilāl b. Umayyah* ; they were loyal *Muslims* whose faith was above suspicion. They missed the expedition from simple inadvertence, not from weakness of faith or fear or danger or consideration of hardship. Their remorse at the mishap was intense and they were, therefore, forgiven by *Allah.*

The crossing of the desert by the *Muslim* army was a grim ordeal. "No marching was carried out until after sunset, but this was not much compensation. The dusk brought relief from the direct rays of the sun on helmets and breast plates, but the night was not long enough for the land and the air to cool off. In the day-time the only shadow was afforded by rocks which were so hot that they could not be touched. The ground blistered the feet as burning coals. The scarcity of water added to the misery. The hot wind made life intolerable. None of the men, not even the oldest nomad, had undergone such a trial of heat and privation."[19]

"*Muḥammad* rose above himself. His behaviour was exemplary. He was not a nomad, he was not young or even middle aged. In addition to the actual physical test, he had to cope with a thousand responsibilities. Yet he never faltered. In just over a week he brought an entire force with all its baggage train to *Tabūk* on the frontier of Roman Empire.[20]

Having reached *Tabūk,* where there was plenty of shade and water, the army halted. The rumours of invasion had by this time reached the border which was found quite peaceful. If

---

19. R. V. C. Bodley, *The Messenger,* Lahore, 1954, pp, 264-65.
20. *Ibid.,* p. 265.

conversion was to be secured, at the point of sword, could there have been a more promising opportunity than this ? The forces of *Muḥammad* (may the peace of *Allah* be upon him) were sufficient in numbers to add Damascus and part of Syria to his dominions. Before him lay a vast field for the gratification of worldly greeds, if he had any. But he had no Alexandrian lust for power, no passion for conquest merely for the display of his strength. His heart was absolutely free from such ambitions. Despite all the expense and trouble, when he felt satisfied that there was no cause for oppression he dropped all ideas of fighting and stirred the hearts of men to the great truth which he had come to preach. The marvellous speech that he delivered in *Tabūk* on this historic occasion beautifully sums up the objective behind his struggle.

The Prophet's Speech at *Tabūk*

He praised *Allah* and thanked Him and said :

> Well, verily the most veracious discourse is the Book of *Allah*. The most trustworthy handhold is the word of piety. The best of the religions is the religion of *Ibrāhīm*. The best of the precedents is the precedent of *Muḥammad*. The noblest speech is the invocation of *Allah*. The finest of the narratives is this *Qur'ān*. The best of the affairs is that which has been firmly resolved upon. The worst in religion are those things which are created without sanction. The best of the ways is the one trodden by the Prophets. The noblest death is the death of a martyr. The most miserable blindness is waywardness after guidance. The best of the actions is that which is beneficent. The best guidance is that which is put into practice. The worst blindness is the blindness of the heart.
>
> The upper hand is better than the lower hand.[21] The little that suffices is better than what is abundant and alluring. The worst apology is that which is tendered when death stares one in the face. The worst remorse is that which is felt on the day of Resurrection.
>
> Some men do not come to Friday prayer, but with

21. The hand which gives charity is better than the one which receives it.

hesitance and delay. And some of them do not remember *Allah* but with reluctance. The tongue which is addicted to false expression is a bubbling spring of sins.

The most valuable possession is the contentment of heart. The best provision is that of piety. The highest wisdom is fear of *Allah*, the Mighty and the Great. The best thing to be cherished in the hearts is faith and conviction ; doubt is infidelity.

Impatient wailing and fulsome laudation of the dead is an act of ignorance. Betrayal leads one to the fire of hell. Drinking amounts to burning. Obscene poetry is the work of the devil. Wine is the mother of all evil. The worst thing eaten is one which belongs to the orphan. Blessed is he who receives admonition from others.

Each one of you must resort to a place of four cubit (grave). Your affairs would be decided ultimately in the next life. The worst dream is false dream. Whatever is in store is near.

To abuse a believer is transgression ; raising arms against him is infidelity. To backbite him is a disobedience to *Allah*. Inviolability (and sacredness) of his property is like that of his blood.

He who swears by *Allah* (falsely), in fact falsifies Him. He who pardon others is himself granted pardon. He who forgives others, is forgiven by *Allah* for his sins.

He who represses anger, *Allah* rewards him. He who faces misfortunes with perseverance, *Allah* compensates him. He who acts only for fame and reputation, *Allah* disgraces him. He who shows patience and forbearance *Allah* gives him a double reward. He who disobeys *Allah*, *Allah* chastises him.

I seek the forgiveness of *Allah*.
I seek the forgiveness of *Allah*.
I seek the forgiveness of *Allah*.[22]

This speech is too eloquent to need any comment.

---

22. Ḥāfiz Ibn Qayyim, *Zād al-Ma'ād*, Vol. iii, pp. 13-14.

The Holy Prophet (peace of *Allah* be upon him) Receives Submission

During his stay at *Tabūk*, the Holy Prophet received the submission of the chieftains of towns adjoining to the frontiers of Syria, as also the homage of the Christian prince, *Yuhanna b. Ru'ba* the governor of *Ayla*. The following treaty was signed between him and the Holy Prophet (peace and blessings of *Allah* be upon him) :

> "In the name of God, the Compassionate and the Merciful. This is a guarantee from God and *Muḥammad*, the Apostle of God, *Yuhanna b. Ru'ba* and the people of *Ayla*, for their ships and their caravans by land and sea. They and all that are with them, men of Syria and those of the Yemen and seamen, all have the protection of *Allah* and that of His Apostle. Whoso contravenes this treaty, his wealth shall not save him ; it shall be the fair prize of him that takes it. Now it should not be lawful to hinder the men of *Ayla* from any springs which they have been in the habit of frequenting, nor from any journey they desire to make, whether by sea or by land."[23]

Several other tribes of *Arab* Christians of *Jibra* and *Adhruh* also made their submission. *Khālid b. Walid*, under the instructions of the Holy Prophet, marched with four hundred men on *Ukaydir al-Kindī*, ruler of *Dummat al-Jandal* (under the Roman influence). He arrested him and brought him before the Prophet. The chief surrendered to *Muḥammad* and was released on an undertaking to be loyal and to pay tribute.

The Holy Prophet had stayed in *Tabūk* for twenty days and reached the capital before the arrival of *Khālid*. The different sections of the population accorded him reception according to their love for *Islam*. The sincere *Muslims*, including men and children gave *Muḥammad* and his men, an enthusiastic welcome. But the Holy Prophet did not adopt the attitude of a conquering hero. As the people thronged around his mule, he addressed them cheerfully by their names. He let the children climb up his stirrups and ride behind him and in front of him. He behaved like the father of a huge family returning after a long

---

23. *Ibn Hishām*, Vol. iv, p. 169.

absence from the house.

The three persons who had lagged behind, not out of insincerity, or from contumacy, or ill-will, but from thoughtless slackness, and human weakness, were excluded from the life of the community. They suffered this pang readily, not in a spirit of defiance, but with a feeling of repentance and remorse for their negligence in their duty towards *Islām.* They freely repented and showed it in their deeds that loyalties to *Allah* and His Apostle were unshaken. The Almighty God, therefore, in His infinite mercy granted them pardon :

> God turned with favour to the Prophet, the *Muhājir* and the *Anṣār*—who followed him in a time of distress. After that the hearts of a part of them had nearly wavered (from duty) ; but He turned towards them (also) ! For He is unto them Most Kind, Most Merciful.
>
> (He turned in mercy also) to the three who were left behind, until the earth became strait to them notwithstanding its spaciousness and their souls were also straitened to them ; and they know it for certain that there was no refuge from *Allah* but in Him ; then He turned to them (mercifully) that they might turn to Him. Surely *Allah* ! He is the Relenting, the Merciful. (ix : 117-118)

In contrast to these were the "dwellers of the desert" who had stayed back notwithstanding the clear refusal of leave. They are admonished by *Allah* for their obedience, obstinacy and ficklessness and for their merely awaiting the turns of fortune :

> The dwellers of the desert are more hard in disbelief and hypocrisy, and more likely to be ignorant of the limits which *Allah* hath revealed unto His Messenger. And *Allah* is Knower, Wise.
>
> And of the wandering *Arabs* there is he who taketh that which he expendeth (for the cause of *Allah*) as a loss, and awaiteth (evil) turns of fortune for you (that he may be rid of it). The evil turn of fortune will be theirs. *Allah* is Hearer, Knower. (ix : 97-98)

The men Holy Prophet had to deal with

A thoughtful reading of *Surah 'Tauba'* (Repentance) clearly reveals that besides sincere *Muslims*, there were three categories of men with whom the Holy Prophet had to deal. Firstly, the hypocrites, who, when found out, made excuses because otherwise they would have suffered ignominy ; they were degenerated to the core and there was no hope for them.

> And among those around you of wandering *Arabs*, there are hypocrites, and among the town people of *Al-Medina* (there are some who) persist in hypocrisy who thou (O Prophet) knowest not. We know them, and We shall chastise them twice ; then they will be relegated to a painful doom. (ix : 101)

The second category comprised of those *Muslims* who were honest in their faith but under the transitory influence of human weakness had failed to carry out the commands of *Allah*. They repented, however, on their failings, and tried to make amends for their shortcomings and offered sincere and unqualified apologies. The Merciful Lord pardoned them :

> And others have confessed their faults, they have mingled a good deed and evil one ; may be *Allah* will turn to them (mercifully) ; surely *Allah* is Forgiving, Merciful. (ix : 102)

Thirdly, there were doubtful cases who would be judged later by *Allah* when He deems fit :

> And others are made to await *Allah's* command, whether He chastises them or whether He turns to them (mercifully) and *Allah* is Knowing, Wise. (ix : 106)

Hypocrites' Mosque Destroyed

Besides these three categories of hypocrites, there was the fourth class of insidious evil doers who carried their nefarious activities in a mosque at *Qubā'* which they had built not out of devotion to *Allah*, but for providing a rendezvous for conspirators against *Islām*. When the Holy Prophet had arrived at *Medina* he rested four days in *Qubā'* before entering the new city. Here was built the first mosque. The mosque based on true devotion and piety. Taking advantage of these sacred associations, some hypocrites of the tribe *Banū Ghanam* built an opposition mosque at *Qubā'*, pretending to advance the cause of *Islām*. In reality they were in league with a notorious enemy of *Islām*, one *Abū 'Āmir*, who had fought against *Islām* at *Uḥud* and who was now, after the battle of *Ḥunayan*, in Syria. This mosque was erected at his instigation to provide shelter to him and his associates wherefrom they could safely hatch conspiracy against the faithful. They approached the Holy Prophet with the request that he should come and consecrate that place by praying in it himself. As he was at the moment about to start for *Tabūk*, he deferred compliance with their request till his return. Meanwhile he came to know through Divine revelation that it was not a mosque meant for devotion and prayer but a meeting place of the anti-*Islamic* elements. On his return, therefore, the Holy Prophet sent a party to demolish the new edifice. The Holy *Qur'ān* denounced activities of these hypocrites in the following verse :

> And those who built a mosque to cause harm and for unbelief and to cause disunion among the believers and an ambush to him who made war against *Allah* and His Apostle before ; and they will certainly swear, 'we did not desire aught but good,' and *Allah* bears witness that they are most surely liars. (ix : 107)

The Holy Prophet set out for *Tabūk* in the *Rajab* of ninth year of *Hijrah* and came back in *Ramaḍan* of the same year. It was the last expedition which he himself led.[24]

Prophet's Large-Heartedness

About two months after the return of the *Muslim* army from *Tabūk*, the recognized leader of the hypocrites, *'Abd Allah b. Ubayy* died. His son who was a true *Muslim*, came to the Holy Prophet on his father's death and requested him to grant him his shirt so that he might use it as a shroud for the dead body of his father. He further asked him to conduct the burial ceremony. The Holy Prophet got up but *'Umar* took hold of his garment and objected on the ground that *'Abd Allah* was a hypocrite and that *Allah* had forbidden the Holy Prophet to offer

---

24. The account of *Tabūk* is based upon *Zād al-Ma'ād* of Ḥāfiz Ibn Qayyim : for details see Vol. iii, pp. 1-52.

prayer for him. The Holy Prophet replied : "I have been given the choice,[25] for *Allah* says : Ask forgiveness for them or do not ask forgiveness for them. If you ask forgiveness for them (even) seventy times, *Allah* will not forgive them. (ix : 80) The Prophet also said that if he only knew that by an addition to the seventy, they would be forgiven, he would add thereto." He even followed the bier and prayed over the grave and stood over it until he was buried. "I was astonished at myself and my boldness," says *'Umar*, "being well aware of the fact that *Allah* and His Apostle knew best." It was not long before that these two verses were revealed :

> Any pray thou not ever over any of them that may die nor stand thou over his grave. Verily they have disbelieved in *Allah* and His Apostle and died while they are ungodly. (ix : 84)

Afterwards the Apostle never offered prayer over the dead body of a hypocrite.[26]

The incident shows what intense love he had for mankind and how kind and forgiving he was even to his worst enemies. He was always looking forward for an opportunity when he could save the "erring people" from falling into the fire of hell.

'Urwa Embraces *Islam*

Ṭā'if in general maintained a hostile position yet. *'Urwa b. Mas'ūd al-Thaqafī*, one of its talented chiefs, who was with *Suhayl* in negotiating the treaṭy of *Ḥudaybiyāh*, and had learnt much about *Muḥammad* (peace be upon him) and the faith that he preached, felt an irresistible revulsion of feelings, went over fondly to the Holy Prophet, embraced *Islām* and became an active, faithful and devoted servant of *Allah*. Full of the new spirit and faith he returned to his men and proclaimed his abjuration of idolatry and called them enthusiastically to share in the blessings of the Divine religion. He was confident that his sound position would not expose him to any peril. But it proved to be a miscalculation of the situation. His men could not tolerate his conversion. They surrounded his house one day

---

25. Ibn Ḥajar 'Asqalānī, *Fatḥ al-Bāri*, Cairo 1959, Vol. xii, Kitāb al-Janā'iz, p. 381.

26. *Ibn Hishām*, Vol. iv, p, 197.

and killed him by a shower of arrows. While he was breathing his last he was asked, "What do you think about your death?" He said, "It is a gift with which God has honoured me and a martyrdom which God has led me to. I am like the martyrs who were killed with the Apostle before he went away from them, so bury me with them." "The dying words of *'Urwa,*" says Syed Ameer Ali, "had a great effect upon his compatriots than all his endeavours whilst living. The martyr's blood blossomed into faith in the hearts of murderers. Seized with sudden compunction, perhaps also weary of their hostility with the tribes of the desert, the Tayefites sent the deputation for forgiveness,"[27]

Deputation from *Ṭa'if*

The Holy Prophet received the deputation gladly and pitched the tent for their accommodation close by the mosque so that they should be able to hear the *Qur'ān* and see the *Muslims* offering their prayers to *Allah.* They were deeply impressed by the words of *Allah* and the devotion of the faithful. They were also impressed by the new style of public address adopted by *Muḥammad* (peace be upon him) in which he never allowed himself to protrude. When they heard his eloquent, well-knit utterances in which there was no rambling, no self-exhibition, no account of his personal sorrows, they observed : Our minds are stirred to acknowledge the truth that *Muḥammad* is the Apostle of *Allah,* for he does not project his own self in his utterances.[28]

As the faith in the apostlehood of *Muḥammad* is one of the fundamentals of *Islām,* the Holy Prophet stressed its basic importance and said, "I am the first to profess that I am the Prophet of *Allah.*"[29] It is by belief in the unity of *Allah* and the apostlehood of all the earlier prophets and that of Prophet *Muḥammad* (peace be upon him) that a man is admitted into the fold of *Islām.* The Holy Prophet, therefore, proclaimed it in unequivocal terms that belief in his apostlehood is not a matter of choice. It is the basis of *Islām* and as such one should be very clear about it before making any decision.

The memhers of the deputation freely communicated their apprehensions to the Holy Prophet who removed all their doubts

27. Syed Ameer Ali, *The Spirit of Islam* p. 98.
28. Ḥāfiẓ Ibn Qayyim, *Zād al-Ma'ād,* Vol. III, p. 55.
29. *Ibid.*

and misgivings with the Divine Wisdom endowed to him and instructed them in the faith so nicely that they were all convinced of the truth of his mission. They, however, put forward certain conditions before the Holy Prophet and requested him that some allowance should be given to them as regards faith, devotion and canons of morality. The one thing they begged for was that fornication should not be banned for them. "The overwhelming majority amongst us," they argued, "does not undertake the responsibilities of a married life, and they have, therefore, to satisfy their sexual lust through adultery." "No it can't be," replied the Holy Prophet, "for it is forbidden by *Allah* as he says, 'And go not nigh fornication.[30] Surely it is ever an abomination and vile as a pathway' (xvii: 32) They then asked that no check should be imposed on the system of their lending money on interest. But the Prophet would not agree. He told them frankly that he could grant them no concession in that respect. They were entitled to recover the principal only, whereas the rest of the amount obtained by way of interest would not be given to them as the Holy *Qur'ān* observes: "O you who believe! observe your duty to *Allah*, and give up what remaineth (due to you) from usury,[31] if ye are

30. The *Arabic* word '*zinā*' (زنا) is much more comprehensive than either fornication which is restricted to the illicit sexual intercourse of unmarried person or adultery which also denotes the sexual intercourse of two persons either of whom is married to a third person. *Zinā*' in general denotes sexual intercourse between any man and woman, whether married or not, who do not stand to each other in the relation of husband and wife. The enormity of this evil in *Islām* can be well judged from the fact that *Allah* not only forbids it with vehemence but enjoins men not to go near it, thus avoiding any approach or temptation to it.

Adultery is an evil through and through. It is not only shameful in itself and inconsistent with any self-respect or respect for others, but it opens the road to so many sins and crimes. It undermines the basis of self-control and discipline. It deprives a man of the sense of decency, modesty and chastity. It destroys the very foundation of the family and darkens the life of the children not yet born. Moreover it causes so many diseases to spread in society. Then it leads to murders and the vicious circle which lasts for many years bringing ruination and destruction to so many valuable lives and property.

31. The Arabic word '*ribā*' is but partially covered by the English word 'usury', which in modern parlance, signifies only an exorbitant, or extortionate interest. The word '*ribā*' means an addition over and above the

[*Contd.*

(in truth) believers." (ii : 278). They again demanded that they should be permitted to drink, for it was the extract of their soil, and their very existence depended upon it. The Holy Prophet turned down their demand and recited the following verses of the Holy *Qur'ān* : [32]

> Oh ye who believe ! intoxicants[33] and gambling,[34] and stone altars and divining arrows are only an abomination, and handiwork of Satan. Eschew such (abomination) that ye may prosper. (v : 90)

They went back to their tents and discussed the situation at length with one another and then they again turned up and asked the Holy Prophet what treatment they should accord to their goddess *al-Lāt*. The Prophet said without the least hesitation. "Destroy that." There arose a cry amongst them and they expressed their fear that if the idol knew their intention, it would immediately kill the inhabitants of the city. Upon

---

principal sum that is lent (*Mufradāt* of Imam Rāghib) and includes usury as well as interest. The devastating propensities of usury are visible to every eye. It is through charity that selflessness is inculcated in man which forms the basis of human sympathy, usury engenders callousness and greed which annihilate any tenderly feelings in a man and make him the worshipper of Mammon. It is the most effective weapon of the ruthless exploitation of the toiling masses and its grip on the economy of the country leads to the concentration of wealth in a few hands much to the harm of the lower strata of society who are driven to extreme poverty. Then this interest is one of the great causes of trade cycles in which the 'have nots' receive the hardest blow. It also promotes habits of idleness, but its worst effect is on morals, as it causes man to be obsessed with greed and selfishness.

32. Ḥāfiẓ Ibn Qayyim, *Zād al-Ma'ād*, Vol. iii, p. 56.

33. '*Khamr*' includes all inebriating liquors. It may be added that according to *Islām* the small quantity of anything of which a large quantity is intoxicating is also prohibited.

34. The original word is '*maisir*' (ميسر) derived from '*yasra*' (يسر) meaning 'he divided anything in parts.' *Maysir* was a game of hazard of the Arabs, and in the legal language of *Islām*, it includes all games of chance. Some derive it from *yusr* (يسر) meaning 'ease', because of the ease with which wealth could be attained in that manner.

The close relationship between drinking, gambling and other sins and crimes is well-known. Drinking and gambling lead a man to nervous excitement and he loses his hold upon himself. The taverns and gambling houses are almost everywhere the notorious dens of crime and prostitution. Wine, women and gambling very often go together and lead a man to some very grave excesses and the whole fabric of society is disrupted.

this *'Umar* who was standing by the side of the Holy Prophet remarked :

> *'Abd Yalil* ! How ignorant you are ! It is nothing but an idol carved out of lifeless stone.[35] They, however, then begged a favour that *al-Lāt* should be spared for some time. First, they asked for three years, then two years and then one year and finally for one month only.[36] But the Holy Prophet (may peace of *Allah* be upon him) declined firmly as *Islām* and idol-worship could not co-exist. There was no midway between believing in *Allah* and accepting other deities as objects of worship. Finally, they asked that they might be exempted from the daily prayers and should be permitted not to break the idols with their own hands. The Apostle said : "We excuse you from destroying the idols with your own hands, but as for prayer, no concession can be granted in it since there is no virtue in faith in which there is no prayer."[37]

Prayer is in fact the heart and soul of religion. It is the first, the highest and the most solemn phenomenon in which a religious man expresses his devotion to God, a fundamental element in all genuine piety. It has been called the *mi'rāj* (ascent) of the *Muslims*. All the forms which the communions of the human soul with God is able to assume, will be found there in unexampled nobility and splendour.

The principal elements which distinguish the prayers of *Islām* are :

1. A vivid consciousness of *Allah*, as Ever Wakeful and Merciful, Ever-living and All-Powerful.

2. An unfailing realisation of His Greatness, involving the conviction that only through moral goodness can men become acceptable in His sight.

3. The consciousness of man's own failings and his weaknesses and in contrast to them the Power of the Almighty *Allah*, His unbounded favours. This finds expression in intercession, thanksgiving, petition, gratitude and

35. Ḥāfiẓ Ibn Qayyim, *Zād al-Ma'ād*, Vol. iii, p. 56.
36. *Ibn Hishām*, Vol. iv, pp. 184-185.
37. *Ibid.*, p. 185.

love, repentance and solicitation.

Thus God as the Living, Merciful Lord, and righteousness as He visualizes it, can elevate man and can bring harmony between man, the universe and its Creator. These are the essentials of *Islamic* beliefs and form the distinguishing marks of *Islamic* prayer.

These aspects of prayer have been clearly set forth in the *Qur'ān* :

> Recite thou that which hath been revealed unto thee of the Book and establish thou the prayer ; Verily prayer preventeth man from indecency and that which is disreputable ; and surely the remembrance of *Allah* is the greatest. And *Allah* Knoweth that which ye perform. (xxix : 45)

Nothing else which the Men of *Thaqīf* could say was left unsaid. The Holy Prophet had elucidated before them all aspects of the Divine Faith and had fully convinced them of the responsibilities that would fall upon them and the changes that they would be obliged to make in the patterns of their individual and social life. Before they left *Medina,* they had agreed to an unconditional surrender to *Allah* and had expressed their faith in all the teachings of *Islām.*

The Preachers sent

The Holy Prophet was fully alive to the needs of new converts. Someone was required to guide them in the principles of religion. He appointed *'Uthmān b. Abi al-Ās* as their teacher and leader as he was the most zealous in acquiring the teachings of the *Qur'ān.*

The deputation stayed at *Medina* during the month of *Ramaḍān* and then returned home. The Holy Prophet (peace be upon him) sent *Abū Sufyān* and *al-Mughīrah* along with them to destroy the idols. Both of them were old friends of *Banū Thaqīf.* They smote the idols whilst the women wept, but no one could say anything in protest for they had already agreed to the destruction of idols.

Abu Bakr leads the Pilgrimage

With the turn of the year, the time came again for the

pilgrimage to *Mecca*. This time *Muḥammad* (peace be upon him) did not go himself. In his place he sent a caravan under leadership of his trusted lieutenant *Abū Bakr*. Soon after its departure there came a revelation from *Allah* : the opening passage of the chapter entitled "Repentance" in which 'freedom from obligation' is proclaimed from *Allah* in regard to those idolatrous tribes who had shown no respect for the treaties which they had entered into with the Holy Prophet (peace and blessings of *Allah* be upon him).

'Alī, the cousin and the son-in-law of *Muḥammad*, was deputed to make this declaration on behalf of the Prophet which concerned mainly the problems of status and security of their lives and property. On coming up with it, and communicating the nature of his errand, *Abū Bakr* inquired whether the Prophet had put him in command or had he been just commissioned to make the announcement. "I have been deputed to make the proclamation only," replied *'Alī*.[38]

Towards the close of the pilgrimage, on the day of the ritual sacrifice, *'Alī* read aloud to the multitudes that thronged around him the heavenly command as follows :

> Quittance is this from *Allah* and His Apostle towards those of the idolaters with whom ye covenanted. Let them go about, then, in the land for four months. And know that verily *Allah* is the Humiliator of the infidels. And a proclamation from *Allah* and His Messenger to all men on the day of the greater pilgrimage that *Allah* is free from the obligation to the idolaters, and (so is) His Messenger. So if ye repent, it will be better for you ; but if you are averse, then know that ye cannot escape *Allah*. And announce unto those who disbelieve of a painful doom.
>
> Excepting those of the idolaters with whom ye (*Muslims*) have a treaty, and who have since abated nothing of your right nor have supported anyone against you (as for these) fulfil (the terms of) the treaty with them till their term. Verily, *Allah* loveth those who keep their duty (unto Him).

---

38. *Ibn Hishām*, Vol. iv, p. 237.

Then, when the sacred months have passed, slay[39] the idolaters wherever you find them and take them (captive) and besiege them, and prepare for them each ambush. But if they repent and establish worship and pay the poor due, then leave their way free. Verily *Allah* is Forgiving, Merciful.

And if anyone of the idolaters seeketh thy protection (O Prophet) then protect him so that he may hear the Word of *Allah,* and afterwards convey him to his place of safety. This is because they are a folk who know not. How can there be agreement for the idolaters with *Allah* and His Apostle, except those with whom you made an agreement at the sacred Mosque? So long as they are true to you, be true to them ; Surely *Allah* loveth those who are careful (of their duty).

How (can there be any treaty for the others) when, if they have the upper hand on you, they regard not pact nor honour in respect of you ; they please you with their mouths while their hearts do not consent and most of them are transgressors. (ix : 1-8)

Having finished the recitation of these verses *'Alī* (*Allah* be pleased with him) expounded the edict thus :

"I am ordered to declare unto you that no unbeliever shall enter paradise. No unbeliever shall, after this year, perform the pilgrimage ; nor shall any one be allowed to make the circuit of the Holy House unclothed. Whosoever has a treaty with the Apostle, it shall be respected until its time expires. Four months are given to the tribes that they may return to their homes in security. After that the obligations of the Messenger shall cease."[40]

At the conclusion of *'Alī's* speech, the pilgrims dispersed.

39. The clear exception of the last verse shows that the command is not of general application, but refers to the particular groups of *Meccan* idolaters who showed no designs of desisting from their treacherous designs. Here the emphasis is on the first clause : The essential fact to be borne in mind is that all the polytheists of the world, even all the idolaters of Arabia, are not spoken of in the verse. The persons spoken of are those who had repeatedly violated their treaties and inflicted severe injuries upon the *Muslims.*

40. Ibn Qayyim, *Zād al-Ma'ād,* Vol. iii, p. 53.

In groups and companies as well as individually, they made way to their homes. As they went, they spread the news that from now on *Islām* was the religion of every part of Arabia. The tribes of the desert had fully seen by this time that *Muḥammad* (peace be upon him) was a true Prophet ; that his message was divine and the words which came out of his lips were based on sincerity ; that no mortal could have even thought or done what the Prophet had thought and done under the most trying circumstances. All this had undermined the basis of opposition and the small seed of *Islām* had grown into a mighty tree.

Embassies pour in from all Parts of Arabia

The supremacy of *Islām* was thus fully established. The age of ignorance with all its attendant evils, had given place to an era of enlightenment, knowledge, and human kindness. To *Medina,* therefore, flowed streams of deputations from all quarters to render homage to *Islām* and to the Last of the Prophets (peace be upon him). There came deputations from *Banū Tamim, Banū Sa'ad, b. Bakr, Tayy, Farwa b. Musayk al-Muradi, Banū Zubayd, Kindah,* from the kings of *Ḥimyar.*

By the tenth year of the *Hijrah* nearly all the pagan *Arabs* had embraced *Islām* and most of those who still remained Christians and Jews were under *Muḥammad's* protection. But an overwhelming majority of the *Muslims* who lived far from *Medina* needed instruction in the Divine Faith. The Holy Prophet, therefore, sent forth teachers to instruct the new converts in the teachings of *Islām* and collect poor due. It is narrated on the authority of *'Abd Allāh b. Abū Bakr* that when the Apostle of God deputed *Mu'ādh* to undertake this heavy task, he gave him the following principles for his guidance :

> Deal gently with the people and show no harshness towards them. You are going to one of the peoples with Scripture who will ask you about the key of heaven. Say to them ; Verily the key of Paradise is to testify that there is no god, but *Allah* ; with Him there is no partner.[41]

As *Islām* knows of no division between religious and secular activities the envoys who were commissioned to give religious

---

41. *Ibn Hishām,* Vol. iv, p. 237.

instructions to the people were also invested with judicial authority. Acceptance of the new faith implied of necessity the simultaneous recognition of its social, political, moral and spiritual code, and thus the whole life of the new converts required to be regulated by the teachings of *Islām*. Every action was to be adjudged in the light of the *Qur'ān* and the *Sunnah* of the Holy Prophet. The exponents of these teachings became, therefore, also the judges of the land.

Towards the close of the Prophet's life, the sound of war had almost died away, but there were conversions to *Islām* on an amazingly large scale. It is hardly credible that this sudden and unexpected change of behaviour could have been the result of warfare. These warlike sons of Arabia, still strong and proud of their racial traditions, could not have been coerced into submission at the point of the sword. They were strong enough to hold their own against the *Muslims* in battle, or could easily form a federation against the growing power of *Medina*. Furthermore, in case of war they could always contract treaties with the *Muslims* of good neighbourliness and retain the right of worship in their own way as the terms accorded to Jews and Christians. But they did nothing to hold themselves back from *Islām*. They had been convinced of the great truth that it preached and the sincerity and genuineness of the Holy Prophet who delivered it. Their hearts had been changed and nothing could deter them from accepting the Divine Faith.

Farewell Address

Muḥammad (peace and blessings of *Allah* be upon him), the Prophet, was now in the sixty-third year of his life which coincided with the close of the tenth year of the *Hijrah*. His mission was completed. To a people steeped in ignorance, the Holy Prophet gave light and inspired them with belief in *Allah*, the sole Creator, Master and Sustainer of the universe. To a disunited mass, engaged in perpetual warfare, he gave unity of thought and action and locked them in ties of brotherhood and love. His life is the noblest record of a mission nobly and faithfully performed and "he performed it with an enthusiasm and fervour which admitted of no compromise, conceived no halting ; with indomitable courage which brooked no resistance and allowed no fear of consequence ; with a singleness of purpose which thought of no self.''[42]

The completion of his mission implied his departure from his earthly home to his heavenly abode. The Prophet visualised it clearly and, therefore, spent most of his time in making preparations for the journey on which he was about to set.

The month of pilgrimage was at hand, and the Prophet decided to avail himself of this opportunity. The *Ka'bah* had been completely purified and there was no vestige of an image or heathen rite left which could offend his eyes. He set on what is called the Farewell Pilgrimage, because it was the last pilgrimage performed by him. Messengers were sent to all the parts of Arabia inviting people to join him in this great pilgrimage. It was necessary for them since they should learn by first hand knowledge the several injunctions and practices of pilgrimage—free from all taints of ignorance—an ideal pattern which was to be kept intact in its pristine glory for all times to come.

Five days before *Dhul Ḥijjah*, the Prophet (peace be upon him) put on the pilgrim's garb and set out to *Mecca* with more than 114,000 *Muslims* along with him. All his wives accompanied him. As he rode, he recited "*Labbaik ! Labbaik !*" signifying, "Here I am at Thy service, here I am O Lord ! Here I am to declare that there is no partner with Thee. All praise and blessings belong to Thee and all sovereignty is Thine. I am here at Thy service, and Thou has no partner, O *Allah* !" As the Holy Prophet recited the above call, all his companions repeated the same loudly.

What the psychologists call the sudden outburst of crowd psychology was changed into sublime spiritual expression. There is something marvellously sacred with this ritual of *Islām* which raises a man to the lofty heights of love for God. It symbolises self-sacrifice and devotion to the Great Master. It is an assembly where human equality reigns supreme and where no mark of distinction between a king and peasant is seen, where all meet as brethren to do homage to their Lords.

The Holy Prophet reached *Mecca* on the 5th *Dhul Ḥijjah*. He made seven circuits (*ṭawāf*) of the *Ka'bah*, offered two *raka'hs* of prayer at the "station of *Ibrāhīm*" and climbing up the Mount of *Safā* declared, "There is no god, but *Allah*. He has no partner.

42. Syed Ameer Ali, *The Spirit of Islam*, p. 105.

All sovereignty and praise belong to Him. He gives life and brings death. He is All-Powerful and Supreme over everything. He fulfilled His promise, He helped His servant, and He alone crushed all the forces of disbelief." Meanwhile *'Alī* (*Allah* be pleased with him) also joined the Prophet with the pilgrims of Yemen.

On the 8th of *Dhul Ḥijjah* the Prophet left with his companions for *Minā* and passed the night there, and on the 9th, after the morning prayer, he proceeded to *'Arafāt* where he delivered the following celebrated address :

> All praise be to *Allah*. We glorify Him and seek His help and pardon ; and we turn to Him. We take refuge with *Allah* from the evils of ourselves and from the evil consequences of our deeds. There is none to lead him astray whom *Allah* guides aright, and there is none to guide him aright whom He leads astray. I bear witness that there is no god but *Allah* alone ; having no partner with Him, and I bear witness that *Muḥammad* is His bondman and His Messenger. I admonish you, O bondmen of *Allah* ! to fear *Allah* and I urge you to His obedience and I open the speech with that what is good.
>
> Ye people ! Listen to my words : I will deliver a message to you, for I know not whether, after this year, I shall ever be amongst you here again. O people ! Verily your blood, your property and your honour are sacred and inviolable until you appear before your Lord, as this day and this month is sacred for all. Verily you will meet your Lord and you will be held answerable for your actions. Have I not conveyed the message ? O *Allah* ! Be my witnesses.
>
> He who has any trust with him he should restore it to the person who deposited it with him.
>
> Beware, no one committing a crime is responsible for it but he himself. Neither the son is responsible for the crime of his father, nor the father is responsible for the crime of his son.
>
> O people ! Listen to my words and understand them. You must know that a *Muslim* is the brother of the *Muslim*

and they form one brotherhood. Nothing of his brother is lawful for a *Muslim* except what he himself allows willingly. So you should not oppress one another. O *Allah* ! have I not conveyed the message ?

Behold ! all practices of paganism and ignorance are now under my feet. The blood-revenges of the days of Ignorance are remitted. The first claim on blood I abolish is that of *Ibn Rabi'ah Ibn Hārith* who was nursed in the tribe of Sa'd and whom the *Hudhayl* killed.

Usury is forbidden, but you will be entitled to recover your principal. Wrong not and you would not be wronged. *Allah* has decreed that there should be no usury and I make a beginning by remitting the amount of interest which *'Abbās b. 'Abd al-Muṭṭalib* has to receive. Verily it is remitted entirely.

O people ! fear *Allah* concerning women. Verily you have taken them on the security of *Allah* and have made their persons lawful unto you by words of *Allah* ! Verily you have got certain rights over your women and your women have certain rights over you. It is incumbent upon them to honour their conjugal rights and, not to commit acts of impropriety which, if they do, you have authority to chastise them, yet not severely. If your wives refrain from impropriety and are faithful to you, clothe and feed them suitably.

Behold ! Lay injunctions upon women but kindly.

O people ! Listen and obey though a mangled Abyssinian slave is your *amīr* if he executes [the ordinances of] the Book of *Allah* among you.

O people ! Verily *Allah* has ordained to every man the share of his inheritance. The child belongs to the marriage-bed and the violator of wedlock shall be stoned. He who attributes his ancestry to other than his father or claims his clientship to other than his masters, the curse of *Allah*, that of the angels, and of the people be upon him. *Allah* will accept from him neither repentance nor righteousness.

O people ! Verily the Satan is disappointed at being

ever worshipped in this land of yours, but he can be obeyed in anything short of worship he will be pleased in matters you may be disposed to think of little account, so beware of him in your matters of religion.

Verily, I have left amongst you the Book of *Allah* and the *Sunnah* of His Apostle which if you hold fast, you shall never go astray.

"And if you were asked about me, what would you say ?" They replied : "We bear witness that you have conveyed the message, and discharged your ministry."

The Holy Prophet addressed the assembly again on Friday, *Dhul Ḥijjah* 10 A.H. and besides repeating some of the important points of the previous address, he threw a good deal of light on some new questions.

As usual, he opened his oration with praising *Allah* and expressing his gratitude to Him.

O people ! Verily the intercalation[43] (of a prohibited month) aggravates infidelity. Thereby the unbelievers are led to wrong. For they make it lawful one year and forbid it in another year to be in conformity with the number [of months] which *Allah* declared unlawful so they consider violable that which *Allah* declared to be inviolable and they consider inviolable what *Allah* declared to

---

43. This was an invention or innovation of the idolatrous Arabs, whereby they avoided keeping a sacred month, when it suited to their convenience. The Holy *Qur'ān* condemns the arbitrary and selfish conduct of the pagan Arabs in changing the months, or making addition or deduction in them s o as to get an unfair advantage over the enemy. The four prohibited months were *Dhu al-Qa'dah, Dhul-Ḥijjah, Muḥarram* and *Rajab*. If it suited them they postponed one of these months, and so a prohibited month became an ordinary month, while their opponents might hesitate to fight, they got an undue advantage. This practice interfered with the security of life and was therefore denounced by the Prophet. It also desecrated the sanctity of the month of pilgrimage. The *Qur'ān* says :

"Verily the transposing of a prohibited month is an addition unto infidelity, whereby the infidels are led astray, allowing it one year and forbidding it another year, that they make up the number which *Allah* has sanctified and then they allow that which *Allah* hath forbidden. The evil of their course seems pleasing to them. But *Allah* guideth not those who reject the Faith." (ix : 37)

be violable.

Verily the time has revolved in its own way from the day when the heavens and the earth were created. The number of months to *Allah* is twelve of which four are sacred ; three are consecutive—*Dhul Qa'dah, Dhul Ḥijjah, Muḥarram,* and *Rajab* which is between *Jumadah* and *Sha'ban.*

O people ! Do you know what day it is, what territory it is, what month it is ?

To this the people answered : The day is the day of sacrifice ; and the territory is the sacred territory, the month is the sacred month. At each reply the Holy Prophet said :

So I apprise you that your lives, your property and your honour must be as sacred to one another as this sacred day, in this sacred month, in this sacred town.

And your slaves ! See that you feed them with such food as you eat yourselves ; and clothe them with the clothes that you yourselves wear. And if they commit a fault which you are not inclined to forgive, then part with them for they are the servants of *Allah* and are not to be chastised.

Behold ! Listen to me. Worship your Lord ; offer prayers five times a day ; observe fast in the month of *Ramaḍān* ; make pilgrimage to the House (*Ka'bah*) ; pay readily the *Zakāt* (poor-rate) on your property and obey whatever I command you, only then will you get into the heaven.

Let him that is present convey it unto him who is absent. For happily, many people to whom the message is conveyed may be more mindful of it than the audience."

The Holy Prophet picked up the thread of his oration on the next day also and added :

O people ! Verily your Lord is one and your father is one. All of you belong to one ancestry of *Adam* and *Adam* was created out of clay. There is no superiority for an *Arab* over a non-*Arab* and for a non-*Arab* over an *Arab* ; nor for white over the black nor for the black over the white except in piety. 'Verily the noblest among you is he who is the most pious.' (xlix : 13)

Behold, the nearer ones of you should convey the message to the remoter ones. I have conveyed the message.

Then looking up to the heaven, he said :

"O Lord ! I have delivered the message and discharged my ministry."

"Yes," cried all the people crowding round him, "Yes, verily you have."

"O Lord ! I beseech Thee bear Thou witness unto it."

And with these words, the Prophet concluded his address.[44]

He alighted from his camel and offered the noon and afternoon prayers together. It was at this time that the verse regarding the completion of religion was revealed to him :

This day I have perfected for you your faith, And completed My favour upon you, And I am well-pleased with *al-Islām* as your religion. (v : 3)

The Prophet immediately recited this verse to all those who were present on this occasion.[45]

The *Muslims* were happy on receiving this information, but *Abū Bakr* was sad as he perceived in it a clear indication of the departure of Holy Prophet (peace and blessings of *Allah* be upon him) to his eternal abode. *Abū Bakr* rightly realized that the Prophet had been raised in order to bring the religious truth to

---

44. The different parts of this address are scattered in various chapters of the authentic books of *Ḥadīth*. It has been narrated with a little bit of variation of words by various narrators in many ways *Shāh Walīullāh* of Delhi has recorded this address in his book *Izālat al-Khifā'* with eighty different chains of narrators. Although there is some difference of words, they all convey the same meaning. I have pieced together the fragments into one whole. The material is selected from the following books :

(*a*) *Ibn Hishām*, Vol. iv, Cairo, 1936 A.D., pp. 250-752.
(*b*) Ibn Kathīr, *Al-Bidāya wan-Nihāya*, Cairo, 1932 A.D.
(*c*) *Fatḥ al-Bārī*, Kitāb al-Maghāzī, Vol. ix, Cairo, 1959 A.D., pp. 170-172.

45. *Fatḥ al-Barī*, Vol. ix, p. 172.

perfection. Evidently when the mission of *Muḥammad* (peace and blessings of *Allah* be upon him) had been fulfilled, it meant that his physical presence on the earth was no longer needed and that the time had come for him to take eternal rest in his heavenly abode far from the cares and worries of worldly of life.

The farewell address of the Holy Prophet is not only remarkable for its eloquence, but also for its sublime message for the whole of human race. The world has not been able to lay down better principles of ethics than those enunciated in it. Every word of it breathes a spirit of magnanimity and aims at establishing righteousness and fair dealings among men on a workable basis. It establishes brotherhood among *Muslims* irrespective of the divergences of their geographical, racial and colour backgrounds and puts finishing touches to a social order, perfectly free from oppression and injustice :

> "Three days were allowed for the *Medina* contingent to recuperate before returning home. The atmosphere was cordial and different from what it had been at the time of the last visit. Relatives met relatives and friends recognized friends without that watchful glance for the concealed sword. Parties were given and the brotherhood of which *Muḥammad* had preached was put into practice. It was perhaps less gay than in the days of *Abu Jahl* and *Abu Lahab*, but it was more sincere."[46]

Muḥammud (peace be upon him) was happy. His mind was at peace. He had completed the pilgrimage and established a religious practice in its ideal form, free from all taints of paganism. He had delivered the message which sums up beautifully the fundamentals of *Islām* and the responsibilities which fall upon the shoulders of *Muslims* as the standard-bearers of the Divine faith. "The Prophet", observes *Ibn Hishām*, "completed the *Hajj* and showed to the people the rites and ceremonies which are essential and taught them what God had made incumbent upon them with regard to pilgrimage, the "*station*," the throwing of stones, the circumambulation of the House, and what He had permitted and forbidden in this connection. It was the pilgrimage of message and proclamation

46. R. V. C. Bodley, *The Messenger*, Lahore, p. 279.

and that of the Farewell also, since it was the last *Hajj* which the Holy Prophet performed in his life."[47]

After the Farewell Pilgrimage, the concourse broke and returned to *Medina*. The Holy Prophet accompanied his men in their homeward journey and reached the city of *Medina* at the end of *Ḍhul-Hijjah*.

He had no doubt realized that he would soon be called back to his heavenly abode, but he was not to be disheartened or dismayed. He was entrusted with a heavy responsibility by *Allah* and he was therefore very anxious to spend every moment of his sacred life in the discharge of his ministry. The idea of fast-approaching death did not droop his spirit ; it rather provided him incentive to give finishing touches to the work assigned to him, so that nothing should be left undone before he presented himself to his Lord in heaven.

Prophet's Activities After the Pilgrimage

The Holy Prophet in the last year of his life spent most of his time in *Medina*. He settled the organization of the provinces and tribal communities which had adopted *Islām* and become the component parts of the *Muslim* state. Officers were sent to the provinces and to various tribes for the purpose of teaching the people the precepts and practices of *Islām*, administering justice according to the *Qur'ān* and the *Sunnah* and collecting *zakāt*.

The *Arabs* had embraced *Islām*, he thought, but what about Syria, Egypt and Abyssinia ? These countries and in fact the whole world must bear the message of *Islām*. Arrangements were made to send missions to these countries also.

Illness

The Holy Prophet was up till now in good health and had performed all his duties with zeal and fervour ; leading prayers, issuing despatches, appointing governors, and arranging administration throughout Arabia. He, however, became indisposed during the middle of *Safar*, 11 A.H. after his return from *Mecca*. The poison which had been given to him by a Jewess at *Khaybar* and which had slowly penetrated into his system, began to show

47, *Ibn Hisham*, Vol. iv. p. 253.

its effects and his health deteriorated with alarming rapidity.

The Holy Prophet had said good-bye to his people at *Mecca* but his mind was occupied with the thought that he had not prayed for the martyrs of *Uḥud* ; and so to their graves he now turned his steps. There, standing besides the graves of his brave and faithful companions, he prayed and with such earnestness that although they were now buried for eight long years, one would have believed as if a departing soul was bidding farewell to living persons.[48] Then he went to the pulpit and said :

> I am to precede you and I have been made a witness upon you. By God, you will meet me at the "Fountain" very soon. I have been given the keys of the worldly treasures. By *Allah,* I do not fear for you that you will turn polytheists after me. But I do fear that you may strike one another's necks for the acquisition of worldly riches.[49]

On the 18th of *Safar* he went to *Baqi' al-Gharaqad* in the middle of the night and prayed for the dead. He, then, returned to his wife *Maimunah's* apartment. The fever became violent and the pain considerably increased. But he bore all these sufferings with remarkable calmness and serenity. He led the prayers in the mosque as long as his health supported him but he could not continue that as his health was failing alarmingly. One day water had to be poured over his head before he could come out and he had a bandage round his head to relieve headache. He called his wives and said: "You see that I am very sick. I am not able to visit you in turn. If it be pleasing unto you, I may be permitted to stay in the apartment of *'Ā'ishah.*" They all agreed and he walked with the support of *'Alī* and *'Abbās* (*Āllah* be pleased with them) to her apartment.

Abū Bakr was commanded by the Holy Prophet to lead the prayer during his illness. *'Ā'ishah* suggested to her husband that her father should be relieved of this for he had a tender heart and might burst into tears while reciting the Holy *Qur'ān.* The Holy Prophet insisted on his continuing to officiate for him so that *Abū Bakr* had no other choice but to lead the prayers.

---

48. Ibn Ḥajar Asqalānī, *Kitāb-ul-Janā'iz, Fatḥ al-Bārī,* Vol. iii, p. 454.
49. *Ibid.*

Last Instructions

On Thursday he again asked his family to pour water upon him. Refreshed by the bath he felt relieved and went forth to the mosque, supported by *'Alī* and *'Abbās*, to offer his noonday prayer. At the conclusion of the prayer he seated himself upon the pulpit and addressed the people around him :

> There is a servant whose Lord has given him option between this life and that which is nigh unto the Lord, and the servant has chosen the latter.

Abū Bakr seems to have been the only one in the mosque who recognised what *Muḥammad* (peace be upon him) really meant and tears filled his eyes at the idea that soon the Prophet would be no more among them.

Then the Apostle of *Allah* (peace be upon him) said :

> There is none more bountiful to us for his unwavering loyalty and devotion and for his sacrifice of wealth than *Abū Bakr*. If I were to choose a bosom friend it would be he : but *Islām* has made a closer brotherhood among us all.
>
> The fact is that your companion is the friend of *Allah*. Let every door that leads into the mosque be closed, except the door of *Abū Bakr*.[50]
>
> O people ! It has reached me that you are afraid of the approaching death of your Prophet. Has any previous Prophet lived for ever among those to whom he was sent ? So think not that I would ever live among you ?
>
> Behold, I am about to go to my Lord. You too will go sooner or later. I instruct you to do good to the first Emigrants and I recommend the Emigrants to do good among themselves.

Verily *Allah*, the Exalted says :

> "By the time, Verily man is in the loss, except those who themselves believe and do righteous works, and enjoin upon each other the truth and enjoin upon each other endurance." (ciii : 1-3)

---

50. Ibn Ḥajar 'Asqalānī, *'Fath al-Bari, Kitāb al-Faḍā'il*, Vol. ix, pp. 12-13.

Verily, the affairs take their course according to the Will of *Allah*. Delay in dispensation should not in any way urge you to be impatient in demand. *Allah*—the Mighty and the Great—does not submit to the haste of anybody. He who contends with *Allah*—*Allah* overpowers him. He who tries to play fast and loose with *Allah*, he is outwitted by Him. In the near future, if you get power in the world, then do not spread mischief on earth and do not cut off your blood relations. I instruct you to do good to the Helpers. They are those who provided facilities for the promotion of the faith. So you should behave unto them well. Did they not provide accommodation for you in their homes? Did they not give you preference over themselves, while they were confronted with poverty?

The number of believers would increase, but the *Anṣar* would decrease to the extent that they would be among men as salt in the food. They are my family and with them I found shelter.

By Him in Whose Hand my life is, verily I love you. The Helpers have acquitted themselves creditably of the responsibility that fell upon them and now there remains what you have to do.

So he who from among you occupies a position of responsibility and is powerful enough to do harm or good to the people, he should fully acknowledge and appreciate the favour that has been shown by these benefactors and should overlook their faults.

Verily do not give preference to yourselves over them.

Beware, he who is anxious to come to the 'fountain' along with me tomorrow should hold his tongue and restrain his hands.

O people! Verily sins deprive people of blessings and bring about changes in their lot. When people are good, their rulers do good to them and when the people are wrong-doers their rulers oppress them.

There may be some amongst you whom I owe anything. I am, after all a human being. So if there is any man whose honour I have injured, here I am to answer for it.

If I have done any injury to the skin of anybody, here is my skin; he can take his recompense. If I owe aught to anyone here is my property; he may take it.

Know that among you the most faithful to me is the one who has such a claim against me and then he either takes it from me or absolves me so that I meet my Lord after I have been absolved.

Nobody should say : "I fear enmity and grudge of the Apostle of *Allah.*" I nurse no grudge towards anyone. These are the things which are alien to my nature and temperament. I abhor them.[51]

The Holy Prophet received the news that there was some grumbling in certain quarters about the appointment of *Usāmah* to the post of the commander of the intended expedition to Syria. He summoned the people in question and addressed them in the following words :

> O people ! What is this which has reached my ears, that some amongst you murmur against my appointing *Usāmah* as the commander ? Now if you criticise my appointing *Usāmah* as *amīr,* [it is not a new thing for] you have indeed criticised my appointing his father [*Zayd*] as *amīr* before him. And I swear by the Lord, that he verily was well-fitted for the command, and that his son after him is well-fitted also. Truly, *Usāmah* is one of the men most dearly loved by me, as his father was. They both are indeed loved by me.[52]

One day, while he was in a precarious condition, he said to his Companions around him :

> Come here, I will cause you to write something so that you may never fall into error. Upon this some[53] of those present said : "The Prophet of God is suffering from acute pain and you have the *Qur'ān* with you ; the Book of *Allah* is sufficient unto us." Others, however, wanted the writing to be made. When *Muḥammad* (peace be upon him) saw them debating over it, he was perturbed

51. *Sharḥ Al-Mawāhib-al-Ladduniyah,* Vol. viii, p. 268. *Ibn Kathīr, Al-Bidāya wan Nihayah,* Vol. v, pp. 330-31.
Ibn Sa'd, Leiden, 1330 A.H. Series, II, Vol. ii, pp. 42 46.

52. *Ibn Sa'd,* Series II, Vol. ii, p. 41.

53. In *Saḥiḥ Muslim,* the name of *'Umar* has been mentioned in this connection.

and ordered them to go away and leave him alone.[54]

Muḥammad (peace be upon him) had a great love for his only daughter *Fāṭimah* (may *Allah* be pleased with her).

She visited her departing father very frequently and received his blessings and love. On one such occasion he whispered to her something and she began to weep. Then he again whispered to her something and she laughed.

'Ā'ishah questioned her after the Prophet's death, about this weeping and laughing to which *Fāṭimah* replied: "The first time, he disclosed to me that he would not recover from his illness and I wept. The second time he revealed that I would be the first of the family to join him and that made me laugh.[55]

The sickness of the Prophet on the Saturday night assumed a serious turn. Fever rose to such a pitch that the hand could hardly be placed upon the Prophet's body owing to the burning heat. His body was racking with pain ; but he was still busy in calling people to the path of righteousness. Turning to the women who sat close by he said : 'O *Fatimah* ! my daughter and thou *Safiyyah*, my aunt ! Work ye out that which shall please the Lord. For verily I have no power with Him to save you in any way.'[56]

Even in this hour of illness, when he had grown very weak, his mind was alert and perceived all that went on around him. Some of the women, who had been in exile in Abyssinia mention-

---

54. *Ṣaḥiḥ Bukhāri* : *Kitāb al-Maghāzi*, Cairo, Vol. iii, p. 91.

This *Hadith* has provoked a good deal of controversy among *Muslims*. A section of the people contends that it pertains to the problem of succession which the Holy Prophet was going to decide in favour of *'Ali*, whereas the others argue that it refers to his instruction which he later on issued verbally concerning the Jews, the Christians and the offering of presents to the deputations at the time of their departure, etc.

On thoughtful examination of the statements recorded by *Bukhāri* and *Muslim* one comes to the conclusion that it has nothing to do with the matter of succession. This order was given on Thursday, *viz.*, four days before his death. After this he deputed *Abū Bakr* to lead the prayer, appeared in the mosque, admonished his Companions on various issues, delivered sermons and spoke on various topics. Had the Prophet any intention of nominating *'Alī* as his successor, he could have easily carried it into effect on any other occasion during the four days that he lived.

55. *Ṣaḥiḥ Bukhāri* : *Kitāb al-Maghāzi*, Cairo, Vol. iii, p. 92.

56. *Ibn Sa'd*, Series II, Vol ii, p. 46.

ed about the cathedral of Maria and of the wonderful picture on its walls. Overhearing it, the Holy Prophet (may peace and blessings of *Allah* be upon him) was displeased and remarked :

> These are the people who, when a saint among them dies, build over his tomb a place of worship and they adorn it with his pictures—in the eyes of Lord, the worst part of all creation.

He then raised his hand in prayer and said :

> O Lord ! Let my grave be not adopted as an idol. God has cursed the people who have turned the graves of their Prophets into places of worship.[57]

Meanwhile it occurred to him that he had given to *'Ā'ishah* some gold coins. He desired that these should be given at once in charity to the needy, as he did not like that he should meet his Lord when he had some material wealth in his possession.[58]

The Last Day

The last night of *Muḥammad's* life, i.e., the 11th of *Rabi' al-Awwal*, 11 A.H. was heavy upon him. He was overheard praying constantly to his Lord for His blessings. The morning brought him some relief. Fever and pain had somewhat abated, and there was some recovery of strength. He moved the curtain of his apartment and saw the *Muslims* offering their prayers in the Mosque with *Abū Bakr* as their leader.

Having paused thus for a moment at the door of his apartment, the Holy Prophet, supported by a companion, walked slowly to the place where *Abū Bakr* stood. People made way for him, opening their ranks as he advanced. *Abū Bakr* heard the rustle and guessing the cause, stepped backward to vacate the leader's place ; but the Holy Prophet asked him by motion of his hand to keep on leading the prayer. When he had finished, *Muḥammad* (peace be upon him) set on the step of the pulpit and addressed once more his devoted followers :

> By the Lord ! As for myself, I have not made lawful anything except that which God has declared lawful ;

57. *Ibn Sa d,* Series II, Vol. ii, p. 34-36.
58. *Ibid.*, pp. 33-34.

> nor have I prohibited aught but that which God has forbidden.[59]

This is the last occasion on which he appeared in public. *Muslims* were happy that the Prophet had recovered and there was no danger to his life. *Usāmah* came to the Prophet and asked his permission to proceed with his army to Syria *Abū Bakr* greeted the Holy Prophet on his recovery and sought his permission to go out of *Medina* to see his wife at *al-Sunah*. *'Alī* told the eager crowd that the Holy Prophet had recovered and there was no cause for worry. The people, therefore, dispersed well pleased and happy at this news.

Muḥammad (peace be upon him), however, seemed quite exhausted and returned to the apartment of *'Ā'ishah*. As the day advanced his strength failed rapidly. *'Ā'ishah*, seeing him to be too weak, raised his head from the pillow and laid it tenderly in her lap. She moistened his forehead with damp cloth. His fever was very high. But the Holy Prophet remained calm and forbearing. He had resigned himself to the Will of God and repeated these words again and again :

> "In the company of those on whom is the Grace of *Allah*." (iv : 69)

He felt as if he was drifting towards the irresistible end. But as ever, he was without fear. He did not, for a moment, lose his courage. He constantly called his Master to help him :

> "O Lord ! I beseech Thee assist me in the agony of death."

At this juncture *'Abd al-Raḥmān*, the brother of *'Ā'ishah*, entered with a green twig in his hand. Seeing that his eyes rested on it, and knowing it to be such as he liked, she asked whether he would like to have it. He signified assent. Chewing it a little to make it soft and pliable, she placed it in his hand. This pleased him. He brushed his teeth energetically and then put it down.

The Holy Prophet Breathes his Last

His strength now rapidly sank and he was heard saying :

---

59. *Ibn Sa'd*, Series II, Volume ii, p. 46.

"Lord ! grant me pardon ; and join me to the companionship on high."

Then at intervals he uttered these words :

"The most exalted companionship on high."

He also murmured admonition :

"Prayer and the persons who have been entrusted to your care."

This he repeated several times. Then after a pause of silence, his strength ebbed back. His eyes opened widely and he said clearly :

"Lord ! blessed is the companionship on high."

Then his limbs relaxed. His head fell back in *'Ā'ishah's* lap. She fixed her eyes upon him anxiously, almost hopefully to get a response from him but she found to her great sorrow that the faint suggestion of a smile which relaxed her husband's lips did not belong to this world. *Muḥammad* (peace and blessings of *Allah* be upon him), after having rendered his obligations towards his earthly companions, had now returned to the companionship of the One on high. It was Monday, the twelfth of *Rabī' al-Awwal* that he left for his heavenly abode, at the age of sixty-three :

May the Lord shower His choicest blessings on him, his family and his companions !

So ended a life consecrated from first to last, to the service of God and humanity.

The Companions' Concern over Prophet's Death

The news of the Prophet's death spread to all corners of the city. Consternation and fear blazed through the ranks of the people who had just seen their master alive. Some wept bitterly ; some were struck dumb ; some disbelieved the news of death and held that it was only a swoon. Even *'Umar* in the state of agonv, forgot that the Prophet was a mortal and death was, therefore, a natural phenomenon with him.

It was an unusual scene, an extraordinary situation. *Muḥammad* (peace be upon him) had never in any manner or by suggestion direct or indirect given any indication that he was immortal. Rather he had emphasised his humanness and mortality time and again. His followers, however, who had received a heavenly life by his teachings, who had developed the consciousness of *Allah* in full glory through him, and had constantly witnessed the manifestations of Divine help, mercy and power in his words and actions, could not look upon him as a mere human being. They could not associate their master with anything mortal. It was indeed painful for them to imagine that the man who had brought them out of darkness and superstition into light and wisdom ; who had changed their lives from gross materialism to sublime spirituality, was no longer within their reach to guide them. Such a feeling was quite natural.

'Umar stood there in the throng with his sword unsheathed and announced that anybody who dared say that *Muḥammad* (may the peace and blessings of *Allah* be upon him) was dead, would do so at the cost of his life.

Abu Bakr Handles the Situation

Just then appeared *Abū Bakr*. Passing through the mosque and disregarding the crowds which pressed about him, asking a thousand questions, he walked onward into the apartment of *'Ā'ishah*. He did not say anything but lifted the *Yamanī* mantle which had covered the face of the Holy Prophet. For a moment he looked sadly at the finely drawn features of his great and illustrious friend. Then he knelt beside him and kissed the broad forehead, and said : "Sweet you were in life and sweet too in death. Yes, you are dead." He continued, "Alas ! my friend, my chosen one, dearer than father and mother to me ! you have tasted the death which God had decreed ; a second death will never overtake you."[60]

Gently putting down the head upon the pillow, he stooped again and kissed the face ; then replaced the covering and withdrew.

He went out and became aware of the tumult outside the Prophet's chamber. He hurried toward it and heard *'Umar's* voice reiterating that *Muhammad* was not dead. *Abū Bakr*

---

60. *Ibn Sa'd*, Series II, Vol. ii, pp. 54-55.

tried to silence him, but it was no use. He would not listen to him. He, therefore, left him to himself and moved towards the people who had thronged round him. He addressed them in his natural calm and soft measured tone :

> Has not the Almighty revealed this verse unto His Prophet saying :
>
> 'Verily thou shalt die, and they shall die.' (xxx : 30) Again :
>
> 'And *Muḥammad* is naught but an Apostle ; apostles have surely passed away before him. Will ye then, if he dieth or be slain, turn round on your heels.' (iii : 144)

Let him who worshipped *Muḥammad* know that *Muḥammad* (peace and blessings of *Allah* be upon him) is dead ; but whosoever worshipped *Allah*, let him know that *Allah* is alive, and He shall never die.[61]

The short sermon had a very salutary effect upon the assembly and it brought solace to the wounded hearts of the *Muslims* in this unbearably sad bereavement. They submitted with a cheerful resignation to the Will of *Allah* with an understanding that like all other mortals the Holy Prophet had also left this earthly abode. They felt that the *Quranic* verse which *Abū Bakr* had recited before them was squarely applicable to the situation, as if it had been revealed just then on that occasion.

Abū Bakr in spite of his intense grief, kept his head cool. He knew that at that moment *Islām* was faced with grave dangers. The shock of *Muḥammad's* death had been great, but the reaction might even be greater. He, therefore, kept a watch over the affairs lest they should take a serious turn. On hearing the report that *Anṣār* had gathered in the Hall of *B. Sā'idah* in order to decide the issue of *Muḥammad's* successor, he hurried to the spot. He was urgently needed there. *'Umar* and *Abū 'Ubaydah* accompanied him to that place. *Abū Bakr* listened to the arguments of the Helpers calmly and then placed the matter before them dispassionately and asked them to decide the issue. He told them :

61. *Ibn Sa'd*, Series II, Vol. ii, pp. 54-55.

> All that you speak of your excellence is perfectly true. There is no people upon earth deserving all this praise more than you do. But the *Arabs* will not accept a chief other than a man of the *Quraysh*. *Quraysh* will be the administrators and you will be their ministers.

He spoke very persuasively, trying to make the *Anṣār* realise the gravity of the situation and make them decide the matter coolly and in the best interest of *Islām*. *Abū Bakr's* words touched a chord that vibrated in every heart and thus had the desired effect. The spirit of opposition soon disappeared and he was unanimously elected as the first caliph of the departed Prophet (peace be upon him).

While all this was going on *'Alī* and *'Abbās* and some other members of the Prophet's family bathed his body. It was wrapped in three coverings and laid in state in *'A'ishah's* apartment. People were allowed to catch the last glimpse of their benefactor's face and say the funeral prayers. Each group did that and moved on. This went on the whole day long : women followed men and children followed women.

When the time for burial approached, it was discovered that no one had a clear idea where the Holy Prophet should be laid to rest. Some were in favour of burying him in the mosque, while others wanted to bury him along with his Companions. *Abū Bakr* solved the problem by announcing : "I heard the Apostle say, 'No Prophet dies but he is buried where he dies.' So the bed on which he died was removed and a grave was dug there. The sacred body was lowered in the grave by *'Alī, Usāmah* and *Al-Faḍl*. A vault of unbaked bricks was built over it and the rest was filled in with gravel and sand."[62]

> May Lord shower upon him the choicest of His blessings and favours !

A General Estimate of the Prophet's Character

It is meet and proper that before bringing this work to a

---

62. The account of the death of the Holy Prophet is based on the following book :

(1) *Ibn Sa'd*, Leiden Series II, Vol. ii, pp. 1-79.

(2) *Saḥiḥ Bukhāri* : *Kitāb al-Maghāzi*.

(3) *Ibn Hishām*, Vol. iv, pp. 298-316.

close, I should sum up the chief traits of the character of the Holy Prophet, which, at different stages of his life and from various points of view, have been presented in these pages. This I will now briefly attempt.

Personal Appearance

The person of *Muḥammad* (peace be upon him) was extremely graceful. His form, a little above average height, was stately and commanding. The depth of feeling in his dark black eyes and the winning expression of the face, gained the confidence and love of strangers, even at first sight. 'He was', says an admiring follower, 'the handsomest, the brightest faced and most generous of men. It was as though the sunlight beamed in his countenance.'

The Prophet—an Exemplar

When the Prophet's wife *'Ā'ishah* (may *Allah* he pleased with him) asked to describe the mode of his life and conduct she replied : "His morals are the *Qur'ān*. In other words, his daily life was a true picture of the *Qur'ānic* teachings." He was an embodiment of all the virtues enunciated by the Holy *Qur'ān*. The record of his life which sheds light on his conduct as a child, as a father, as a husband, as a neighbour, as a merchant, as a preacher, as a persecuted emigrant, as a friend, as a warrior, as an army commander, as a conqueror, as a judge, as a ruler, as a law-giver and above all as a devotee of *Allah* was all an exemplification of the Book of *Allah*.

Simple Habits

In his habits he was very simple, though elegant. His eating and drinking, his dress and his household goods retained, even when he reached the apex of his power, their original simplicity. In all matters he stood far too high above to fall a prey to material temptations so much so that he had no wealth or riches with him when he left this earthly abode. For he had set his slaves free and distributed his money in all conceivably good causes. His personal belongings at the time of his death consisted merely of an armour (and even this had been mortgaged with a Jew), a mattress of dried palm leaves and a water-skin.

He was gifted with uncommon power of imagination, sublimity of thought and delicacy and refinement of feeling. He was most indulgent to his inferiors, and would never allow his young servant to be scolded, regardless of what he did. "Ten years," said *Anas*, his faithful servant, "I was with the Prophet, and he never said as much as 'fie to me." He was very affectionate towards his family. He loved the little children dearly ; stopped them in the street and patted their heads with great affection. In times of leisure he even joined them in their innocent games.

Though his living was simple, yet he did not shun the use of the good things of life. He relished tasty food, enjoyed the beauty of flowers, the fragrance of perfumes, and was even fond of light jokes. He gave love for love. He had a large heart, overflowing with the milk of human kindness, especially kindness towards the weak and the oppressed. He admired the good qualities in others and readily accepted good counsel, no matter from which quarter it came.

Muḥammad (peace be upon him) was a warmhearted and faithful friend. He loved *Abū Bakr* with the close affection of a brother. In the same way he loved *'Alī*, his cousin and son-in-law and *Zayd*, his freed slave, with the fondness of a father. This freed slave of the Prophet, in his turn, was so deeply attached to him that he preferred to stay on at *Mecca* with his kind and affectionate master, rather than return home with his own father. *Muḥammad* (peace be upon him) had a great regard for him and after the death of *Zayd*, his son *Usāmah* was treated with the same favour and love which his father had received from the Holy Prophet. *'Uthmān* and *'Umar* were also very dear to his heart. He had a very great regard for the *Anṣār* and frankly and gracefully acknowledged their valuable services to the cause of *Islām*. His affections were in no instance misplaced ; they were ever reciprocated by a warm and self-sacrificing love on the part of his followers.

He was very sweet and kind and with the exception of one instance, in which an open challenge was thrown to him, he never struck any one with his own hand.

The worst expression he ever made use of in his conversation was: 'What has come to him? May his forehead become darkened with mud.' When asked to curse someone he replied : "I have not been sent to curse but to be a mercy to mankind." He visited the sicks, followed any bier that he saw, accepted the invitation of everyone, even of slaves, to dinner, mended his own clothes, repaired his own shoes, milked his goats. While shaking hands, he never was the first to withdraw his hand out of another man's palm and turned not away before the other had turned.

> He was the most faithful protector of those he protected, the sweetest and most agreeable in conversation. Those who saw him were suddenly filled with reverence; those who came near him loved him; they who described him would say, 'I have never seen his like either before or after.' He was of great taciturnity, but when he spoke it was with emphasis and deliberation and no body could forget what he said.[63]

He was very courteous to all those who met him. He is never reported to have said 'nay' to anyone. He never contradicted anybody unless what he said was opposed to the teachings of *Islām*, nor did he get angry with any man because of personal matters. He paid equal regard to the humble and the rich. He claimed no distinction for himself and lived amongst his friends as if he was not their leader, but a sincere companion and a devoted brother. When walking, people would walk in front of him and behind him. When seated among his followers, who loved him dearer than their own lives, he would occupy no special seat in order to make himself conspicuous. Strangers were at times puzzled to recognise him from his companions. All his actions and movements were characterized by simplicity and humility. Anything savouring of artificiality was repugnant to his nature.

Calm and Self-Possessed

The Holy Prephet (peace and blessings of *Allah* be upon him) did not make decisions in hot haste, he decided matters after having weighed their pros and cons carefully and after having taken his companions in full confidence. Once the matter was resolved, he spared no pains in giving it a practical shape.

His generosity not only towards his own friends but even

63. Stanley Lane Poole, *The Speeches and Table Talk of the Prophet Muhammad*, London 1882, pp. 27-29.

towards his enemies is unparalleled in history. The long and obstinate struggle carried on ceaselessly by the *Meccans* against him, and the atrocities which they perpetrated without any qualm of conscience, would have induced any other conqueror to take revenge, leaving behind him indelible traces of fire and blood. "But *Muḥammad*, excepting a few criminals, granted general pardon, and nobly casting into oblivion the memory of the past, with all its mockery, its affronts and persecutions, he treated even the foremost of his opponents with a gracious and even friendly consideration. Not less marked was the forbearance shown to *'Abdullah* and the disaffected citizens of *Medina*, who for so many years persistently thwarted his designs and resisted his authority, nor the clemency with which he received the submissive advances of tribes that before had been the most hostile, even in the hour of victory."[64]

His Implicit Faith in *Allah*

The most striking point in the life of *Muḥammad* (peace be upon him) is his implicit faith in *Allah* and his constant endeavour to be always in communion with Him. God was the vital spark of his spiritual flame. Such was the Prophet's close relation with his Creator that no one can read the account of his sacred life without having deepened within him a sense of the Majesty of *Allah* and of His overruling Providence. It was sublime and unshakable faith in Providence which may be called the keynote of the Prophet's character. Prayer and communion with *Allah* were the basic sources of his strengh. His constant and vivid sense of an all-pervading providence influenced all his thoughts and actions. He never took up any work, major or minor, without mentioning the Name of *Allah*. In trouble and affliction, as well as in joy and sorrow, he always saw and humbly acknowledged the Majesty and Power of *Allah*, the Benevolent, the Merciful.

Humble and meek to the highest degree, the Holy Prophet had the courage of the bravest man. He had the conviction that the mighty hand of *Allah* would protect him from all evil designs of the enemies. Filled with this faith he showed unflinching fortitude and unswerving steadfastness under the most trying

64. William Muir, *The Life of Muhammad*, p. 497.

circumstances. Despair and despondency were unknown to him. He was always calm, self-possessed, contented and happy, both in prosperity and adversity. He had to endure privation and hardships throughout his life. He remained, nevertheless, strong and steadfast amidst the severest opposition and apparent helplessness. "Surrounded by a little group of faithful men and women, he met insults, menaces, dangers and persecutions with a lofty and patient trust in the power of his Maker." He and his family often had to pass several days without food and frequently had to content themselves with a handful of dates, but nobody ever heard a word of complaint from their lips. He was the Messenger of *Allah* and as such he had made the preaching of the Divine Message the sole purpose of his life. All other considerations were subservient to it. Even in the most adverse circumstances, his heart was aglow with the belief that he would receive a reward from the Creator for all the hardships that he had endured.

Daily Routine

The daily routine of his life was extremely rigorous. After the morning prayer he received people so as to educate them. He even settled disputes and administered justice ; received envoys and dictated despatches and then the assembly was adjourned. The public function now over, he used to go to one of his wives, and do any job which she wanted him to do. He even went to the market for shopping. Then another short prayer was performed, after which he visited the sick, and the poor, and called at the houses of his friends and then he went to the mosque for the noonday prayer. After coming back from the mosque he took his meal, if it was available, and then retired to his private apartment for some rest and then again went to the mosque for the afternoon prayer.

After the prayer, the Holy Prophet would go to his wives and would sit with them till children claimed his time. He led the evening prayer and then took his supper and attended either to his household affairs or spent his time in the company of his devoted followers and explained to them the teachings of *Islām*. He led the night prayer in the mosque and then returned to his home for prayers in solitude and rest. He slept for a few hours only and then rose and prayed and meditated and again retired to the bed only for a brief time, rising again for the morning prayer, when the day's work began once again. His energy was extraordinary. He seldom complained of fatigue.

One is simply astonished when one reviews the greatness of the purpose, the meagreness of the sources and yet the astounding results which the Holy Prophet achieved in the brief span of his ministry. "The most famous men created arms, laws and empires only. They founded, if anything at all, no more than material powers, which often crumbled before their eyes. This man moved not only armies, legislation, empires, peoples, dynasties, but millions of men in one-third of the then inhabited world ; and more than that, he moved the altars, the gods, the religions, the ideas, the beliefs and souls."[65]

Judged by all standards of human greatness, we find him on the loftiest height which can possibly be conceived of. The most amazing aspect of his life, however, is that in spite of his astounding achievements and his close intimacy with *Allah*, he never claimed to be anything but a mortal who had been bidden to announce the Message of his Lord to humanity so that it might live in harmony with the Will of the Creator. He not only forcefully disclaimed any divinity for himself, but also warned his followers to attribute any such thing to him. He was entrusted with the sacred task of propagating the Divinity of *Allah*, the Sole Creator, Sustainer, Master and Sovereign of the universe and this work he performed most eminently.

May *Allah* and His angels shower their choicest blessings on him—the Mercy of both the worlds ! Amen !

---

65. Lamartine, *Histoire de La Turquie*, Paris, 1854, Vol. II, pp. 276-277 quoted in *Charm of Islam*, p. 15, published by 'A'isha Bawani Wakf, Karachi.

INDEX

E

F

G

H

I

J

K

L

M

N

O

P

Q

R

BIBLIOGRAPHY

Al-Qur'an :

For translating the passages of the Holy Qur'ān the following translations have been freely consulted :

(*i*) Sale's *Preliminary Discourse to the Translation of the Koran* prefixed as Introduction to *Wherry Commentary on the Kuran,* 4 Vols. (Trubner, London).

(*ii*) M. 'Abdul Mājid Daryābādi's Translation & Commentary, 2 Vols. (Taj Company, Lahore).

(*iii*) Marmaduke Pickthall : *The Meaning of the Glorious Quran,* 2 Volumes (Hyderabad-Deccan, India 1938).

(*iv*) 'Abdullah Yusuf 'Ali : *The Holy Quran : An Interpretation in English* (Sh. Muhammad Ashraf, Lahore 1934).

For the proper understanding of the full import and meaning of the verses the following commentaries have been made use of :

Arabic :

(*i*) Ḥāfiz 'Imād-al-Dīn Abu-l-Fidā Ismā'īl ibn 'Umar ibn Kathīr Qarshi (774 A.H.) : *Tafsīr al-Qurān al-'Azīm* ; popularly known as *Tafsīr Ibn Kathīr* ; (Published by al-Maktaba al-Malkiya, 1948).

(*ii*) 'Allāma Shihāb-ud-Dīn Sayed Maḥmūd Alusi : *Rūḥ al-Ma'ani* (Cairo).

(*iii*) Imām Abu 'Abdullah Muḥammad b. Aḥmad Anṣāri Qurtubi : *Al-Jami'li-Aḥkām-al-Qurān,* popularly known as *Tafsīr Qurtubi*.

(*iv*) Jar-ullah Maḥmūd Ibn 'Umar Zamakhshari, *Kashshāf* ; edited by Muṣṭafā Ḥussain Aḥmad (Cairo 1365 A.H.)

(*v*) Fakhr al-Dīn Muḥammad 'Ibn Omar Rāzi, *Mafātiḥ al-Ghaib* (*Tafsīr Kabīr*). (Printed at al-Amirah Press, 1307 A.H.)

(*vi*) Imām Abu-l-Qāsim al-Ḥussain b. Muḥammad Ibn al-Faḍl al-Rāghib : *Al-Mufradāt fi Gharībi-l-Qur'ān* (Cairo).

(*vii*) *Tanwīr-ul-Miqyās min Tafsīr Ibn 'Abbās*, edited by Abu Ṭāhir b. Muḥammad b. Ya'qūb al-Ferozeābādi Al-Shāfi'ī. Published by ('Abdul Ḥamīd Aḥmad Ḥanifi, Egypt).

(*viii*) *Jāmi' al-bayan 'an Tāwīl al-Qur'ān*, popularly known as *Tafsīr al-Tabari*, by Abu Ja'far Muḥammad ibn Jarīr Tabari. Published by Maṭba' Muṣṭafā Albābī al-Ḥalbī. (Egypt, 1954.)

Urdu :

(*i*) Maulānā Ashraf 'Ali Thānwī, *Bayān-ul-Qur'an* (Taj Company, Lahore).

(*ii*) Sayyed Abul A'lā Maudoodi, *Tafhīm-ul-Qur'ān*. (6 volumes) Idara Tarjaman-ul-Quran, Lahore.

(*iii*) Maulānā Abdul Mājid Daryābādi : *Tafsir-i-Majidi*. (Taj Company, Lahore).

(*iv*) Translation of the Holy Quran in Urdu with short explanatory notes by Sheikh-ul-Hind Mahmood Hasan and Maulānā Shabbir Ahmad 'Uthmani.

Hadith :

After the Holy Quran, the most authentic source of Prophet's life is the Hadith. The following important collections of traditions have been made use of :—

(*i*) *Sahih al-Bukhari* by Abu 'Abd Allah Muhammad b. Ismail al-Bukhari (Cairo).

(*ii*) *Sahih Muslim* : Abu al-Hussain 'Asakir al-Din Muslim b. Hajjaj b. Muslim al-Qushayri al-Nishapuri (Cairo).

(*iii*) *Sunan Abu Dawud al-Sijistani* (Karachi 1953).

(*iv*) *Jāmi' al-Tirmidhi* : Abu Isa Muhammad b. Isa (Delhi).

(*v*) *Sunan al-Nasai* : 'Abd al-Rahman Ahmad b. Shu'ayb al-Nasai.

(*vi*) *Sunan al-Darimi* : Abu Muhammad 'Abd Allah b. 'Abd al-Rahman (Kanpur), 1293 A.H.

(*vii*) *Sunan Ibn Majah* : Abu 'Abd Allah Muhammad b. Yazid, Edited by Muhammad Fawad Abdul Baqi (Egypt, 1952), 2 Volumes.

(*viii*) *Musnad* : al-Imam Abu 'Abd Allah Ahmad b. Muhammad Ibn Hanbal, Ed. by Ahmad Shakir. Cairo (1949-55), Vols. (i-xvi).

(*ix*) *Mishkāt al-Masabih* : Waliy al-Din Muhammad b. 'Abd Allah al-Khatib al-'Umari al-Tibrizi, Lucknow, 1326 A.H.

(*x*) *Al-Adab al-Mufrad*, compiled by Imam Bokhari (translated into Urdu by M. Khalil-ur-Rahman Nu'mani), Published in Karachi.

(*xi*) *Shamail Tirmidhi* : Abu Isā Muhammad b. Isā Tirmidhi with explanatory notes in Urdu by M. Muhammad Zakriya (Karachi).

(*xii*) *Mu'atta* : Imam Malik Abū 'Abd-Allah Malik ibn Anas. Edited by Muhammad Fawad Abdul Baqi (2 Volumes).

(*xiii*) *Kanz al-Ummal fi Sunan-e-Aqwal wa-l-Af'al*, by Sheikh 'Alā' al-Din al-Muttaqi ibn Hisham al-Din Hyderabad Deccan, 1312 A.H.

(*xiv*) *Kitab-al-Sunan* of Abu Bakr Ahmad ibn al-Husain, commonly known as Baihaqi.

(*xv*) *Mustadrak 'Ala al-Sahihein fil al-Hadith* : completed by Imam Abu 'Abd Allah Muhammad b. 'Abd Allah known as Hakim al-Nishapuri. Published in Hyderabad Deccan.

(This book is popularly known as *Mustadrak Hakim*).

Commentaries of the Hadith :

1. *Fath al-Bari* (commentary on Sahih al-Bokhari), Hafiz Ibn Hajar 'Asqalani (852 A.H.), Cairo 1959.
2. *Commentary on Sahih Muslim* : Abu Zakriya, Yahya al-Nawwi. It is appended to the original Text, published by Karkhana Tajarit-Kutab, Delhi, in 1930.
3. *'Aun al-Ma'bud 'ala Sunani Abu Dawud* ; by Abu 'Abd al-Rahman Sharf al-Haqq, commonly known as

Muhammad Ashraf, according to the Edition printed at Ansari Press, Delhi, 4 volumes, 1318 A.H.

4. *'Umdat-ul-Qari*, by Badr-ud-Din Mahmud ibn Ahmad, al-'Ayni Hanafi : This is the commentary of Sahih Bokhari according to the Hanifite point of view (Cairo).
5. *Nail-ul-Autar* by Imam Muhammad b. Abu b. Muhammad al-Shaukani (1255 A.H.), Cairo 1357 A.H.
6. *Tuhfat al-Ahwadhi* by 'Abd al-Rahman Mubarakpuri. Delhi 1353 A.H., 4 volumes.
7. *At-taliq-us-Sabih 'ala Mishkat-il-Masabih,* Muhammad Idris Kandhalvi, Damascus, 4 volumes.

BIOGRAPHIES

Arabic :

Besides the Holy Qur'an and the famous compilations of Hadith, the following books are of utmost importance for the biography of Muhammad :

1. *Al-Sirat al-Nabawiyyah* by Abu Muhammad 'Abd al-Malik ibn Muhammad ibn Hisham (213 A.H.). Edited by Mustafa Alsaqqa, Ibrahim al-Abyari and Abdul Hafeez Shalbi, Egypt (1355 A.H./1936 A.D.).

2. *Kitab-al-Rouḍ, al-Unuf* by Abul Qasim, 'Abd al-Rahman b. 'Abd Allah b. Ahmad b. 'Ali, Al-Hasan al-Khth'ami-al-Soheili (508 A.H).

   This is the famous commentary of Ibn Hisham. It was published in two volumes in Maṭba'a al-Jamaliya, Egypt.

3. *Z'ad al-Ma'ad fi Hadyi Khair-al-'Ibad* by Hafiz Abu 'Abdallah Muhammad b. Abu Bakr, popularly known as Hafiz Ibn Qayyim. Edited by Muhammad Hamid al-Fiqi, published in Cairo in October 1953.

4. *Al-Bidaya wa al-Nihaya* by Hafiz 'Imad al-Din, Abu-l-Fida Ismail ibn Umar ibn Kathir Qarshi (744 A.H.) 9 vols. Volumes II to VI deal with the life of the Holy Prophet.

5. *Al-Sharh 'ala-l-Mawahib al-Ladunniyyah* by 'Allama ibn 'Abd al-Baqi al-Zarqani (8 volumes).
It is a well known commentary of Shahab-ud-Din Ahmad b. Abu Bakr Qastlani's Al-Mawahib al-Ladunniyyah. Published in Mataba' al-Azhariya, Egypt in 1325.

6. *Kitab al-Tabaqat al-Kabir** : Muhammad Ibn Sa'd, (845 A.H.) Katib al-Waqidi. Edited by E. Miltwoch and E. Sachau, Leiden 1904-1918. (Only the first two volumes deal with the life of the Holy Prophet.)

7. *Tarikh al-Rusul wa al-Muluk,* by Abu Ja'far Muhammad ibn Jarir Tabari. Edited by M. J. de Goeje, Leiden, 1879-1901.

8. *Al-Kamil fi al-Tarikh Ibn al-Athir Jazri,* published in Idara al-Taba'at al-Muniryya, Egypt. Volume II records the life of Prophet Muhammad.

9. *Insanul 'Uyun fi Sirat al-Amin al-Mamun,* popularly known as Al-Sirat al-Halbiyyah by 'Ali, b. Burhanud-din Halabi, al-Shafa'i.

10. *'Uyun-al-Athar fi funun al-Maghazi-wa al-Siyar* by Abu al-Fatih Muhammad b. Yahya ibn Sayyid Al-Nas. (734 A.H.) Al-Maktaba Al-Qudsi, Cairo, 1356 A.H.

11. *Kitab Futuh al-Buldan* by Abu al-'Abbas Ahmad Ibn Yahya ibn Jabir al-Baladhuri, edited by M. J. de Goeje, Leiden, 1866.

12. *Kitab-al-Maghazi* by 'Ali 'Abd Allah b. 'Omar al-Waqidi. Edited by A. Von Kremer. Published by Asiatic Society Bengal (Calcutta) in 1855.

13. *Al-Shifa bi-Ta'rif Huquq al-Mustafa,* by Al-Qaḍi Abu Al-Faḍl Ayaḍ by Musa Alyasibi (544) Vol. I and Vol. II. Matba' Mustafa al-Babi al-Halbi, Egypt, 1950.

14. *Al-Khasais al-Kubra* : by Imam Jalal-ud-Din al-Suyuti :

---

*There is also a very fine edition of this book which was published from Beirut in 1957 in 8 volumes. In the first eight chapters of the book this edition has been used of whereas in the last four chapters I have depended upon Leiden edition.

published by Dairat al-Ma'arif, Hyderabad, Deccan (1319-20 A.H.)

15. *Hayat Muhammad*; Muhammad Hussain Haikal, Cairo, 1947.

16. *Muhammad* by Muhammad Riḍa, Cairo, 1368 A.H.

17. *Ansab al-Ashraf* : Abu al-'Abbas Ahmad ibn Yaha ibn Jabir Baladhuri. Edited by Dr. Hamid-Ullah, Egypt, 1959.

Persian :

1. *Madarij al-Nubuwwat* by Sheikh Abdul Haqq Muhaddith Dehlavi (1052 A.H.). Two volumes. Published by Matba' Nasri, Delhi.

2. *Mi'raj al-Nubuwwat fi Madarij al-Nubuwwat* by M. Moeen Kashfi Harvi, 1926.

Urdu :

1. *Sirat al-Nabi*,* M. Shibli Nu'mani, and M. Sayyid Sulaiman Nadvi, 6 volumes, Azamgarh.

2. *Khutbat-i-Madras* : Sayyid Sulaiman Nadvi, Azamgarh.

3. *Asahh Al-Siyyar fi Hadyi Khair-al-Bashar*, by Abul-Barakat 'Abd al-Rauf Danapuri, Karachi.

4. *Rahmat-ul-Lil Alamin*, 3 volumes. Qazi Sulaiman Mansurpuri, Lahore 1962.

5. *Sirat al-Mustafa*, M. Idris Kandhalvi, 3 volumes, published by Ilmi Markaz, Anarkali.

6. *Mohsin-i-Insaniat* : Fazl-ur-Rahman Na'im Siddiqui (2 volumes) published by Islamic Publications Ltd., Lahore.

7. *Khutabat-i-Majidi* : Abdul Majid Daryabadi : It is a compilation of nine lectures which the author delivered in Madras dealing with the different aspects of Prophet's life. These lectures are based only on the Holy

*The first two volumes were written by M. Shibli Nu'mani and the rest were completed by his illustrious disciple late S. Sulaiman Nadvi.

Qur'an ; published by Sidq-i-Jadeed Book Agency, Lucknow.

8. *Maqalat-i-Sirat* : Dr. Muhammad Asif Qidwai, published by Majlis-i-Tahqiq wa Nashriyat-i-Islam, Lucknow (India).
9. *Al-Nabi al-Khatim* : Maulana Manazar Ahsan Gilani, Karachi (Fourth edition).

English :

1. *The Life of Mahomet** by Sir William Muir, London, 1894.
2. *Mohammad and Mohammedanism* by Bosworth Smith, London, 1876.
3. *Muhammad at Mecca* by W. Montgomery Watt, Oxford, 1953.
4. *Muhammad at Madina* by W. Montgomery Watt, Oxford, 1956.
5. *Muhammad, Prophet and Statesman* by W. Montgomery Watt, Oxford University Press, 1961.
6. *The Spirit of Islam* by Ameer Ali, Calcutta, 1920.
7. *A Short History of Saracens* by Amir Ali, London 1951.
8. *Mohammad and the Rise of Islam* by D. S. Margoliouth, London, 1905.
9. *Mohammad, The Man and His Faith* by Tor Andrae, Translated from German by Theophil Menzel, London, 1936.
10. *Muhammad and His Power* by P. De Lacy Johnstone ; Edited by Oliphant Smeaton, New York, 1901.
11. *Islam and its Founder* by J. W. H. Stobart, London, 1876.
12. *The Life of Mahomet* by Emile Dermengham, London, 1930.

---

*I have written Muhammad instead of Mahomet in all those places where I have referred to this book since the word Mahomet is derogatory.

13. *Life of Mahomet* by Washington Iriving, London, 1850.

14. The Life and Religion of Mohammad as contained in the Sheeah Traditions of the H'yaṭ-ul-Kuloob. Translated from Persian by James L. Merwick, Boston 1850.

15. *The Life of Mohammad, the Prophet of Allah* by E. Dinet and Saliman ben Ibrahim, Paris, 1918.

16. *Mohamed : The Prophet* by Sirdar Ikbal 'Ali Shah, London, 1932.

17. *Mohamed : The Holy Prophet* by Hafiz Ghulam Sarwar, Lahore, 1961.

18. *The Prophet and Islam* (Abridged from an Edition of 1879) by Stanley Lane-Poole, Lahore, 1959.

19. *Muhammad : The Prophet* by M. Muhammad 'Ali, Lahore, 1951.

20. *The Prophet of the Desert* : by K. L. Gauba, Lahore, 1959.

21. *The Messenger : The Life of Mohammad* by R. V. C. Bodley, Lahore, 1954.

22. *The Greatness of Muhammad* by S. D. Kudsey, Lahore.

23. The Great Prophet by F. K. Khan Durrani, Lahore, 1931.

24. *The Orations of Muhammad* by M. Muhammad 'Ubaidul Akbar, Lahore, 1954.

25. *Muhammad and Christ* by M. Muhammad 'Ali, Lahore, 1921.

26. *Muhammad and Teachings of Quran* by John Davenport Edited by Muhammad Amin, Lahore, 1944.

27. *Half Hours with Muhammad* by Arthur N. Wollaston.

28. *The Living Thoughts of Prophet Muhammad* by M. Muhammad 'Ali, Cassel, 1947.

29. *Essays on the Life of Muhammad* by Syed Ahmed Khan, Trubner and Company.

30. *The Wives of Muhammad* by Fida Hussain Malik,

Lahore, 1952.

31. *History of the Arabs* (7th Edition) by Philip K. Hitti, Macmillan and Company Limited, New York, 1960.

32. *Islam and the Arabs* by Rom Landau, London, 1958.

33. *Mystical Elements in Muhammad* by John Clark Archer, Yale University Press.

34. *The Religion of Islam* by Dr. Ahmad A. Galwash, Cairo, 1945.

35. *The Ideal World Prophet* by M. Faḍal Karim, Dacca, East Pakistan, 1955.

36. *The Prophet and Islam or the Mirror of Islam* by Dr. Muhammad Abdul Hakim Khan, M.B., Rajindra Press, Patiala.